SOPHOCLES

AJAX

Board game between Achilles and Ajax. Black figure painting by Exekias (Vat. 344)

ARIS & PHILLIPS CLASSICAL TEXTS

SOPHOCLES

Ajax

edited with introduction, translation and commentary by

A. F. Garvie

Aris & Phillips Classical Texts
are published by
Oxbow Books, Park End Place, Oxford OX1 1HN

ISBN 0-85668-660-3

A CIP record for this book is available from the British Library.

Printed and bound by Antony Rowe Ltd, Eastbourne

Contents

Preface

This edition of *Ajax* is intended both for students who are reading the play in Greek and for those who are studying it in English. For the benefit of the latter the Commentary, as is normal in this series, is based not on the Greek text but on the translation, and while help is given to the former category of reader with the understanding of the Greek, Greek words and phrases in the Commentary are generally followed by an English translation. Discussion of the many textual problems of the play has been kept to a minimum, and much that was present in earlier drafts has been eliminated from the final one. As for the translation, in the difficult task of trying to find the right balance between a literal rendering of the Greek and one which bears some resemblance to modern idiomatic English, I have, if anything, veered towards the former. It certainly makes no pretension to literary merit. Where I have felt obliged to translate more freely, for the sake of the readers who are trying to understand the Greek a more literal rendering is often included in the Commentary.

My debt to earlier editions of *Ajax* will be obvious, particularly to the Oxford Classical Text of H. Lloyd-Jones and N.G. Wilson. Unfortunately, their *Sophocles: second thoughts* (Göttingen 1997) appeared too late for me to use. I am grateful to many people: to Elizabeth Moignard for her help with vase-paintings, to Vayos Liapis, with whom, while he was a research student at Glasgow, I spent many happy hours discussing *Ajax* and other Sophoclean plays, to my wife for her patience and encouragement, to my son David for his expertise in word-processing, to my daughter Margaret for her comments on the Translation, and above all to Malcolm Willcock, the General Editor of the Series, who read the whole of an earlier draft, and who, by his wise suggestions, saved me from many errors and vastly improved the whole book. Finally I must thank Adrian Phillips and Janet Davis of Aris & Phillips for their never-failing advice and assistance and for their professional skill in producing this book.

Glasgow February 1998

Introduction

The Myth

Ajax is a major character in Homer's *Iliad*, in which he is regarded as the best warrior on the Greek side after Achilles.[1] His qualities as a doughty and stubborn fighter are revealed especially in the battles at the ships in the second part of the poem, and it is he who rescues Odysseus when he is in difficulties at *Il.* 11.473-88. Though not as distinguished as Odysseus for intelligence and diplomacy, he nevertheless is chosen for, and with his blunt speech plays an important part in, the Embassy to Achilles in Book 9. Hector praises him for his understanding, as well as for his physical strength, at 7.288. He is the only major hero who never directly receives the help of a god.[2] It is as a defensive fighter that he stands out, and he is rarely presented as an outright winner.[3] He has the better of the duel with Hector in Book 7 and it ends honourably but inconclusively, as does his wrestling-match with Odysseus in the Funeral Games in Book 23.708-39, the first occasion on which these two heroes compete with each other, but as yet in friendly fashion. In the same Games Diomedes wins 'on points' in the fight in armour (23.811-25), and Ajax is defeated by Polypoetes in the throwing of a mass of metal (23.826-49).

It is in the *Odyssey* that we find the earliest reference to the story with which Sophocles is concerned in *Ajax*. After the death of Achilles his arms were awarded to Odysseus, and not to Ajax. In a poignant scene at *Od.* 11.541-65 Odysseus encounters his soul in the Underworld, when the angry Ajax refuses Odysseus' attempt at a reconciliation and turns away without a word. The story is told so allusively that one must suppose that it was already familiar to Homer's audience. Odysseus in his narrative says (11.547; the line was athetised, we do not know why, by Aristarchus) that the judgement was made by the sons of the Trojans and by Pallas Athena, but gives no clue as to how it was arranged. The part played by Athena seems to foreshadow the role that the goddess plays in Sophocles' play, but in Sophocles there is no suggestion that she influenced the judgement of the arms. We are not even explicitly told that Ajax commits suicide, though we may take it for granted that he does so, in shame and anger at the loss of honour which he has sustained. It is unlikely, but not impossible, that already, at this early stage of the

---

1   *Il.* 2.768-9, 7.227-8, 289, 17.279-80; cf. *Od.* 11.469-70 = 24.17-18, 11.550-1, Alcaeus 387 LP, *Carm. Conviv.* 898 and 899 *PMG*, P. *Nem.* 7.27, S. *Aj.* 423-6n.

2   See Scodel 12.

3   See Kirkwood (1965) 60, Sorum 364, E.A. Moignard, *CA News* 14 (1996) 2-3, and her whole article, 2-4, on the black-figure amphora of c. 540-30 by Exekias (Vat.344; J.D. Beazley, *Attic black-figure vase-painters* (Oxford 1956) 145.13), which shows Ajax evidently losing to Achilles in a board-game.

tradition, Ajax tried, as in Sophocles' play, to take revenge on Agamemnon, Menelaus, and Odysseus, and was prevented from doing so by Athena.

We know from fragments and from the summaries of the late writer Proclus that the story was treated or referred to in several poems of the post-Homeric Epic Cycle. The *Aethiopis*, ascribed to the probably seventh-century Arctinus of Miletus,[4] having told how Achilles' corpse was carried off the battlefield by Ajax while Odysseus fought off the Trojans, ends in Proclus' summary with the dispute between them over the dead hero's arms. Jebb (xv-xvi) argued that to the *Aethiopis* belongs the account in Σ *Od.* 11.547 (cf. Eust. 1698) of how Agamemnon, not wishing to show partiality to either hero, asked his Trojan prisoners which of them had caused them more trouble, and they replied that it was Odysseus, so that he was judged to be the better.[5] According to Σ P. *Isthm.* 4.58 (fr. 1 Davies) Ajax committed suicide at dawn, which, if correct, would mean that the poem continued after the judgement, or at least referred to its consequences, but it is possible that Σ confuses this poem with the *Little Iliad*,[6] usually attributed to Lesches of Mytilene, which began with the judgement. Greeks sent, on the advice of Nestor, to cavesdrop under the walls of Troy overheard two Trojan girls arguing as to whether Ajax or Odysseus was the greater warrior (fr. 2 D). The first girl pointed to Ajax' carrying of Achilles' corpse,[7] but the second won the argument 'by the forethought of Athena'. As far as we can deduce, the judgement in both these versions was presented as fair, and there is no suggestion of improper behaviour on the part of the judges. In this poem for the first time we hear of Ajax' madness and his attack on the booty (Proclus, p. 52 Davies), which led to his suicide, but there is no indication that the madness was caused by Athena, rather than by his natural anger, or that he returned to sanity before he killed himself. Agamemnon, angry with Ajax, no doubt because of his attack on the booty, refused him cremation, and his corpse had to be buried in a coffin (fr. 3 D; cf. Apollod. *Ep.* 5.7), which was evidently a mark of humiliation.[8] Sophocles maintains the tradition that Agamemnon wished to humiliate Ajax in death, but he nowhere

---

4   For the possibility that this poem is *pre*-Homeric see J.T. Kakridis, *Homeric researches* (Lund 1949) 89-90, J.A. Notopoulos, *HSPh* 68 (1964) 34-5, 40-1, K. Dowden, *JHS* 116 (1996) 47-61.

5   *Contra* C. Robert, *Bild und Lied* (Berlin 1881) 221.

6   See March 2.

7   This seems to have been the normal version (cf. S *Il.* 17.719). But there was another in which Ajax had the more difficult task of warding off the Trojans while Odysseus carried the corpse: Σ *Od.* 5.310, *P.Oxy.* 2510 (fourth century AD); see J.T. Kakridis, *WS* 20 (1986) 63-7.

8   See Holt (1992), who argues (against J. Bremmer, *The early Greek concept of the soul* (Princeton 1983) 95-6, M. Davies, *The Epic Cycle* (Bristol 1989) 65) that Ajax' interment was not originally humiliation, but goes back to predominant Mycenaean practice, and that the explanation of Philostratus, *Her.* 35.15, that it was considered wrong to cremate suicides, is Philostratus' own innovation.

suggests that burial was in any way inferior to cremation. Finally, we learn from fr.
1.8 D of the *Sack of Troy*, a poem which, like the *Aethiopis*, was ascribed to Arctinus
of Miletus, that the physician Podaleirius was the first to notice the anger of Ajax
from his flashing eyes and heaviness of spirit. It is unclear whether the flashing eyes
are a symptom of madness (so W. Kullmann, *Die Quellen der Ilias* (Wiesbaden
1960) 80), as in the *Little Iliad*, or whether (Jebb xiii-xiv) in this version the natural
anger of Ajax was followed immediately by his suicide.

From the seventh century onwards the story provided a popular subject for
artists.[9]   From about 700 BC the judgement of the arms is often represented, with
Ajax and Odysseus vigorously confronting each other,[10] while representations of the
actual suicide may well have influenced Sophocles.[11] A sixth-century black-figure
amphora by Exekias (Boulogne 558; *LIMC* 329.104, Beazley, *Attic black-figure
vase-painters* (Oxford 1956) 145.18, *The Development of Attic black-figure* (rev.
edn. Berkeley, Los Angeles 1986) 64, Pl. 32.1) shows Ajax heaping up a mound of
earth and fixing his sword, while an Attic lekythos of c. 460, perhaps by the
Alcimachus Painter (Basel Antikenmuseum (on loan from private collection); *LIMC*
329.105; K. Schefold, *AK* 19 (1976) 71-8; M.I. Davies, in *ΕΙΔΩΛΟΠΟΙΙΑ* (Rome
1985) 83-117), shows him kneeling in prayer before he kills himself. Sometimes he
falls on his sword, sometimes he thrusts it into himself with his hand. The covering
of the corpse by Tecmessa at *Aj.* 915-16 is evidently anticipated on the tondo of the
kylix attributed to the Brygos Painter (see n. 10; *LIMC* 332.140; Davies (1973);
Taplin (1978) Pl. 11), and on a lost black-figure Etruscan oinochoe attributed to the
Micali Painter (*LIMC* 330.115; Beazley, *EVP* 15, 139). In one version of the myth
Ajax was invulnerable except in his armpit or side, and this seems to be reflected in a
bronze Etruscan statuette of c. 460 in Basel,[12] which, unlike the usual representations

---

9   See J.D. Beazley, *Etruscan vase-painting* (Oxford 1947) 137-41; E. Kunze, *Archaische
       Schildbänder* (= *Olympische Forschungen* 2 (1950)) 154-7; O. Touchefeu, in *Lexicon
       Iconographicum Mythologiae Classicae* I 1 (Zurich and Munich 1981) 325-32; March
       4-7.
10   The voting by the Greek chieftains in the presence of Athena is shown, for example, on
       one side of the exterior of a cup of c. 500-475 by the Brygos Painter from the Bareiss
       Collection (New York Metropolitan Museum L 69.11.35; *LIMC* 325.72, 326.83;
       Davies (1973) 67-9), while the other side presents the quarrel between Ajax and
       Odysseus.
11   The earliest is a proto-Corinthian aryballos (Berlin 3319; *LIMC* 330.118; K. Friis
       Johansen, *The Iliad in early Greek art* (Copenhagen 1967) 30, fig. 4 on 33), which
       shows Ajax throwing himself on his sword. Cf. also a steatite sealstone in New York
       Metropolitan Museum of Art (42.11.13) of the second half of the seventh century (K.
       Schefold, *Myth and legend in early Greek art* (tr. London 1966) Pl. 32 a, a metope (c.
       570-50) from the Temple of Hera at Foce del Sele near Paestum (*LIMC* 331.128).
12   Antikenmuseum Kä 531; *LIMC* 331.133; Davies (1971) 148-56. Cf. also an Etruscan
       mirror in Boston (99.494; *LIMC* 331.135; Beazley, *EVP* 140). On an Etruscan stamnos

of Ajax crouching over his sword, shows him face up and wild-eyed, with the sword entering his left armpit.

Some of the fifth-century paintings may be indebted to Aeschylus, who was the first to present the story on stage, but only a few fragments survive [13] of his Judgement of the Arms, Thracian Women, and Women of Salamis, which were evidently produced together as a trilogy. In the first of these Ajax and Odysseus quarrelled in speeches on stage (fr. 175 R). Whether Jebb was right to suppose that Aeschylus followed the Aethiopis in making the Trojan prisoners the judges it is impossible to say. March 8 surmises that he was the first to present the voting as unfair, on the grounds that, while this motif is evidently not epic, Sophocles treats it so allusively that it must already have been familiar to his audience. But he may have derived it from Pindar (see below). The suicide took place in the Thracian Women, but offstage, and it was reported by a Messenger (Σ Aj. 815, fr. 83). Aeschylus, unlike Sophocles, seems to have followed the version according to which Ajax' invulnerability made his suicide difficult. The Women of Salamis dealt with the return of Teucer and Eurysaces to Salamis, and with the expulsion of Teucer to found Salamis in Cyprus. A cloak is mentioned at fr. 216, which has suggested to some scholars (e.g. March 6) that Tecmessa's covering of the corpse is referred to in this play, and that Aeschylus is the source of this motif. But we should expect it rather in the Thracian Women, and Davies (1973) 65-6 is more probably right that it appeared already in epic.

In three of his epinikian odes the fifth-century poet Pindar is concerned to vindicate the reputation of Ajax after his suicide.[14] At Nem. 7.20-30, in a poem variously dated by modern scholars in the 480s or 460s, Pindar complains that it was the power of Homer's poetry that unduly enhanced the reputation of Odysseus, and secondly that if the army at Troy had been able to see the truth, Ajax would have been awarded Achilles' arms, and would never in his anger have committed suicide with his sword (cf. later Pl. Ap. 41b). All the emphasis, as the context makes clear, is on the unfairness of the judgement by the Greeks. Rather different is the tone of Isth. 4.35-9, perhaps to be dated to 478 BC, where Ajax' suicide brings blame on all the Greeks, but he has nevertheless been honoured by Homer throughout the world. At Nem. 8.21-34, usually dated in the 460s or 450s (but 445 by N.O. Brown), Pindar returns to the theme in the context of human envy and malignant representation, and refers explicitly to the 'secret votes' of the Greeks (cf. S. Aj. 1135). Pindar evidently means, not that it was a secret ballot, but that some kind of cheating was involved.

---

of 425-400 (Palermo, Cat. Ant. 1490; LIMC 329.107; Beazley, EVP 42) Athena directs the sword to the vulnerable part of his body.

13   See H.J. Mette, Der verlorene Aischylos (Berlin 1963) 121-7.

14   For Pindar's treatment of the story see especially G.W. Most, The measures of praise: structure and function in Pindar's Second Pythian and Seventh Nemean odes (Göttingen 1985) 152-6.

He may have been the first to say so. In none of these passages is there any
reference to Ajax' madness or to his attack on the cattle.

Most of what we find in Sophocles' play derives, directly or indirectly, from
one or other of these traditional versions - the judgement of the arms by the Greeks,
Ajax' madness, his attack on the cattle, the suicide, the presence of Tecmessa, the
problem of how to dispose of his corpse. So does the hostility of Athena, though we
cannot be certain that in any earlier version it was she who drove him mad.
Sophocles is possibly the first to bring him back to sanity before his suicide.[15] He
takes it for granted that his audience is familiar with the enmity between Ajax and
Odysseus, and uses it as the starting-point of his play (see 1-33n.). What the
audience does not expect is that at the end of the play it will be Odysseus who
restores the reputation of Ajax by persuading Agamemnon to allow his burial.
Odysseus' surprising behaviour is almost certainly Sophocles' own contribution to
the story. As for the fairness of the voting, there is no doubt that in the play Ajax
and his friends all believe that the arms should not have been awarded to Odysseus
(see 442-6n.), but only Teucer suggests that there was actual tampering with the
votes (1135n.). Agamemnon, not surprisingly, takes a different line (1246-9n.; cf.
1136). It is curious that Sophocles never makes it clear whether there is any
substance to Teucer's accusation, perhaps because in the last resort it makes no
difference. Even if, to an unprejudiced observer, the voting was conducted fairly,
Ajax' reaction to the defeat would have been the same.[16] His claim has been
rejected, and his honour has therefore suffered. Like Pindar, Sophocles is concerned
to rehabilitate his hero, but, unlike him, he does not suppress his embarrassing
exploits (see March 4).

To Sophocles' Athenian audience Ajax was not merely a character from
literature and art but also a figure of hero-cult. He came from Salamis, an island
which since the sixth century had belonged to Athens, and he had come to be
regarded as one of the major Athenian heroes (see 202n.). Salamis is associated with
Athens already at Hom. Il. 2.557-8, a passage which was thought by some in
antiquity to be an Athenian interpolation. There, in the Catalogue of Ships, he
positions his ships at Troy beside those of the Athenians. Before the Battle of
Salamis in 480 BC the Athenians summoned Ajax to help them, and they believed
that they had his support (Hdt. 8.64, Plut. Them. 15). After the victory they
dedicated a captured trireme to him (Hdt. 8.121). As the eponymous hero of one of
the Athenian tribes he had a statue in the agora (Hdt. 5.66, Plut. Mor. 628b-629a,
Paus. 1.5.1), and he had a temple and a festival on Salamis (Paus. 1.35.3, IG II²

---

15   So Mazon 4, Rose 64, March 21-2. But the iconographic evidence on this point is
     inconclusive; see Touchefeu in LIMC I 1. 335-6.
16   'Even if the election had been perfectly fair and proper, nothing would have been
     different. The use of the ballot expresses the views of the people, and the hero must not
     be subject to their whims' (Rosenmeyer 171).

1227.32, Hesych. A 67). His son Eurysaces had an altar in Athens. Miltiades, the victor of Marathon, and Cimon claimed descent from him (Hdt. 6.35, Paus. 2.29.4).[17] It may seem strange that at Megara there was a temple of Athena Aiantis (Paus. 1.42.4), in which the hero and his divine opponent were evidently associated (Pausanias surmises that the statue was made by Ajax himself), but this is not the only example of such an association in cult between a hero and his divine opponent, sometimes a god who has killed him. 'Myth has separated into two figures what in the sacrificial ritual is present as a tension' (W. Burkert, *Greek religion* (tr. J. Raffan, Oxford 1985) 202-3; see also Seaford 130 n.121). Some have thought that Sophocles wrote his play to show his audience how their hero could have triumphed over his defeat and disgrace to become the object of their veneration.[18] His consecration as a hero is probably implied at the end of the play (see 1166-7, 1172nn.), but it is never directly stated, and it is going too far to think of it as the main concern of the drama.

The Play

Of the seven surviving plays of Sophocles the dates of only *Philoctetes* (409 BC) and *Oedipus at Colonus* (produced posthumously in 401) are known for certain. *Antigone* is usually dated to the late 440s, on the strength of a story that connects his election to a generalship in 441/40 with the success of that play. Most, but not quite all, scholars agree that *Ajax*, *Antigone*, and *Trachiniae* together are the earliest of the surviving plays, and of these most scholars believe *Ajax* to be the earliest of all, some putting it as far back as the 450s.[19] They do so on various grounds. Some try to connect the play with the political situation in Athens in the 440s. Whitman, for example, thought that the statesman Cimon, who died in 449, may lie behind the character of Ajax with his simple aristocratic values,[20] while F. Robert dates the play to 446-5, with reference to Pericles' citizen-law of 451-50 (see 1260-1n.). See further pp. 15-16 below. Other scholars have relied on supposed borrowings from, or dependence on, the work of other poets: e.g. Euripides' *Telephus* (see 1100-8n.) or his *Cretan Women* (1295-7n.), which, if true, would bring the play down to the

---

17   See L. Deubner, *Attische Feste* (Berlin 1932) 228, E. Kearns, *The heroes of Attica, BICS* Suppl. 57 (1989) 81-2, 141-2, H.A. Shapiro, *Art and cult under the tyrants in Athens* (Mainz am Rhein 1989) 154-7.

18   E.g. Jebb xxx-xxxii, Bowra 16-19, Rosenmeyer 186-9, Poe 9-18, Seaford 129-30, 136, 398-402; *contra* Pearson, *CQ* 16 (1922) 129, Kitto (1956) 182-3, (1961) 119, Winnington-Ingram 57 n.2; Segal (1981) 142.

19   For discussion of chronology see Whitman 42-55, Webster 2-7, Reinhardt 7-33 (with Lloyd-Jones' Introduction xx-xxiii). J. Kott, *The eating of the gods: an interpretation of Greek tragedy* (tr. London 1974) 289 n.42, is unusual in arguing for the 420s.

20   Whitman 45-6, 61; see also N.O. Brown, Webster 196, Evans, March 32-4.

430s.[21] Reinhardt (11-12) thought that Sophocles was influenced by Aeschylus' *Niobe* (against this see Lloyd-Jones' note on p. 236 of his translation of Reinhardt). For N.O. Brown the play is closely connected with Pindar *Nemean* 8, which he dates to 445 (with 154 7 an echo of *Nem.* 8.22), and must have been written soon after it: it is about the mid fifth-century Athenian crisis which was finally resolved by the Thirty Years' Peace.

The iconographic evidence has sometimes been adduced for dating purposes. Schefold suggested that the Basel lekythos (p. 3 above) was inspired by the play, and indeed was dedicated by the winning choregus as a votive offering after the performance.[22] This would date the play to c. 460, which for most scholars is improbably early.

Most discussions of dating have concentrated on the supposed development of Sophocles in matters of dramatic technique, structure, and style. Those who put *Ajax* before or close to *Antigone* and *Trachiniae* point to the comparative lack of three-actor dialogue, to the anapaestic prelude to the parodos (see 134-200n.), to anapaests used to round off a scene or to introduce a new character (1163-7n.), or to the technique of stichomythia, which seems to be freer in the later plays.[23] For Kirkwood (1958) 86-9, 93, 289, the play shows signs of structural stiffness and abruptness of technique,[24] while Reinhardt, 7-11, 15-18, 32-3, thought that the whole structure was archaic, in that Sophocles had not yet learnt to combine form and content in a perfect unity. On the other hand, it has often been remarked that *antilabē*, the division of an iambic trimeter between two speakers, is found already in *Ajax*, but not in *Antigone*,[25] and that in terms of metrical technique *Ajax*, with its greater frequency of resolution in iambic trimeters, *looks* later than *Trachiniae*, *Antigone*, and *Electra*.

Many scholars have claimed to find a development in Sophocles' style, vocabulary, diction, and imagery. His first production, which was apparently also his first victory, was in 468 BC. Plutarch *Mor.* 79b attributes to Sophocles himself a statement that his style had passed through three phases, the first in which he still employed the inflated style (ὄγκος) of Aeschylus, the second which was displeasing,

---

21   See Tycho von Wilamowitz, *Die dramatische Technik des Sophokles* (Berlin 1917) 51 n. 1; *contra* Lesky 180 n. 2, Reinhardt 234 n. 3.

22   K. Schefold, *AK* 19 (1976) 71-8; see also Stanford (1978) 195-6, M.I. Davies, in *ΕΙΔΩΛΟΠΟΙΙΑ* (Rome 1985) 83-117, March 32-3. *Contra* Scullion 105-6, who remarks that the iconographic tradition has nothing to do with the theatre.

23   Three-actor dialogue, Webster 122, K. Aichele in Jens n. 64 on 64; anapaests, Jebb li, Webster 140, more cautiously Burton 8-9, Heath 174-5; stichomythia, see B. Seidensticker in Jens 200-9, but he is rightly reluctant (209) to explain the differences from the other plays in terms of a simple chronological development.

24   Contrast Mazon 6-7, for whom the dialogue is more subtle than in *Antigone*.

25   Jebb liii-liv, Tycho von Wilamowitz 51 n. 1, Seidensticker 201; Dalmeyda 3 suspected a late revision of the text.

harsh or crude, and artificial, and the third which was most suited to the portrayal of character and the best.[26] Few scholars would ascribe *Ajax* to the first of these periods, but more would place it, perhaps along with *Trachiniae* and *Antigone*, in the second.[27] F.R. Earp, *The style of Sophocles* (Cambridge 1944), traced a straight-line development from an elaborate and artificial style, marked for example by the use of heavy compounds, to a simpler and more natural style, and argued that of the surviving plays *Ajax* shows most clearly the influence of Aeschylus.[28] He detected also a greater number of direct borrowings from Homer. Polemon, the head of the Academy from 314-c.276 BC, is said (*TGrF* IV T 115; cf. 116) to have described Homer as the epic Sophocles, and Sophocles as the tragic Homer. That the Sophoclean Ajax is closer to the Iliadic hero than any other Sophoclean character, and that certain passages of the play are closely modelled on the *Iliad* is undeniable.[29] Whether this has any bearing on its dating is quite another matter. There is no intrinsic reason why the most 'Homeric' play must be the earliest.

Indeed many of the criteria are subjective. None is conclusive in itself, and even cumulatively the evidence does not amount to a great deal. It was the same kind of evidence that before 1952 led most scholars to the false conclusion that *Supplices* was the earliest surviving play of Aeschylus.[30] Some at least of the differences should be explained in terms of the subject-matter (e.g. the Homeric echoes) or the dramatic purpose of the play. All that we can say in the present state of the evidence is that nothing contradicts a date in the 440s, but that certainty is impossible.

Most discussion of dramatic structure has centred on the apparent division of the play into two parts, the first leading up to the suicide of Ajax at 865, and the second dealing with the question of whether he is to receive an honourable burial. In this respect, more than any other, *Ajax* has been grouped with *Trachiniae* and *Antigone*,

---

26 What he meant is not entirely clear; see C.M. Bowra, *Problems in Greek poetry* (Oxford 1953) 108-25, H. Lloyd-Jones, *JHS* 75 (1955) 158-9. For possible borrowings from Aeschylus in *Ajax* see Garner 50-1, 59.

27 First period, J.H. Finley, *HSPh* 50 (1939) 57-8, Webster 166; second period, Bowra, *Problems* 125, Dalmeyda 2, Musurillo 143 n. 1, Webster 143-4, Reinhardt 7, Lesky 265. For Kirkwood (1958) 89 *Ajax* is perhaps one of the earliest plays of the third stage.

28 See also Jebb lii, Whitman 43-4, Kirkwood (1958) 293, Webster 143-62, Lesky 265, Burton 18. For imagery see Musurillo 144, 150-2, for ornamental epithets L. Bergson, *L' Épithète ornementale dans Eschyle, Sophocle et Euripide* (Lund 1956), but his conclusion (173-5) is that they are not sufficient in themselves to determine relative chronology.

29 See 485-524n. (also 1273-80n.), Kirkwood (1965), Reinhardt n. 9 on 237, Easterling (1984), Garner 51-64.

30 See Garvie, *Aeschylus' Supplices: play and trilogy* (Cambridge 1969). For this as a warning to those who try to date *Ajax* see Lloyd-Jones, Introduction to Reinhardt xxi.

and the term 'diptych' is often used by scholars to describe this kind of play. For most the word carries a derogatory sense, which often reflects the feeling that with the death of Ajax the play loses much of its interest.[31] The ancient writer of the scholion on 1123 already complained about a lack of dramatic unity, remarking that after the suicide Sophocles, wishing to extend his drama, indulged in bad taste (for this as the mark of a bad poet cf. Arist. *Po.* 1451b 37-52a 1), and of modern scholars Waldock (49-75) goes furthest in this direction: for him Sophocles' material was insufficient for a proper full-length tragedy, and so he had to pad it out by adding the last 555 lines. Others are less extreme in their criticism, but agree that Sophocles had not yet found the perfect form to match the content of his tragedies.[32] Others again, more reasonably, use the term 'diptych', but in a purely factual and non-derogatory sense: *Ajax*, like *Trachiniae* and *Antigone*, falls into two parts, but Sophocles knew very well what he was doing, and there is no real disintegration of the plot.[33]

Even this approach, however, is too defensive, and it may be better to abandon the term 'diptych' altogether. If we are prepared to take a more positive view from the beginning,[34] we may recognise that the play does in fact possess a carefully planned and highly satisfactory dramatic unity. Heath 195-7 remarks that the structural break before the suicide speech is greater than the break after it, and that 'the audience's expectations are manipulated in such a way as to avoid a premature sense of closure or completeness, thus binding the earlier and later scenes of the play together as integral parts of a single dramatic whole'. First we see the mad Ajax, exulting in his supposed vengeance over his enemies. Then, when he returns to sanity and realises that instead of killing his foes he has slaughtered helpless animals, we watch him resisting all the attempts of his friends to save him, and resolving on suicide, on the grounds that 'the noble man must either live well or die well (479-80). Since the former is no longer possible for him he sees no alternative to death. The Greeks of Sophocles' day may well have held different views about the morality and justification of suicide.[35] For Pythagoreans (Athen. 4.157c; cf. Pl. *Phaedo* 62b,

---

31   See, for example, Dalmeyda 8, Earp 169, Letters 112, 132.

32   E.g. Whitman 44, 63 (Sophocles is struggling with the problem of evolving a single play out of Aeschylus' trilogic form); Tyler 31-6 (Sophocles has unsuccessfully combined two separate plots in one play); see further Tycho von Wilamowitz, *Die dramatische Technik des Sophokles* (Berlin 1917) 51-3, Torrance 294-7, 320-1, Webster 102-3, 166-8. For a useful summary of scholarly opinion see Davidson (1985).

33   See Kirkwood (1958) 42-54, Gellie 190-3, Lesky 188, Scodel 20-2.

34   See Kitto (1961) 119, Knox (1964) 166 n. 13, March 24. Machin 377-93 (esp. 378) argues that *Trachiniae* and *Antigone*, but not *Ajax*, are diptych plays. For Bergson 48-9 the play has a *triptych* form.

35   See 473n.; Pearson on fr. 952, Bowra 46, K.J. Dover, *Greek popular morality in the time of Plato and Aristotle* (Oxford 1974) 168-9, R. Garland, *The Greek way of death* (London 1985) 95-9, E.P. Garrison, *TAPhA* 121 (1991) 1-34, *Groaning tears: ethical*

Laws 873c) it was evidently wrong, and according to Aristotle *EN* 1138a 12-14 there were public sanctions against it. According to R. Parker, *Miasma: pollution and purification in early Greek religion* (Oxford 1983) 41-2, more pollution attached to it than to an ordinary death (but see also Garrison (1995) 11-33). The disgraced Heracles at E. *HF* 1347-51 (cf. 1246-54; also Odysseus at Hom. *Od.* 10.49-53) decides not to kill himself because that would be an act of cowardice.[36] Yoshitake shows, however, that from Homer to Plato suicide was commonly held to be justified as a means of preserving one's honour, and that it is this line that Ajax follows. Despite Kott, for whom his death is a final mockery, 'a heroic gesture in a void',[37] nothing in the play suggests that we are meant to reject his evaluation, or to disagree with Demosthenes (60.31), who cites Ajax' suicide as an example of heroism.[38]

With Ajax' suicide, however, there is no relaxation at all in the tension. He died to save his honour, but death by itself is not sufficient for that purpose. For it is not enough for Ajax himself and his friends to be conscious of his merit. According to the traditional heroic code one's merit must be recognised also by other people. The question of his burial becomes the symbol of that recognition. The point is not that without burial Ajax' soul will be denied peace in Hades and condemned to endless wandering;[39] for nothing whatsoever is said about this in the play (or in *Antigone*). Nor is there any need to apologise for the final part of the play on the grounds that burial was a matter of importance to fifth-century Greeks, as if it were unimportant in other cultures, including our own. Rather, if Menelaus and Agamemnon can prevent his burial, or even if he receives only a clandestine funeral, his suicide has merely saved him from the horror of having to face continued life in permanent disgrace. It has not restored him to his status as a hero. The concern of the whole play, from the moment when his disgrace is discovered in the prologue, to the final sad but triumphant exit of the funeral procession, is designed to rehabilitate him, to show how a man who has fallen so low can be recognised at the end as the

---

   and dramatic aspects of suicide in Greek tragedy (Leiden, New York, Cologne 1995)(45-53 on *Ajax*), Yoshitake. For the six suicides in Sophocles' plays, and for discussion of Ajax' suicide in terms of modern psychological theory, see Seidensticker 105-44.

36   For similarity and difference between Euripides' Heracles and Sophocles' Ajax see Perrotta 81-2, S.A. Barlow, *Ramus* 10 (1981) 112-28, Seidensticker 143, and esp. Yoshitake, who argues that Euripides is not putting forward the doctrine that *all* suicide is cowardice. Garrison shows that a clear distinction was made in general between honourable (e.g. suicide to restore one's honour) and cowardly suicide.

37   J. Kott, *The eating of the gods: an interpretation of Greek tragedy* (tr. London 1974) 70; see also Sorum 372-3, Poe 49.

38   See Nielsen 24, Seidensticker 142-3, Garland 97, Garrison (1995) 53.

39   So Letters 133-5; *contra* Kitto (1956) 181-2; for the idea cf. Hom. *Il.* 23.69-74.

hero that he really is. Visually too he remains at the centre of our attention from the beginning to the end of the play. In the final scenes his corpse lies on the stage, from 1184 forming the centre of a powerful tableau that includes his concubine Tecmessa, his child Eurysaces, and his half-brother Teucer. The final part of the play is no mere coda, but an indispensable development of the drama as a whole.[40]

The Tragedy of Ajax

Ajax falls not because he is wicked but because he is a great man, or rather because of the qualities which make him a great man. This statement would not meet with universal agreement. Some scholars believe that he has done something wrong and is properly punished for it by the gods:[41] the play then teaches us how we should live our lives so as to avoid such punishment. According to one interpretation Ajax' punishment is for his attack on the Greek commanders.[42] But for a fifth-century Greek audience, as for Greeks throughout the classical period, it was as normal and acceptable for someone to take vengeance on his enemies as it was to help his friends.[43] Nowhere in the prologue does Athena say that his conduct was wicked, or that this is why she is punishing him. Nor does Ajax himself ever express guilt or contrition for his attempted action. Cairns (230 n. 48) argues that this lack of concern with the morality of what he has done is 'part of his *extreme* concern with his honour' (my italics), but in the play itself no one, apart from his enemies, explicitly condemns him for it.[44] His intended victims will naturally object to it, but that is a different matter. Other critics too have found Ajax' reaction to be, though understandable, extreme.[45] But, despite Kirkwood (1958) 174, Hester 251, Fisher 327, Cairns 228, his behaviour is not so very different from that of Achilles, who was prevented from killing Agamemnon in *Iliad* 1, not by his sense of morality, nor

---

40   See March 8; for a different view Gellie 23.

41   I have discussed these matters more fully in Garvie (1993) 243-53.

42   For Poe 22 (also 36-8) any convincing defence of Ajax' *arete* must deal with the problem of his attempted attack on his colleagues. For an extreme statement of this view see R.W. Minadeo, *Eranos* 85 (1987) 19-23, for whom (23) Ajax 'betrays the heroic code of conduct outright'. See also Letters 137, Lawall, Webster 30 n. 3, 102, Nielsen 22, Knox (1979) 131.

43   See especially Blundell, but with the qualification (55-9) that stronger disapproval might be directed against those who failed to help friends than against those who failed to harm enemies; also D.A. Hester, *Antichthon* 11 (1977) 22-41, on *OC* (33, 'helping one's friends and harming one's enemies is the duty of the hero, alike in life and death'), Knox (1979) 127-34 (though for him (133) the rule, while proper for the gods, is not necessarily right for men, who can never be sure who their friends and enemies are), Goldhill ch. 4 (esp. 85-8 on *Ajax*). For ancient evidence see X. *Mem.* 2.3.14, 2.6.35, *Hiero* 2.2, 6.12, Pl. *Meno* 71e, *Rep.* 331e, 332d, 334b, 335e.

44   See Linforth 8-10, March 11 n. 60.

45   E.g. Heath 173, Fisher 314, 326-8.

by his recognition of the need to compromise, but by the intervention of Athena and her promise (1.212-14) of splendid gifts in compensation for Agamemnon's *hybris*. That Ajax attempted to take his revenge deceitfully by night has seemed to some critics to detract from his *arete*.[46] The paradox is certainly striking (see 47n.), but it is difficult to see what other option was available to him. The truth is that Ajax is disgraced, not because he sought vengeance on his enemies, but because he failed to achieve it. The great hero turned his sword instead against helpless animals, and he has in consequence become the victim of his enemies' laughter.

A common interpretation of the play,[47] that Ajax has incurred Athena's anger not, or not so much, because of his attack on his foes, but because of his *hybris* in general, depends largely on Athena's speech at 127-32, and on the Messenger's account of Ajax' foolish words on two previous occasions (762-7). That neither passage provides a satisfactory reason for his fall will be shown in the Commentary at 127-33, 719-865, 758-61nn. For the present we may note merely that in neither passage does the word *hybris* occur. The term has all too often been understood to describe a religious offence committed by a human being against the gods, and in particular the presumption or pride which leads a person to step across the line that should separate men from gods. But this is not its normal meaning. It describes, not, or not primarily, a state of mind, though it may result from a state of mind, and it should not be translated as 'pride' (see, however, 1087-8n.). It describes specific behaviour, or the intention to commit such behaviour, and it is usually behaviour committed against another human being, behaviour which is seen by the victim as bringing dishonour to himself. In Homer's *Iliad*, where *hybris* and its cognates occur only five times, the word is used by Achilles when he complains that Agamemnon has robbed him of Briseis (1.203, picked up by Athena at 214). In the *Odyssey*, where it is much more frequent, it is most often applied to the outrageous behaviour of the suitors in Odysseus' palace, behaviour which is directed against Odysseus, not the gods. The word is naturally used most often by the victim complaining about the behaviour of the aggressor. In the *Iliad* Thetis, and in the *Odyssey* Athena, help their human favourites to secure their vengeance, but that does not mean that it was against the gods that the *hybris* was committed. The victims naturally hope that the gods, and Zeus in particular, will punish those who are guilty of it, as they are expected to punish all offences against morality (see Fisher 74), no doubt because the weak who feel threatened by an aggressor naturally hope to have the gods on their side. But that does not turn it into a peculiarly religious offence, even in the

---

46   E.g. Winnington-Ingram 17, Scodel 17. For Ebeling 287 Athena's concern is not to
      punish Ajax, but merely to protect the commanders.
47   See, for example, Perrotta 63-4, Bowra 11-12, 27-38, Letters 137, 144, Kitto (1956) 179-
      98, (1961) 122, Kirkwood (1958) 274 ('he suffers the anger of the gods for as clear a
      demonstration of *hybris* as one could imagine'), Stanford xxvi, Webster 65.

less frequent cases in which the specific outrageous behaviour is actually directed against a god or his cult.[48]

The usage of Sophocles is entirely consistent with this picture. He uses the word and its cognates 37 times in the seven surviving plays (far more often than Aeschylus, who has 18 occurrences in six plays, not counting PV), and of the total no fewer than 14 belong to Ajax. The next highest figure is seven for Electra. Only Euripides' Bacchae has as many occurrences. Almost always the word is put into the mouth of someone who is complaining about the behaviour of his enemies, but who would feel it perfectly proper to retaliate in kind. Only at Trach. 280 are the gods said to disapprove of it. In Electra it is used three times to describe the behaviour of Clytaemestra towards Electra or Orestes, once to describe the adultery of Aegisthus. The same is true of Ajax. Nowhere in the play is the word used in the context of Ajax' attitude towards the gods. Nine times it describes the behaviour of his enemies that is directed, or likely to be directed, against him, or in one case against his son.[49] Only twice is it clearly used of Ajax' behaviour against his enemies (1061, 1081), and there it is put into the mouth of Menelaus, who is not an attractive character in the play. One may add 1088, where Menelaus remarks triumphantly that Ajax used to be a *hybristes*, but now the tables are turned. And at 1258 Teucer, the representative of Ajax, is accused of it by Agamemnon. For the remaining, ambiguous, occurrence see 304n.[50] The conclusion must be that the use

---

48   In most of this I agree with Fisher, for whom *hybris* is the deliberate infliction of shame or dishonour on another, often for the purpose of expressing a sense of superiority, or the drive to engage in such behaviour. See also D.M. MacDowell, *G&R* 23 (1976) 14-31. However, Fisher's interpretation of *Ajax* (312-29) lays too much stress on the *hybris* committed by the hero. For pertinent criticism of his view in general see D.L. Cairns, *CR* 44 (1994) 76-9, *JHS* 116 (1996) 1-32, arguing that *hybris* is not confined to actions, but may describe 'a disposition of excessive self-assertion', an overestimate of one's own honour in a way that threatens the honour of others. For the question of whether 'thinking big' is merely associated with (or an element in) *hybris*, or whether it can actually be equated with it, see 1087-8n. Fisher's view is opposed also by Dickie 101-9, but, even while defending the traditional view that *hybris* is basically an arrogant or presumptuous and complacent state of mind, he concedes (109) that it, 'perhaps in the majority of the instances of its use, does mean "an act of outrage", "an insult"'.

49   153, 196, 367, 560, 955, 971, 1092, 1151, 1385.

50   Fisher (11; cf. also 16, 57 n. 71) goes perhaps too far in his statement that 'acts of aggression done in retaliation or revenge are emphatically not *hybris*'. Occasionally the punishment inflicted on a *hybristes* is itself described in terms of reciprocal *hybris* (see Fisher himself, 96, 250, and cf. [A.] *PV* 970, Gorg. 82 B 6 1.14-15, E. *Ph.* 620, *Ba.* 616; see 304, 1087-8nn.). Certainly excessive revenge does seem to be described, esp. in Euripides, as *hybris* (Fisher 116, 424ff.); for the refusal of burial in revenge see 1129n.

of the word in the play provides little support for the view that Ajax is punished by Athena for his *hybris*, whether it was directed against herself or against his enemies.

It is, however, true that at 132-3 Athena declares that the gods love those who are *sophron* ('sound-minded', 'temperate', 'self-controlled') and hate the wicked. It is equally true that one who commits *hybris* cannot be described as temperate or self-controlled (cf. 1258-9 where the ideas are opposed to each other).[51] *Sophrosyne* (self-control) is certainly not one of Ajax' virtues. Like all Sophoclean heroes he is prone to excess (Greek *perissos*) in everything that he does and says. He talks big (386, 422-3n.), and always refuses to heed the advice of ordinary people, the minor characters, to learn moderation or common-sense, to adapt himself to changing circumstances, to accept compromises.[52] Against all opposition the Sophoclean hero insists on doing what he believes to be right. He is cut off from his community, the *polis*, or, in Ajax' case, the army.[53] In the eyes of his victims his behaviour may seem to be *hybris*, but it is for these qualities that we admire him.[54] As in the case of Ajax they may lead to his ruin, and to this extent we may say that he falls because of his *hybris*.[55] But, as we have seen, Sophocles himself does not put it in these terms, and it is better to avoid the word in this context. It remains true that it is the qualities which arouse our admiration that almost inevitably lead to his ruin.[56] Had he not been proud he would not have fallen. But all Sophoclean heroes are proud, and to qualify his pride by 'megalomaniac' (Winnington-Ingram 15, 19-20, 41, 305; see also Knox (1979) 132) introduces a misleadingly derogatory note. That Ajax' preoccupation with his own honour leads him to exclude the claims of his friends is the unattractive side of his character (see p. 17 below), but Blundell (68-72)

---

51   See Winnington-Ingram 6 n. 11, 'since the man who is *sophron* will not act hubristically and the man who acts hubristically cannot be *sophron*, *hubris* and *sophrosune* can, with due reserve, be regarded as antithetical'. The noun *sophrosyne* does not itself occur in any of Sophocles' surviving plays (nor in Aeschylus), and even the adjective *sophron* and the verb *sophronein* are not common; see Knox (1964) 67 n. 20, who comments that 'they are often used to describe not what the hero should be but what he should not'. They occur more frequently in *Ajax* than in the other plays; see Blundell 61 n. 6.

52   See esp. Knox (1964); also Whitman 59-80, Rosenmeyer 169-70, Winnington-Ingram 9, 304-7.

53   For this aspect of the Sophoclean hero see B. Knox, in *Sophocle* (*Entretiens Fondation Hardt* 29, Vandoeuvres-Geneva 1982) 1-27 (10-13 on *Ajax*).

54   Despite Minadeo (n. 42 above) 23, for whom 'he no more deserves our admiration than he did the arms of Achilles', Gardiner (1987) 77, for whom Sophocles did not intend his audience to admire any aspect of Ajax' actions during the play.

55   'Such heroism contains an inherent *hybris*, and *hybris* an inherent *atê* [ruin]' (Torrance 274-6); see also Kirkwood (1958) 175.

56   We should wonder whether perhaps tragedy is inherent, not only in the human condition and the individual destiny, but in the very standards of heroism' (Winnington-Ingram 310-11; see also Knox (1964) 6, Segal (1981) 8.

overstates this when she describes this preoccupation in terms of 'ruthless indulgence of his own desires' (68). It is honour rather than 'delight' that he elevates 'into a supreme goal' (cf. 72). In Sophocles' plays it is the minor characters, the ordinary mediocre people, who regularly advocate the quiet virtue of *sophrosyne*, and it is his rejection of it that sets the Sophoclean hero apart from them. In *Ajax* its principal proponent is Menelaus, a character who is, compared with Ajax, not only minor, but also contemptible in his presentation. It should therefore disturb the believers in a pious and conventional Sophocles that he pairs Menelaus with Athena in her praise of the *sophron* man at 132-3. It is scarcely credible that Sophocles means these lines to contain the moral of the play, or that he wrote his tragedy to persuade his audience to practise *sophrosyne* and to avoid the *hybris* of Ajax.

There is, however, another character, Odysseus, who is not so obviously minor and certainly not contemptible, but who, although he does not use the word or preach sermons about *sophrosyne*, nevertheless practises it at the end of the play in a manner that far transcends the arguments of Athena and Menelaus. Many scholars have strangely argued that in some sense Odysseus represents a merciful Athena in the final scene, having learnt the lesson of *sophrosyne* as she expounded it in the prologue.[57] On the contrary, Athena is now quite forgotten, and Odysseus' attitude is very different from hers (see 127-33, 132-3nn.). It is Odysseus, the worst enemy of Ajax, who secures his burial and his recognition as a hero. He does so because he shares a common humanity with Ajax, and because he understands the lesson of alternation, an idea which is of crucial importance for our understanding of the play (see 131-2, 383, 646-7, 1087-8nn.): everything changes, so that it is not always right to hate one's enemy, and one should be prepared to accept him as one's friend. So attractive is Odysseus' behaviour that some modern scholars have been tempted to suppose that Sophocles is setting him up, rather than Ajax, as a role-model for the audience. So for Kitto (1961) 122, 'in effect, the play has almost been asking the Socratic question... "How are we to live?" Not like Ajax, and certainly not like Menelaus'.[58] It is often said that Ajax is presented as the last of the traditional aristocratic heroes, his values already out of place in a more modern world which needs rather the flexible and co-operative approach of men like Odysseus.[59] It might, then, be significant that at 1381 (n.) and 1399 the traditional language of *arete* is used for this new kind of hero. Some critics try to explain this in terms of the particular concerns of Athens at the time when the play may have been written (see p. 6 above). So for Segal (1995) 6, 17 the play focuses on the tension between competitive and co-operative values in the fifth-century democratic *polis*, while for

---

57   E.g. Camerer 295, Wigodsky 157, Leinieks 200, Scodel 25, Bergson 38-9.
58   See also Webster 71. For an *un*favourable - and unfair - view of Odysseus' behaviour see Nielsen.
59   E.g. Rosenmeyer 171-2, L.R. Cresci, *Maia* 26 (1974) 223-5, Knox (1979) 126, 144, S.A. Barlow, *Ramus* 10 (1981) 116, Sorum 362-3, 374-6, Golder 14-18, 28-9.

C. Meier, *The political art of Greek tragedy* (tr. Cambridge 1993) 167-87, *Ajax* is a strongly political play, in which Sophocles advocates *sophrosyne* and reconciliation between the leaders and the common people of Athens. H. Gasti, *QUCC* 40 (1992) 81-93, sees Ajax' *hybris* as his refusal to accept the new civic and co-operative conception of hoplite warfare.[60] There is some truth in this approach, but it should not be exaggerated. The attitude of Odysseus will not seem after all so new, if we remember how the traditional hero Achilles treated Priam in *Iliad* 24, while as early as *Odyssey* 22.411-2 it is said by Odysseus to be wrong to exult excessively over dead enemies.[61] Conversely (see n. 66 below) Menelaus and Agamemnon, the opponents of Ajax, share many of his traditional values. It is better to understand the play as demonstrating the excellence of both Ajax and Odysseus. In fifth-century society, as in the heroic age, both types are required.[62] But all the emphasis at the end of the play is on the vindication of Ajax, and ultimately the unexpected behaviour of Odysseus is merely a means to that end.[63] So in *Philoctetes* we find attractive the conversion of Neoptolemus, but it is Philoctetes whom we admire. The recognition of Ajax by Odysseus is more important for what it tells us about Ajax than for what it tells us about Odysseus.[64] The final testimony to the greatness of Ajax is that even his enemy accepts it. Ajax is at the centre of the final procession, and Odysseus will already have left the stage.

A sense of tragedy remains, however, not only because of the suffering and waste that come before the end, but because we are left with unsolved paradoxes and problems. It is ironical that Agamemnon, who is persuaded by Odysseus to permit the burial, never understands the principle of alternation but thinks that Odysseus is acting selfishly (1366), and yields only because he feels obliged to treat Odysseus as a friend (1370-3, cf. 1328-31). On this occasion the traditional obligation to harm

---

60   See further N.O. Brown, Whitman 45-6, Knox (1961), Musurillo 24-5, Rosenmeyer 171-2, Bradshaw, Evans, Rose. For interesting discussion of the complex interrelation between fifth-century civic ideology and the values of the Homeric world see Goldhill 77-8, 146, 155-61, 195.

61   Cairns 240-1 rightly stresses that Odysseus' values are themselves traditional; see also W.E. Brown 120-1, Heath 169, 203-4 (for whom the ethical polarity is not between old and new but between admirable and contemptible), Blundell 100 n. 195.

62   See Rose 71, J. Gould, in T. Winnifrith, P. Murray, K.W. Gransden (edd.), *Aspects of the epic* (London 1983) 40, 'the Ajax of Sophocles' play is...an image of an absolute "morality of honour" which had lost nothing of its relevance for the contemporaries of Alcibiades'.

63   'This appearance of Odysseus is the necessary final word on the tragedy', and 'it is Ajax, not Odysseus, who achieves real sublimity' (Kirkwood (1958) 48-9); see also Perrotta 74, Seale 172-3.

64   Despite Winnington-Ingram 65, for whom Odysseus' defence of Ajax will be 'the supreme testimony to his own *sophrosune*', and Fisher 328, for whom 'the most admirable character by far is of course Odysseus'.

his enemies conflicts with his obligation towards his friends.[65] If Agamemnon had not preferred the latter Ajax would never have secured his burial. More disturbing is that these traditional standards are those of Ajax himself.[66] He too, although he found the principle of alternation attractive, rejected it for himself. In some of the most poignant lines of the play (1381-99) Teucer politely declines Odysseus' offer to help with the funeral, and we feel that the representative of Ajax is right to do so. Odysseus no longer hates Ajax, but it is certain that the reverse could never be true. The audience will remember *Odyssey* 11 (p. 1 above). For Ajax, as for Agamemnon, an enemy must always be an enemy. Yet he himself has rejected the claims of his friends. And it is on his enemy, not his friends, that his recognition and restitution depend.[67] Ajax has the unyielding soul of which Odysseus expresses disapproval at 1361. It is Ajax whom we admire, but, as with so many Sophoclean heroes, it is sad that in rising to his full status as a hero, in transcending the limitations of ordinary human beings, he has had to forfeit some of the attractive graces of human life. Even the burial does not mark a complete resolution of the conflict. It will take place, not in the centre of the community, but on the lonely seashore. Menelaus and Agamemnon will not be present, and even Odysseus will have only a restricted role in it. The play began with Odysseus seeking his enemy Ajax; it ends with him excluded from the presence of Ajax whom he now sees as his friend.[68] The drama concludes with a typically Sophoclean blend of achievement and loss.

The Distribution of the Parts

Various distributions of the parts among the three actors are possible (see Jebb 7-8). The likeliest is that the protagonist played Ajax and Teucer, the deuteragonist Odysseus and Tecmessa, while the tritagonist took the roles of Athena, the Messenger, Menelaus, and Agamemnon. For the possible dramatic significance of such an arrangement see 974-1184n.

The Text

Of the seven surviving plays of Sophocles three, *Ajax*, *Electra*, and *Oedipus Tyrannus*, which were selected in the Byzantine period for study in schools, and are known as the Byzantine triad, are represented by no fewer than about 150 medieval manuscripts, the oldest of which is L, written in the second half of the tenth century, and now in the Laurentian Library in Florence. The fullest account and collation of the manuscripts is to be found in R.D. Dawe, *Studies on the text of Sophocles*

---

65 For the problems inherent in this kind of conflict between the two principles see Blundell 263-4; also Sorum 374-5.

66 'Despite the enormous difference in heroic stature, the values of the Atreidae are essentially the same as Teucer's and Ajax's own' (Blundell 91 n. 161).

67 For this irony see Kirkwood (1958) 255-6, Segal (1995) 6.

68 See Bowie, Fisher 318 n. 124.

(Leiden 1973; Vol. I *The manuscripts and the text* , Vol. II *The collations*), and the fullest apparatus criticus in his Teubner edition (3rd edn. Stuttgart and Leipzig 1996). The apparatus criticus of the present edition is based on that of H. Lloyd-Jones and N.G. Wilson in their 1990 Oxford Classical Text, and it follows their system of reporting readings. But it is more selective in recording both manuscript disagreements and the conjectures of modern scholars. In particular minor matters of orthography are usually ignored.

Discoveries of papyrus fragments have contributed little to the text of *Ajax*, and only four are to be recorded - P.Colon. 251 (2nd cent.), P. Oxy. 2093 (2nd or 3rd cent.), P.Oxy. 1615 (4th cent.), and P.Berol. 21208 (5th or 6th cent.). More important is the evidence of the scholia (Σ), explanatory notes written usually in the margins of the manuscripts, which sometimes explain a text that is clearly different from that of the manuscript itself, and thus provide evidence for an earlier stage of the tradition. The textual critic must take into account also quotations in later authors, e.g. Stobaeus (probably 5th cent.), Eustathius (the 12th cent. Archbishop of Thessalonica), and the lexicographical work of Hesychius (5th cent.), and especially the *Suda,* a lexicon *cum* encyclopaedia of about 1000 AD, which quotes extensively from *Ajax* (A. Adler, in the index of her edition cites over 250 such quotations).

The symbols used in the apparatus criticus, and the manuscripts or groups of manuscripts which they represent are as follows:

l   L (Laur. 32.9, mid-10th cent.), Λ (Leiden, BPG 60A, 10th cent.), K (Laur. 31.10, second half of 12th cent.)

r   the Roman family, consisting of G (Laur. conv. soppr. 152, 1282 AD), R (Vat. gr. 2291, 15th cent.), Q (Par. supp. gr. 109, 16th cent.)

p   two or more of C (Par. gr. 2735), F (Laur. 28.25), H (Laur. 32.40), N (Matrit. gr. 4677), O, (Leiden, Voss. gr. Q.6), P (Heidelberg, Pal. gr. 40), Pa (Vaticanus gr. 904), S (Vaticanus Urb. Gr. 141), V (Venice, Marc. gr. 468), Wa (Milan, Ambr. E. 103 sup.), all of the 13th or 14th centuries

a   two or more of A (Par. gr. 2712, early 14th cent.), D (Neapol. II. F. 9, early 14th cent.), Xr (Vindob. phil. gr. 161, 1412 AD), Xs (Vindob. phil. suppl. gr. 71, second half of 14th cent.), Zr (Marc. gr. 616, 15th cent.)

t   the recension of the 14th cent. scholar Demetrius Triclinius, as it is found in T (Par. gr. 2711) and Ta (Venice, Marc. gr. 470)

Occasionally cited are Zc (Vat. gr. 1333, about 1310-20 AD), which apparently provides evidence for the work of Triclinius at an earlier stage than that represented by T and Ta,[69] and J (Jena, Bos. Q. 7, late 15th cent.)

---

69   See O.L. Smith, *C&M* 32 (1980) 35-43.

L^{ac}	L before correction (ante correctionem)
L^{pc}	L after correction (post correctionem)
L^{sl}	above the line in L
cett.	the remaining manuscripts
codd.	manuscripts (codices)
del.	deleted (delevit)
gl	explanatory gloss
γρ	variant reading (γράφεται)
om.	omitted (omisit)
plerique	the majority of manuscripts
Σ	scholia
v.l.	variant reading (varia lectio)

Quarrel over the arms of Achilles.   Red figure painting by the Brygos Painter (London, British Museum E69)

Bibliography

The following editions of *Ajax*, whether as a single play or as part of the complete works of Sophocles, are most often cited:

L. Campbell (1881; with *Paralipomena Sophoclea*, 1907), R.C. Jebb (1896), A.C. Pearson (OCT 1924), A. Dain and P. Mazon (Budé 1958), J.C. Kamerbeek (2nd edn. 1963), W.B. Stanford (1963), J. de Romilly (1976), H. Lloyd-Jones and N.G. Wilson (OCT 1990), R.D. Dawe (3rd edn. Teubner 1996).

Adams, S.M.   'The *Ajax* of Sophocles', *Phoenix* 9 (1955) 93-110
Adkins, A.W.H. *Merit and responsibility: a study in Greek values* (Oxford 1960)
Bergson, L.   'Der Aias des Sophokles als "Trilogie"', *Hermes* 114 (1986) 36-50
Biggs, P.   'The disease theme in Sophocles' *Ajax, Philoctetes* and *Trachiniae*, *CPh* 61 (1966) 223-35
Blundell, M.W. *Helping friends and harming enemies: a study in Sophocles and Greek ethics* (Cambridge 1989)
Bowie, A.M.   'The end of Sophocles' *Ajax*', *LCM* (1983) 114-15
Bowra, C.M.   *Sophoclean tragedy* (Oxford 1944)
Bradshaw, D.J. 'The Ajax myth and the polis: old values and new', in Pozzi, D.C. and Wickersham, J.M. (edd.), *Myth and the polis* (Ithaca and London 1991) 99-125
Brown, N.O.   'Pindar, Sophocles, and the Thirty Years' Peace', *TAPhA* 82 (1951) 1-28
Brown, W.E.   'Sophocles' Ajax and Homer's Hector, *CJ* 61 (1965/6) 118-21
Burian, P.   'Supplication and hero cult in Sophocles' *Ajax*', *GRBS* 13 (1972) 151-6
Burton, R.W.B. *The chorus in Sophocles' tragedies* (Oxford 1980)
Cairns, D.L.   *AIDOS: the psychology and ethics of honour and shame in ancient Greek literature* (Oxford 1993)
Camerer, R.   'Zu Sophokles' *Aias*', *Gymnasium* 60 (1953) 289-327
Christodoulou, G.A. Τὰ ἀρχαῖα σχόλια εἰς Αἴαντα τοῦ Σοφοκλέους (Athens 1977)
Cohen, D.   'The imagery of Sophocles: a study of Ajax's suicide', *G&R* 25 (1978) 24-36
Coray, M.   *Wissen und Erkennen bei Sophokles* (Basle/Berlin 1993)
Dalmeyda, G.   'Sophocle, Ajax', *REG* 46 (1933) 1-14
Davidson, J.F. 'The parodos of Sophocles *Ajax*', *BICS* 22 (1975) 163-77
———   'Sophocles, Ajax 192-200', Mnem. 29 (1976) 129-35
———   'Sophoclean dramaturgy and the Ajax burial debates', *Ramus* 14 (1985) 16-29

Davies, M.I.   'The suicide of Ajax: a bronze Etruscan statuette from the Käppeli Collection', *AK* 14 (1971) 148-56
———   'Ajax and Tecmessa: a cup by the Brygos Painter in the Bareiss Collection', *AK* 16 (1973) 60-70

Dawe, R.D.   *Studies on the text of Sophocles I: the manuscripts and the text* (Oxford 1973)

Denniston, J.D.   *The Greek particles* (2nd edn. Oxford 1954)

Dickie, M.   'Hesychia and *hybris in Pindar'*, in Gerber, D.E. (ed.), *Greek poetry and philosophy: studies in honour of L. Woodbury* (Chico 1984) 83-109

Easterling, P.E.   'The tragic Homer', *BICS* 31 (1984) 1-8
———   'Notes on tragedy and epic', in *Papers in honour of R.P. Winnington-Ingram* (London 1987) 52-62

Ebeling, R.   'Missverständnisse in den Aias des Sophokles', *Hermes* 76 (1941) 283-314

Errandonea, I.   'Les quatre monologues d' *Ajax* et leur signification', *LEC* 26 (1958)

Evans, J.A.S.   'A reading of Sophocles' *Ajax'*, *QUCC* 38 (1991) 69-85

Ferguson, J.   'Ambiguity in *Ajax'*, *Dioniso* 44 (1970) 12-29

Ferrari, F.   *Ricerche sul testo di Sofocle* (Pisa 1983)

Fisher, N.R.E.   *Hybris: a study in the values of honour and shame in ancient Greece* (Warminster 1992)

Fraenkel, Ed.   *Due seminari romani* (ed. L.E. Rossi, Rome 1977

Fritz, K. von   *Antike und moderne Tragödie* (Berlin 1962)

Gardiner, C.P.   'The staging of the death of Ajax', *CJ* 75 (1979) 10-14
———   *The Sophoclean chorus* (Iowa City 1987)

Garner, R.   *From Homer to tragedy: the art of allusion in Greek poetry* (London, 1990)

Garvie, A.F.   'L'*hybris*, particulièrement chez Ajax', in Machin, A. and Pernée, L. (edd.), *Sophocle: le texte, les personnages* (Aix-en-Provence 1993) 243-53

Gellie, G.H.   *Sophocles: a reading* (Melbourne 1972)

Golder, H.   'Sophocles' Ajax: beyond the shadow of time', *Arion* 1 (1990) 9-34

Goldhill, S.   *Reading Greek tragedy* (Cambridge 1986)

Goodwin, W.W.   *Syntax of the moods and tenses of the Greek verb* (London 1897)

Heath, M.   *The poetics of Greek tragedy* (Stanford 1987)

Henrichs, A.   'The tomb of Aias and the prospect of hero cult in Sophokles'. *ClAnt* 12 (1993) 165-80

Hester, D.A.   'The heroic distemper: a study in the Ajax of Sophocles'. *Prometheus* 5 (1979) 241-55

Holt, P.   'Ajax' ailment', *Ramus* 9 (1980) 22-33

——————— 'The debate-scenes in the Ajax', *AJPh* 102 (1981) 275-88

——————— 'Ajax's burial in early Greek epic', *AJPh* 113 (1992) 319-31

Jackson, J. *Marginalia scaenica* (Oxford 1955)

Jens, W. (ed.), *Die Bauformen der griechischen Tragödie* (Munich 1971)

Jouanna, J. 'La métaphore de la chasse dans le prologue de l' "Ajax" de Sophocle, *Bull de l' Assoc. G. Budé* (1977) 168-86

Kirkwood, G.M. *A study of Sophoclean drama* (Ithaca NY 1958)

——————— 'Homer and Sophocles' "Ajax"', in Anderson, M.J. (ed.), *Classical drama and its influence: essays H.D.F. Kitto* (London 1965) 51-70

Kitto, H.D.F. *Form and meaning in drama* (London 1956)

——————— *Greek tragedy* (3rd edn. London 1961)

Knox, B. 'The *Ajax* of Sophocles', *HSPh* 65 (1961) 1-37

——————— *The heroic temper: studies in Sophoclean tragedy* (Berkeley, Los Angeles, London 1964)

——————— *Word and action: essays on the ancient theater* (Baltimore and London 1979)

Kühner, R. *Ausführliche Grammatik der griechischen Sprache* II. 2 vols (3rd edn. rev. B. Gerth, Hanover and Leipzig 1898-1904)

Lawall, S.N. 'Sophocles' Ajax: ἄριστος after Achilles', *CJ* 54 (1958-9) 290-4

Leinieks, V. 'Aias and the day of wrath', *CJ* 69 (1974) 193-201

Lesky, A. *Die tragische Dichtung der Hellenen* (3rd edn. Göttingen 1972)

Letters, F.J.H. *The life and work of Sophocles* (London and New York 1953)

Ley, G. 'A scenic plot of Sophocles' *Ajax* and *Philoctetes*', *Eranos* 86 (1988) 85-115

Linforth, I.M. 'Three scenes in Sophocles "Ajax"', *Univ. of California Pubs. In Class. Philol.* 15 (1954) 1-28

Lloyd-Jones, H. and Wilson, N.G *Sophoclea: studies on the text of Sophocles* (Oxford 1990)

Long, A.A. *Language and thought in Sophocles: a study of abstract nouns and poetic technique* (London 1968)

Machin, A. *Cohérence et continuité dans le théâtre de Sophocle* (Quebec 1981)

March, J.R. 'Sophocles' *Ajax*: the death and burial of a hero', *BICS* 38 (1991-3) 1-36

Mills, S.P. 'The death of Ajax', *CJ* 76 (1980-81) 129-35

Moore, J. 'The dissembling-speech of Ajax' *YClS* 25 (1977) 47-66

Moorhouse, A.C.*The syntax of Sophocles* (Leiden 1982)

Musurillo, H. *The light and the darkness: studies in the dramatic poetry of Sophocles* (Leiden 1967)

Nielsen, R.M. 'Sophocles' *Ajax*: a matter of judgment', *Antichthon* 12 (1978) 18-27

Padel, R.   *In and out of the mind: Greek images of the tragic self* (Princeton 1992)

Pearson, A.C.   'Critical notes on Sophocles and in particular on the Ajax', *PCPhS* 121 (1922) 14 29

Perrotta, G.   'L' "Aiace" di Sofocle', *Atene e Roma* 2 (1934) 63 98

Podlecki, A.J.   'Ajax's gods and the gods of Sophocles', *AC* 49 (1980) 45-86

Poe, J.P.   *Genre and meaning in Sophocles' Ajax* (Frankfurt am Main 1987)

Poehlmann, E.   'Bühne und Handlung im Aias des Sophokles', *A&A* 32 (1986) 20-32

Reeve, M.D.   'Interpolation in Greek tragedy III', *GRBS* 14 (1973) 145-71

Reinhardt, K.   *Sophocles* (tr. H. Harvey and D. Harvey, intro. by H. Lloyd-Jones; Oxford 1979)

Renehan, R.   Review of Lloyd-Jones and Wilson, *CPh* 87 (1992) 335-75

Robert, F.   'Sophocle, Périclès, Hérodote et la date d'*Ajax*', *RPh* 38 (1964) 213-27

Rose, P.W.   'Historicizing Sophocles' *Ajax*', in Goff, B. (ed.), *History, tragedy, theory: dialogues in Athenian drama* (Austin 1995) 59-90

Rosenmeyer, T.G. *The masks of tragedy: essays on six Greek dramas* (New York 1971)

Schefold, K.   'Sophokles' Aias auf einer Lekythos', *AK* 19 (1976) 71-8

Schlesinger, E. 'Erhaltung im Untergang: Sophokles' *Aias* als pathetische Tragödie', *Poetica* 3 (1970) 359-87

Scodel, R.   *Sophocles* (Boston 1984)

Scott, W.C.   *Musical design in Sophoclean theater* (Hanover NH 1996)

Scullion S.   *Three studies in Athenian dramaturgy* (Stuttgart/Leipzig 1994)

Seaford, R.   *Reciprocity and ritual: Homer and tragedy in the developing city-state* (Oxford 1994)

Seale, D.   *Vision and stagecraft in Sophocles* (London and Canberra 1982)

Segal, C.   *Tragedy and civilization: an interpretation of Sophocles* (Cambridge MA and London 1981)

_____   *Sophocles' tragic world: divinity, nature, society* (Cambridge MA and London 1995)

Seidensticker, B. 'Die Wahl des Todes bei Sophokles', in *Entretiens Fondation Hardt* 29 (Vandoeuvres - Geneva 1982) 105-44

Sicherl, M.   'The tragic issue in Sophocles' *Ajax*', *YClS* 25 (1977) 67-98

Simpson, M.   'Sophocles' Ajax: his madness and transformation', *Arethusa* 2 (1969) 88-103

Sorum, C.E.   'Sophocles' *Ajax* in context', *CW* 79 (1985-6) 361-77

Stanford, W.B.   'Light in darkness in Sophocles' *Ajax*', *GRBS* 19 (1978) 189-97

Stevens, P.T.   'Ajax in the *Trugrede*', *CQ* 36 (1986) 327-36

Synodinou, K.   'Tecmessa in the *Ajax* of Sophocles', *A&A* 33 (1987) 99-107

Taplin, O.   *The stagecraft of Aeschylus: the dramatic use of exits and entrances in Greek tragedy* (Oxford 1977)
————   *Greek tragedy in action* (London 1978)
————   in Bowersock, G. et al.(edd.), *Arktouros: Hellenic studies presented to B.M.W. Knox* (Berlin/New York 1979) 122-9
Torrance, R.M.   'Sophocles: some bearings', *HSPh* 69 (1965) 269-327
Tyler, J.   'Sophocles' Ajax and Sophoclean plot construction', *AJPh* 95 (1974) 24-42
Vandvik, E.   'Ajax the insane', *SO* Suppl. 11 (1942) 169-75
Waldock, A.J.A. *Sophocles the dramatist* (Cambridge 1951)
Webster, T.B.L. *An introduction to Sophocles* (2ⁿᵈ edn. London 1969)
West, M.L.   'Tragica II', *BICS* 25 (1978) 106-22
Whitman, C.H. *Sophocles: a study of heroic humanism* (Cambridge MA 1951)
Wigodsky, M.M. The "salvation" of Ajax', *Hermes* 90 (1962) 149-58
Wilamowitz-Moellendorff, T. von *Die dramatische Technik des Sophokles* (Berlin 1917)
Winnington-Ingram, R.P. *Sophocles: an interpretation* (Cambridge 1980)
Yoshitake, S.   'Disgrace, grief and other ills: Herakles' rejection of suicide', *JHS* 114 (1994) 135-53
Zanker, G.   'Sophocles' *Ajax* and the heroic values of the *Iliad*', *CQ* 42 (1992) 20-5

SOPHOCLES

AJAX

ΑΙΑΣ

ΑΘΗΝΑ

Ἀεὶ μέν, ὦ παῖ Λαρτίου, δέδορκά σε
πεῖράν τιν' ἐχθρῶν ἁρπάσαι θηρώμενον·
καὶ νῦν ἐπὶ σκηναῖς σε ναυτικαῖς ὁρῶ
Αἴαντος, ἔνθα τάξιν ἐσχάτην ἔχει,
5 πάλαι κυνηγετοῦντα καὶ μετρούμενον
ἴχνη τὰ κείνου νεοχάραχθ', ὅπως ἴδῃς
εἴτ' ἔνδον εἴτ' οὐκ ἔνδον. εὖ δέ σ' ἐκφέρει
κυνὸς Λακαίνης ὥς τις εὔρινος βάσις.
ἔνδον γὰρ ἀνὴρ ἄρτι τυγχάνει, κάρα
10 στάζων ἱδρῶτι καὶ χέρας ξιφοκτόνους.
καί σ' οὐδὲν εἴσω τῆσδε παπταίνειν πύλης
ἔτ' ἔργον ἐστίν, ἐννέπειν δ' ὅτου χάριν
σπουδὴν ἔθου τήνδ', ὡς παρ' εἰδυίας μάθῃς.

ΟΔΥΣΣΕΥΣ

ὦ φθέγμ' Ἀθάνας, φιλτάτης ἐμοὶ θεῶν,
15 ὡς εὐμαθές σου, κἂν ἄποπτος ᾖς ὅμως,
φώνημ' ἀκούω καὶ ξυναρπάζω φρενί,
χαλκοστόμου κώδωνος ὡς Τυρσηνικῆς.
καὶ νῦν ἐπέγνως εὖ μ' ἐπ' ἀνδρὶ δυσμενεῖ
βάσιν κυκλοῦντ', Αἴαντι τῷ σακεσφόρῳ·
20 κεῖνον γάρ, οὐδέν' ἄλλον, ἰχνεύω πάλαι.
νυκτὸς γὰρ ἡμᾶς τῆσδε πρᾶγος ἄσκοπον
ἔχει περάνας, εἴπερ εἴργασται τάδε·
ἴσμεν γὰρ οὐδὲν τρανές, ἀλλ' ἀλώμεθα·
κἀγὼ 'θελοντὴς τῷδ' ὑπεζύγην πόνῳ.
25 ἐφθαρμένας γὰρ ἀρτίως εὑρίσκομεν
λείας ἁπάσας καὶ κατηναρισμένας
ἐκ χειρὸς αὐτοῖς ποιμνίων ἐπιστάταις.
τήνδ' οὖν ἐκείνῳ πᾶς τις αἰτίαν τρέπει.
καί μοί τις ὀπτὴρ αὐτὸν εἰσιδὼν μόνον

AJAX

[*Enter Odysseus by an eisodos (side-passage), followed by Athena probably by the same eisodos.*

ATHENA   I am for ever seeing you, son of Laertes, hunting down some enterprising way of attacking your enemies; so now I see you at the huts by Ajax' ships, where he holds the post at the end of the line, hunting all this time and measuring his newly-furrowed tracks, to see whether he is at home or away from home. It is like the keen-scented course of some Laconian bitch that brings you surely to your goal. For Ajax has just arrived home, his head and sword-killer's hands dripping with sweat. There is no longer any need for you to peer inside this gate, but you should tell me why you have taken this trouble; since I already know the answer to your question you may learn it from me.

ODYSSEUS   O voice of Athena, dearest of gods to me, how easily I hear and recognise your utterance, invisible though you are, and grasp it in my mind as if it were from a bronze-mouthed Etruscan trumpet. Now you have done well to recognise that it is in quest of an enemy that I circle round, Ajax the bearer of the shield. For it is he, none other, that I have long been tracking. Last night he has performed against us an inconceivable deed, if indeed he *has* done this; for we have no clear knowledge, but are perplexed; and that is why I volunteered to undertake this task. For we have just discovered all the plundered animals destroyed and killed by human hand, together with the overseers of the flocks. So everyone attributes the blame

30 πηδῶντα πεδία σὺν νεορράντῳ ξίφει
φράζει τε κἀδήλωσεν· εὐθέως δ' ἐγὼ
κατ' ἴχνος ᾄσσω, καὶ τὰ μὲν σημαίνομαι,
τὰ δ' ἐκπέπληγμαι, κοὐκ ἔχω μαθεῖν ὅπου.
καιρὸν δ' ἐφήκεις· πάντα γὰρ τά τ' οὖν πάρος
35 τά τ' εἰσέπειτα σῇ κυβερνῶμαι χερί.
ΑΘ. ἔγνων, Ὀδυσσεῦ, καὶ πάλαι φύλαξ ἔβην.
τῇ σῇ πρόθυμος εἰς ὁδὸν κυναγίᾳ.
ΟΔ. ἦ καί, φίλη δέσποινα, πρὸς καιρὸν πονῶ;
ΑΘ. ὡς ἔστιν ἀνδρὸς τοῦδε τἄργα ταῦτά σοι.
40 ΟΔ. καὶ πρὸς τί δυσλόγιστον ὧδ' ᾖξεν χέρα;
ΑΘ. χόλῳ βαρυνθεὶς τῶν Ἀχιλλείων ὅπλων.
ΟΔ. τί δῆτα ποίμναις τήνδ' ἐπεμπίπτει βάσιν;
ΑΘ. δοκῶν ἐν ὑμῖν χεῖρα χραίνεσθαι φόνῳ.
ΟΔ. ἦ καὶ τὸ βούλευμ' ὡς ἐπ' Ἀργείοις τόδ' ἦν;
45 ΑΘ. κἂν ἐξεπράξατ', εἰ κατημέλησ' ἐγώ.
ΟΔ. ποίαισι τόλμαις ταῖσδε καὶ φρενῶν θράσει;
ΑΘ. νύκτωρ ἐφ' ὑμᾶς δόλιος ὁρμᾶται μόνος.
ΟΔ. ἦ καὶ παρέστη κἀπὶ τέρμ' ἀφίκετο;
ΑΘ. καὶ δὴ 'πὶ δισσαῖς ἦν στρατηγίσιν πύλαις.
50 ΟΔ. καὶ πῶς ἐπέσχε χεῖρα μαιμῶσαν φόνου;
ΑΘ. ἐγώ σφ' ἀπείργω, δυσφόρους ἐπ' ὄμμασι
γνώμας βαλοῦσα, τῆς ἀνηκέστου χαρᾶς,
καὶ πρός τε ποίμνας ἐκτρέπω σύμμεικτά τε
λείας ἄδαστα βουκόλων φρουρήματα·
55 ἔνθ' ἐσπεσὼν ἔκειρε πολύκερων φόνον
κύκλῳ ῥαχίζων· κἀδόκει μὲν ἔσθ' ὅτε

33 ὅπου LᵃᶜKa: ὅτου rpat
35 χερί] φρενί ΣL, γρ in N
44 βούλευμ' pat, ΣL: βούλημ' Lrp
45 ἐξεπράξατ' L, ΣL: -αξεν rpa
50 μαργῶσαν H: διψῶσαν γρ in G, gl in p
51 ἀπείργω Lpat: ἀπεῖρζα rp, Aˢˡ

for this to him. And an eyewitness who saw him all by himself leaping over the plain with freshly-sprinkled sword informed me and revealed it to me. I immediately rushed on the trail, and I can identify some of the signs, but as for the rest I am confused and I cannot discover where he is. You have arrived at the right time; for in all things both past and future I am guided by your hand.

Athena	I knew it Odysseus, and that is why I came out on the road a while ago, zealous to promote your hunting-expedition.
Odysseus	Dear mistress, am I really labouring to good effect?
Athena	Yes, you should know that it *is* this man's work.
Odysseus	For what purpose then did he put his hand to so irrational an attack?
Athena	Anger overwhelmed him because of Achilles' armour.
Odysseus	Why then was it on the flocks that he fell with such an onslaught?
Athena	He thought that it was with your blood that he was staining his hand.
Odysseus	Was this intention really directed against the Argives?
Athena	Yes, and he would have accomplished it, had I been careless.
Odysseus	What kind of rashness was this and how was his mind so bold?
Athena	He set out alone against you, by night and stealthily.
Odysseus	Did he really get there and arrive at his goal?
Athena	Yes, he was already at the gates of the two generals.
Odysseus	Then how was it that he stayed his hand when it was so eager for blood?
Athena	I cast grievous imaginations on his eyes and kept him from this incurable joy, by diverting him against the flocks and the mixed booty, still undivided, that the herdsmen guarded; then he fell on the many horned beasts and slaughtered them, hewing at them all around him and cutting through their spines, and he thought at times that he had in his power

δισσοὺς ᾿Ατρείδας αὐτόχειρ κτείνειν ἔχων,
ὅτ᾽ ἄλλοτ᾽ ἄλλον ἐμπίτνων στρατηλατῶν.
ἐγὼ δὲ φοιτῶντ᾽ ἄνδρα μανιάσιν νόσοις

60 ὤτρυνον, εἰσέβαλλον εἰς ἕρκη κακά.
κἄπειτ᾽, ἐπειδὴ τοῦδ᾽ ἐλώφησεν φόνου,
τοὺς ζῶντας αὖ δεσμοῖσι συνδήσας βοῶν
ποίμνας τε πάσας ἐς δόμους κομίζεται,
ὡς ἄνδρας, οὐχ ὡς εὔκερων ἄγραν ἔχων.

65 καὶ νῦν κατ᾽ οἴκους συνδέτους αἰκίζεται.
δείξω δὲ καὶ σοὶ τήνδε περιφανῆ νόσον,
ὡς πᾶσιν ᾿Αργείοισιν εἰσιδὼν θροῇς.
θαρσῶν δὲ μίμνε, μηδὲ συμφορὰν δέχου,
τὸν ἄνδρ᾽· ἐγὼ γὰρ ὀμμάτων ἀποστρόφους

70 αὐγὰς ἀπείρξω σὴν πρόσοψιν εἰσιδεῖν.
οὗτος, σὲ τὸν τὰς αἰχμαλωτίδας χέρας
δεσμοῖς ἀπευθύνοντα προσμολεῖν καλῶ·
Αἴαντα φωνῶ· στεῖχε δωμάτων πάρος.

ΟΔ. τί δρᾷς, ᾿Αθάνα; μηδαμῶς σφ᾽ ἔξω κάλει.
75 ΑΘ. οὐ σῖγ᾽ ἀνέξῃ μηδὲ δειλίαν ἀρῇ;
ΟΔ. μὴ πρὸς θεῶν· ἀλλ᾽ ἔνδον ἀρκείτω μένων.
ΑΘ. τί μὴ γένηται; πρόσθεν οὐκ ἀνὴρ ὅδ᾽ ἦν;
ΟΔ. ἐχθρός γε τῷδε τἀνδρὶ καὶ τανῦν ἔτι.
ΑΘ. οὔκουν γέλως ἥδιστος εἰς ἐχθροὺς γελᾶν;
80 ΟΔ. ἐμοὶ μὲν ἀρκεῖ τοῦτον ἐν δόμοις μένειν.
ΑΘ. μεμηνότ᾽ ἄνδρα περιφανῶς ὀκνεῖς ἰδεῖν;
ΟΔ. φρονοῦντα γάρ νιν οὐκ ἂν ἐξέστην ὄκνῳ.
ΑΘ. ἀλλ᾽ οὐδὲ νῦν σε μὴ παρόντ᾽ ἴδῃ πέλας.
85 ΟΔ. πῶς, εἴπερ ὀφθαλμοῖς γε τοῖς αὐτοῖς ὁρᾷ.
ΑΘ. ἐγὼ σκοτώσω βλέφαρα καὶ δεδορκότα.
ΟΔ. γένοιτο μεντἂν πᾶν θεοῦ τεχνωμένου.

57   δοιοὺς P.Oxy. 2093[ac]
58   ὅτ᾽] τότ᾽ P.Oxy. 2093   ἐμπεσὼν γρ in L, ἐμπίπτειν RP
60   εἰς ἐρινῦν κακήν γρ in L
61   φόνου Lrpat: πόνου a
63   post 64, omisso 65, P.Oxy. 2093
75   ἀρῇ Hesych.: εἶς at, ἄρῃς LrpZr
80   ἐν δόμοις Waa: εἰς δόμους Lrpt, Σ

the two sons of Atreus and was killing them with his own hand, at other times that he was killing now this, now that commander, as he fell on them. I urged the man on in his frenzied movement with attacks of madness, and threw him into evil hunting-nets. And then, when he rested from this killing, he turned to the surviving cattle and bound them with chains and brought home all the flocks, as if he had men in his power, not prey with fine horns. And now he has them tied up at home and tortures them.

To you too I shall display this sickness in full view, so that when you have seen it you may tell of it aloud to all the Argives. Wait for the man with confidence, do not expect any mishap; for I shall turn away the beams of his eyes and prevent them from seeing your face.

You there, you who are pulling back your prisoners' arms with ropes, I summon you to approach. I call 'Ajax'; come out in front of the house.

Odysseus	What are you doing, Athena? On no account summon him outside.
Athena	Won't you face him quietly and avoid the charge of cowardice?
Odysseus	Please no; be content that he should stay indoors.
Athena	In case what may happen? Was he not a man before?
Odysseus	Yes he was my enemy before and still he is.
Athena	Why, is it not the sweetest laughter to laugh at one's enemies?
Odysseus	I am content that he should stay in the house.
Athena	Do you shrink from seeing a madman in full view?
Odysseus	Yes, if he had been sane I should not have kept out of his way or shrunk from him.
Athena	Well even now he will certainly not see you though you are here and close to him.
Odysseus	How so, if he sees with the same eyes as before?
Athena	I shall darken his eyes even though they can still see.
Odysseus	Well anything may happen if a god contrives it.

60

65

70

75

80

85

32

ΑΘ. σίγα νυν ἑστώς, καὶ μέν' ὡς κυρεῖς ἔχων.
ΟΔ. μένοιμ' ἄν· ἤθελον δ' ἂν ἐκτὸς ὢν τυχεῖν.
ΑΘ. ὦ οὗτος, Αἴας, δεύτερόν σε προσκαλῶ,
90   τί βαιὸν οὕτως ἐντρέπῃ τῆς συμμάχου;

ΑΙΑΣ

       ὦ χαῖρ', Ἀθάνα, χαῖρε, Διογενὲς τέκνον,.
       ὡς εὖ παρέστης· καί σε παγχρύσοις ἐγὼ
       στέψω λαφύροις τῆσδε τῆς ἄγρας χάριν.
ΑΘ.   καλῶς ἔλεξας. ἀλλ' ἐκεῖνό μοι φράσον,
95   ἔβαψας ἔγχος εὖ πρὸς Ἀργείων στρατῷ;
ΑΙ.   κόμπος πάρεστι κοὐκ ἀπαρνοῦμαι τὸ μή.
ΑΘ.   ἦ καὶ πρὸς Ἀτρείδαισιν ἤχμασας χέρα;
ΑΙ.   ὥστ' οὔποτ' Αἴανθ' οἵδ' ἀτιμάσουσ' ἔτι.
ΑΘ.   τεθνᾶσιν ἄνδρες, ὡς τὸ σὸν ξυνῆκ' ἐγώ.
100 ΑΙ. θανόντες ἤδη τἄμ' ἀφαιρείσθων ὅπλα.
ΑΘ.   εἶεν· τί γὰρ δὴ παῖς ὁ τοῦ Λαερτίου;
       ποῦ σοι τύχης ἔστηκεν; ἦ πέφευγέ σε;
ΑΙ.   ἦ τοὐπίτριπτον κίναδος ἐξήρου μ' ὅπου;
ΑΘ.   ἔγωγ'· Ὀδυσσέα τὸν σὸν ἐνστάτην λέγω.
105 ΑΙ. ἥδιστος, ὦ δέσποινα, δεσμώτης ἔσω
       θακεῖ· θανεῖν γὰρ αὐτὸν οὔ τί πω θέλω.
ΑΘ.   πρὶν ἂν τί δράσῃς ἢ τί κερδάνῃς πλέον;
ΑΙ.   πρὶν ἂν δεθεὶς πρὸς κίον' ἑρκείου στέγης
ΑΘ.   τί δῆτα τὸν δύστηνον ἐργάσῃ κακόν;
110 ΑΙ. μάστιγι πρῶτον νῶτα φοινιχθεὶς θάνῃ.
.ΑΘ.   μὴ δῆτα τὸν δύστηνον ὧδέ γ' αἰκίσῃ.
ΑΙ.   χαίρειν, Ἀθάνα, τἄλλ' ἐγώ σ' ἐφίεμαι,
       κεῖνος δὲ τείσει τήνδε κοὐκ ἄλλην δίκην.
ΑΘ.   σὺ δ' οὖν, ἐπειδὴ τέρψις ἥδε σοι τὸ δρᾶν,
115   χρῶ χειρί, φείδου μηδὲν ὧνπερ ἐννοεῖς.
ΑΙ.   χωρῶ πρὸς ἔργον· τοῦτο σοὶ δ' ἐφίεμαι,

89 Αἴας K: Αἴαν cett., *Suda*
97 χέρα pat: -αι L, -ας rH
98 οἵδ' L
112 ἐγώ σ' QRpa: ἔγωγέ σ' LGpZrt: ἔγωγ' Jackson 155-6
114 ἥδε Lap: ὧδε rpt: ἐπειδὴ τέρψις ἥδ', ἐν σοὶ τὸ δρᾶν Jackson 156-7

Athena	Be quiet then, stand there and stay just as you are.
Odysseus	I'll stay; but I could have wished to be safely out of the way.
Athena	You there, Ajax, I summon you a second time. Why do you pay so little heed to your ally?

90

[Enter Ajax from the hut]

Ajax	Oh hail, Athena, hail daughter of Zeus, how well you have stood by my side; and I shall honour you with golden spoils in gratitude for this hunt.
Athena	Well said. But tell me this, did you dye your sword thoroughly in the army of the Argives?
Ajax	I can freely boast of it, and I don't deny that I did it.
Athena	Did you really turn your armed hand on the sons of Atreus?
Ajax	The result is that these men will never again dishonour Ajax.
Athena	The men are dead, as I understand your word.
Ajax	They are dead. Now let them deprive me of my arms.
Athena	Well then, what of Laertes' son? In what state do you have him? Has he escaped you?
Ajax	Are you asking me where the villainous fox is?
Athena	I am; I mean Odysseus your adversary.
Ajax	He is sitting inside, mistress, a most welcome prisoner; for I do not want him to die for a while yet.
Athena	Until you do what or gain what benefit?
Ajax	Until tied to a pillar of my house -
Athena	What harm, pray, will you do to the wretched man?
Ajax	Until his back is first reddened with the whip before he dies.
Athena	Pray do not torture so the wretched man.
Ajax	In everything else, Athena, I bid you have your way, but this, and no other, is the punishment that he will receive.
Athena	Very well then, since it is your pleasure to act like this, take action, spare none of the things you plan.

95

100

105

110

115

34

τοιάνδ' ἀεί μοι σύμμαχον παρεστάναι.
ΑΘ. ὁρᾷς, Ὀδυσσεῦ, τὴν θεῶν ἰσχὺν ὅση;
τούτου τίς ἄν σοι τἀνδρὸς ἢ προνούστερος
120 ἢ δρᾶν ἀμείνων ηὑρέθη τὰ καίρια;
ΟΔ. ἐγὼ μὲν οὐδέν' οἶδ'· ἐποικτίρω δέ νιν
δύστηνον ἔμπας, καίπερ ὄντα δυσμενῆ,
ὁθούνεκ' ἄτῃ συγκατέζευκται κακῇ,
οὐδὲν τὸ τούτου μᾶλλον ἢ τοὐμὸν σκοπῶν.
125 ὁρῶ γὰρ ἡμᾶς οὐδὲν ὄντας ἄλλο πλὴν
εἴδωλ' ὅσοιπερ ζῶμεν ἢ κούφην σκιάν.
ΑΘ. τοιαῦτα τοίνυν εἰσορῶν ὑπέρκοπον
μηδέν ποτ' εἴπῃς αὐτὸς ἐς θεοὺς ἔπος,
μηδ' ὄγκον ἄρῃ μηδέν', εἴ τινος πλέον
130 ἢ χειρὶ βρίθεις ἢ μακροῦ πλούτου βάθει.
ὡς ἡμέρα κλίνει τε κἀνάγει πάλιν
ἅπαντα τἀνθρώπεια· τοὺς δὲ σώφρονας
θεοὶ φιλοῦσι καὶ στυγοῦσι τοὺς κακούς.

ΧΟΡΟΣ

Τελαμώνιε παῖ, τῆς ἀμφιρύτου
135 Σαλαμῖνος ἔχων βάθρον ἀγχίαλον,
σὲ μὲν εὖ πράσσοντ' ἐπιχαίρω·
σὲ δ' ὅταν πληγὴ Διὸς ἢ ζαμενὴς
λόγος ἐκ Δαναῶν κακόθρους ἐπιβῇ,
μέγαν ὄκνον ἔχω καὶ πεφόβημαι
140 πτηνῆς ὡς ὄμμα πελείας.
ὡς καὶ τῆς νῦν φθιμένης νυκτὸς
μεγάλοι θόρυβοι κατέχουσ' ἡμᾶς
ἐπὶ δυσκλείᾳ, σὲ τὸν ἱππομανῆ
λειμῶν' ἐπιβάντ' ὀλέσαι Δαναῶν
145 βοτὰ καὶ λείαν,
ἥπερ δορίληπτος ἔτ' ἦν λοιπή,
κτείνοντ' αἴθωνι σιδήρῳ.

119 ἄν σοι τἀνδρὸς Lpat: ἀνδρῶν ἄλλος rD ἢ LGZrt: ἦν QRpa
129 ἄρῃ Lpa: ῃς rpat
130 βάθει Lrpat: βάρει pa
135 ἀγχίαλον H: -άλου cett.
146 λοιπή] κοινή γρ in G, gl in Q, cf. Σp

Ajax	I am off to work; but this I bid you, always stand beside me as an ally of this kind.

[*Exit Ajax into the hut*]

Athena	Do you see, Odysseus, the greatness of the strength of the gods? Whom could you have found with greater prudence than this man or better at doing what had to be done?
Odysseus	I know of no one; but I pity him in his wretchedness nonetheless, although he is my enemy, because he has been harnessed to an evil delusion; I look not to his case more than to my own. For I see that all we who live are nothing more than phantoms or an insubstantial shadow.
Athena	Look then on such things, and never speak yourself any arrogant word against the gods, nor be puffed up with self-importance, if you outweigh someone else in might or in the depth of your great wealth. For a day can cause all human affairs to sink and bring them up again; it is the sound-minded whom the gods love, while they hate the wicked.

120

125

130

[*Exeunt Athena and Odysseus, probably by different eisodoi. Enter the chorus of Ajax' sailors*]

CHORUS

Son of Telamon, possessor of sea-girt Salamis, firmly based beside the sea, when you prosper I rejoice over it; but whenever the stroke of Zeus or a violent word from the Danaans comes upon you slanderously, I feel great alarm and I become afraid like the eye of a winged dove.

135

140

So too in the course of the night that is now past great clamour assails us to our discredit, the rumour that you have gone over the meadow which abounds in horses, and that you have destroyed the Danaans' cattle and the booty, which had been captured by their spear and still remained to be divided, killing the animals with your flashing sword.

145

150

155

160

165

170

175

τοιούσδε λόγους ψιθύρους πλάσσων
εἰς ὦτα φέρει πᾶσιν Ὀδυσσεύς,
καὶ σφόδρα πείθει. περὶ γὰρ σοῦ νῦν
εὔπειστα λέγει, καὶ πᾶς ὁ κλύων
τοῦ λέξαντος χαίρει μᾶλλον
τοῖς σοῖς ἄχεσιν καθυβρίζων.
τῶν γὰρ μεγάλων ψυχῶν ἱεὶς
οὐκ ἂν ἁμάρτοι· κατὰ δ' ἄν τις ἐμοῦ
τοιαῦτα λέγων οὐκ ἂν πείθοι.
πρὸς γὰρ τὸν ἔχονθ' ὁ φθόνος ἕρπει.
καίτοι σμικροὶ μεγάλων χωρὶς
σφαλερὸν πύργου ῥῦμα πέλονται·
μετὰ γὰρ μεγάλων βαιὸς ἄριστ' ἂν
καὶ μέγας ὀρθοῖθ' ὑπὸ μικροτέρων.
ἀλλ' οὐ δυνατὸν τοὺς ἀνοήτους
τούτων γνώμας προδιδάσκειν.
ὑπὸ τοιούτων ἀνδρῶν θορυβῇ·
χἠμεῖς οὐδὲν σθένομεν πρὸς ταῦτ'
ἀπαλέξασθαι σοῦ χωρίς, ἄναξ.
ἀλλ' ὅτε γὰρ δὴ τὸ σὸν ὄμμ' ἀπέδραν,
παταγοῦσιν ἅτε πτηνῶν ἀγέλαι·
μέγαν αἰγυπιόν ‹δ'› ὑποδείσαντες
τάχ' ἄν, ἐξαίφνης εἰ σὺ φανείης,
σιγῇ πτήξειαν ἄφωνοι.

ἦ ῥά σε Ταυροπόλα Διὸς Ἄρτεμις -   στρ.
ὦ μεγάλα φάτις, ὦ
μᾶτερ αἰσχύνας ἐμᾶς -
ὥρμασε πανδάμους ἐπὶ βοῦς ἀγελαίας,
ἦ πού τινος νίκας ἀκαρπώτου χάριν,
ἤ ῥα κλυτῶν ἐνάρων

149 πᾶσιν **rpat**: πάντων Lp 155 ἁμάρτοι **rpat**: -ῃ Kp, v.l. in r, ͅοις *Suda*, fort. Lᵃᶜ
168 ἅτε GQpat: ἅπερ LRp
169 ‹δ'› Dawes
176 ἀκαρπώτου Johnson: ἀκάρπωτον codd.

Such are the whispering words that Odysseus
fabricates and insinuates into everybody's ears,
150   strongly persuading them. For he now speaks
plausibly about you, and everyone who hears it, even
more than the speaker, enjoys arrogantly mocking
your distress.

155   For one who shoots at great souls could not miss;
but if someone were to say such things against *me* he
would not carry persuasion. It is against the man who
has that envy creeps. And yet small men without the
great are a treacherous defensive tower; for with the
160   great to help him a humble man might best be kept
upright, and a great man too if served by smaller men.
But it is impossible to teach these maxims in advance
to those who are incapable of understanding them.

     Such are the men whose clamour is raised against
165   you, and we have no strength to defend ourselves
against this without you, my lord. For indeed when
they escape from your sight, they chatter like flocks of
birds; but they would soon shrink in fear from the
170   great vulture, if you were suddenly to appear, and they
would cower down speechless in silence.

str.   Was it then Artemis Tauropolos, daughter of Zeus –
oh mighty rumour, oh mother of my shame – who
175   sent you out against the herds of cattle, the property of
all the people, perhaps because of some victory that
brought her no profit, because she was cheated of her
glorious spoils, or because of a deer-hunt in

ψευσθεῖσ', ἀδώροις εἴτ' ἐλαφαβολίαις;
ἦ χαλκοθώραξ σοί τιν' Ἐνυάλιος
180   μομφὰν ἔχων ξυνοῦ δορὸς ἐννυχίοις
μαχαναῖς ἐτείσατο λώβαν;

οὔποτε γὰρ φρενόθεν γ' ἐπ' ἀριστερά,   ἀντ.
παῖ Τελαμῶνος, ἔβας
τόσσον ἐν ποίμναις πίτνων·
185   ἥκοι γὰρ ἂν θεία νόσος· ἀλλ' ἀπερύκοι
καὶ Ζεὺς κακὰν καὶ Φοῖβος Ἀργείων φάτιν.
εἰ δ' ὑποβαλλόμενοι
κλέπτουσι μύθους οἱ μεγάλοι βασιλῆς,
χὠ τᾶς ἀσώτου Σισυφιδᾶν γενεᾶς,
190   μὴ μή, ἄναξ, ἔθ' ὧδ' ἐφάλοις κλισίαις
ὄμμ' ἔχων κακὰν φάτιν ἄρῃ.

ἀλλ' ἄνα ἐξ ἑδράνων   ἐπ.
ὅπου μακραίωνι
στηρίζῃ ποτὲ τᾷδ' ἀγωνίῳ σχολᾷ,
195   ἄταν οὐρανίαν φλέγων.
ἐχθρῶν δ' ὕβρις ὧδ' ἀτάρβηθ'
ὁρμᾶται ἐν εὐανέμοις βάσσαις,
πάντων καγχαζόντων
γλώσσαις βαρυάλγητ'·
200   ἐμοὶ δ' ἄχος ἔστακεν.

ΤΕΚΜΗΣΣΑ
ναὸς· ἀρωγοὶ τῆς Αἴαντος,
γενεᾶς χθονίων ἀπ' Ἐρεχθειδᾶν,
ἔχομεν στοναχὰς οἱ κηδόμενοι
τοῦ Τελαμῶνος τηλόθεν οἴκου.
205   νῦν γὰρ ὁ δεινὸς μέγας ὠμοκρατὴς
Αἴας θολερῷ
κεῖται χειμῶνι νοσήσας.

178 ψευσθεῖσ' ἀδώροις H. Stephanus: ψευσθεῖσα δώροις codd.
179 σοί Reiske: ἦ codd.
189 χὠ τᾶς Morstadt: ἦ τᾶς Lrpat, ἦ τῆς p
190 μὴ μή μ' codd.: μ' del. Blaydes: μὴ μηκέτ', ὦναξ, ὧδ' Morstadt, μὴ μηκέθ' ὧδ', ἄναξ Jackson
191 ἄρῃ Lrpa: ἄρῃς pat
196 ἀτάρβηθ' Lobeck: -ητα Lrpat, -ήτως p, Suda
197 ὁρμᾶται t: ὁρμᾶτ' Lrpa
198 καγχαζόντων pat, Suda: βακχ- L^{ac}r, βαγχ- L^{pc}

180 which she received no gifts? Or did the War-god with his bronze breastplate have some complaint against you at your partnership in battle, and punish the outrage with the scheme that he adopted in the night?

ant.

For it was never of your own mind, son of Telamon, that you went so far astray, and fell upon the flocks; for it may turn out that divine sickness has come from the gods; but may Zeus and Phoebus avert the evil rumour of the Argives. If the great kings and the king who is of the abandoned race of the sons of Sisyphus are uttering secret suggestive words, no longer, my lord, no longer keep your face thus hidden in your huts beside the sea, bearing the burden of the evil rumour.

epode

But rise up from the seat where you have too long been firmly set in this lengthy retirement from the conflict, making your ruin blaze up to heaven. Your enemies' outrageous behaviour stirs so fearlessly in the glens where the winds blow freely, while they all mock with their tongues and cause you sore pain; for me distress is my constant state.

[*Enter Tecmessa from Ajax' hut*]
TECMESSA

Crew of Ajax' ship, men of the race descended from the earth-born line of Erechtheus, we have cause to wail, we who care for the house of Telamon so far away. For now lies the terrible great Ajax, so fierce in his might, after falling sick with a storm of turbulence.

40

XO. τί δ' ἐνήλλακται τῆς ἀμερίας
     νὺξ ἥδε βάρος;
210 παῖ τοῦ Φρυγίου Τελεύταντος,
     λέγ', ἐπεί σε λέχος δουριάλωτον
     στέρξας ἀνέχει θούριος Αἴας·
     ὥστ' οὐκ ἂν ἄϊδρις ὑπείποις.
TE. πῶς δῆτα λέγω λόγον ἄρρητον;
215 θανάτῳ γὰρ ἴσον πάθος ἐκπεύσῃ.
     μανίᾳ γὰρ ἁλοὺς ἡμὶν ὁ κλεινὸς
     νύκτερος Αἴας ἀπελωβήθη.
     τοιαῦτ' ἂν ἴδοις σκηνῆς ἔνδον
     χειροδάϊκτα σφάγι' αἱμοβαφῆ,
220 κείνου χρηστήρια τἀνδρός.

XO. οἵαν ἐδήλωσας   στρ.
     ἀνέρος αἴθονος ἀγγελίαν
     ἄτλατον οὐδὲ φευκτάν,
225 τῶν μεγάλων Δαναῶν ὕπο κληζομέναν,
     τὰν ὁ μέγας μῦθος ἀέξει.
     ὤμοι, φοβοῦμαι τὸ προσέρπον· περίφαντος ἀνὴρ
230 θανεῖται, παραπλήκτῳ χερὶ συγκατακτὰς
     κελαινοῖς ξίφεσιν βοτὰ καὶ
     βοτῆρας ἱππονώμας.

TE. ὤμοι· κεῖθεν κεῖθεν ἄρ' ἡμῖν
     δεσμῶτιν ἄγων ἤλυθε ποίμναν·
235 ὧν τὰ μὲν εἴσω σφάζ' ἐπὶ γαίας,

208 ἀμερίας] ἡρεμίας Thiersch
210 Τελλεύταντος p: Τελεύτ– Lrpat: σὺ Τελεύταντος Porson, Φρυγίοιο
     Τελεύταντος Jaeger
212 στέρξας ἀνέχει rpat: στέρξασαν ἔχει LᵃᶜK, γρ in Σ
215 πάθος LQpa: βάρος Lᵃᶜˢˡ, GRpt
222 ἀνέρος Hermann: ἀνδρὸς codd. αἴθονος LᵖᶜKN: -οπος at, -ωνος Lᵃᶜrpa
235 τὰ t: τὸ Xs, τὴν Lrpa σφάζ' Krat: σφάξ' LrF εἴσω t: ἔσω Lpa, ἔξω r

	Chorus	What heavy burden has this night received in
210		exchange for the burden of the day? Daughter of
		Phrygian Teleutas, tell us, since to you, the bedmate
		captured by his spear, impetuous Ajax shows constant
		affection; you are not then without knowledge to
		suggest an explanation.
	Tecmessa	How then am I to tell a tale that is unspeakable? You
215		will hear of a misfortune that is as bad as death.
		Seized by madness our famous Ajax fell into disgrace
		in the night. Such is the sight that you could see inside
		the hut, victims slaughtered by his hand, bathed in
220		blood, his sacrificial victims.
	Chorus *str.*	What dreadful tidings you have revealed of the hot-
		tempered man, news that is unbearable yet
225		inescapable, news reported by the great men of the
		Danai, and it is increased by mighty rumour. Alas, I
		fear what is coming. The man will die conspicuously,
230		because with frenzied hand he has killed the cattle
		with his black sword, and with them the horse-
		mounted herdsmen.
	Tecmessa	Alas! So it was from there, from there, that he came to
		me bringing the flock as prisoners; some of which he
235		slaughtered inside on the ground, while the rest he
		broke in two by striking their ribs. But he took up two
		white-footed rams, cut off the head of one and the tip
		of its tongue, and threw them down, while the

42

τὰ δὲ πλευροκοπῶν δίχ᾽ ἀνερρήγνυ.
δύο δ᾽ ἀργίποδας κριοὺς ἀνελών,
τοῦ μὲν κεφαλὴν καὶ γλῶσσαν ἄκραν
ῥιπτεῖ θερίσας, τὸν δ᾽ ὀρθὸν ἄνω
240   κίονι δήσας,
μέγαν ἱπποδέτην ῥυτῆρα λαβὼν
παίει λιγυρᾷ μάστιγι διπλῇ,
κακὰ δεννάζων ῥήμαθ᾽, ἃ δαίμων
κοὐδεὶς ἀνδρῶν ἐδίδαξεν.

245   ΧΟ. ὥρα τιν᾽ ἤδη τοι   ἀντ.
κρᾶτα καλύμμασι κρυψάμενον
ποδοῖν κλοπὰν ἀρέσθαι,
ἢ θοὸν εἰρεσίας ζυγὸν ἑζόμενον
250   ποντοπόρῳ ναῒ μεθεῖναι.
τοίας ἐρέσσουσιν ἀπειλὰς δικρατεῖς Ἀτρεῖδαι
καθ᾽ ἡμῶν· πεφόβημαι λιθόλευστον Ἄρη
255   ξυναλγεῖν μετὰ τοῦδε τυπείς,
τὸν αἶσ᾽ ἄπλατος ἴσχει.

      ΤΕ. οὐκέτι· λαμπρᾶς γὰρ ἄτερ στεροπᾶς
ᾆξας ὀξὺς νότος ὣς λήγει,
καὶ νῦν φρόνιμος νέον ἄλγος ἔχει·
260   τὸ γὰρ ἐσλεύσσειν οἰκεῖα πάθη,
μηδενὸς ἄλλου παραπράξαντος,
μεγάλας ὀδύνας ὑποτείνει.

      ΧΟ. ἀλλ᾽ εἰ πέπαυται, κάρτ᾽ ἂν εὐτυχεῖν δοκῶ·
φρούδου γὰρ ἤδη τοῦ κακοῦ μείων λόγος.
265   ΤΕ. πότερα δ᾽ ἄν, εἰ νέμοι τις αἵρεσιν, λάβοις,
φίλους ἀνιῶν αὐτὸς ἡδονὰς ἔχειν
ἢ κοινὸς ἐν κοινοῖσι λυπεῖσθαι ξυνών;

236   τὰ t: τὰς cett.
245   τοι om. pat, Eust.: ὥρα ᾽στιν ἁρμοῖ Lloyd-Jones, CR 28 (1978) 217-18
246   κάρα t
251   ἐρείσουσιν Wieseler
254   Ἄρη La: Ἄρην rpat

240   other he tied upright to a pillar, and taking a great strap, a horse's harness, he beat the ram with the shrill double lash, uttering terrible words of abuse, which a god, no man, must have taught him.

245   Chorus *ant.*   It is time now to hide one's head in a veil and to steal away on foot, or to sit on the swift rower's bench and
250   let the sea-going ship have her way. Such are the threats that the Atreidae, the joint commanders, are setting in motion against us; and I am afraid to share
255   the pain of death by stoning, struck down with him, whom a terrible fate holds in its grip.

        Tecmessa   No longer does it hold him; for there is no more bright lightning-flash - rather it ceases like a south wind that has burst out sharply, and now though sane he has
260   fresh grief; for to look upon one's self-made sufferings, when no one else has helped to inflict them, intensifies great pain.

        Leader   Well, if it has stopped, I think he is very fortunate; for now that the trouble has gone there will be less talk about it.
265   Tecmessa   If someone were to offer you the choice, which would you prefer, to distress your friends but enjoy yourself, or to be one with them and share their pains in common?

44

ΧΟ.	τό τοι διπλάζον, ὦ γύναι, μεῖζον κακόν.
ΤΕ.	ἡμεῖς ἄρ' οὐ νοσοῦντος ἀτώμεσθα νῦν.
270 ΧΟ.	πῶς τοῦτ' ἔλεξας; οὐ κάτοιδ' ὅπως λέγεις.
ΤΕ.	ἀνὴρ ἐκεῖνος, ἡνίκ' ἦν ἐν τῇ νόσῳ,
	αὐτὸς μὲν ἥδεθ' οἷσιν εἴχετ' ἐν κακοῖς,
	ἡμᾶς δὲ τοὺς φρονοῦντας ἠνία ξυνών·
	νῦν δ' ὡς ἔληξε κἀνέπνευσε τῆς νόσου,
275	κεῖνός τε λύπῃ πᾶς ἐλήλαται κακῇ
	ἡμεῖς θ' ὁμοίως οὐδὲν ἧσσον ἢ πάρος.
	ἆρ' ἔστι ταῦτα δὶς τόσ' ἐξ ἁπλῶν κακά;
ΧΟ.	ξύμφημι δή σοι καὶ δέδοικα μὴ 'κ θεοῦ
	πληγή τις ἥκει. πῶς γάρ, εἰ πεπαυμένος
280	μηδέν τι μᾶλλον ἢ νοσῶν εὐφραίνεται;
ΤΕ.	ὡς ὧδ' ἐχόντων τῶνδ' ἐπίστασθαί σε χρή.
ΧΟ.	τίς γάρ ποτ' ἀρχὴ τοῦ κακοῦ προσέπτατο;
	δήλωσον ἡμῖν τοῖς ξυναλγοῦσιν τύχας.
ΤΕ.	ἅπαν μαθήσῃ τοὔργον, ὡς κοινωνὸς ὤν.
285	κεῖνος γὰρ ἄκρας νυκτός, ἡνίχ' ἔσπεροι
	λαμπτῆρες οὐκέτ' ᾗθον, ἄμφηκες λαβὼν
	ἐμαίετ' ἔγχος ἐξόδους ἕρπειν κενάς.
	κἀγὼ 'πιπλήσσω καὶ λέγω, "τί χρῆμα δρᾷς,
	Αἴας; τί τήνδ' ἄκλητος οὔθ' ὑπ' ἀγγέλων
290	κληθεὶς ἀφορμᾷς πεῖραν οὔτε του κλύων
	σάλπιγγος; ἀλλὰ νῦν γε πᾶς εὕδει στρατός."
	ὁ δ' εἶπε πρός με βαί', ἀεὶ δ' ὑμνούμενα·
	"γύναι, γυναιξὶ κόσμον ἡ σιγὴ φέρει."
	κἀγὼ μαθοῦσ' ἔληξ', ὁ δ' ἐσσύθη μόνος.
295 | καὶ τὰς ἐκεῖ μὲν οὐκ ἔχω λέγειν πάθας· |

---

269 νοσοῦντος Hermann: -τες codd.
273 φρονοῦντας] βλέποντας γρ in L
274 κἀπέπαυσε r
279 ἥκει WaZr: ἥκοι cett., ἥκῃ Suda
287 κενάς: νέας Dawe
290 ἀφορμᾷς Lrpa: ἐφ- pat
293 γυναιξὶ codd., P.Oxy. 2093ˢˡ, Stob.: -κὶ P.Oxy. 2093, Aristotle
295 τὰς μὲν ἔνδον Suda   φράζειν J Par.gr. 2598 πάθας] τύχας t, gl in C

	Leader	The double trouble, woman, is surely greater.
	Tecmessa	So we suffer now when he is not ill.
270	Leader	What do you mean by this? I do not understand your meaning.
	Tecmessa	He himself, when he was still sick, enjoyed the troubles which held him in their grip, but to us who were sane his company caused distress; but now that he has stopped and recovered from his sickness, he has
275		been altogether vexed by sore pain, and we alike no less than before. Are these troubles not twice as great after one that was single?
	Leader	Yes, I agree with you, and I fear that some blow has come from god. For how can it be otherwise, if now
280		that his madness has stopped he is no happier than when he was sick?
	Tecmessa	This is in fact the case, and so you must understand it so.
	Leader	How ever did the trouble start to swoop upon him? Explain what happened to us who share your pain.
	Tecmessa	You will learn everything that he did, as you are
285		involved. At dead of night when the evening lamps no longer burned, he took his two-edged sword and was eager to go out on a futile mission. I rebuked him and said, "What are you doing, Ajax? Why are you setting out unsummoned on this enterprise, when you have
290		not been called by messengers nor heard any trumpet-call? The whole army is now asleep." And he said little to me, only the ever-repeated words: "woman, silence adorns women." I understood and stopped, while he rushed off alone. I cannot tell you of what
295		happened to him there. But he came back

46

εἴσω δ’ ἐσῆλθε συνδέτους ἄγων ὁμοῦ
ταύρους, κύνας βοτῆρας, εὔερόν τ’ ἄγραν.
καὶ τοὺς μὲν ηὐχένιζε, τοὺς δ’ ἄνω τρέπων
ἔσφαζε κἀρράχιζε, τοὺς δὲ δεσμίους
300   ᾐκίζεθ’ ὥστε φῶτας ἐν ποίμναις πίτνων.
τέλος δ’ ἀπάξας διὰ θυρῶν σκιᾷ τινι
λόγους ἀνέσπα, τοὺς μὲν Ἀτρειδῶν κάτα,
τοὺς δ’ ἀμφ’ Ὀδυσσεῖ, συντιθεὶς γέλων πολύν,
ὅσην κατ’ αὐτῶν ὕβριν ἐκτείσαιτ’ ἰών.
305   κἄπειτ’ ἐνάξας αὖθις ἐς δόμους πάλιν
ἔμφρων μόλις πως ξὺν χρόνῳ καθίσταται,
καὶ πλῆρες ἄτης ὡς διοπτεύει στέγος,
παίσας κάρα ’θώϋξεν· ἐν δ’ ἐρειπίοις
νεκρῶν ἐρειφθεὶς ἕζετ’ ἀρνείου φόνου,
310   κόμην ἀπρὶξ ὄνυξι συλλαβὼν χερί.
καὶ τὸν μὲν ἧστο πλεῖστον ἄφθογγος χρόνον·
ἔπειτ’ ἐμοὶ τὰ δείν’ ἐπηπείλησ’ ἔπη,
εἰ μὴ φανοίην πᾶν τὸ συντυχὸν πάθος,
κἀνήρετ’ ἐν τῷ πράγματος κυροῖ ποτε.
315   κἀγώ, φίλοι, δείσασα τοὐξειργασμένον
ἔλεξα πᾶν ὅσονπερ ἐξηπιστάμην.
ὁ δ’ εὐθὺς ἐξώμωξεν οἰμωγὰς λυγράς,
ἃς οὔποτ’ αὐτοῦ πρόσθεν εἰσήκουσ’ ἐγώ.
πρὸς γὰρ κακοῦ τε καὶ βαρυψύχου γόους
320   τοιούσδ’ ἀεί ποτ’ ἀνδρὸς ἐξηγεῖτ’ ἔχειν·
ἀλλ’ ἀψόφητος ὀξέων κωκυμάτων
ὑπεστέναζε ταῦρος ὣς βρυχώμενος.
νῦν δ’ ἐν τοιᾷδε κείμενος κακῇ τύχῃ
ἄσιτος ἀνήρ, ἄποτος, ἐν μέσοις βοτοῖς
325   σιδηροκμῆσιν ἥσυχος θακεῖ πεσών,

297   εὔερόν Schneidewin: εὔκερον Q, εὔκερων cett. τ’ om. r
301   ἀπάξας P.Oxy 2093, LQRp: ὑπ- a, ἐπ- Gpat
305   ἐνάξας P.Oxy. 2093: ἐπ- KGapt, ἀπ- L^{pc}QRp
309   ἐρεισθεὶς γρ in L
313   φανοίην Xr: -είην cett.
314   πράγματος Lpat: -ατι rpa κυροῖ LrN: -εῖ pat
322   μυκώμενος t

inside bringing with him hobbled bulls, herdsman's dogs, and his fleecy prey. He cut the throats of some, while others he turned upside down and slaughtered and broke their spines, while the rest which were tied up he tortured like men, falling on the flocks. In the end he rushed off through the door, and talked to some shadow painfully dragging out his words, some against the sons of Atreus, others about Odysseus, and with them he laughed loudly at all the violence he had gone and inflicted on them by way of vengeance; and then he rushed back again into the house and with some difficulty he eventually returned to sanity, and when he saw the house so full of carnage he struck his head and cried aloud; he fell a wreck in the wreckage of the dead sheep's corpses and he sat there, his nails gripping his hair tightly with his hand.

He sat there voiceless for most of the time; then he uttered those terrible threats against me, if I should not reveal to him everything that had happened. And he asked me about the situation in which he found himself. I, friends, was afraid and told him all that had been done, as far as I understood it. And he immediately broke out into painful lamentations, which I had never heard from him before. For he always used to explain that such laments were the mark of a cowardly and dejected man; rather without any sound of shrill wailing he used to utter low moans bellowing like a bull. But now that he lies in such evil plight the man sits quietly, fallen down, without eating, without drinking, in the middle of the animals

48

καὶ δῆλός ἐστιν ὥς τι δρασείων κακόν.
τοιαῦτα γάρ πως καὶ λέγει κὠδύρεται.
ἀλλ᾽, ὦ φίλοι, τούτων γὰρ οὕνεκ᾽ ἐστάλην,
ἀρήξατ᾽ εἰσελθόντες, εἰ δύνασθέ τι.
330 φίλων γὰρ οἱ τοιοίδε νικῶνται λόγοις.
ΧΟ. Τέκμησσα, δεινοῖς, παῖ Τελεύταντος, λέγεις
ἡμῖν τὸν ἄνδρα διαπεφοιβάσθαι κακοῖς.
ΑΙ. ἰώ μοί μοι.
ΤΕ. τάχ᾽, ὡς ἔοικε, μᾶλλον· ἢ οὐκ ἠκούσατε
335 Αἴαντος οἵαν τήνδε θωΰσσει βοήν;
ΑΙ. ἰώ μοί μοι.
ΧΟ. ἀνὴρ ἔοικεν ἢ νοσεῖν, ἢ τοῖς πάλαι
νοσήμασι ξυνοῦσι λυπεῖσθαι παρών.
ΑΙ. ἰὼ παῖ παῖ.
340 ΤΕ. ὤμοι τάλαιν᾽· Εὐρύσακες, ἀμφὶ σοὶ βοᾷ.
τί ποτε μενοινᾷ; ποῦ ποτ᾽ εἶ; τάλαιν᾽ ἐγώ.
ΑΙ. Τεῦκρον καλῶ· ποῦ Τεῦκρος; ἢ τὸν εἰσαεὶ
λεηλατήσει χρόνον, ἐγὼ δ᾽ ἀπόλλυμαι;
ΧΟ. ἀνὴρ φρονεῖν ἔοικεν. ἀλλ᾽ ἀνοίγετε.
345 τάχ᾽ ἄν τιν᾽ αἰδῶ κἀπ᾽ ἐμοὶ βλέψας λάβοι.
ΤΕ. ἰδού, διοίγω· προσβλέπειν δ᾽ ἔξεστί σοι
τὰ τοῦδε πράγη, καὐτὸς ὡς ἔχων κυρεῖ.

ΑΙ. ἰώ   στρ. 1
φίλοι ναυβάται, μόνοι ἐμῶν φίλων
350 μόνοι ἔτ᾽ ἐμμένοντες ὀρθῷ νόμῳ,
ἴδεσθέ μ᾽ οἷον ἄρτι κῦ-
μα φοινίας ὑπὸ ζάλης
ἀμφίδρομον κυκλεῖται.

327 del. Nauck
330 λόγοις γρ in Xs, Stob.: φίλοι cett.
331 δεινοῖς Bentley: δεινά codd.
338 παροῦσι...ξυνών Blaydes
350 ἔτ᾽ Hermann: τ᾽ codd.

that his sword has slain. And it is clear that he wants to do some mischief. For such are the words and lamentations that he utters.

Well, my friends - for this is why I came out - go inside and help him, if you have any power. For such men can be won by the words of friends.

330

Leader   Tecmessa, daughter of Teleutas, terrible, by your account, are the misfortunes which have driven the man frantic.

[*Ajax is heard offstage*]

Ajax   Alas, alas!

Tecmessa   Soon, it seems, it will be worse; or did you not hear what kind of cry this is that Ajax utters?

335

Ajax   Alas, alas!

Leader   It seems either that the man is sick, or that he is suffering from the effects of the former madness which are still with him in his present state.

Ajax   Oh my son, my son!

340

Tecmessa   Oh wretched me! Eurysaces, he is shouting about you. What ever does he want? Where are you? Wretched me!

Ajax   I am calling Teucer. Where is Teucer? Will he for ever be driving booty, while I perish?

Leader   The man seems to be sane. But open the door. Perhaps when he sees me he may acquire a sense of shame towards me too.

345

Tecmessa   There, I am opening the door. You can look on what he has done, and on the plight in which he finds himself.

[*Enter Ajax from his hut*]

Ajax *str.1*   Oh dear sailors, you who alone, alone of my friends, still remain firm in your loyalty, see what a wave now encloses and encircles me, raised by a storm of blood.

350

ΧΟ. οἴμ' ὡς ἔοικας ὀρθὰ μαρτυρεῖν ἄγαν.
355 δηλοῖ δὲ τοὔργον ὡς ἀφροντίστως ἔχει.

ΑΙ. ἰὼ   ἀντ. 1.
     γένος ναΐας ἀρωγὸν τέχνας,
     ἅλιον ὃς ἐπέβας ἑλίσσων πλάταν,
     σέ τοι, σέ τοι μόνον δέδορ-
360 κα ποιμένων ἐπαρκέσοντ'·
     ἀλλά με συνδάϊξον.
ΧΟ. εὔφημα φώνει· μὴ κακὸν κακῷ διδοὺς
     ἄκος πλέον τὸ πῆμα τῆς ἄτης τίθει.

ΑΙ. ὁρᾷς τὸν θρασύν, τὸν εὐκάρδιον,   στρ. 2.
365 τὸν ἐν δαΐοις ἄτρεστον μάχας,
     ἐν ἀφόβοις με θηρσὶ δεινὸν χέρας;
     οἴμοι γέλωτος· οἷον ὑβρίσθην ἄρα.
ΤΕ. μή, δέσποτ' Αἴας, λίσσομαί σ', αὔδα τάδε.
ΑΙ. οὐκ ἐκτός; οὐκ ἄψορρον ἐκνεμῇ πόδα;
370 αἰαῖ αἰαῖ.
ΤΕ. ὦ πρὸς θεῶν, ὕπεικε καὶ φρόνησον εὖ.
ΑΙ. ὦ δύσμορος, ὃς χεροῖν
     μεθῆκα τοὺς ἀλάστορας,
     ἐν δ' ἑλίκεσσι βουσὶ καὶ
375 κλυτοῖς πεσὼν αἰπολίοις
     ἐρεμνὸν αἷμ' ἔδευσα.
ΧΟ. τί δῆτ' ἂν ἀλγοίης ἐπ' ἐξειργασμένοις;
     οὐ γὰρ γένοιτ' ἂν ταῦθ' ὅπως οὐχ ὧδ' ἔχοι.

358 ἅλιον Hermann: ἁλίαν codd.
365 δαΐοις LGQpA: -αις Rpat ἄτρεστον Lrpat: ἄτρεπτον Kp μάχας Blaydes: -
     αις codd.
369 ἐκνεμεῖς K^{pc}D
371 Tecmessae trib. K.O. Müller, choro codd.
372 χεροῖν t: χερσὶ μὲν Lrpa
378 ἔχοι Herwerden (cf. Σ): ἔχῃ C^{pc}, ἔχειν cett.

Leader	Alas, your testimony seems to be all too accurate. The fact shows that he is not thinking properly.

355

Ajax *ant.1*	Oh you people, who helped me in the skill of navigation, who went aboard and rapidly plied the oar at sea, I see that you and you alone of those who care for me will help me. Well join in killing me.
Leader	Don't speak ill-omened words; do not treat evil with an evil cure and make worse the misery of your ruin.

360

Ajax *str.2*	Do you see the bold man, the stout-hearted man, the one who was fearless in battle among the foe, do you see me so terrible in might among unfearing beasts? Alas for the laughter! What insults then have I suffered!
Tecmessa	Don't say these things, lord Ajax, I entreat you.
Ajax	Away with you! Won't you take yourself off to other pastures? Alas, alas!
Tecmessa	Oh, for the gods' sake yield and come to your senses.
Ajax	Oh, unhappy that I am, who from these hands let go the accursed men but fell instead upon the cattle with their twisted horns and the glorious flocks of goats and made dark blood to flow.
Leader	Why then should you grieve at what is over and done? There is no way in which this could be other than it is.

365

370

375

ΑΙ. ἰὼ πάνθ' ὁρῶν, ἅπαντ' ἀΐων,   ἀντ. 2.
380 κακῶν ὄργανον, τέκνον Λαρτίου,
   κακοπινέστατόν τ' ἄλημα στρατοῦ,
   ἦ που πολὺν γέλωθ' ὑφ' ἡδονῆς ἄγεις.
ΧΟ. ξὺν τῷ θεῷ πᾶς καὶ γελᾷ κὠδύρεται.
ΑΙ. ἴδοιμι δή νιν, καίπερ ὧδ' ἀτώμενος –
385 ἰώ μοί μοι.
ΧΟ. μηδὲν μέγ' εἴπῃς· οὐχ ὁρᾷς ἵν' εἶ κακοῦ;
ΑΙ. ὦ Ζεῦ, προγόνων πάτερ,
   πῶς ἂν τὸν αἱμυλώτατον,
   ἐχθρὸν ἄλημα, τούς τε δισσ-
390 άρχας ὀλέσσας βασιλῆς,
   τέλος θάνοιμι καὐτός;
ΤΕ. ὅταν κατεύχῃ ταῦθ', ὁμοῦ κἀμοὶ θανεῖν
   εὔχου· τί γὰρ δεῖ ζῆν με σοῦ τεθνηκότος;
ΑΙ. ἰὼ   στρ. 3.
   σκότος, ἐμὸν φάος,
395 ἔρεβος ὦ φαεννότατον, ὡς ἐμοί,
   ἕλεσθ' ἕλεσθέ μ' οἰκήτορα,
   ἕλεσθέ μ'· οὔτε γὰρ θεῶν γένος
   οὔθ' ἀμερίων ἔτ' ἄξιος
400 βλέπειν τιν' εἰς ὄνησιν ἀνθρώπων.
   ἀλλά μ' ἁ Διός
   ἀλκίμα θεὸς
   ὀλέθριον αἰκίζει.
   ποῖ τις οὖν φύγῃ;
   ποῖ μολὼν μενῶ;
405 † εἰ τὰ μὲν φθίνει,
   φίλοι, τοῖσδ' ὁμοῦ πέλας, †
   μώραις δ' ἄγραις προσκείμεθα,
   πᾶς δὲ στρατὸς δίπαλτος ἂν
   με χειρὶ φονεύοι.
410 ΤΕ. ὦ δυστάλαινα, τοιάδ' ἄνδρα χρήσιμον
   φωνεῖν, ἃ πρόσθεν οὗτος οὐκ ἔτλη ποτ' ἄν.

379 ἅπαντ' ἀΐων Lloyd-Jones et Wilson: ἁπάντων τ' ἀΐων pXs, ἁπάντων τ' ἀεί
   cett.
384 δή t: om. cett.
387 πάτερ t: προπάτωρ (-ορ) cett.
396 ἕλεσθε ἕλεσθε t: ἕλεσθε μ' ἕλεσθε Lrpa, Suda
403 ὀλέθριον] οὔλιον Wunder
404 φύγῃ] τράπῃ γρ in LH
406 τίσις δ' ἐμοῦ πέλας Pearson

380	Ajax *ant.2*	Oh, you see everything, you hear everything, instrument of evil, child of Laertes, filthiest knave in the army, and no doubt you keep on laughing heartily in your pleasure.
	Leader	It depends on the god whether any man laughs or wails.
385	Ajax	I wish indeed I could see him, even in this state of ruin - alas, alas!
	Leader	Do not talk so proud. Don't you see the plight that you are in?
390	Ajax	Oh Zeus, father of my ancestors, how might I destroy the wiliest man, the hateful knave, and the jointly reigning kings before I finally die myself?
	Tecmessa	When you pray for this, pray for death for me as well; for why should I live if you are dead?
395 400 405 410	Ajax *str.3* Tecmessa	Oh darkness, which is my light, darkness of the underworld which for me shines most brightly, take me, take me to live with you, take me; for I no longer deserve to look for any help to the race of gods or of men who live but for a day. The mighty goddess daughter of Zeus tortures me to my destruction. Where then is one to flee? Where shall I go to stay? † If these things perish, my friends, along with these creatures near me †, and I have got involved in a foolish hunt, and the whole army would brandish their swords and lift their hands to kill me. Oh wretched me, that so sound a man should utter such words, words which earlier he would never have brought himself to speak!

54

AI. ⟨ἰ⟩ὼ   ἀντ. 3.
πόροι ἁλίρροθοι
πάραλά τ' ἄντρα καὶ νέμος ἐπάκτιον,
πολὺν πολύν με δαρόν τε δὴ
415   κατείχετ' ἀμφὶ Τροίαν χρόνον·
ἀλλ' οὐκέτι μ', οὐκέτ' ἀμπνοὰς
ἔχοντα· τοῦτό τις φρονῶν ἴστω.
ὦ Σκαμάνδριοι
γείτονες ῥοαί,
420   εὔφρονες Ἀργείοις,
οὐκέτ' ἄνδρα μὴ
τόνδ' ἴδητ' - ἔπος
ἐξερῶ μέγ' - οἶ-
ον οὔτινα Τροία στρατοῦ
425   δέρχθη χθονὸς μολόντ' ἀπὸ
Ἑλλανίδος· τανῦν δ' ἄτι-
μος ὧδε πρόκειμαι.
XO. οὗτοι σ' ἀπείργειν, οὐδ' ὅπως ἐῶ λέγειν
ἔχω, κακοῖς τοιοῖσδε συμπεπτωκότα.

430 AI. αἰαῖ· τίς ἄν ποτ' ᾤεθ' ὧδ' ἐπώνυμον
τοὐμὸν ξυνοίσειν ὄνομα τοῖς ἐμοῖς κακοῖς;
νῦν γὰρ πάρεστι καὶ δὶς αἰάζειν ἐμοὶ
καὶ τρίς· τοιούτοις γὰρ κακοῖς ἐντυγχάνω·
ὅτου πατὴρ μὲν τῆσδ' ἀπ' Ἰδαίας χθονὸς
435   τὰ πρῶτα καλλιστεῖ' ἀριστεύσας στρατοῦ
πρὸς οἶκον ἦλθε πᾶσαν εὔκλειαν φέρων·
ἐγὼ δ' ὁ κείνου παῖς, τὸν αὐτὸν ἐς τόπον
Τροίας ἐπελθὼν οὐκ ἐλάσσονι σθένει,
οὐδ' ἔργα μείω χειρὸς ἀρκέσας ἐμῆς,
440   ἄτιμος Ἀργείοισιν ὧδ' ἀπόλλυμαι.

420   κακόφρονες Lloyd-Jones et Wilson
423   ἐξερῶ Hᵃᶜ: ἐῶ cett.
427   πρόκειμαι GQpa: -κειται lRpt
428   οὐδ' Elmsley: οὔθ' codd.
433   del. Morstadt

Ajax *ant.3*		Oh, you paths of the roaring sea, you caves beside the sea and wooded pastures by the shore, for long for far too long a time you have detained me at Troy; but no longer, no longer will you detain me with the breath of life. Let people know and understand it. Oh streams of nearby Scamander, so kindly to the Argives, you will certainly see this man no longer - I shall boast - I was like no other whom Troy saw coming in the army from the land of Greece; but now I lie thus prostrate in dishonour.

415

420

425

Leader   I can't restrain you, but I don't know how I am to allow you to speak, now that you have fallen into such misfortunes.

430 Ajax   Alas! Who would have thought that the name by which I am called would so correspond with my misfortunes? For now I can say alas even twice or thrice; for such are the misfortunes I encounter; I

435   whose father won the first and fairest prize in the army from this land of Ida for excellence, and carried all the glory when he went home; while I, his son, who came in turn against the same region of Troy with strength no less, who performed services just as great

440   with my hand, I perish so dishonoured in the eyes of the Argives. And yet this much at least I think I

καίτοι τοσοῦτόν γ' ἐξεπίστασθαι δοκῶ,
εἰ ζῶν Ἀχιλλεὺς τῶν ὅπλων τῶν ὧν πέρι
κρίνειν ἔμελλε κράτος ἀριστείας τινί,
οὐκ ἄν τις αὕτ' ἔμαρψεν ἄλλος ἀντ' ἐμοῦ.
445 νῦν δ' αὕτ' Ἀτρεῖδαι φωτὶ παντουργῷ φρένας
ἔπραξαν, ἀνδρὸς τοῦδ' ἀπώσαντες κράτη.
κεἰ μὴ τόδ' ὄμμα καὶ φρένες διάστροφοι
γνώμης ἀπῇξαν τῆς ἐμῆς, οὐκ ἄν ποτε
δίκην κατ' ἄλλου φωτὸς ὧδ' ἐψήφισαν.
450 νῦν δ' ἡ Διὸς γοργῶπις ἀδάματος θεὰ
ἤδη μ' ἐπ' αὐτοῖς χεῖρ' ἐπευθύνοντ' ἐμὴν
ἔσφηλεν ἐμβαλοῦσα λυσσώδη νόσον,
ὥστ' ἐν τοιοῖσδε χεῖρας αἱμάξαι βοτοῖς·
κεῖνοι δ' ἐπεγγελῶσιν ἐκπεφευγότες,
455 ἐμοῦ μὲν οὐχ ἑκόντος· εἰ δέ τις θεῶν
βλάπτοι, φύγοι τἂν χὠ κακὸς τὸν κρείσσονα.
καὶ νῦν τί χρὴ δρᾶν; ὅστις ἐμφανῶς θεοῖς
ἐχθαίρομαι, μισεῖ δέ μ' Ἑλλήνων στρατός,
ἔχθει δὲ Τροία πᾶσα καὶ πεδία τάδε.
460 πότερα πρὸς οἴκους, ναυλόχους λιπὼν ἕδρας
μόνους τ' Ἀτρείδας, πέλαγος Αἰγαῖον περῶ;
καὶ ποῖον ὄμμα πατρὶ δηλώσω φανεὶς
Τελαμῶνι; πῶς με τλήσεταί ποτ' εἰσιδεῖν
γυμνὸν φανέντα τῶν ἀριστείων ἄτερ,
465 ὧν αὐτὸς ἔσχε στέφανον εὐκλείας μέγαν;
οὐκ ἔστι τοὔργον τλητόν. ἀλλὰ δῆτ' ἰὼν
πρὸς ἔρυμα Τρώων, ξυμπεσὼν μόνος μόνοις
καὶ δρῶν τι χρηστόν, εἶτα λοίσθιον θάνω;
ἀλλ' ὧδέ γ' Ἀτρείδας ἂν εὐφράναιμί που.
470 οὐκ ἔστι ταῦτα· πεῖρά τις ζητητέα
τοιάδ' ἀφ' ἧς γέροντι δηλώσω πατρὶ
μή τοι φύσιν γ' ἄσπλαγχνος ἐκ κείνου γεγώς.
αἰσχρὸν γὰρ ἄνδρα τοῦ μακροῦ χρῄζειν βίου,

---

445 αὕτ' Lpat: ὧδ' rD
446 ἔπρασαν Hartung
448 ἀπῇξαν Lpat: ἀπεῖρξαν rXr
451 ἐπευθύνοντ' IC: ἐπεντείνοντ' G[sl] pt, ἐπεντύνοντ' rpa

understand: if Achilles had been alive and was to assign to anyone the victory for excellence in the matter of his own arms, no one else would have seized them instead of me. But now the sons of Atreus have procured them for a man who is at heart a villain, and have thrust aside *my* triumphs. If these eyes and mind had not been distorted and parted company from my intention, they would never have procured by voting such a decision against another man. But as things are, while I was already directing my hand against them, the daughter of Zeus, the Gorgon-eyed unconquerable goddess, inflicted on me the disease of madness and tripped me up, so that it was on animals like these that I bloodied my hands; and they laugh at me because they have escaped, not with *my* consent; but, if some god were to ruin one, even the coward might escape the better man.

And now what should I do? I who am clearly hated by the gods, while the Greek army loathes me, and the whole of Troy and these plains hate me. Am I to cross the Aegean sea for home, leaving my station where the ships are anchored, and the sons of Atreus all alone? Then what expression shall I show to my father Telamon when I appear? How ever will he bear to look on me when I appear naked without the prize of valour, for which he himself gained the great garland of glory? The thing is intolerable. Well then, am I to go to the Trojans' wall, engage with them in duels, and perform some useful service before I finally die? But in this way I would, no doubt, give pleasure to the sons of Atreus. It cannot be. I must seek some such enterprise that from it I shall show my aged father that I, his son, am not naturally a coward. It is shameful

κακοῖσιν ὅστις μηδὲν ἐξαλλάσσεται.
475 τί γὰρ παρ' ἦμαρ ἡμέρα τέρπειν ἔχει
     †προσθεῖσα κἀναθεῖσα τοῦ γε κατθανεῖν;†
     οὐκ ἂν πριαίμην οὐδενὸς λόγου βροτὸν
     ὅστις κεναῖσιν ἐλπίσιν θερμαίνεται.
     ἀλλ' ἢ καλῶς ζῆν ἢ καλῶς τεθνηκέναι
480 τὸν εὐγενῆ χρή. πάντ᾽ ἀκήκοας λόγον.
XO. οὐδεὶς ἐρεῖ ποθ' ὡς ὑπόβλητον λόγον,
     Αἴας, ἔλεξας, ἀλλὰ τῆς σαυτοῦ φρενός.
     παῦσαί γε μέντοι καὶ δὸς ἀνδράσιν φίλοις
     γνώμης κρατῆσαι, τάσδε φροντίδας μεθείς.
485 ΤΕ. ὦ δέσποτ᾽ Αἴας, τῆς ἀναγκαίας τύχης
     οὐκ ἔστιν οὐδὲν μεῖζον ἀνθρώποις κακόν.
     ἐγὼ δ' ἐλευθέρου μὲν ἐξέφυν πατρός,
     εἴπερ τινὸς σθένοντος ἐν πλούτῳ Φρυγῶν·
     νῦν δ' εἰμὶ δούλη· θεοῖς γὰρ ὧδ' ἔδοξέ που
490 καὶ σῇ μάλιστα χειρί. τοιγαροῦν, ἐπεὶ
     τὸ σὸν λέχος ξυνῆλθον, εὖ φρονῶ τὰ σά,
     καί σ' ἀντιάζω πρός τ' ἐφεστίου Διὸς
     εὐνῆς τε τῆς σῆς, ᾗ συνηλλάχθης ἐμοί,
     μή μ' ἀξιώσῃς βάξιν ἀλγεινὴν λαβεῖν
495 τῶν σῶν ὑπ' ἐχθρῶν, χειρίαν ἐφείς τινι.
     ᾗ γὰρ θάνῃς σὺ καὶ τελευτήσας ἀφῇς,
     ταύτῃ νόμιζε κἀμὲ τῇ τόθ' ἡμέρᾳ
     βίᾳ ξυναρπασθεῖσαν Ἀργείων ὕπο
     ξὺν παιδὶ τῷ σῷ δουλίαν ἕξειν τροφήν.
500 καί τις πικρὸν πρόσφθεγμα δεσποτῶν ἐρεῖ
     λόγοις ἰάπτων· "ἴδετε τὴν ὁμευνέτιν

---

476 κἀνεθεῖσα A^{sl}, κἀντιθεῖσα West 109-10 τοῦ γε L^{pc}Krpat, τοῦ δὲ L^{ac}, Stob., τό
     γε p, πλὴν τοῦ Lloyd-Jones et Wilson
478 καλαῖσιν Stob.
481 ἀπόβλητον rpa
495 ἐφείς LGpt: ἀφ- cett.
496 ᾗ Bothe: ἦν a, εἰ cett. τελευτήσας L^{pc}pat: -ήσεις lrp   ἀφῇς Lpat: ἀφείς
     Gp, ἀφ' ἧς rpD

for a man to wish for his life to be long, if he experiences no alternation in his misfortunes. For

475 what pleasure can day after day provide as it brings one near to or moves one back from death? I would not buy at any valuation the mortal who warms

480 himself on empty hopes. The noble man should either live well or die well. You have heard my whole account.

Leader No one, Ajax, will ever say that you have made a false speech; it is one that comes from your own heart. Yet stop, and allow those who are your friends to prevail over your intention, and give up these thoughts.

485 Tecmessa Lord Ajax, no evil is greater for men than the fortune which necessity lays upon them. I was born of a free father, mighty in wealth if any Phrygian was; but now I am a slave. For so it seemed good, I suppose, to the

490 gods and above all to your hand. Since, therefore, I have come to share your bed, I am well-disposed to all that is yours, and I entreat you by Zeus, the god of our hearth, and by your bed, by which you and I were united, do not think it right for me to hear the painful

495 talk that your enemies will utter, if you hand me on to be someone else's possession. For on the day you die, and having died abandon me, consider that on that very day *I* will be violently seized by the Argives, and with your child will have the life of a slave. And one

500 of my masters will describe me and attack me painfully with these words, "Behold the woman who

Αἴαντος, ὃς μέγιστον ἴσχυσε στρατοῦ,
οἵας λατρείας ἀνθ᾽ ὅσου ζήλου τρέφει".
τοιαῦτ᾽ ἐρεῖ τις· κἀμὲ μὲν δαίμων ἐλᾷ,
505 σοὶ δ᾽ αἰσχρὰ τἄπη ταῦτα καὶ τῷ σῷ γένει.
ἀλλ᾽ αἴδεσαι μὲν πατέρα τὸν σὸν ἐν λυγρῷ
γήρᾳ προλείπων, αἴδεσαι δὲ μητέρα
πολλῶν ἐτῶν κληροῦχον, ἥ σε πολλάκις
θεοῖς ἄραται ζῶντα πρὸς δόμους μολεῖν·
510 οἴκτιρε δ᾽, ὦναξ, παῖδα τὸν σόν, εἰ νέας
τροφῆς στερηθεὶς σοῦ διοίσεται μόνος
ὑπ᾽ ὀρφανιστῶν μὴ φίλων, ὅσον κακὸν
κείνῳ τε κἀμοὶ τοῦθ᾽, ὅταν θάνῃς, νεμεῖς.
ἐμοὶ γὰρ οὐκέτ᾽ ἔστιν εἰς ὅ τι βλέπω
515 πλὴν σοῦ. σὺ γάρ μοι πατρίδ᾽ ᾔστωσας δορί,
καὶ μητέρ᾽ ἄλλη μοῖρα τὸν φύσαντά τε
καθεῖλεν Ἅιδου θανασίμους οἰκήτορας.
τίς δῆτ᾽ ἐμοὶ γένοιτ᾽ ἂν ἀντὶ σοῦ πατρίς;
τίς πλοῦτος; ἐν σοὶ πᾶσ᾽ ἔγωγε σῴζομαι.
520 ἀλλ᾽ ἴσχε κἀμοῦ μνῆστιν· ἀνδρί τοι χρεὼν
μνήμην προσεῖναι, τερπνὸν εἴ τί που πάθοι.
χάρις χάριν γάρ ἐστιν ἡ τίκτουσ᾽ ἀεί·
ὅτου δ᾽ ἀπορρεῖ μνῆστις εὖ πεπονθότος,
οὐκ ἂν γένοιτ᾽ ἔθ᾽ οὗτος εὐγενὴς ἀνήρ.
525 ΧΟ. Αἴας, ἔχειν σ᾽ ἂν οἶκτον ὡς κἀγὼ φρενὶ
θέλοιμ᾽ ἄν· αἰνοίης γὰρ ἂν τὰ τῆσδ᾽ ἔπη.
ΑΙ. καὶ κάρτ᾽ ἐπαίνου τεύξεται πρὸς γοῦν ἐμοῦ,
ἐὰν μόνον τὸ ταχθὲν εὖ τολμᾷ τελεῖν.
ΤΕ. ἀλλ᾽ ὦ φίλ᾽ Αἴας, πάντ᾽ ἔγωγε πείσομαι.
530 ΑΙ. κόμιζέ νύν μοι παῖδα τὸν ἐμόν, ὡς ἴδω.
ΤΕ. καὶ μὴν φόβοισί γ᾽ αὐτὸν ἐξελυσάμην.
ΑΙ. ἐν τοῖσδε τοῖς κακοῖσιν, ἢ τί μοι λέγεις;
ΤΕ. μὴ σοί γέ που δύστηνος ἀντήσας θάνοι.

502 ἴσχυε Blaydes
503 οἵας λατρείας Lrpat: οἵαν ᾱνp
516 ἄλλη DZc: ἀλλ᾽ ἡ cett. τε LGp: με QRpat
519 πᾶσ᾽ a: πᾶσιν lrpZrt
521 πάθοι pat, Suda: πάθῃ Lrp
523 γένοιτ᾽] λέγοιτ᾽ Tournier

shared the bed of Ajax, the man who became by far the mightiest in the army, instead of being so envied what a life of servitude she endures!" This is the kind of thing that people will say, and as for me it is my destiny which will drive me, but for you and for your family these are disgraceful words. Feel shame at abandoning your father in his painful old age, feel shame before your mother too who has many years for her portion, who often prays to the gods that you may come home alive; and pity, my lord, your son; if robbed of his youthful nurture he is to pass his life apart from you, controlled by unfriendly guardians, think how great is this misfortune that, when you die, you will bestow on him and on me. For I no longer have anything to look to except for you. You annihilated my country with your spear, and another fate destroyed my mother and my father who now dwell in death in Hades. What country then could I have except for you? What wealth? All my salvation depends on you. Remember even me; a man should keep it in his memory if perhaps he has enjoyed some pleasure. For it is always kindness which breeds kindness; but when someone has been well treated and the recollection slips away, he could no longer be reckoned as a noble man.

Leader Ajax, I could wish you to have compassion as I too do in my heart; for then you would praise this woman's words.

Ajax Yes, she will certainly win praise at least from me, if only she can bring herself to complete properly what she is commanded.

Tecmessa Yes, I shall obey you in everything, dear Ajax.

Ajax Then bring me my son that I may see him.

Tecmessa Indeed I let him go away because I was afraid.

Ajax In these misfortunes of mine? Or how am I to take your meaning?

Tecmessa Yes, in case the wretched boy should perhaps encounter you and die.

62

<table>
<tr><td></td><td>ΑΙ.</td><td>πρέπον γέ τἂν ἦν δαίμονος τοὐμοῦ τόδε.</td></tr>
<tr><td>535</td><td>ΤΕ.</td><td>ἀλλ' οὖν ἐγὼ 'φύλαξα τοῦτό γ' ἀρκέσαι.</td></tr>
<tr><td></td><td>ΑΙ.</td><td>ἐπήνεσ' ἔργον καὶ πρόνοιαν ἣν ἔθου.</td></tr>
<tr><td></td><td>ΤΕ.</td><td>τί δῆτ' ἂν ὡς ἐκ τῶνδ' ἂν ὠφελοῖμί σε;</td></tr>
<tr><td></td><td>ΑΙ.</td><td>δός μοι προσειπεῖν αὐτὸν ἐμφανῆ τ' ἰδεῖν.</td></tr>
<tr><td></td><td>ΤΕ.</td><td>καὶ μὴν πέλας γε προσπόλοις φυλάσσεται.</td></tr>
<tr><td>540</td><td>ΑΙ.</td><td>τί δῆτα μέλλει μὴ οὐ παρουσίαν ἔχειν;</td></tr>
<tr><td></td><td>ΤΕ.</td><td>ὦ παῖ, πατὴρ καλεῖ σε. δεῦρο προσπόλων
ἄγ' αὐτὸν ὅσπερ χερσὶν εὐθύνων κυρεῖς.</td></tr>
<tr><td></td><td>ΑΙ.</td><td>ἕρποντι φωνεῖς, ἢ λελειμμένῳ λόγου;</td></tr>
<tr><td></td><td>ΤΕ.</td><td>καὶ δὴ κομίζει προσπόλων ὅδ' ἐγγύθεν.</td></tr>
<tr><td>545</td><td>ΑΙ.</td><td>αἶρ' αὐτόν, αἶρε δεῦρο· ταρβήσει γὰρ οὔ,
νεοσφαγῆ τοῦτόν γε προσλεύσσων φόνον,
εἴπερ δικαίως ἔστ' ἐμὸς τὰ πατρόθεν.
ἀλλ' αὐτίκ' ὠμοῖς αὐτὸν ἐν νόμοις πατρὸς
δεῖ πωλοδαμνεῖν κἀξομοιοῦσθαι φύσιν.</td></tr>
<tr><td>550</td><td></td><td>ὦ παῖ, γένοιο πατρὸς εὐτυχέστερος,
τὰ δ' ἄλλ' ὅμοιος, καὶ γένοι' ἂν οὐ κακός.
καίτοι σε καὶ νῦν τοῦτό γε ζηλοῦν ἔχω,
ὁθούνεκ' οὐδὲν τῶνδ' ἐπαισθάνῃ κακῶν.
ἐν τῷ φρονεῖν γὰρ μηδὲν ἥδιστος βίος,</td></tr>
<tr><td>555</td><td></td><td>ἕως τὸ χαίρειν καὶ τὸ λυπεῖσθαι μάθῃς.
ὅταν δ' ἵκῃ πρὸς τοῦτο, δεῖ σ' ὅπως πατρὸς
δείξεις ἐν ἐχθροῖς οἷος ἐξ οἵου 'τράφης.
τέως δὲ κούφοις πνεύμασιν βόσκου, νέαν
ψυχὴν ἀτάλλων, μητρὶ τῇδε χαρμονήν.</td></tr>
<tr><td>560</td><td></td><td>οὔτοι σ' Ἀχαιῶν, οἶδα, μή τις ὑβρίσῃ
στυγναῖσι λώβαις, οὐδὲ χωρὶς ὄντ' ἐμοῦ.
τοῖον πυλωρὸν φύλακα Τεῦκρον ἀμφὶ σοὶ
λείψω τροφῆς ἄοκνον ἔμπα κεἰ τανῦν
τηλωπὸς οἰχνεῖ, δυσμενῶν θήραν ἔχων.</td></tr>
</table>

543 λόγου **rpat**: -ων l
546 τοῦτόν γε **rpat**: τοῦτον δὲ **p**, τοῦ τόνδε L, που τόνδε A, ποῦ τόνδε Zc
554a τὸ μὴ φρονεῖν γὰρ κάρτ' ἀνώδυνον κακόν codd., *Suda*, om. Stob.
557 δείξεις L^{pc}at: -ῃς lrp

	Ajax	That would indeed have been appropriate to my destiny.
535	Tecmessa	Well anyway I took care to ward off that misfortune.
	Ajax	I approve of what you did and the forethought which you showed.
	Tecmessa	How then may I help you even in the present situation?
	Ajax	Let me address him and see him face to face.
	Tecmessa	Certainly, he is being guarded by servants nearby.
540	Ajax	Why then the delay in his appearance?
	Tecmessa	My son, your father calls you. Bring him here, servant, you who lead him by the hand.
	Ajax	Is he coming, the man to whom you call, or does he fail to hear your word?
	Tecmessa	Here comes the servant bringing him near.

[Enter Eurysaces, with a servant, by an eisodos]

545   Ajax   Lift him, lift him up here, for he will have no dread, when he looks on this newly-slaughtered blood, if indeed his inheritance makes him rightly mine. He must immediately be broken in like a young horse in his father's savage ways, and be made like him in his 550 nature. My son, may you be more fortunate than your father, but in other respects like him; you could not then be bad. Yet even now I can envy you this at least, that you have no perception of these troubles. For the pleasantest life consists in being aware of nothing, 555 before you learn the meaning of pleasure and pain. But when you reach that stage, you must show among your father's enemies what sort of son you are and what sort of father bred you. Till then be fed by light breezes, nurturing your young soul, a joy to your 560 mother here. None of the Achaeans, I am sure, will insult you with hateful outrage, even when you are separated from me. Such is the warden, Teucer, the resolute guardian of your nurture, that I shall leave for you, even if he has now gone far away hunting down

64

565 ἀλλ', ἄνδρες ἀσπιστῆρες, ἐνάλιος λεώς,
ὑμῖν τε κοινὴν τήνδ' ἐπισκήπτω χάριν,
κείνῳ τ' ἐμὴν ἀγγείλατ' ἐντολήν, ὅπως
τὸν παῖδα τόνδε πρὸς δόμους ἐμοὺς ἄγων
Τελαμῶνι δείξει μητρί τ', Ἐριβοίᾳ λέγω,
570 ὥς σφιν γένηται γηροβοσκὸς εἰσαεί,
[μέχρις οὗ μυχοὺς κίχωσι τοῦ κάτω θεοῦ.]
καὶ τἀμὰ τεύχη μήτ' ἀγωνάρχαι τινὲς
θήσουσ' Ἀχαιοῖς μήθ' ὁ λυμεὼν ἐμός.
ἀλλ' αὐτό μοι σύ, παῖ, λαβὼν τοὐπώνυμον,
575 Εὐρύσακες, ἴσχε διὰ πολυρράφου στρέφων
πόρπακος ἑπτάβοιον ἄρρηκτον σάκος·
τὰ δ' ἄλλα τεύχη κοίν' ἐμοὶ τεθάψεται.
ἀλλ' ὡς τάχος τὸν παῖδα τόνδ' ἤδη δέχου,
καὶ δῶμα πάκτου, μηδ' ἐπισκήνους γόους
580 δάκρυε. κάρτα τοι φιλοίκτιστον γυνή.
πύκαζε θᾶσσον. οὐ πρὸς ἰατροῦ σοφοῦ
θρηνεῖν ἐπῳδὰς πρὸς τομῶντι πήματι.
ΧΟ. δέδοικ' ἀκούων τήνδε τὴν προθυμίαν.
οὐ γάρ μ' ἀρέσκει γλῶσσά σου τεθηγμένη.
585 ΤΕ. ὦ δέσποτ' Αἴας, τί ποτε δρασείεις φρενί;
ΑΙ. μὴ κρῖνε, μὴ 'ξέταζε· σωφρονεῖν καλόν.
ΤΕ. οἴμ' ὡς ἀθυμῶ· καί σε πρὸς τοῦ σοῦ τέκνου
καὶ θεῶν ἱκνοῦμαι, μὴ προδοὺς ἡμᾶς γένῃ.
ΑΙ. ἄγαν γε λυπεῖς. οὐ κάτοισθ' ἐγὼ θεοῖς
590 ὡς οὐδὲν ἀρκεῖν εἴμ' ὀφειλέτης ἔτι;
ΤΕ. εὔφημα φώνει. ΑΙ. τοῖς ἀκούουσιν λέγε.
ΤΕ. σὺ δ' οὐχὶ πείσῃ; ΑΙ. πόλλ' ἄγαν ἤδη θροεῖς.
ΤΕ. ταρβῶ γάρ, ὦναξ. ΑΙ. οὐ ξυνέρξεθ' ὡς τάχος;
ΤΕ. πρὸς θεῶν, μαλάσσου. ΑΙ. μῶρά μοι δοκεῖς φρονεῖν,
595 εἰ τοὐμὸν ἦθος ἄρτι παιδεύειν νοεῖς.

569 δείξει a: -ῃ lrpt
571 del. Elmsley μέχρις ἂν t, Suda
573 μήθ' ὁ λυμεὼν] μητὲ λυμεὼν Schaefer, lac. post μήθ' Jackson 232-3
574 τοὐπώνυμον Fraenkel: ἐπωνύμον codd.
579 δῶμα πάκτου Cᵃᶜ?, Eust.: δῶμ' ἀπάκτου plerique
582 θρηνεῖν LrpA: θροεῖν pat, Suda τραύματι γρ in L, Xs
589 γε] με Elmsley, σε Diggle, Prometheus 2 (1976) 83

565   our enemies. As for you, bearers of the shield, my
seafaring people, I instruct you to share this service,
and report my command to him, that he may take this
boy to my home and show him to Telamon and my
570   mother, Eriboea I mean, so that he may come to
tend them permanently in their old age, [until they
reach the recesses of the god below] and that as far as
my arms are concerned no umpires nor my destroyer
should set them up as a prize for the Achaeans. But
you, my son, Eurysaces, must accept from me the very
575   thing from which you get your name, and keep it,
wielding it with its well-stitched loop, my unbroken
shield, made of the hides of seven bulls; the rest of my
armour shall be buried along with me. But take this
child now as quickly as you can, and make fast the
house, and do not weep in lamentation before the hut.
580   A woman is indeed a creature most prone to wail.
Shut the door quickly. It is not for a wise doctor to
lament with incantations over a disease that calls for
the knife.

Leader   I am afraid when I hear this vehemence of yours. For
your excited tongue gives me no pleasure.

585   Tecmessa   Lord Ajax, what do you mean in your heart to do?

Ajax   Do not question me, do not examine me; self-control
is good.

Tecmessa   Oh, how I despair! I entreat you by your child and by
the gods, do not turn into our betrayer.

Ajax   You vex me too much. Don't you understand that I
590   am no longer under any obligation to serve the gods?

Tecmessa   Do not speak ill-omened words. **Ajax:** Keep your
talk for those who listen.

Tecmessa   Won't you be persuaded? **Ajax:** Already you have
far too much to say.

Tecmessa   That is because I dread, my lord. **Ajax:** Will you not
shut the door as quickly as you can?

Tecmessa   By the gods, be softened! **Ajax:** It seems to me that
595   you are thinking foolishly, if even now you plan to
educate my character.

Exeunt Ajax, Tecmessa, and Eurysaces into the hut]

66

XO. ὦ κλεινὰ Σαλαμίς, σὺ μέν που   στρ. 1.
     ναίεις ἁλίπλακτος εὐδαίμων,
     πᾶσιν περίφαντος αἰεί·
600 ἐγὼ δ᾽ ὁ τλάμων παλαιὸς ἀφ᾽ οὗ χρόνος
     †Ἰδαῖα μίμνων λειμωνίᾳ ποίᾳ† μη-
     νῶν ἀνήριθμος αἰὲν εὐνῶμαι
605 χρόνῳ τρυχόμενος,
     κακὰν ἐλπίδ᾽ ἔχων
     ἔτι μέ ποτ᾽ ἀνύσειν τὸν ἀπότροπον ἀΐδηλον Ἅιδαν.

     καί μοι δυσθεράπευτος Αἴας   ἀντ. 1.
610 ξύνεστιν ἔφεδρος, ὤμοι μοι,
     θείᾳ μανίᾳ ξύναυλος·
     ὃν ἐξεπέμψω πρὶν δή ποτε θουρίῳ
     κρατοῦντ᾽ ἐν Ἄρει· νῦν δ᾽ αὖ φρενὸς οἰοβώ-
615 τας φίλοις μέγα πένθος ηὕρηται,
     τὰ πρὶν δ᾽ ἔργα χεροῖν
     μεγίστας ἀρετᾶς
620 ἄφιλα παρ᾽ ἀφίλοις ἔπεσ᾽ ἔπεσε μελέοις Ἀτρείδαις.

     ἦ που παλαιᾷ μὲν σύντροφος ἁμέρᾳ,   στρ. 2.
625 λευκῷ τὲ γήρᾳ μάτηρ νιν ὅταν νοσοῦν-
     τα φρενοβόρως ἀκούσῃ,
     αἴλινον αἴλινον,
     οὐκ οἰκτρᾶς γόον ὄρνιθος ἀηδοῦς

597 ἁλίπλακτος rpa: -αγκτος lpat
601 μίμνων LCᵃᶜG: μίμνω rpat   ποίᾳ Lpa: πόα rpDt   μηνῶν Hermann: μήλων codd.
604 εὐνῶμαι Bergk: εὐνώμᾳ t, εὐνόμᾳ cett.
613 κρατοῦντ᾽ ἐν] νικῶντ᾽ εἶν t
615 ηὕρηται] γεγένηται γρ in LH (vide Christodoulou ad Σ 617)
616 χεροῖν t: χερσὶν La, χερσὶ rpD
617 μεγίστας t: μέγιστ᾽ Lrpa
620 παρ᾽ ἀφίλοις Gpat: παρὰ φίλοις LQR pD
622 σύντροφος gl in Zc: ἔν- codd.
625 λευκά Schneidewin
626 φρενοβόρως Dindorf: -μόρως vel -μώρως codd.
628 οὐκ Wecklein: οὐδ᾽ codd.

Chor. *str.1*	Oh famous Salamis, you lie, I think, beaten by the sea

Chor. *str.1* Oh famous Salamis, you lie, I think, beaten by the sea
and prosperous, for ever conspicuous to all men's
600   eyes; but as for me in my misery, long is the time that
..... , keeping no count of the months, I make my bed
605   here for ever worn away by time, with the sad
expectation that one day still I shall complete the
journey to inexorable Hades the annihilator.

ant.1   Ajax is here beside me, hard to heal, a fresh
610   competitor that I must wrestle with, alas alas, who
shares his home with divine-sent madness; long ago
you sent him out, mighty in impetuous Ares; but now
615   as he feeds his lonely thoughts he has turned out to be
a source of great grief for his friends, while the former
works of his hands, marked by the highest excellence,
620   have fallen, fallen away friendless in the eyes of the
sons of Atreus, unfriendly and wretched as they are.

str.2   No doubt his mother, the days of whose life are
625   ancient and her old age hoary, when she hears that he
is sick with a disease that eats his heart - sing woe,
sing woe - will in her unhappiness not restrain the

630 σχήσει δύσμορος, ἀλλ' ὀξυτόνους μὲν ᾠδὰς
θρηνήσει, χερόπληκτοι δ'
ἐν στέρνοισι πεσοῦνται
δοῦποι καὶ πολιᾶς ἄμυγμα χαίτας.

635 κρείσσων γὰρ "Αιδᾳ κεύθων ὁ νοσῶν μάταν,   ἀντ. 2.
ὃς ἐκ πατρῴας ἥκων γενεᾶς ἄρισ-
τα πολυπόνων Ἀχαιῶν,
οὐκέτι συντρόφοις
640 ὀργαῖς ἔμπεδος, ἀλλ' ἐκτὸς ὁμιλεῖ.
ὦ τλᾶμον πάτερ, οἵαν σε μένει πυθέσθαι
παιδὸς δύσφορον ἄταν,
ἂν οὔπω τις ἔθρεψεν
645 αἰὼν Αἰακιδᾶν ἄτερθε τοῦδε.

ΑΙ. ἅπανθ' ὁ μακρὸς κἀναρίθμητος χρόνος
φύει τ' ἄδηλα καὶ φανέντα κρύπτεται·
κοὐκ ἔστ' ἄελπτον οὐδέν, ἀλλ' ἁλίσκεται
χὠ δεινὸς ὅρκος χαἰ περισκελεῖς φρένες.
650 κἀγὼ γάρ, ὃς τὰ δείν' ἐκαρτέρουν τότε
βαφῇ σίδηρος ὥς, ἐθηλύνθην στόμα
πρὸς τῆσδε τῆς γυναικός· οἰκτίρω δέ νιν
χήραν παρ' ἐχθροῖς παῖδά τ' ὀρφανὸν λιπεῖν.
ἀλλ' εἶμι πρός τε λουτρὰ καὶ παρακτίους
655 λειμῶνας, ὡς ἂν λύμαθ' ἁγνίσας ἐμὰ
μῆνιν βαρεῖαν ἐξαλύξωμαι θεᾶς·
μολών τε χῶρον ἔνθ' ἂν ἀστιβῆ κίχω
κρύψω τόδ' ἔγχος τοὐμόν, ἔχθιστον βελῶν,
γαίας ὀρύξας ἔνθα μή τις ὄψεται·

629 σχήσει Reiske: ᾔσει LGpat, ἄσει tF, Suda
634 ἄμυγμα Bothe: -ατα codd., Eust.
635 ὁ Lobeck: ἢ codd.
636 ἐκ] εἰς Lloyd-Jones, JHS 76 (1956) 112   ἄριστα cod. Livinei: -ος tZc, om.
cett.
641 τλᾶμον **rpat**: τλάμων L, v.l. in **r, a**
649 χαἰ Musgrave: καὶ codd.
650 ἐκαρτέρουν τότε] ἐπηπείλησ' ἔπη γρ in L
656 ἐξαλύξωμαι Hesych.: ἐξαλέξομαι Oac, ἐξαλεύσωμαι plerique, ἐξαλέξωμαι West
111-12

630   dirge of the piteously wailing bird, the nightingale, but will utter high-pitched lamentations, and the thud of her beating hands will fall on her breast and she will tear her grey hair.

635   *ant.2*   For better hidden in Hades is the man who suffers from an empty sickness, whose inheritance from his father's family was better than that of any other of the toiling Achaeans; he no longer remains constant to the

640   temperament he grew up with, but has become a stranger to it. Wretched father, how grievous is your son's ruin, which you have yet to hear about, ruin which life's destiny has never before engendered for

645   any of the sons of Aeacus except for him.

[*Enter Ajax from his hut, carrying his sword, and followed by Tecmessa*]

Ajax   Long and immeasurable time brings forth all things that are obscure and when they have come to light hides them again; there is nothing that is beyond expectation, but even the terrible oath falls into time's power, and minds which are too strict. For even I,

650   who at that time was so terribly firm, like iron hardened by dipping, have been softened like a woman in my speech, thanks to the woman here; I pity her that I should leave her a widow with my enemies and my son an orphan. Well, I shall go the bathing-place

655   and the meadows by the shore, to wash away my defilement and escape from the heavy anger of the goddess; I shall go to where I can find an untrodden place and I shall hide this sword of mine, the most hateful of my weapons, digging in the ground where

660   ἀλλ' αὐτὸ νὺξ "Αιδης τε σῳζόντων κάτω.
ἐγὼ γάρ, ἐξ οὗ χειρὶ τοῦτ' ἐδεξάμην
παρ' Ἕκτορος δώρημα δυσμενεστάτου,
οὔπω τι κεδνὸν ἔσχον Ἀργείων πάρα.
ἀλλ' ἔστ' ἀληθὴς ἡ βροτῶν παροιμία,
665   ἐχθρῶν ἄδωρα δῶρα κοὐκ ὀνήσιμα.
τοιγὰρ τὸ λοιπὸν εἰσόμεσθα μὲν θεοῖς
εἴκειν, μαθησόμεσθα δ' Ἀτρείδας σέβειν.
ἄρχοντές εἰσιν, ὥσθ' ὑπεικτέον· τί μήν;
καὶ γὰρ τὰ δεινὰ καὶ τὰ καρτερώτατα
670   τιμαῖς ὑπείκει· τοῦτο μὲν νιφοστιβεῖς
χειμῶνες ἐκχωροῦσιν εὐκάρπῳ θέρει·
ἐξίσταται δὲ νυκτὸς αἰανὴς κύκλος
τῇ λευκοπώλῳ φέγγος ἡμέρᾳ φλέγειν·
δεινῶν δ' ἄημα πνευμάτων ἐκοίμισε
675   στένοντα πόντον· ἐν δ' ὁ παγκρατὴς Ὕπνος
λύει πεδήσας, οὐδ' ἀεὶ λαβὼν ἔχει.
ἡμεῖς δὲ πῶς οὐ γνωσόμεσθα σωφρονεῖν;
ἔγωγ'· ἐπίσταμαι γὰρ ἀρτίως ὅτι
ὅ τ' ἐχθρὸς ἡμῖν ἐς τοσόνδ' ἐχθαρτέος,
680   ὡς καὶ φιλήσων αὖθις, ἔς τε τὸν φίλον
τοσαῦθ' ὑπουργῶν ὠφελεῖν βουλήσομαι,
ὡς αἰὲν οὐ μενοῦντα. τοῖς πολλοῖσι γὰρ
βροτῶν ἄπιστός ἐσθ' ἑταιρείας λιμήν.
ἀλλ' ἀμφὶ μὲν τούτοισιν εὖ σχήσει· σὺ δὲ
685   ἔσω θεοῖς ἐλθοῦσα διὰ τέλους, γύναι,
εὔχου τελεῖσθαι τοὐμὸν ὧν ἐρᾷ κέαρ.
ὑμεῖς θ', ἑταῖροι, ταὐτὰ τῇδέ μοι τάδε
τιμᾶτε, Τεύκρῳ τ', ἢν μόλῃ, σημήνατε
μέλειν μὲν ἡμῶν, εὐνοεῖν δ' ὑμῖν ἅμα.

668 τί μήν Linwood: τί μή vel τιμῇ codd.
672 αἰανὴς L: -ῆς cett.
674 δεινῶν GQpat· -ὸν IR, Suda
678 ἔγωγ' Brunck: ἐγὼ δ' codd.
679 ἡμῖν K, Suda· ἤμην (ἤ- O) codd., Suda ἐχθαρτέος Lp: ἐχθραντέος rpat, Suda
685 τέλους] τάχους v.l. in LGp
689 ἡμῶν...ὑμῖν] ὑμῶν...ἡμῖν West 112-13 ὑμῖν ἅμα pat: ὑμῶν ἅμα lrp, ὑπέρμεγα γρ in LH, μετὰ γρ in K, ὑμῶν ὕπερ Dawe

660 nobody shall see it; let night and Hades keep it safely down below. For ever since I received it in my hand as a gift from Hector, my worst enemy, I have never yet had any good from the Argives. True is men's 665 proverb, that the gifts of enemies are no gifts and bring no benefit. Therefore we shall know in future to yield to the gods, and we shall learn to reverence the sons of Atreus. They are the rulers, so one ought to yield - of course one ought. For even things that are terrible and 670 very strong yield to what is held in honour; firstly, winters which cover the roads with snow give way to summer with its lovely fruit; and the eternal rotation of the night withdraws for day with its white horses to kindle its light; and the breath of terrible winds puts to 675 sleep the groaning sea; moreover omnipotent Sleep releases when it has fettered, and what it has caught it does not hold for ever. Then how shall *we* not learn good sense? I shall; for at this late hour I understand that our enemy is to be hated only to the extent that he 680 will later become our friend, while as far as a friend is concerned I shall want to serve and help him only so far, believing that he will not always so remain. For to most mortals the haven of comradeship is not to be trusted. But in these matters it will turn out well; as 685 for you, madam, go inside and pray to the gods that what my heart desires may be accomplished right to the end. And you, my comrades, pay me this same honour as she does, and, if Teucer should come, bid

690 ἐγὼ γὰρ εἶμ' ἐκεῖσ' ὅποι πορευτέον,
ὑμεῖς δ' ἃ φράζω δρᾶτε, καὶ τάχ' ἄν μ' ἴσως
πύθοισθε, κεἰ νῦν δυστυχῶ, σεσωμένον.

XO. ἔφριξ' ἔρωτι, περιχαρὴς δ' ἀνεπτάμαν.   στρ.
   ἰὼ ἰὼ Πὰν Πάν,
695 ὦ Πὰν Πὰν ἁλίπλαγκτε, Κυλ-
   λανίας χιονοκτύπου
   πετραίας ἀπὸ δειράδος φάνηθ', ὦ
   θεῶν χοροποί' ἄναξ, ὅπως μοι
   Μύσια Κνώσι' ὀρ-
700 χήματ' αὐτοδαῆ ξυνὼν ἰάψῃς.
   νῦν γὰρ ἐμοὶ μέλει χορεῦσαι <∪ – ∪ –>.
   Ἰκαρίων δ' ὑπὲρ †πελαγέων†
   μολὼν ἄναξ Ἀπόλλων
   ὁ Δάλιος εὔγνωστος
705 ἐμοὶ ξυνείη διὰ παντὸς εὔφρων.

   ἔλυσεν αἰνὸν ἄχος ἀπ' ὀμμάτων Ἄρης.   ἀντ.
   ἰὼ ἰώ, νῦν αὖ,
   νῦν, ὦ Ζεῦ, πάρα λευκὸν εὐ-
   άμερον πελάσαι φάος
710 θοᾶν ὠκυάλων νεῶν, ὅτ' Αἴας
   λαθίπονος πάλιν, θεῶν δ' αὖ
   πάνθυτα θέσμι' ἐξ-
   ήνυσ' εὐνομίᾳ σέβων μέγιστα.
   πάνθ' ὁ μέγας χρόνος μαραίνει τε καὶ φλέγει·
715 κοὐδὲν ἀναύδητον φατίσαιμ'
   ἄν, εὖτέ γ' ἐξ ἀέλπτων

---

693 ἔφριξ' ἐν **t**
695 ἁλίπλαγκτε LQpa: -ακτε GRpat
699 Μύσια *P.Oxy.* 1615, *Suda*: Νύσια codd.
701 lacunam posuit Hermann et Lobeck
702 πελαγέων] πελαγίων **p**Zc, κελεύθων Lloyd-Jones et Wilson
705 ξυνείη **lpr**: -είης **pa**
706 ἔλυσεν Lᵃᶜ: ἔλυσε(ν) γὰρcett.
714 τε καὶ φλέγει om. Stob.
715 φατίσαιμ' cod. Livinei: φατίξαιμ' **Lrpa**, φατίζαιμ' Lᵃᶜ, Fᵃᶜ, om. **t**

him care for us and also remain loyal to yourselves;
690   for I am going where I must journey, but you must do
what I tell you, and perhaps you may soon learn that,
even if I am unhappy now, I have been saved.

[*Exit Ajax by an eisodos, exit Tecmessa into the hut*]

Chor. *str*   I thrill with rapture, I soar on wings with exceeding
695   joy. Oh oh Pan, Pan, oh Pan, Pan, sea-roaming god,
appear to me from Cyllene's snow-beaten rocky ridge,
you, lord, who make the gods to dance, that in my
700   company you may move in the rapid Mysian and
Cnossian steps which you have taught yourself. For
now it is in my mind to dance <...> And may the lord
Apollo, the Delian god, come over the Icarian sea, and
keep company with me, fully recognisable, well-
705   disposed to me through all time.

ant.   Ares has dissolved the dread grief from my eyes. Oh
oh, now once more, now, oh Zeus, the white light of a
710   happy day can come near to the swift ships that speed
across the sea, now that Ajax has again forgotten his
troubles, and once more has performed with full
sacrifice the rites of the gods, reverencing them with
the greatest loyalty to their divine law. Great time
extinguishes all things and kindles them; and I would
715   say that nothing can be declared impossible, when

Αἴας μετανεγνώσθη
θυμῶν τ᾽ Ἀτρείδαις μεγάλων τε νεικέων.

ΑΓΓΕΛΟΣ

ἄνδρες φίλοι, τὸ πρῶτον ἀγγεῖλαι θέλω,
720 Τεῦκρος πάρεστιν ἄρτι Μυσίων ἀπὸ
κρημνῶν· μέσον δὲ προσμολὼν στρατήγιον
κυδάζεται τοῖς πᾶσιν Ἀργείοις ὁμοῦ.
στείχοντα γὰρ πρόσωθεν αὐτὸν ἐν κύκλῳ
μαθόντες ἀμφέστησαν, εἶτ᾽ ὀνείδεσιν
725 ἤρασσον ἔνθεν κἄνθεν οὔτις ἔσθ᾽ ὃς οὔ,
τὸν τοῦ μανέντος κἀπιβουλευτοῦ στρατῷ
ξύναιμον ἀποκαλοῦντες, ὡς τ᾽ οὐκ ἀρκέσοι
τὸ μὴ οὐ πέτροισι πᾶς καταξανθεὶς θανεῖν.
ὥστ᾽ ἐς τοσοῦτον ἦλθον ὥστε καὶ χεροῖν
730 κολεῶν ἐρυστὰ διεπεραιώθη ξίφη.
λήγει δ᾽ ἔρις δραμοῦσα τοῦ προσωτάτω
ἀνδρῶν γερόντων ἐν ξυναλλαγῇ λόγου.
ἀλλ᾽ ἡμὶν Αἴας ποῦ 'στιν, ὡς φράσω τάδε;
τοῖς κυρίοις γὰρ πάντα χρὴ δηλοῦν λόγον.
735 ΧΟ. οὐκ ἔνδον, ἀλλὰ φροῦδος ἀρτίως, νέας
βουλὰς νέοισιν ἐγκαταζεύξας τρόποις.
ΑΓ. ἰοὺ ἰού.
βραδεῖαν ἡμᾶς ἆρ᾽ ὁ τήνδε τὴν ὁδὸν
πέμπων ἔπεμψεν, ἢ 'φάνην ἐγὼ βραδύς.
740 ΧΟ. τί δ᾽ ἐστὶ χρείας τῆσδ᾽ ὑπεσπανισμένον;
ΑΓ. τὸν ἄνδρ᾽ ἀπηύδα Τεῦκρος ἔνδοθεν στέγης
μὴ 'ξω παρεῖναι, πρὶν παρὼν αὐτὸς τύχῃ.
ΧΟ. ἀλλ᾽ οἴχεταί τοι, πρὸς τὸ κέρδιον τραπεὶς
γνώμης, θεοῖσιν ὡς καταλλαχθῇ χόλου.

---

717 μετανεγνώσθη **Lrpat**: μετεγνώσθη **pa**
718 θυμῶν γρ in G, Nˢˡ t: ὃν cett., *Suda*   τ᾽ A: om. cett.
726 στρατῷ Schaefer: -οῦ codd.
727 ἀρκέσοι **Lrpa**: -έσει **pt**
742 παρεῖναι Hartung: παρείκειν H, παρήκειν cett.   τύχῃ **LQpat**: -οι **GRH**
743 κέρδιον Kᵃᶜ?, **p**: κέρδιστον **Lrpat**

beyond my hopes Ajax has been converted from his anger against the sons of Atreus and from his mighty quarrels.

[*Enter by an eisodos a messenger from the Greek army*]
MESSENGER

720 Friends, first I wish to report, Teucer has just arrived from the cliffs of Mysia; he came to the general's tent in the middle of the camp and was abused by the whole body of the Argives. For when they recognised from a distance that he was approaching, they stood round him in a circle, and then they all without

725 exception assailed him on all sides with reproaches, calling him the kinsman of the madman who conspired against the army, saying that he would not be strong enough to avoid death completely mangled with stones. So they came to such a pitch that in their

730 hands swords were actually drawn and unsheathed from their scabbards. But when it had run as far as it could go the quarrel ceased through old men's reconciling words. But where, pray, is Ajax, that I may tell him this? For I must reveal the whole story to my lord.

735 Leader He is not at home, but has just left; for he has reformed his plans to suit his new temper.

Messenger Oh, no! Too slow then was this mission on which the one who sent me dispatched me, or I have turned out to be slow.

740 Leader Where have you fallen short in the execution of this duty?

Messenger Teucer said that Ajax should not be allowed out from inside the house, until he himself should arrive.

Leader Well, I tell you he has gone, his intention changed for the better, to be reconciled to the gods after his anger.

76

745 ΑΓ. ταῦτ' ἐστὶ τἄπη μωρίας πολλῆς πλέα,
εἴπερ τι Κάλχας εὖ φρονῶν μαντεύεται.
ΧΟ. ποῖον; τί δ' εἰδὼς τοῦδε πράγματος πάρει;
ΑΓ. τοσοῦτον οἶδα καὶ παρὼν ἐτύγχανον·
ἐκ γὰρ συνέδρου καὶ τυραννικοῦ κύκλου
750 Κάλχας μεταστὰς οἶος 'Ατρειδῶν δίχα,
ἐς χεῖρα Τεύκρου δεξιὰν φιλοφρόνως
θεὶς εἶπε κἀπέσκηψε παντοίᾳ τέχνῃ
εἶρξαι κατ' ἦμαρ τοὐμφανὲς τὸ νῦν τόδε
Αἴανθ' ὑπὸ σκηναῖσι μηδ' ἀφέντ' ἐᾶν,
755 εἰ ζῶντ' ἐκεῖνον εἰσιδεῖν θέλοι ποτέ.
ἐλᾷ γὰρ αὐτὸν τήνδ' ἔθ' ἡμέραν μόνην
δίας 'Αθάνας μῆνις, ὡς ἔφη λέγων.
τὰ γὰρ περισσὰ κἀνόητα σώματα
πίπτειν βαρείαις πρὸς θεῶν δυσπραξίαις
760 ἔφασχ' ὁ μάντις, ὅστις ἀνθρώπου φύσιν
βλαστὼν ἔπειτα μὴ κατ' ἄνθρωπον φρονῇ.
κεῖνος δ' ἀπ' οἴκων εὐθὺς ἐξορμώμενος
ἄνους καλῶς λέγοντος ηὑρέθη πατρός.
ὁ μὲν γὰρ αὐτὸν ἐννέπει, "τέκνον, δορὶ
765 βούλου κρατεῖν μέν, σὺν θεῷ δ' ἀεὶ κρατεῖν".
ὁ δ' ὑψικόμπως κἀφρόνως ἠμείψατο,
"πάτερ, θεοῖς μὲν κἂν ὁ μηδὲν ὢν ὁμοῦ
κράτος κατακτήσαιτ'· ἐγὼ δὲ καὶ δίχα
κείνων πέποιθα τοῦτ' ἐπισπάσειν κλέος".
770 τοσόνδ' ἐκόμπει μῦθον. εἶτα δεύτερον
δίας 'Αθάνας, ἡνίκ' ὀτρύνουσά νιν
ηὐδᾶτ' ἐπ' ἐχθροῖς χεῖρα φοινίαν τρέπειν,
τότ' ἀντιφωνεῖ δεινὸν ἄρρητόν τ' ἔπος·
"ἄνασσα, τοῖς ἄλλοισιν 'Αργείων πέλας

747 πάρει Reiske: πέρι codd.
756 την δε θ]ημερανμονην P.Oxy. 1615: τῇδέ θ' ἡμέρᾳ μόνῃ codd.
758 κἀνόητα Zcᵃᶜ: κἀνόνητα cett
761 φρονῇ P.Oxy. 1615, LP: -εῖ cett.
770 δεύτερον] δ' ἀντίον Jebb
771 δίας 'Αθάνας] Αἴας 'Αθάναν anon.
773 τότ' Lpat: ὅδ' t, τόδ' H   ἀντιφωνεῖ Lrpat: ἀντεφώνει p

745	Messenger	These words are very foolish, if indeed with sound understanding Calchas utters prophecy.
	Leader	What prophecy? With what knowledge of this affair do you come?
	Messenger	So much I know, and I was present. Calchas moved

745 Messenger These words are very foolish, if indeed with sound understanding Calchas utters prophecy.

Leader What prophecy? With what knowledge of this affair do you come?

Messenger So much I know, and I was present. Calchas moved

750 from the council and the royal circle, separating himself from the sons of Atreus, and putting his right hand in friendly fashion into Teucer's hand he spoke and enjoined upon him by all means for as long as the present daylight lasts to keep Ajax in his hut and not

755 allow him to go out freely, if he wished ever again to see him alive. For it is only for today that the wrath of divine Athena still drives him, as he said in his speech. The prophet declared that it is bodies grown too great and stupid that fall through grievous afflictions at the

760 hands of the gods, whenever a man is born with a human nature, but does not then think in accordance with his human status. He, from the very moment when he was setting out from home and his father gave him good advice, was found to be lacking in understanding. For his father addressed him, "My son,

765 you must wish to win the victory with your spear, but always to win it with the help of god." And he boastfully and thoughtlessly replied, "Father, together with the gods even the nonentity could achieve victory; but *I* trust that even without them I shall win

770 this glory." So great was the boast he uttered. Then on a second occasion, in the presence of divine Athena, when she encouraged him and told him to direct his murderous hand against the foe, he then replied with a terrible word, one that should never

775   ἴστω, καθ' ἡμᾶς δ' οὔποτ' εἰσρήξει μάχη".
        τοιοῖσδέ τοι λόγοισιν ἀστεργῆ θεᾶς
        ἐκτήσατ' ὀργήν, οὐ κατ' ἄνθρωπον φρονῶν.
        ἀλλ' εἴπερ ἔστι τῇδ' ἔθ' ἡμέρᾳ, τάχ' ἂν
        γενοίμεθ' αὐτοῦ σὺν θεῷ σωτήριοι.
780   τοσαῦθ' ὁ μάντις εἶφ'· ὁ δ' εὐθὺς ἐξ ἕδρας
        πέμπει μέ σοι φέροντα τάσδ' ἐπιστολὰς
        Τεῦκρος φυλάσσειν. εἰ δ' ἀπεστερήμεθα,
        οὐκ ἔστιν ἀνὴρ κεῖνος, εἰ Κάλχας σοφός.
ΧΟ.   ὦ δαΐα Τέκμησσα, δυσμόρων γένος,
785   ὅρα μολοῦσα τόνδ' ὁποῖ' ἔπη θροεῖ.
        ξυρεῖ γὰρ ἐν χρῷ τοῦτο μὴ χαίρειν τινά.
ΤΕ.   τί μ' αὖ τάλαιναν, ἀρτίως πεπαυμένην
        κακῶν ἀτρύτων, ἐξ ἕδρας ἀνίστατε;
ΧΘ.   τοῦδ' εἰσάκουε τἀνδρός, ὡς ἥκει φέρων
790   Αἴαντος ἡμῖν πρᾶξιν ἣν ἤλγησ' ἐγώ.
ΤΕ.   οἴμοι, τί φής, ἄνθρωπε; μῶν ὀλώλαμεν;
ΑΓ.   οὐκ οἶδα τὴν σὴν πρᾶξιν, Αἴαντος δ' ὅτι,
        θυραῖος εἴπερ ἐστίν, οὐ θαρσῶ πέρι.
ΤΕ.   καὶ μὴν θυραῖος, ὥστε μ' ὠδίνειν τί φής.
795 ΑΓ.   ἐκεῖνον εἴργειν Τεῦκρος ἐξεφίεται
        σκηνῆς ὕπαυλον, μηδ' ἀφιέναι μόνον.
ΤΕ.   ποῦ δ' ἐστὶ Τεῦκρος, κἀπὶ τῷ λέγει τάδε;
ΑΓ.   πάρεστ' ἐκεῖνος ἄρτι· τήνδε δ' ἔξοδον
        Αἴαντος εἰς ὄλεθρον ἐλπίζει φέρειν.

775   εἰσρήξει West 113: ἐκ- codd., ἐνρήξει Lloyd-Jones et Wilson
776   τοι Hermann: τοῖς codd.
778   ἔθ' Lobeck: θ' Λrpat, ἐν L^{ac}Kp
780   τοσαῦθ' at: τοιαῦθ' Lrp
782   ἀφυστερήμεθα Wakefield
784   δυσμόρων R. Paehler: δύσμορον codd.
790   πρᾶξιν] βάξιν Reiske
794   μὴν rpat: νῦν l, γρ in G, p
799   Αἴαντος εἰς ὄλεθρον Jebb (post Blaydes): ὀλεθρίαν Αἴαντος codd., τὴν ὀλεθρίαν Αἴαντος Lloyd-Jones et Wilson

have been spoken: "Queen, stand near the rest of the
775 Argives, but where I am stationed the battle will never
break in." With such words he acquired the intolerant
hatred of the goddess, because he did not think in
accordance with his human status. Yet if indeed he is
still alive today, perhaps we might turn out to be his
780 saviours with the help of god. So much the prophet
said, and Teucer immediately from where he sat sent
me with these orders for you to observe. But if we
have been frustrated, Ajax no longer lives, if Calchas
is a wise man.

Leader Wretched Tecmessa, offspring of an ill-fated family,
785 come and see what words this man speaks. This will
be a close shave to prevent someone from rejoicing.

[Enter Tecmessa from the hut]

Tecmessa Why have you once more disturbed me from where I
was sitting, an unhappy woman who has only just
gained respite from unwearying troubles?

Leader Listen to this man; for he comes with news for us of
790 an affair concerning Ajax which has caused me pain.

Tecmessa Alas, man, what is it you say? Surely we are not
undone?

Messenger I do not know how *you* are faring, only that as far as
Ajax is concerned, if indeed he is out of doors, I have
no confidence.

Tecmessa Yes he is out of doors, so that I am full of anguish at
what you mean.

795 Messenger Teucer commands that he be kept in the shelter of his
hut and not be allowed out alone.

Tecmessa But where is Teucer, and for what reason does he say
this?

Messenger He has only just arrived; and he expects that this
departure of Ajax will lead to his death.

800 ΤΕ.　οἴμοι τάλαινα, τοῦ ποτ' ἀνθρώπων μαθών;
　　ΑΓ.　τοῦ Θεστορείου μάντεως, καθ' ἡμέραν
　　　　　τὴν νῦν, ὃ τούτῳ θάνατον ἢ βίον φέρει.
　　ΤΕ.　οἳ 'γώ, φίλοι, πρόστητ' ἀναγκαίας τύχης,
　　　　　καὶ σπεύσαθ' οἱ μὲν Τεῦκρον ἐν τάχει μολεῖν,
805　　　οἱ δ' ἑσπέρους ἀγκῶνας, οἱ δ' ἀντηλίους
　　　　　ζητεῖτ' ἰόντες τἀνδρὸς ἔξοδον κακήν.
　　　　　ἔγνωκα γὰρ δὴ φωτὸς ἠπατημένη
　　　　　καὶ τῆς παλαιᾶς χάριτος ἐκβεβλημένη.
　　　　　οἴμοι, τί δράσω, τέκνον; οὐχ ἱδρυτέον.
810　　　ἀλλ' εἶμι κἀγὼ κεῖσ' ὅποιπερ ἂν σθένω.
　　　　　χωρῶμεν, ἐγκονῶμεν, οὐχ ἔδρας ἀκμή,
　　　　　σῴζειν θέλοντες ἄνδρα γ' ὃς σπεύδει θανεῖν.
　　ΧΟ.　χωρεῖν ἕτοιμος, κοὐ λόγῳ δείξω μόνον.
　　　　　τάχος γὰρ ἔργου καὶ ποδῶν ἅμ' ἕψεται.

815 ΑΙ.　ὁ μὲν σφαγεὺς ἕστηκεν ᾗ τομώτατος
　　　　　γένοιτ' ἄν, εἴ τῳ καὶ λογίζεσθαι σχολή,
　　　　　δῶρον μὲν ἀνδρὸς Ἕκτορος ξένων ἐμοὶ
　　　　　μάλιστα μισηθέντος, ἐχθίστου θ' ὁρᾶν.
　　　　　πέπηγε δ' ἐν γῇ πολεμίᾳ τῇ Τρῳάδι,
820　　　σιδηροβρῶτι θηγάνῃ νεηκονής·
　　　　　ἔπηξα δ' αὐτὸν εὖ περιστείλας ἐγώ,
　　　　　εὐνούστατον τῷδ' ἀνδρὶ διὰ τάχους θανεῖν.
　　　　　οὕτω μὲν εὐσκευοῦμεν· ἐκ δὲ τῶνδέ μοι
　　　　　σὺ πρῶτος, ὦ Ζεῦ, καὶ γὰρ εἰκός, ἄρκεσον.
825　　　αἰτήσομαι δέ σ' οὐ μακρὸν γέρας λαβεῖν.
　　　　　πέμψον τιν' ἡμῖν ἄγγελον, κακὴν φάτιν
　　　　　Τεύκρῳ φέροντα, πρῶτος ὥς με βαστάσῃ
　　　　　πεπτῶτα τῷδε περὶ νεορράντῳ ξίφει,
　　　　　καὶ μὴ πρὸς ἐχθρῶν του κατοπτευθεὶς πάρος

802　ὃ τούτῳ Pearson: ὅτ' αὐτῷ Lat, ἥτ' αὐτῷ rp
812　θέλοντες rpat: -ας L　ὃς ἂν Lp　σπεύδει rpat: ῃ Lᵃᶜp
816　del. Herwerden
825　γέρας λαβεῖν L, γρ in G, pt: γέρας λαχεῖν a, λαχεῖν γέρας rp

800	Tecmessa	Alas, unhappy me, who was the man from whom he learned it?
	Messenger	The prophet son of Thestor, a pronouncement which on this very day brings death or life to him.
	Tecmessa	Alas, my friends, protect me from this misfortune that is forced upon me, and some of you urge Teucer to
805		come quickly, while others go to the western bays, and others to the east, and try to find my husband's unhappy destination. For I have come to realise that I have been deceived in the man and cast out from my former favour. Alas, what am I to do, my son? I must
810		not sit still. No, I too shall go as far as I have the strength. Let us go, let us hurry, it is no time for sitting down, if we wish to save a man who is hastening to his death.
	Leader	I am ready to go, as I shall prove not only in my words. For speed of action and of foot will match them.

[*Exeunt Tecmessa, the Messenger, and the divided chorus by the two eisodoi. After an interval Ajax enters by an eisodos*]

815	Ajax	The killer stands where, if one has the leisure for calculation, it might cut most effectively, the gift of Hector, the man who was loathed by me more than any other of my guest-friends, and most hateful to my sight. It is fixed in the hostile land of Troy, newly
820		sharpened on an iron-consuming whetstone; I fixed it with great care, that it might be very kind to me and grant me a speedy death. So we are well-equipped; and after this, you first, oh Zeus, for that is reasonable,
825		must help me. It is no large gift that I shall ask from you. Send some messenger, I pray you, with the bad news to Teucer, that he may be the first to lift me up when I have fallen round this freshly-sprinkled sword,

82

830 ῥιφθῶ κυσὶν πρόβλητος οἰωνοῖς θ' ἕλωρ.
τοσαῦτά σ', ὦ Ζεῦ, προστρέπω· καλῶ δ' ἅμα
πομπαῖον Ἑρμῆν χθόνιον εὖ με κοιμίσαι,
ξὺν ἀσφαδάστῳ καὶ ταχεῖ πηδήματι
πλευρὰν διαρρήξαντα τῷδε φασγάνῳ.
835 καλῶ δ' ἀρωγοὺς τὰς ἀεί τε παρθένους
ἀεί θ' ὁρώσας πάντα τὰν βροτοῖς πάθη,
σεμνὰς Ἐρινῦς τανύποδας μαθεῖν ἐμὲ
πρὸς τῶν Ἀτρειδῶν ὡς διόλλυμαι τάλας.
[καί σφας κακοὺς κάκιστα καὶ πανωλέθρους
840 ξυναρπάσειαν, ὥσπερ εἰσορῶσ' ἐμὲ
αὐτοσφαγῆ πίπτοντα· τὼς αὐτοσφαγεῖς
πρὸς τῶν φιλίστων ἐκγόνων ὀλοίατο.]
ἴτ', ὦ ταχεῖαι ποίνιμοί τ' Ἐρινύες,
γεύεσθε, μὴ φείδεσθε πανδήμου στρατοῦ.
845 σὺ δ', ὦ τὸν αἰπὺν οὐρανὸν διφρηλατῶν
Ἥλιε, πατρῴαν τὴν ἐμὴν ὅταν χθόνα
ἴδῃς, ἐπισχὼν χρυσόνωτον ἡνίαν
ἄγγειλον ἄτας τὰς ἐμὰς μόρον τ' ἐμὸν
γέροντι πατρὶ τῇ τε δυστήνῳ τροφῷ.
850 ἦ που τάλαινα, τήνδ' ὅταν κλύῃ φάτιν,
ἥσει μέγαν κωκυτὸν ἐν πάσῃ πόλει.
ἀλλ' οὐδὲν ἔργον ταῦτα θρηνεῖσθαι μάτην·
ἀλλ' ἀρκτέον τὸ πρᾶγμα σὺν τάχει τινί.
ὦ Θάνατε Θάνατε, νῦν μ' ἐπίσκεψαι μολών·
855 [καίτοι σὲ μὲν κἀκεῖ προσαυδήσω ξυνών.
σὲ δ' ὦ φαεννῆς ἡμέρας τὸ νῦν σέλας,
καὶ τὸν διφρευτὴν Ἥλιον προσεννέπω,
πανύστατον δή κοὔποτ' αὖθις ὕστερον.]
ὦ φέγγος, ὦ γῆς ἱερὸν οἰκείας πέδον
860 Σαλαμῖνος, ὦ πατρῷον ἑστίας βάθρον,
κλειναί τ' Ἀθῆναι, καὶ τὸ σύντροφον γένος,

836   om. AXr^ac, *Suda*
839-42 del. P. Wesseling
842   φιλτάτων r
854-8 del. Campe, 856-8 Jahn, 857 Radermacher

830 and that I may not be spotted first by any of my enemies and cast out as a prey for the dogs and birds. That is all my prayer to you, Zeus, but at the same time I call on Hermes, the escort and the underworld god, to put me carefully to sleep, when with a swift leap and without a struggle I have torn my side with this sword.

835 And I summon as helpers the everlasting virgins, who for ever observe all human suffering, the holy Furies with their long strides, to learn how in my wretchedness I am being destroyed by the sons of Atreus. [And may they snatch them away the wretches in utter wretchedness and total destruction, 840 even as they look upon me falling at my own hands; so may they perish at the hands of their closest descendants.] Come, you swift avenging Furies, devour them, spare not the whole body of the army.

845 And you Sun, who drive your chariot over the steep heaven, when you see my fatherland, check your gold-decked rein and report my ruin and my death to my old father and my unhappy nurse. No doubt the 850 wretched woman, when she hears this news, will utter loud wailing all through the city.

Well there is no point in lamenting this in vain; the affair must be begun with some speed. Oh death, 855 death, come now and visit me[; yet there too I shall speak to you in your presence. And you I address, bright light of the present shining day, and Sun the charioteer, for the last time, never again to do so]. Oh light, oh holy soil of my native Salamis, oh foundation 860 of my father's hearth, and famous Athens, and the race

84

κρῆναί τε ποταμοί θ' οἵδε, καὶ τὰ Τρωϊκὰ
πεδία προσαυδῶ, χαίρετ', ὦ τροφῆς ἐμοί·
τοῦθ' ὑμῖν Αἴας τοὖπος ὕστατον θροεῖ,
865   τὰ δ' ἄλλ' ἐν Ἅιδου τοῖς κάτω μυθήσομαι.

HMIXOPION
πόνος πόνῳ πόνον φέρει.
πᾷ πᾷ
πᾷ γὰρ οὐκ ἔβαν ἐγώ;
κοὐδεὶς †ἐπίσταταί† με συμμαθεῖν τόπος.
870   ἰδοὺ ἰδού·
δοῦπον αὖ κλύω τινά.
Ημ.   ἡμῶν γε ναὸς κοινόπλουν ὁμιλίαν.
Ημ.   τί οὖν δή;
Ημ.   πᾶν ἐστίβηται πλευρὸν ἕσπερον νεῶν.
875 Ημ.   ἔχεις οὖν;
Ημ.   πόνου γε πλῆθος κοὐδὲν εἰς ὄψιν πλέον.
Ημ.   ἀλλ' οὐδὲ μὲν δὴ τὴν ἀφ' ἡλίου βολῶν
κέλευθον ἀνὴρ οὐδαμοῦ δηλοῖ φανείς.

ΧΟ.   τίς ἂν δῆτά μοι, τίς ἂν φιλοπόνων   στρ.
880   ἁλιαδᾶν ἔχων ἄϋπνους ἄγρας,
ἢ τίς Ὀλυμπιάδων θεᾶν, ἢ ῥυτῶν
Βοσπορίων ποταμῶν,
885   τὸν ὠμόθυμον εἴ ποθι
πλαζόμενον λεύσσων
ἀπύοι; σχέτλια γὰρ
ἐμέ γε τὸν μακρῶν ἀλάταν πόνων
οὐρίῳ μὴ πελάσαι δρόμῳ,
890   ἀλλ' ἀμενηνὸν ἄνδρα μὴ λεύσσειν ὅπου.

864   ἔσχατον r
869   ἐπίσταται] †...† Garvie, ἐπισπᾶται Wecklein   με συμμαθεῖν] μ' ἐς ὄμμ'
ἄγειν West 115   τόπος] τόδε E.. Viketos, Hermes 117 (1989) 499
877   οὐδὲ   μὲν Lrpt: οὐδ' ἐμοὶ pa   βολῶν Lpa: βολῆς Λrp, μολὼν t
879   δῆτα Hermann: δή codd.
884   ποταμῶν ἴδρις codd. plerique
886   πλαζόμενον λεύσσων] πλάζοιτ' ἂν προσβλέπων t
890   ἀμένηνον] μεμηνότ' N, gl in P

that has grown up with me, these springs and rivers,
and the Trojan plains I call on, farewell, my nurses;
this is the last word that Ajax speaks to you; the rest I
865   shall say in the house of Hades to those below.

[*Ajax falls on his sword. Enter the two half-choruses by the two eisodoi*]

Chorus 1   Trouble brings trouble on trouble.
Where where
where have I not been?
There is no place that †...† me to share its knowledge
of his whereabouts.
870   Listen, listen!
Now again I hear some sound.

Chorus 2   Yes, it is we your comrades who shared your voyage
in the ship.

Chorus 1   What news then?

Chorus 2   We have trodden all the side to the west of the ships.

875   Chorus 1   Do you have anything, then?

Chorus 2   Yes, an abundance of trouble and nothing more to see.

Chorus 1   Nor does the man reveal his presence anywhere on the
road that comes from the rising sun.

Chor. *str.*   Which, then, which of the toiling sons of the sea who
880   is engaged in sleepless hunting, or which of the
goddesses of Olympus, or of the flowing rivers of the
Bosphorus, might tell me if he sees somewhere the
885   fierce-hearted man approaching? For it is hard that
despite my long troublesome wanderings I should not
have come near to success in my course, but fail to
890   spot the whereabouts of the feeble man.

86

TE.　ἰώ μοί μοι.

XO.　τίνος βοὴ πάραυλος ἐξέβη νάπους;

TE.　ἰὼ τλήμων.

XO.　τὴν δουρίληπτον δύσμορον νύμφην ὁρῶ
895　　　Τέκμησσαν, οἴκτῳ τῷδε συγκεκραμένην.

TE.　οἴχωκ', ὄλωλα, διαπεπόρθημαι, φίλοι.

XO.　τί δ' ἔστιν;

TE.　Αἴας ὅδ' ἡμῖν ἀρτίως νεοσφαγὴς
　　　κεῖται κρυφαίῳ φασγάνῳ περιπτυχής.

900　XO.　ὤμοι ἐμῶν νόστων·
　　　ὤμοι, κατέπεφνες, ἄναξ,
　　　τόνδε συνναύταν, τάλας·
　　　ὦ ταλαίφρων γύνη.

TE.　ὡς ὧδε τοῦδ' ἔχοντος αἰάζειν πάρα.

905　XO.　τίνος ποτ' ἄρ' ἔπραξε χειρὶ δύσμορος;

TE.　αὐτὸς πρὸς αὑτοῦ, δῆλον· ἐν γάρ οἱ χθονὶ
　　　πηκτὸν τόδ' ἔγχος περιπετοῦς κατηγορεῖ.

XO.　ὤμοι ἐμᾶς ἄτας, οἶος ἄρ' αἱμάχθης,
910　　　ἄφαρκτος φίλων·
　　　ἐγὼ δ' ὁ πάντα κωφός, ὁ πάντ' ἄϊδρις,
　　　κατημέλησα. πᾷ πᾷ
　　　κεῖται ὁ δυστράπελος
　　　δυσώνυμος Αἴας;

915　TE.　οὔτοι θεατός· ἀλλά νιν περιπτυχεῖ
　　　φάρει καλύψω τῷδε παμπήδην, ἐπεὶ
　　　οὐδεὶς ἂν ὅστις καὶ φίλος τλαίη βλέπειν
　　　φυσῶντ' ἄνω πρὸς ῥῖνας ἔκ τε φοινίας
　　　πληγῆς μελανθὲν αἷμ' ἀπ' οἰκείας σφαγῆς.
920　　　οἴμοι, τί δράσω; τίς σε βαστάσει φίλων;

902　τόνδε τὸν t　τάλας Hermann: ὦ τάλας t, ἰὼ τάλας cett.
903　ταλαίφρων L^{rc}Rpa: -φρον GQpXrt　γυνή p: γύναι Lrpat
906　αὑτοῦ] L^{ac}Krp: αὐτοῦ pat
907　περιπετοῦς Musgrave: -πετὲς codd.
909　οἶος Lpat: οἷος rpZr
913　δυστράπελος ὁ codd. praeter OD, Suda

[*Enter Tecmessa by an eisodos*]

Tecmessa	Alas, alas!
Leader	Whose is the cry that sounded nearby from the grove?
Tecmessa	Oh, unhappy me!
Leader	I see the ill-fated bride, the captive of his spear,
895		Tecmessa, steeped in this pitiless wailing.
Tecmessa	I am lost, I am undone, I am totally destroyed, my friends.
Chorus	What is it?
Tecmessa	Here lies our Ajax, newly slaughtered, folded round his hidden sword.
900 Chorus		Alas for my return home! Alas, my lord, you have killed me your shipmate, unhappy man! Oh wretched woman!
Tecmessa	This is how he is - you may well lament.
905 Leader		By whose hand then did the ill-fated man do the deed?
Tecmessa	By his own hand, it is clear; for this sword fixed by him in the ground accuses him of having fallen on it.
Chorus	Alas for my delusion, alone your blood was shed,
910 | | unprotected by your friends! And I, deaf to everything, ignorant in everything, paid no heed. Where, where lies inflexible Ajax, of the ill-omened name? |
915 Tecmessa | | He is not to be seen; I shall cover him completely with this enfolding cloak, since no one who is really his friend could bear to look on him as up to his nostrils from the fatal wound he gasps his blackened blood, the result of his self-inflicted slaughter. Alas, |
920 | | what am I to do? Which of your friends will lift you |

πο̂υ Τεῦκρος; ὡς ἀκμαῖος ἂν βαίη μολὼν
πεπτῶτ᾽ ἀδελφὸν τόνδε συγκαθαρμόσαι.
ὢ δύσμορ᾽ Αἴας, οἷος ὢν οἵως ἔχεις,
ὡς καὶ παρ᾽ ἐχθροῖς ἄξιος θρήνων τυχεῖν.

925	ΧΟ.	ἔμελλες, τάλας, ἔμελλες χρόνῳ

                                                     ἀντ.

στερεόφρων ἄρ᾽ ἐξανύσσειν κακὰν
μοῖραν ἀπειρεσίων πόνων· τοῖά μοι
πάννυχα καὶ φαέθοντ᾽
930   ἀνεστέναζες ὠμόφρων
ἐχθοδόπ᾽ Ἀτρείδαις
οὐλίῳ σὺν πάθει.
μέγας ἄρ᾽ ἦν ἐκεῖνος ἄρχων χρόνος
935   πημάτων, ἦμος ἀριστόχειρ
        ‹– ∪∪ –› ὅπλων ἔκειτ᾽ ἀγὼν πέρι.

	ΤΕ.	ἰώ μοί μοι.
	ΧΟ.	χωρεῖ πρὸς ἧπαρ, οἶδα, γενναία δύη.
	ΤΕ.	ἰώ μοί μοι.
940	ΧΟ.	οὐδέν σ᾽ ἀπιστῶ καὶ δὶς οἰμῶξαι, γύναι,
		τοιοῦδ᾽ ἀποβλαφθεῖσαν ἀρτίως φίλου.
	ΤΕ.	σοὶ μὲν δοκεῖν ταῦτ᾽ ἔστ᾽, ἐμοὶ δ᾽ ἄγαν φρονεῖν.
	ΧΟ.	ξυναυδῶ.
	ΤΕ.	οἴμοι, τέκνον, πρὸς οἷα δουλείας ζυγὰ
945		χωροῦμεν, οἷοι νῷν ἐφεστᾶσιν σκοποί.
	ΧΟ.	ὤμοι, ἀναλγήτων
		δισσῶν ἐθρόησας ἄναυδ᾽
		ἔργ᾽ Ἀτρειδᾶν τῷδ᾽ ἄχει.
		ἀλλ᾽ ἀπείργοι θεός.
950	ΤΕ.	οὐκ ἂν τάδ᾽ ἔστη τῇδε μὴ θεῶν μέτα.
	ΧΟ.	ἄγαν ὑπερβριθές γε τάχθος ἤνυσαν.

921   ἀκμαῖος P.Berol.21208, codd.: ἀκμαῖ᾽ ἂν Wakefield, ἀκμὴν ἂν Vauvilliers
     ἂν βαίη μολὼν Pantazides: εἰ βαίη μόλοι codd.
923-4 choro trib. GR^ac
936   Ἀχιλλέως ὅπλων t
947-8 ἄναυδ᾽ ἔργ᾽ Hermann: ἄναυδον ἔργον codd.
951   γε τάχθος Blaydes: τε ἄχθος r, ἄχθος Lpat

up? Where is Teucer? If he came his arrival would be timely for him to join in composing for burial this his fallen brother. Oh ill-fated Ajax, what a man you were to suffer such a fate, how worthy even among your enemies to receive lamentations!

925	Chor. *ant.*	Wretched stubborn-hearted man, so you were finally, finally to accomplish your evil destiny of infinite troubles; such were the groans I heard you utter, fierce
930		in your heart, all night long as well as by day, full of hatred for the sons of Atreus, with deadly passion. Yes, that time was a mighty source of troubles, when
935		the competition for the <...> arms was set up for the best fighter.
	Tecmessa	Alas, alas!
	Leader	It is noble anguish, I know, that pierces your heart.
	Tecmessa	Alas, alas!
940	Leader	I can well believe, madam, that you wail twice, when you are so recently bereft of such a loved one.
	Tecmessa	You can *think* these things, but I must be aware of them all too much.
	Leader	I agree with you.
	Tecmessa	Alas, my child, to what a yoke of slavery are we
945		going, what overseers now stand over us both!
	Chorus	Alas, with this woe you have spoken of the unspeakable deeds that will be performed by the two heartless sons of Atreus. But may god avert them!
950	Tecmessa	These things would not have turned out like this if not with the help of the gods.
	Leader	Yes, all too heavy is the burden that they have brought to pass.

ΤΕ. τοιόνδε μέντοι Ζηνὸς ἡ δεινὴ θεὸς
     Παλλὰς φυτεύει πῆμ' Ὀδυσσέως χάριν.
955 ΧΟ. ἦ ῥα κελαινώπαν θυμὸν ἐφυβρίζει
     πολύτλας ἀνήρ,
     γελᾷ δὲ τοῖσδε μαινομένοις ἄχεσιν
     πολὺν γέλωτα, φεῦ φεῦ,
     ξύν τε διπλοῖ βασιλῆς
960 κλύοντες Ἀτρεῖδαι.

ΤΕ. οἱ δ' οὖν γελώντων κἀπιχαιρόντων κακοῖς
     τοῖς τοῦδ'. ἴσως τοι, κεἰ βλέποντα μὴ 'πόθουν,
     θανόντ' ἂν οἰμώξειαν ἐν χρείᾳ δορός.
     οἱ γὰρ κακοὶ γνώμαισι τἀγάθ' ἐν χεροῖν
965 ἔχοντες οὐκ ἴσασι, πρίν τις ἐκβάλῃ.
     ἐμοὶ πικρὸς τέθνηκεν ἢ κείνοις γλυκύς,
     αὑτῷ δὲ τερπνός· ὧν γὰρ ἠράσθη τυχεῖν
     ἐκτήσαθ' αὑτῷ, θάνατον ὅνπερ ἤθελεν.
     τί δῆτα τοῦδ' ἐπεγγελῷεν ἂν κάτα;
970 θεοῖς τέθνηκεν οὗτος, οὐ κείνοισιν, οὔ.
     πρὸς ταῦτ' Ὀδυσσεὺς ἐν κενοῖς ὑβριζέτω.
     Αἴας γὰρ αὐτοῖς οὐκέτ' ἔστιν, ἀλλ' ἐμοὶ
     λιπὼν ἀνίας καὶ γόους διοίχεται.
ΤΕΥΚΡΟΣ
     ἰώ μοί μοι.
975 ΧΟ. σίγησον· αὐδὴν γὰρ δοκῶ Τεύκρου κλύειν
     βοῶντος ἄτης τῆσδ' ἐπίσκοπον μέλος.
ΤΕΥ. ὦ φίλτατ' Αἴας, ὦ ξύναιμον ὄμμ' ἐμοί,
     ἆρ' ἠμπόληκας ὥσπερ ἡ φάτις κρατεῖ;
ΧΟ. ὄλωλεν ἀνήρ, Τεῦκρε, τοῦτ' ἐπίστασο.
980 ΤΕΥ. ὤμοι βαρείας ἆρα τῆς ἐμῆς τύχης.

---

955 κελαινώπαν θυμὸν P.Berol. 21208, **Lrpat**: –ῶπα θυμὸν OW^ac, Vat. gr. 1332,
Hesych., Eust., κελαινώπᾳ θυμῷ Lloyd-Jones et Wilson
957 τοῖσδε Elmsley: τοῖσι t, τοῖς cett.
964 τἀγάθ' ἐν J: τἀγαθὸν ἐν Q, τἀγαθὸν cett.
966 ἢ Schneidewin (cf. Eust. 1521.40): ἦ codd., *Suda*
969 τί **Lrpt**: πῶς pa
969-73 choro trib. XrXsZrZc

	Tecmessa	Yes, such is the pain that Pallas, the terrible daughter of Zeus, produces to please Odysseus.
955	Chorus	No doubt he grows insolent in his black heart, the much-enduring man, and laughs with much laughter at Ajax' frenzied sorrows, alas alas, and with him the two
960		kings, the sons of Atreus, when they hear of them.
	Tecmessa	Then let them laugh and rejoice over this man's misfortunes; even if they did not miss him while he was alive, they may perhaps lament his death when they turn out to need his spear. For people of poor judgement do not realise the advantages that they have
965		in their hands until they are thrown away. His death is as painful to me as it is sweet to them, and pleasant for himself; for he has got for himself what he longed to obtain, the death which he wanted. Why then should
970		they laugh at him? It is for the gods that he has died, no not for them. Therefore let Odysseus display his futile insolence. For them Ajax no longer lives, but in his passing he has left me with sorrows and lamentation.

[Enter Teucer by an eisodos]

	Teucer	Alas, alas!
975	Leader	Be quiet; for I think I hear the voice of Teucer shouting in a strain that bears on this calamity.
	Teucer	Oh dearest Ajax, oh beloved face of my brother, have you fared as the prevailing rumour suggests?
	Leader	The man is dead, Teucer, you must know this.
980	Teucer	Alas then for my heavy fortune!

92

ΧΟ. ὡς ὧδ' ἐχόντων— ΤΕΥ. ὦ τάλας ἐγώ, τάλας.
ΧΟ. πάρα στενάζειν· ΤΕΥ. ὦ περισπερχὲς πάθος.
ΧΟ. ἄγαν γε, Τεῦκρε. ΤΕΥ. φεῦ τάλας. τί γὰρ τέκνον
τὸ τοῦδε; ποῦ μοι γῆς κυρεῖ τῆς Τρῳάδος;
985 ΧΟ. μόνος παρὰ σκηναῖσιν. ΤΕΥ. οὐχ ὅσον τάχος
δῆτ' αὐτὸν ἄξεις δεῦρο, μή τις ὡς κενῆς
σκύμνον λεαίνης δυσμενῶν ἀναρπάσῃ;
ἴθ', ἐγκόνει, σύγκαμνε. τοῖς θανοῦσί τοι
φιλοῦσι πάντες κειμένοις ἐπεγγελᾶν.
990 ΧΟ. καὶ μὴν ἔτι ζῶν, Τεῦκρε, τοῦδέ σοι μέλειν
ἐφίεθ' ἁνὴρ κεῖνος, ὥσπερ οὖν μέλει.
ΤΕΥ. ὦ τῶν ἁπάντων δὴ θεαμάτων ἐμοὶ
ἄλγιστον ὧν προσεῖδον ὀφθαλμοῖς ἐγώ,
ὁδός θ' ὁδῶν πασῶν ἀνιάσασα δὴ
995 μάλιστα τοὐμὸν σπλάγχνον, ἣν δὴ νῦν ἔβην,
ὦ φίλτατ' Αἴας, τὸν σὸν ὡς ἐπῃσθόμην
μόρον διώκων κἀξιχνοσκοπούμενος.
ὀξεῖα γάρ σου βάξις ὡς θεοῦ τινος
διῆλθ' Ἀχαιοὺς πάντας ὡς οἴχῃ θανών.
1000 ἀγὼ κλυὼν δύστηνος ἐκποδὼν μὲν ὢν
ὑπεστέναζον, νῦν δ' ὁρῶν ἀπόλλυμαι.
οἴμοι.
ἴθ', ἐκκάλυψον, ὡς ἴδω τὸ πᾶν κακόν.
ὦ δυσθέατον ὄμμα καὶ τόλμης πικρᾶς,
1005 ὅσας ἀνίας μοι κατασπείρας φθίνεις.
ποῖ γὰρ μολεῖν μοι δυνατόν, εἰς ποίους βροτούς,
τοῖς σοῖς ἀρήξαντ' ἐν πόνοισι μηδαμοῦ;
ἦ πού με Τελαμών, σὸς πατὴρ ἐμός θ' ἅμα,
δέξαιτ' ἂν εὐπρόσωπος ἵλεώς τ' ἰδὼν
1010 χωροῦντ' ἄνευ σοῦ. πῶς γὰρ οὔχ; ὅτῳ πάρα

988   θανοῦσί] σθένουσί Seyffert, ἐχθροῖσι Herwerden
1000 κλυὼν West: κλύων codd.   δύστηνος lQpt: δείλαιος GRHa   μένων L^{ac}rp
1008 με add. Küster   θ' ἅμα Hat: τ' ἴσως lrp, Suda·
1009 τ' ἰδὼν Hermann (ἰδὼν γρ ad 1008 in Wa): τ' ἴσως plerique, θ' ἅμα p

93

Leader	Since this is the situation -	**Teucer:** Oh unhappy me, unhappy me!
Leader	You may well lament.	**Teucer:** Oh, over-hasty misfortune!
Leader	Yes, all too much so, Teucer.	**Teucer:** Alas, unhappy me! What of his child, where shall I find him in the land of Troy?

985 Leader   He is alone beside the huts. **Teucer:** Won't you then bring him here as quickly as possible, in case one of our enemies should snatch him away like the whelp of a bereaved lioness? Go, hurry, share the labour. It is true that all men are accustomed to laugh at the dead when they are down.

[*Exit Tecmessa*]

990 Leader   Indeed while he was still alive, Teucer, he instructed you to care for this child, as now in fact you do care.

Teucer   Oh most painful of all the sights that I have seen with my eyes, mission which of all missions has most
995 grieved my heart, the mission on which I have now come, oh dearest Ajax, after I heard of your fate when I was pursuing and tracking you down! For a keen rumour about you, as from some god, passed through all the Achaeans that you are dead and gone. When I
1000 heard it at a distance I mourned low in my wretchedness, but now that I see it I am undone.

Alas!

Come, uncover him, so that I may see the whole calamity. Oh face that I can hardly bear to look on, the face which reveals your cruel rashness, how many
1005 sorrows you have sown for me by dying! For where can I go, to what people, after I have supported you nowhere in your troubles? Telamon, no doubt, your father and mine alike, would receive me cheerfully and
1010 graciously when he sees me coming without you. Of

μηδ' εὐτυχοῦντι μηδὲν ἥδιον γελᾶν.
οὗτος τί κρύψει; ποῖον οὐκ ἐρεῖ κακόν
τὸν ἐκ δορὸς γεγῶτα πολεμίου νόθον,
τὸν δειλίᾳ προδόντα καὶ κακανδρίᾳ
1015   σέ, φίλτατ' Αἴας, ἢ δόλοισιν, ὡς τὰ σὰ
κράτη θανόντος καὶ δόμους νέμοιμι σούς.
τοιαῦτ' ἀνὴρ δύσοργος, ἐν γήρᾳ βαρύς,
ἐρεῖ, πρὸς οὐδὲν εἰς ἔριν θυμούμενος.
τέλος δ' ἀπωστὸς γῆς ἀπορριφθήσομαι,
1020   δοῦλος λόγοισιν ἀντ' ἐλευθέρου φανείς.
τοιαῦτα μὲν κατ' οἶκον· ἐν Τροίᾳ δέ μοι
πολλοὶ μὲν ἐχθροί, παῦρα δ' ὠφελήσιμα,
καὶ ταῦτ' ἄφαντα σοῦ θανόντος ηὑρόμην.
οἴμοι, τί δράσω; πῶς σ' ἀποσπάσω πικροῦ
1025   τοῦδ' αἰόλου κνώδοντος, ὦ τάλας, ὑφ' οὗ
φονέως ἄρ' ἐξέπνευσας; εἶδες ὡς χρόνῳ
ἔμελλέ σ' Ἕκτωρ καὶ θανὼν ἀποφθίσειν;
σκέψασθε, πρὸς θεῶν, τὴν τύχην δυοῖν βροτοῖν·
Ἕκτωρ μέν, ᾧ δὴ τοῦδ' ἐδωρήθη πάρα
1030   ζωστῆρι πρισθεὶς ἱππικῶν ἐξ ἀντύγων
ἐκνάπτετ' αἰέν, ἔστ' ἀπέψυξεν βίον·
οὗτος δ' ἐκείνου τήνδε δωρειὰν ἔχων
πρὸς τοῦδ' ὄλωλε θανασίμῳ πεσήματι.
ἆρ' οὐκ Ἐρινὺς τοῦτ' ἐχάλκευσεν ξίφος
1035   κἀκεῖνον Ἅιδης, δημιουργὸς ἄγριος;
ἐγὼ μὲν οὖν καὶ ταῦτα καὶ τὰ πάντ' ἀεὶ
φάσκοιμ' ἂν ἀνθρώποισι μηχανᾶν θεούς·
ὅτῳ δὲ μὴ τάδ' ἐστὶν ἐν γνώμῃ φίλα,
κεῖνός τ' ἐκεῖνα στεργέτω κἀγὼ τάδε.

1011 ἥδιον Fat: ἵλεων lrp, ἴδιον HZc
1016 δόμους] θρόνους F.W. Schmidt νέμοιμι Lrpat: ἔχοιμι KWa
1022 παῦρα Lat: -οι rpa, Suda ὠφελήσιμα Johnson: -οι codd., Suda
1023 ταῦτ' ἄφαντα Jackson: ταῦτα πάντα Lrpat, ταῦθ' ἄπαντα p, Eust.
1032 δωρειὰν Bamberg: δωρεὰν codd.
1028-39 del. Morstadt
1035 Ἅιδης Lrpat: Ἄρης p

course he will; he who even in good fortune finds it just as impossible to laugh with pleasure. What will he keep back? What kind of insult will he not utter against the bastard born from the enemy's spear, the

1015

man who betrayed you, dearest Ajax, by cowardice and unmanliness, or by deceit, so that I might administer your power and house when you are dead! This is the kind of thing that he will say, a bad-tempered man, stern in his old age, one who gets angry at nothing for the sake of a quarrel. And in the end I shall be driven from the land and banished, having

1020

been reduced by his words to the appearance of a slave instead of a free man. So much for home; at Troy I have many enemies, and few advantages, and these I have found to disappear now that you are dead. Alas, what am I to do? How am I to pull you away from this

1025

cruel glittering sword, unhappy man, the killer which after all made you breathe your last? Did you see how Hector, even after death, was finally going to kill you? Consider, I entreat you, the two men's fortune. Hector, with the belt which he received as a gift from

1030

this man here, was fastened to the chariot-rail and continuously mangled, until he breathed out his life; while Ajax, the possessor of this gift of Hector, has been killed by it in fatal fall. Was it not a Fury that

1035

forged that sword, and Hades that belt, a savage craftsman? I would say therefore that it is the gods who contrived these things just as they always contrive everything for mankind; whoever does not find this acceptable in his judgement, let him be content with his opinion and I with mine.

1040 ΧΟ. μὴ τεῖνε μακράν, ἀλλ' ὅπως κρύψεις τάφῳ
φράζου τὸν ἄνδρα, χὥ τι μυθήσῃ τάχα.
βλέπω γὰρ ἐχθρὸν φῶτα, καὶ τάχ' ἂν κακοῖς
γελῶν ἃ δὴ κακοῦργος ἐξίκοιτ' ἀνήρ.
ΤΕΥ. τίς δ' ἐστὶν ὅντιν' ἄνδρα προσλεύσσεις στρατοῦ;
1045 ΧΟ. Μενέλαος, ᾧ δὴ τόνδε πλοῦν ἐστείλαμεν.
ΤΕΥ. ὁρῶ· μαθεῖν γὰρ ἐγγὺς ὢν οὐ δυσπετής.
ΜΕΝΕΛΑΟΣ
οὗτος, σὲ φωνῶ, τόνδε τὸν νεκρὸν χεροῖν
μὴ συγκομίζειν, ἀλλ' ἐᾶν ὅπως ἔχει.
ΤΕΥ. τίνος χάριν τοσόνδ' ἀνήλωσας λόγον;
1050 ΜΕ. δοκοῦντ' ἐμοί, δοκοῦντα δ' ὃς κραίνει στρατοῦ.
ΤΕΥ. οὔκουν ἂν εἴποις ἥντιν' αἰτίαν προθείς;
ΜΕ. ὁθούνεκ' αὐτὸν ἐλπίσαντες οἴκοθεν
ἄγειν Ἀχαιοῖς ξύμμαχόν τε καὶ φίλον,
ἐξηύρομεν ξυνόντες ἐχθίω Φρυγῶν·
1055 ὅστις στρατῷ ξύμπαντι βουλεύσας φόνον
νύκτωρ ἐπεστράτευσεν, ὡς ἕλοι δόρει·
κεἰ μὴ θεῶν τις τήνδε πεῖραν ἔσβεσεν,
ἡμεῖς μὲν ἂν τήνδ' ἣν ὅδ' εἴληχεν τύχην
θανόντες ἂν προὐκείμεθ' αἰσχίστῳ μόρῳ,
1060 οὗτος δ' ἂν ἔζη. νῦν δ' ἐνήλλαξεν θεὸς
τὴν τοῦδ' ὕβριν πρὸς μῆλα καὶ ποίμνας πεσεῖν.
ὧν οὕνεκ' αὐτὸν οὔτις ἔστ' ἀνὴρ σθένων
τοσοῦτον ὥστε σῶμα τυμβεῦσαι τάφῳ,
ἀλλ' ἀμφὶ χλωρὰν ψάμαθον ἐκβεβλημένος
1065 ὄρνισι φορβὴ παραλίοις γενήσεται.

1040 κρύψεις at: -ῃς Lrp
1053 ἄγειν Lrpa: ἄξειν Lˢˡ, γρ in G, pt
1054 ξυνόντες Reiske: ζητοῦντες codd.
1056 ἐλοιδόρει V, γρ in LGp
1058 τήνδ'...τύχην] τῇδ'...τύχῃ Lloyd-Jones et Wilson
1059 θανόντες] παθόντες Pearson, φθανόντες Seyffert   αἰσχίστῳ Lpa: ἀθλίῳ rH, ἐχθίστῳ t
1061 del. Nauck, Reeve 161-2
1063 τοσοῦτον rpt: τοιοῦτον Lpa

1040	Leader	Do not prolong your speech, but consider how you are going to hide the man in a grave, and what you will soon say. For I see an enemy coming, and perhaps when he arrives he will be laughing, as a scoundrel would, at our misfortunes.
	Teucer	Which man from the army do you see?
1045	Leader	Menelaus, in whose interest we undertook this voyage.
	Teucer	I see him; for he is near and not difficult to recognise.

[*Enter Menelaus, probably accompanied by one or two attendants*]

MENELAUS

		You there, I call on you not to put your hand to burial-arrangements for this corpse, but to leave it as it is.
	Teucer	Why have you wasted your breath on such arrogant words?
1050	Menelaus	Because that is my decision, and the decision of the one who commands the army.
	Teucer	Won't you then tell me what reason he put forward for his decision?
	Menelaus	Because, when we hoped that we were bringing him from home to be the ally and friend of the Achaeans, we have found him in our dealings with him to be a
1055		worse enemy than the Phrygians; in that he plotted murder against the whole army and marched against us by night, to destroy us by the spear; and, if one of the gods had not quenched this attempt, we should have died and suffered this fortune which is his lot and would be lying exposed in a most shameful death,
1060		while he would be alive. But as things are a god has turned his outrageous behaviour so that it fell on sheep and herds. That is why there is no man strong enough to entomb his body in a grave; rather he will be cast
1065		out on the yellow sand to become fodder for the birds

πρὸς ταῦτα μηδὲν δεινὸν ἐξάρῃς μένος.
εἰ γὰρ βλέποντος μὴ 'δυνήθημεν κρατεῖν,
πάντως θανόντος γ' ἄρξομεν, κἂν μὴ θέλῃς,
χερσὶν παρευθύνοντες. οὐ γὰρ ἔσθ' ὅπου
1070   λόγων ἀκοῦσαι ζῶν ποτ' ἠθέλησ' ἐμῶν.
καίτοι κακοῦ πρὸς ἀνδρὸς ὄντα δημότην
μηδὲν δικαιοῦν τῶν ἐφεστώτων κλύειν.
οὐ γάρ ποτ' οὔτ' ἂν ἐν πόλει νόμοι καλῶς
φέροιντ' ἄν, ἔνθα μὴ καθεστήκῃ δέος,
1075   οὔτ' ἂν στρατός γε σωφρόνως ἄρχοιτ' ἔτι,
μηδὲν φόβου πρόβλημα μηδ' αἰδοῦς ἔχων.
ἀλλ' ἄνδρα χρή, κἂν σῶμα γεννήσῃ μέγα,
δοκεῖν πεσεῖν ἂν κἂν ἀπὸ σμικροῦ κακοῦ.
δέος γὰρ ᾧ πρόσεστιν αἰσχύνη θ' ὁμοῦ,
1080   σωτηρίαν ἔχοντα τόνδ' ἐπίστασο·
ὅπου δ' ὑβρίζειν δρᾶν θ' ἃ βούλεται παρῇ,
ταύτην νόμιζε τὴν πόλιν χρόνῳ ποτὲ
ἐξ οὐρίων δραμοῦσαν ἐς βυθὸν πεσεῖν.
ἀλλ' ἑστάτω μοι καὶ δέος τι καίριον,
1085   καὶ μὴ δοκῶμεν δρῶντες ἃν ἡδώμεθα
οὐκ ἀντιτείσειν αὖθις ἃν λυπώμεθα.
ἕρπει παραλλὰξ ταῦτα· πρόσθεν οὗτος ἦν
αἴθων ὑβριστής, νῦν δ' ἐγὼ μέγ' αὖ φρονῶ.
καί σοι προφωνῶ τόνδε μὴ θάπτειν, ὅπως
1090   μὴ τόνδε θάπτων αὐτὸς ἐς ταφὰς πέσῃς.
ΧΟ.   Μενέλαε, μὴ γνώμας ὑποστήσας σοφὰς
εἶτ' αὐτὸς ἐν θανοῦσιν ὑβριστὴς γένῃ.
ΤΕΥ.   οὐκ ἄν ποτ', ἄνδρες, ἄνδρα θαυμάσαιμ' ἔτι,
ὃς μηδὲν ὢν γοναῖσιν εἶθ' ἁμαρτάνει,
1095   ὅθ' οἱ δοκοῦντες εὐγενεῖς πεφυκέναι
τοιαῦθ' ἁμαρτάνουσιν ἐν λόγοις ἔπη.
ἄγ', εἴπ' ἀπ' ἀρχῆς αὖθις, ἢ σὺ φὴς ἄγειν

1070 λόγων **pat**: λόγων τ' **Lrp**, λόγων γ' Campbell
1071 ὄντα Reiske: ἄνδρα codd.
1074 καθεστήκῃ L^{Px}K, A in linea: –κοι **pat**, -κει pD, -κε rC, παρεστήκει Stob.
1081 παρῇ **LrpT**: πάρα **a**, T^{sl}Ta

of the shore. So make no terrible display of might.
For if we could not master him when he was alive, we
shall at all events rule him now that he is dead,
whether or not you wish it, disciplining him with our
hands. For on no occasion was he ever willing to
listen to my words while he was alive. Yet it is the
characteristic of a bad man that though he is only a
commoner he claims the right not to listen to those set
over him. For never in a city would laws have a
successful course, where there is no fear established,
nor would an army be governed any longer in a
disciplined way, if it did not have fear or respect as a
defence. A man should think that, even if he grows a
great body, he could fall as a result even of a small
misfortune. You should understand that the man who
enjoys security is the one to whom fear, and with it a
sense of shame, belongs; but where one can act
outrageously and do what one wants, consider that this
city though it has run before fair winds sooner or later
falls to the depths. For me let timely fear also be
firmly established, and let us not think that if we do
what pleases us we shall not in turn pay a penalty that
will cause us pain. These things go in alternation.
This man was formerly full of hot-tempered insolence,
but now it is my turn to be proud. And so I order you
before everyone not to bury this man, so that you may
not by burying him fall yourself into your grave.

Leader

Menelaus, having laid down wise sentiments do not
then turn out to behave outrageously yourself at the
expense of the dead.

Teucer

Men, I should never again be surprised at a man who
is born a nobody and then goes wrong, when those
who seem to be born noble speak words that are so
wrong. Come, start again from the beginning and tell
me, do you really claim that it was you who took

τόνδ᾽ ἄνδρ᾽ Ἀχαιοῖς δεῦρο σύμμαχον λαβών;
οὐκ αὐτὸς ἐξέπλευσεν ὡς αὐτοῦ κρατῶν;
1100 ποῦ σὺ στρατηγεῖς τοῦδε; ποῦ δὲ σοὶ λεὼν
ἔξεστ᾽ ἀνάσσειν ὧν ὅδ᾽ ἦγεν οἴκοθεν;
Σπάρτης ἀνάσσων ἦλθες, οὐχ ἡμῶν κρατῶν.
οὐδ᾽ ἔσθ᾽ ὅπου σοὶ τόνδε κοσμῆσαι πλέον
ἀρχῆς ἔκειτο θεσμὸς ἢ καὶ τῷδε σέ.
1105 [ὕπαρχος ἄλλων δεῦρ᾽ ἔπλευσας, οὐχ ὅλων
στρατηγός, ὥστ᾽ Αἴαντος ἡγεῖσθαί ποτε.]
ἀλλ᾽ ὧνπερ ἄρχεις ἄρχε, καὶ τὰ σέμν᾽ ἔπη
κόλαζ᾽ ἐκείνους· τόνδε δ᾽, εἴτε μὴ σὺ φῇς
εἴθ᾽ ἅτερος στρατηγός, ἐς ταφὰς ἐγὼ
1110 θήσω δικαίως, οὐ τὸ σὸν δείσας στόμα.
οὐ γάρ τι τῆς σῆς οὕνεκ᾽ ἐστρατεύσατο
γυναικός, ὥσπερ οἱ πόνου πολλοῦ πλέῳ,
ἀλλ᾽ οὕνεχ᾽ ὅρκων οἷσιν ἦν ἐπώμοτος,
σοῦ δ᾽ οὐδέν· οὐ γὰρ ἠξίου τοὺς μηδένας.
1115 πρὸς ταῦτα πλείους δεῦρο κήρυκας λαβὼν
καὶ τὸν στρατηγὸν ἧκε· τοῦ δὲ σοῦ ψόφου
οὐκ ἂν στραφείην, ἕως ἂν ᾖς οἷός περ εἶ.
ΧΟ. οὐδ᾽ αὖ τοιαύτην γλῶσσαν ἐν κακοῖς φιλῶ·
τὰ σκληρὰ γάρ τοι, κἂν ὑπέρδικ᾽ ᾖ, δάκνει.
1120 ΜΕ. ὁ τοξότης ἔοικεν οὐ σμικρὸν φρονεῖν.
ΤΕΥ. οὐ γὰρ βάναυσον τὴν τέχνην ἐκτησάμην.
ΜΕ. μέγ᾽ ἄν τι κομπάσειας, ἀσπίδ᾽ εἰ λάβοις.
ΤΕΥ. κἂν ψιλὸς ἀρκέσαιμι σοί γ᾽ ὡπλισμένῳ.
ΜΕ. ἡ γλῶσσά σου τὸν θυμὸν ὡς δεινὸν τρέφει.
1125 ΤΕΥ. ξὺν τῷ δικαίῳ γὰρ μέγ᾽ ἔξεστιν φρονεῖν.
ΜΕ. δίκαια γὰρ τόνδ᾽ εὐτυχεῖν κτείναντά με;

1098 τόνδ᾽ L: τὸν cett.
1101 ἦγεν Porson: ἡγεῖτ᾽ plerique, ἤγαγ᾽ P, ἤγετ᾽ anon.
1105-6 del. Schneidewin
1111-14 del. Wecklein
1113 ἐπώμοτος Krpat: ἐν- L^{K}Va
1117 ἕως gl in Fat: ὡς codd.
1118-19 choro trib. Σ, 1118 Men., 1119 Teuc. codd.
1124 δεινὸν] μέγαν ṭ

and brought this man here as an ally for the Achaeans? Did he not sail out himself as his own master? By what right are you his general? How do you have the authority to command the host which he led from home? You came as ruler of Sparta, not as our commander; there is no established ordinance of command that you should discipline him any more than that he for his part should discipline you. [You sailed here as a commander subordinate to others, not as the general of the whole army, to rule some day over Ajax.] Well, command those whom you command, and chastise *them* with those proud words of yours; but as for him, whether you or the other general say no, I shall duly put him in his grave, with no fear of what you may say. For it was not for your wife's sake that he made the expedition, like those who have their fill of labour, but for the sake of the oath by which he was sworn, and not at all for your sake; for he placed no value on nobodies. Therefore come back here with extra heralds and with the general as well; I won't pay attention to any noise you make, as long as you are the kind of man you are.

Leader	Again I dislike such talk in time of trouble; for harsh words sting, even if they are more than just.
Menelaus	The archer apparently has no small pride.
Teucer	Yes, for the skill I have acquired is not a vulgar one.
Menelaus	Big would be your boast, if you were to get a shield.
Teucer	Even lightly armed I should be a match for you at least, though you be fully armed.
Menelaus	How terrible is the spirit that is fostered by your tongue!
Teucer	Yes, for with justice on one's side one is entitled to display pride.
Menelaus	What, is it just that he should prosper after killing me?

102

ΤΕΥ. κτείναντα; δεινόν γ' εἶπας, εἰ καὶ ζῆς θανών.
ΜΕ. θεὸς γὰρ ἐκσῴζει με, τῷδε δ' οἴχομαι.
ΤΕΥ. μὴ νῦν ἀτίμα θεούς, θεοῖς σεσωμένος.
1130 ΜΕ. ἐγὼ γὰρ ἂν ψέξαιμι δαιμόνων νόμους;
ΤΕΥ. εἰ τοὺς θανόντας οὐκ ἐᾷς θάπτειν παρών.
ΜΕ. τούς γ' αὐτὸς αὑτοῦ πολεμίους· οὐ γὰρ καλόν.
ΤΕΥ. ἦ σοὶ γὰρ Αἴας πολέμιος προὔστη ποτέ;
ΜΕ. μισοῦντ' ἐμίσει· καὶ σὺ τοῦτ' ἠπίστασο.
1135 ΤΕΥ. κλέπτης γὰρ αὐτοῦ ψηφοποιὸς ηὑρέθης.
ΜΕ. ἐν τοῖς δικασταῖς, οὐκ ἐμοί, τόδ' ἐσφάλη.
ΤΕΥ. πόλλ' ἂν καλῶς λάθρᾳ σὺ κλέψειας κακά.
ΜΕ. τοῦτ' εἰς ἀνίαν τοὔπος ἔρχεταί τινι.
ΤΕΥ. οὐ μᾶλλον, ὡς ἔοικεν, ἢ λυπήσομεν.
1140 ΜΕ. ἕν σοι φράσω· τόνδ' ἐστὶν οὐχὶ θαπτέον.
ΤΕΥ. ἀλλ' ἀντακούσῃ τοῦθ' ἕν, ὡς τεθάψεται.
ΜΕ. ἤδη ποτ' εἶδον ἄνδρ' ἐγὼ γλώσσῃ θρασὺν
      ναύτας ἐφορμήσαντα χειμῶνος τὸ πλεῖν,
      ᾧ φθέγμ' ἂν οὐκ ἐνηῦρες, ἡνίκ' ἐν κακῷ
1145 χειμῶνος εἶχετ', ἀλλ' ὑφ' εἵματος κρυφεὶς
      πατεῖν παρεῖχε τῷ θέλοντι ναυτίλων.
      οὕτω δὲ καὶ σὲ καὶ τὸ σὸν λάβρον στόμα
      σμικροῦ νέφους τάχ' ἄν τις ἐκπνεύσας μέγας
      χειμὼν κατασβέσειε τὴν πολλὴν βοήν.
1150 ΤΕΥ. ἐγὼ δέ γ' ἄνδρ' ὄπωπα μωρίας πλέων,
      ὃς ἐν κακοῖς ὕβριζε τοῖσι τῶν πέλας.
      κᾆτ' αὐτὸν εἰσιδών τις ἐμφερὴς ἐμοὶ
      ὀργήν θ' ὅμοιος εἶπε τοιοῦτον λόγον,
      "ὤνθρωπε, μὴ δρᾶ τοὺς τεθνηκότας κακῶς·

1130 νόμους LQpat: γένος GR, γρ in F
1134 ἐμίσει Lrpat: -ουν pXr
1137 καλῶς L: κακῶς Lˢˡ, cett.
1141 ἀλλ' LpZr: σὺ δ' rpat   τοῦθ' ἕν Wecklein: τοῦθ' P, τοῦτον plerique, τοὔπος
      Dawe
1143 ναύταις rpt
1144 ἐνηῦρες Hartung: ἂν ηὗρες codd.
1146 ναυτίλων Lrpat: -ῳ a

	Teucer	Killing you? That is a strange thing to say, if you are in fact alive when you have died.
	Menelaus	The reason is that god is my saviour, while as far as he is concerned I am dead.
	Teucer	Do not then dishonour the gods, if it is by the gods that you were saved.
1130	Menelaus	Would *I* criticise the laws of the gods?
	Teucer	If you stand here and do not allow the dead to be buried.
	Menelaus	Yes, my own enemies; for it is not right.
	Teucer	Did Ajax really ever stand before you as an enemy?
	Menelaus	He hated me as I hated him; you knew it.
1135	Teucer	Yes, for you were found to have cheated him in the arrangement of the votes.
	Menelaus	He met this setback with the judges, not with me.
	Teucer	You would be good at secretly performing much furtive mischief.
	Menelaus	These words are going to lead to grief for someone.
	Teucer	No more, it seems, than the pain that we shall inflict.
1140	Menelaus	I shall say one thing to you: this man is not to be buried.
	Teucer	Well, you will hear this one thing in return, that he *shall* be buried.
	Menelaus	I once saw a man bold of tongue who urged on the sailors to sail in a storm, but in whom you would have found no voice when he was in the grip of trouble in the storm, when he hid beneath his garment and submitted to being trampled on by any of the crew who wished. So also with you and your violent mouth, a great storm might blow up quickly from a little cloud and extinguish your loud shouting.
1145		
1150	Teucer	And I have seen a man full of folly, who triumphed insolently in the misfortunes of his neighbours. And then someone resembling me and like me in his temper looked at him and said something like this,

1155   εἰ γὰρ ποήσεις, ἴσθι πημανούμενος".
        τοιαῦτ' ἄνολβον ἄνδρ' ἐνουθέτει παρών.
        ὁρῶ δέ τοί νιν, κἄστιν, ὡς ἐμοὶ δοκεῖ,
        οὐδείς ποτ' ἄλλος ἢ σύ. μῶν ἡνιξάμην;
    ΜΕ. ἄπειμι· καὶ γὰρ αἰσχρόν, εἰ πύθοιτό τις,
1160   λόγοις κολάζειν ᾧ βιάζεσθαι πάρα.
    ΤΕΥ. ἄφερπέ νυν. κἀμοὶ γὰρ αἴσχιστον κλύειν
        ἀνδρὸς ματαίου φλαῦρ' ἔπη μυθουμένου.

    ΧΟ. ἔσται μεγάλης ἔριδός τις ἀγών.
        ἀλλ' ὡς δύνασαι, Τεῦκρε, ταχύνας
1165   σπεῦσον κοίλην κάπετόν τιν' ἰδεῖν
        τῷδ', ἔνθα βροτοῖς τὸν ἀείμνηστον
        τάφον εὐρώεντα καθέξει.

    ΤΕΥ. καὶ μὴν ἐς αὐτὸν καιρὸν οἵδε πλησίοι
        πάρεισιν ἀνδρὸς τοῦδε παῖς τε καὶ γυνή,
1170   τάφον περιστελοῦντε δυστήνου νεκροῦ.
        ὦ παῖ, πρόσελθε δεῦρο, καὶ σταθεὶς πέλας
        ἱκέτης ἔφαψαι πατρός, ὅς σ' ἐγείνατο.
        θάκει δὲ προστρόπαιος ἐν χεροῖν ἔχων
        κόμας ἐμὰς καὶ τῆσδε καὶ σαυτοῦ τρίτου,
1175   ἱκτήριον θησαυρόν. εἰ δέ τις στρατοῦ
        βίᾳ σ' ἀποσπάσειε τοῦδε τοῦ νεκροῦ,
        κακὸς κακῶς ἄθαπτος ἐκπέσοι χθονός,
        γένους ἅπαντος ῥίζαν ἐξημημένος,
        αὕτως ὅπωσπερ τόνδ' ἐγὼ τέμνω πλόκον.
1180   ἔχ' αὐτόν, ὦ παῖ, καὶ φύλασσε, μηδέ σε
        κινησάτω τις, ἀλλὰ προσπεσὼν ἔχου.
        ὑμεῖς τε μὴ γυναῖκες ἀντ' ἀνδρῶν πέλας
        παρέστατ', ἀλλ' ἀρήγετ', ἔστ' ἐγὼ μόλω
        τάφου μεληθεὶς τῷδε, κἂν μηδεὶς ἐᾷ.

1160   πάρα Nᵖᶜat: παρῇ lrp
1168   πλησίοι Lrpat: ⅃ον p
1183   μολὼν LᵃᶜO, Etym. Magn.
1184   μεληθῶ Etym. Magn.

1155 "Man, do not treat the dead badly; for if you do so, be sure that you will suffer for it." Such was the advice that he stood and gave to the worthless fellow. Indeed I see him, and he is, as it seems to me, none other than yourself. I have not spoken in riddles, have I?

Menelaus I am going; for indeed it is disgraceful, if anyone
1160 should hear that I am using words to chastise you, I who have the power to use force.

Teucer Go away then. For it is most disgraceful for me too to listen to a foolish man speaking petty words.

[*Exit Menelaus*]

Chorus There is going to be a very contentious quarrel. But as
1165 fast as you can, Teucer, hurry and see to some hollow trench for him, where he will possess his dank grave that mortals will always remember.

[*Enter Tecmessa and Eurysaces*]

Teucer Look in the very nick of time here come his child and
1170 wife, to arrange the burial of the wretched corpse. My child, come here, stand near and in supplication take hold of your father who begot you. Sit as a suppliant with locks of hair in your hands, hair from me and from this woman and thirdly from yourself, a
1175 suppliant's treasure. And if anyone from the army were to drag you by force from this corpse, may he the wretch be wretchedly cast out unburied from the land, with the root of his whole family mown down, even as
1180 now I cut off this lock of hair. Hold it, my child, keep close, and let no one move you, but fall down before him and hold him tight; and as for you stand near him, not like women when you should be men, but support him, until I return after I have seen to his grave, even if all forbid it.

[*Exit Teucer by an eisodos*]

1185 ΧΟ. τίς ἄρα νέατος, ἐς πότε λή-   στρ. 1.
        ξει πολυπλάγκτων ἐτέων ἀριθμός,
        τὰν ἄπαυστον αἰὲν ἐμοὶ δορυσσοή-
        των μόχθων ἄταν ἐπάγων
1190   ἂν τὰν εὐρώδη Τροΐαν,
        δύστανον ὄνειδος Ἑλλάνων;

        ὄφελε πρότερον αἰθέρα δῦ-   ἀντ. 1.
        ναι μέγαν ἢ τὸν πολύκοινον Ἅιδαν
1195   κεῖνος ἀνήρ, ὃς στυγερῶν ἔδειξεν ὅ-
        πλων Ἕλλασιν κοινὸν Ἄρη.
        ὦ πόνοι πρόγονοι πόνων·
        κεῖνος γὰρ ἔπερσεν ἀνθρώπους.

        ἐκεῖνος οὐ στεφάνων οὔ-   στρ. 2.
1200   τε βαθειᾶν κυλίκων νεῖ-
        μεν ἐμοὶ τέρψιν ὁμιλεῖν,
        οὔτε γλυκὺν αὐλῶν ὅτοβον, δυσ-
        μόρῳ, οὔτ᾽ ἐννυχίαν τέρψιν ἰαύειν·
1205   ἐρώτων δ᾽ ἐρώτων ἀπέπαυσεν, ὤμοι.
        κεῖμαι δ᾽ ἀμέριμνος οὕτως,
        ἀεὶ πυκιναῖς δρόσοις
        τεγγόμενος κόμας,
1210   λυγρᾶς μνήματα Τροίας.

        καὶ πρὶν μὲν ἐννυχίου δεί-   ἀντ. 2.
        ματος ἦν μοι προβολὰ καὶ
        βελέων θούριος Αἴας·
        νῦν δ᾽ οὗτος ἀνεῖται στυγερῷ δαί-

1186 πολυπλάγκτων Lpat: -άκτων rOD
1187 δορυσσοήτων L: -σσόντων plerique, Suda
1190 ἂν τὰν Ahrens: ἀνὰ τὰν codd., τάνδ᾽ ἂν Lobeck
1199 οὐ Hermann: οὔτε codd.
1202 δυσμόρῳ Blaydes: -μορος codd.
1205 ἐρώτων δ᾽ ἐρώτων r: ἐρώτων ἐρώτων δ᾽ Lpat ἀπέπαυσεν Lrpat:
      ἀπέσπασέ μ᾽ N, ἀπέσπασεν Zr
1210 λυγρᾶς Brunck: -ᾶς codd.
1211 μὲν οὖν t
1214 ἀνεῖται at: ἔγκειται Krp

1185	Chor. *str.1*	Which then will be the last, when will it stop, the number of the wandering years, which imposes on me
1190		for ever in wide Troy the unceasing bane of battle-toil, a sad reproach for the Greeks?
	ant.1	Would that he had first disappeared into the great sky
1195		or into hospitable Hades, that man who showed the Greeks warfare with hateful weapons for all to share. Oh troubles which engender further troubles! It was he who ruined men.
	str.2	He did not dispense the pleasure of garlands or deep
1200		cups for me to consort with, nor the sweet sound of pipes, ill-starred as I am, nor the pleasure of sleep at
1205		night; he has cut me off from the passion of love, of love, alas! And I lie like this uncared for, my hair wet
1210		always with thick dew, to make me remember baneful Troy.
	ant.2	Until now impetuous Ajax was my defence against terror in the night and missiles; but now he is given

1215 μονι. τίς μοι, τίς ἔτ' οὖν τέρψις ἐπέσται;
γενοίμαν ἵν' ὑλᾶεν ἔπεστι πόντῳ
πρόβλημ' ἁλίκλυστον, ἄκραν
1220 ὑπὸ πλάκα Σουνίου,
τὰς ἱερὰς ὅπως
προσείποιμεν 'Αθάνας.

ΤΕΥ. καὶ μὴν ἰδὼν ἔσπευσα τὸν στρατηλάτην
'Αγαμέμνον' ἡμῖν δεῦρο τόνδ' ὁρμώμενον·
1225 δῆλος δέ μοὔστὶ σκαιὸν ἐκλύσων στόμα.

ΑΓΑΜΕΜΝΩΝ
σὲ δὴ τὰ δεινὰ ῥήματ' ἀγγέλλουσί μοι
τλῆναι καθ' ἡμῶν ὧδ' ἀνοιμωκτεὶ χανεῖν.
σέ τοι, τὸν ἐκ τῆς αἰχμαλωτίδος λέγω·
ἦ που τραφεὶς ἂν μητρὸς εὐγενοῦς ἄπο
1230 ὑψήλ' ἐφώνεις κἀπ' ἄκρων ὡδοιπόρεις,
ὅτ' οὐδὲν ὢν τοῦ μηδὲν ἀντέστης ὕπερ,
κοὔτε στρατηγοὺς οὔτε ναυάρχους μολεῖν
ἡμᾶς 'Αχαιῶν οὔτε σοῦ διωμόσω,
ἀλλ' αὐτὸς ἄρχων, ὡς σὺ φής, Αἴας ἔπλει.
1235 ταῦτ' οὐκ ἀκούειν μεγάλα πρὸς δούλων κακά;
ποίου κέκραγας ἀνδρὸς ὧδ' ὑπέρφρονα,
ποῖ βάντος ἢ ποῦ στάντος οὗπερ οὐκ ἐγώ;
οὐκ ἆρ' 'Αχαιοῖς ἄνδρες εἰσὶ πλὴν ὅδε;
πικροὺς ἔοιγμεν τῶν 'Αχιλλείων ὅπλων
1240 ἀγῶνας 'Αργείοισι κηρῦξαι τότε,
εἰ πανταχοῦ φανούμεθ' ἐκ Τεύκρου κακοί,
κοὐκ ἀρκέσει ποθ' ὑμῖν οὐδ' ἡσσημένοις
εἴκειν ἃ τοῖς πολλοῖσιν ἤρεσκεν κριταῖς,
ἀλλ' αἰὲν ἡμᾶς ἢ κακοῖς βαλεῖτέ που
1245 ἢ σὺν δόλῳ κεντήσεθ' οἱ λελειμμένοι.

1215 ἐπέσται] ἔτ' ἔσται Blaydes
1218 πόντῳ Morstadt: -ου codd.
1230 ἐφώνεις L^{rc}a: ἐφρόνεις L^{ac}Krp, Suda, ἐκόμπεις t, Σ Ar. Ach. 638
1241 φανούμεθ' Lpa: -οίμεθ' rpat
1242 ἀρκέσοι Pt
1245 λελημμένοι Η

1215   up to a hateful fate. What pleasure, what pleasure then, will still be my portion? I wish I might be where the wooded sea-washed promontory stands over the

1220   sea, below the flat top of Sunium, that we might greet holy Athens.

[*Enter Teucer*]

Teucer   Look, I have hurried because I saw the commander Agamemnon rushing here to us; it is clear to me that

1225   he is about to unloose his foolish tongue.

[*Enter Agamemnon, probably with attendants*]

Agamemnon   You there, they tell me that you have dared to open your big mouth with such impunity to say these terrible things against us. Yes you I say, I mean the son of the captive-woman; no doubt if you had been bred from a nobly-born woman you would be speaking

1230   proudly and walking on tiptoe, when, nonentity that you are, you have opposed us on a nonentity's behalf; you have sworn that we did not come as your or the Achaeans' generals or admirals, but that Ajax sailed as his own commander, as you claim. Are these not

1235   monstrous insults to hear from the mouths of slaves? What kind of man have you been shouting about so arrogantly, where did he go or where did he stand that I did not? Do then the Achaeans have no men except for him? It was evidently to our sorrow that on that

1240   occasion we proclaimed to the Argives the competition for the arms of Achilles, if we are to be denounced everywhere by Teucer as knaves, and if you will never be content even in defeat to submit to the resolution of the majority of judges, but will for ever sting us, I

1245   suppose, with abuse or stab us deceitfully, you who

ἐκ τῶνδε μέντοι τῶν τρόπων οὐκ ἄν ποτε
κατάστασις γένοιτ' ἂν οὐδενὸς νόμου,
εἰ τοὺς δίκῃ νικῶντας ἐξωθήσομεν
καὶ τοὺς ὄπισθεν ἐς τὸ πρόσθεν ἄξομεν.
1250 ἀλλ' εἰρκτέον τάδ' ἐστίν· οὐ γὰρ οἱ πλατεῖς
οὐδ' εὐρύνωτοι φῶτες ἀσφαλέστατοι,
ἀλλ' οἱ φρονοῦντες εὖ κρατοῦσι πανταχοῦ.
μέγας δὲ πλευρὰ βοῦς ὑπὸ σμικρᾶς ὅμως
μάστιγος ὀρθὸς εἰς ὁδὸν πορεύεται.
1255 καὶ σοὶ προσέρπον τοῦτ' ἐγὼ τὸ φάρμακον
ὁρῶ τάχ', εἰ μὴ νοῦν κατακτήσῃ τινά·
ὃς τἀνδρὸς οὐκέτ' ὄντος, ἀλλ' ἤδη σκιᾶς,
θαρσῶν ὑβρίζεις κἀξελευθεροστομεῖς.
οὐ σωφρονήσεις; οὐ μαθὼν ὃς εἶ φύσιν
1260 ἄλλον τιν' ἄξεις ἄνδρα δεῦρ' ἐλεύθερον,
ὅστις πρὸς ἡμᾶς ἀντὶ σοῦ λέξει τὰ σά;
σοῦ γὰρ λέγοντος οὐκέτ' ἂν μάθοιμ' ἐγώ·
τὴν βάρβαρον γὰρ γλῶσσαν οὐκ ἐπαΐω.
ΧΟ. εἴθ' ὑμῖν ἀμφοῖν νοῦς γένοιτο σωφρονεῖν·
1265 τούτου γὰρ οὐδὲν σφῷν ἔχω λῷον φράσαι.
ΤΕΥ. φεῦ· τοῦ θανόντος ὡς ταχεῖά τις βροτοῖς
χάρις διαρρεῖ καὶ προδοῦσ' ἁλίσκεται,
εἰ σοῦ γ' ὅδ' ἁνὴρ οὐδ' ἐπὶ σμικρὸν λόγον,
Αἴας, ἔτ' ἴσχει μνῆστιν, οὗ σὺ πολλάκις
1270 τὴν σὴν προτείνων προὔκαμες ψυχὴν δορί·
ἀλλ' οἴχεται δὴ πάντα ταῦτ' ἐρριμμένα.
ὦ πολλὰ λέξας ἄρτι κἀνόητ' ἔπη,
οὐ μνημονεύεις οὐκέτ' οὐδέν, ἡνίκα
ἑρκέων ποθ' ὑμᾶς ἐντὸς ἐγκεκλημένους,
1275 ἤδη τὸ μηδὲν ὄντας ἐν τροπῇ δορός,

1253 πλευρὰ (-ᾶ) Lᵃ'Krpt. Eust.: -ἀν Lᴾᶜa, -ᾶς pA
1257 τἀνδρὸς Wecklein: ἀνδρὸς codd.
1259 σωφρονήσεις Lrpat: εὖ φρονήσεις p
1268 σμικρὸν λόγον Reiske: -ῶν -ων Lrpa, -ῶν πόνων t
1272 κἀνόητ' LOaTᵃᵏ: κἀνόηητ' rpaTᵖᶜ
1274 ἐντὸς a: οὗτος Lrpat

lost the decision. Yes, as a result of such practices no law could ever be soundly established, if we are to reject those who fairly win and bring forward those
1250   who are behind. No, this must be prevented; for it is not burly nor broad-backed men that are safest, but it is men of sound mind who are everywhere the best. An ox may have large flanks, yet it is a small whip that
1255   keeps it straight on the road. I see that this remedy is soon on its way for you, if you are not going to acquire some sense; the man no longer lives, but is already a shade, yet you behave so confidently and outrageously and speak so freely. Won't you learn to be reasonable? Won't you recognise what kind of man
1260   you are by birth and bring here someone else, a free man, who will plead your case to us instead of you? For when *you* are the speaker I could have nothing more to learn; for I do not understand the barbarian tongue.

Leader   I wish that you would both acquire the sense to be
1265   reasonable; I can give you both no better advice than this.

Teucer   Alas, how quickly slips away men's gratitude to the dead and it proves treacherous, if this man no longer, even for a brief mention, remembers you, Ajax, on
1270   whose behalf you so often laboured offering your own life to the spear! But all of this is thrown away and lost. Oh as for you who just now spoke so many senseless words, do you no longer remember anything of the time when you were once shut up inside your
1275   defences, and were now reduced to nothing when the

ἐρρύσατ' ἐλθὼν μοῦνος, ἀμφὶ μὲν νεῶν
ἄκροισιν ἤδη ναυτικοῖς θ' ἐδωλίοις
πυρὸς φλέγοντος, ἐς δὲ ναυτικὰ σκάφη
πηδῶντος ἄρδην Ἕκτορος τάφρων ὕπερ;
1280 τίς ταῦτ' ἀπεῖρξεν; οὐχ ὅδ' ἦν ὁ δρῶν τάδε,
ὃν οὐδαμοῦ φής, οὗ σὺ μή, βῆναι ποδί;
ἆρ' ὑμὶν οὗτος ταῦτ' ἔδρασεν ἔνδικα;
χὥτ' αὖθις αὐτὸς Ἕκτορος μόνος μόνου,
λαχών τε κἀκέλευστος, ἦλθεν ἀντίος,
1285 οὐ δραπέτην τὸν κλῆρον ἐς μέσον καθείς,
ὑγρᾶς ἀρούρας βῶλον, ἀλλ' ὃς εὐλόφου
κυνῆς ἔμελλε πρῶτος ἅλμα κουφιεῖν;
ὅδ' ἦν ὁ πράσσων ταῦτα, σὺν δ' ἐγὼ παρών,
ὁ δοῦλος, οὐκ τῆς βαρβάρου μητρὸς γεγώς.
1290 δύστηνε, ποῖ βλέπων ποτ' αὐτὰ καὶ θροεῖς;
οὐκ οἶσθα σοῦ πατρὸς μὲν ὃς προὔφυ πατὴρ
ἀρχαῖον ὄντα Πέλοπα βάρβαρον Φρύγα;
Ἀτρέα δ', ὃς αὖ σ' ἔσπειρε, δυσσεβέστατον
προθέντ' ἀδελφῷ δεῖπνον οἰκείων τέκνων;
1295 αὐτὸς δὲ μητρὸς ἐξέφυς Κρήσσης, ἐφ' ᾗ
λαβὼν ἐπακτὸν ἄνδρ' ὁ φιτύσας πατὴρ
ἐφῆκεν ἐλλοῖς ἰχθύσιν διαφθοράν.
τοιοῦτος ὢν τοιῷδ' ὀνειδίζεις σποράν;
ὃς ἐκ πατρὸς μέν εἰμι Τελαμῶνος γεγώς,
1300 ὅστις στρατοῦ τὰ πρῶτ' ἀριστεύσας ἐμὴν
ἴσχει ξύνευνον μητέρ', ἣ φύσει μὲν ἦν
βασίλεια, Λαομέδοντος· ἔκκριτον δέ νιν
δώρημ' ἐκείνῳ 'δωκεν Ἀλκμήνης γόνος.
ἆρ' ὧδ' ἄριστος ἐξ ἀριστέοιν δυοῖν
1305 βλαστὼν ἂν αἰσχύνοιμι τοὺς πρὸς αἵματος,

1277 ναυτικοῖς: ναυτίλων Dawe   θ' add. Bothe
1281 οὗ σὺ μή, βῆναι J. Krauss: οὐδὲ συμβῆναι codd.
1282 ἆρ'] ἄμ' Musgrave ἔνδικα] ἦ δίχα Reiske
1284 ἦλθεν ἀντίος pat: ἦλθ' ἐναντίος Lrp
1290 ποῦ t
1292 τἀρχαῖον Campbell
1303 γόνος Lrpa: τόκος pt

battle turned, and he came alone and protected you, as
fire already blazed around the tops of the ships and the
ships' quarter-decks, and Hector leapt high over the
trenches on to the vessels' hulls? Who prevented this?
Was it not he who did this, who never set foot
anywhere, you claim, where you did not? In your
judgement was this his duty that he performed? And
again when by himself he faced Hector in single
combat, because he had drawn the lot and not because
he was ordered, and had put in the middle no
runaway's lot, a clod of wet earth, but one which was
likely to be the first to jump lightly out of the well-
plumed helmet? It was he who did this, along with me
who stood beside him, I the slave, the one who was
born from the barbarian mother. You wretch, when
you *say* it where can you look? Do you not know that
your father's father was ancient Pelops, a Phrygian
barbarian? And that Atreus, who in turn begot you,
served his brother a most impious banquet of his own
children? You yourself were born of a Cretan mother,
with whom her sire and father caught a man she had
brought into her bed, and handed her over to be a prey
for dumb fish. When this is the kind of man you are
do you reproach a man like me with his procreation? I
am born from Telamon my father, the man who won
the first prize for valour in the army, and acquired my
mother to share his bed, who was a queen by birth, the
daughter of Laomedon; the son of Alcmene gave her
to him as a choice gift. Being thus by birth the
excellent son of two excellent parents would I bring
shame on my blood-relations, who now lie in such

114

οὓς νῦν σὺ τοιοῖσδ' ἐν πόνοισι κειμένους
ὠθεῖς ἀθάπτους, οὐδ' ἐπαισχύνῃ λέγων;
εὖ νυν τόδ' ἴσθι, τοῦτον εἰ βαλεῖτέ που,
βαλεῖτε χἠμᾶς τρεῖς ὁμοῦ συγκειμένους.
1310   ἐπεὶ καλόν μοι τοῦδ' ὑπερπονουμένῳ
θανεῖν προδήλως μᾶλλον ἢ τῆς σῆς ὑπὲρ
γυναικός, ἢ σοῦ τοῦ θ' ὁμαίμονος λέγω;
πρὸς ταῦθ' ὅρα μὴ τοὐμόν, ἀλλὰ καὶ τὸ σόν.
ὡς εἴ με πημανεῖς τι, βουλήσῃ ποτὲ
1315   καὶ δειλὸς εἶναι μᾶλλον ἢ 'ν ἐμοὶ θρασύς.
ΧΟ.   ἄναξ Ὀδυσσεῦ, καιρὸν ἴσθ' ἐληλυθώς,
εἰ μὴ ξυνάψων, ἀλλὰ συλλύσων πάρει.
ΟΔΥΣΣΕΥΣ
τί δ' ἔστιν, ἄνδρες; τηλόθεν γὰρ ᾐσθόμην
βοὴν Ἀτρειδῶν τῷδ' ἐπ' ἀλκίμῳ νεκρῷ.
1320 ΑΓ.   οὐ γὰρ κλυόντες ἐσμὲν αἰσχίστους λόγους,
ἄναξ Ὀδυσσεῦ, τοῦδ' ὑπ' ἀνδρὸς ἀρτίως;
ΟΔ.   ποίους; ἐγὼ γὰρ ἀνδρὶ συγγνώμην ἔχω
κλυόντι φλαῦρα συμβαλεῖν ἔπη κακά.
ΑΓ.   ἤκουσεν αἰσχρά· δρῶν γὰρ ἦν τοιαῦτ' ἐμέ.
1325 ΟΔ.   τί γάρ σ' ἔδρασεν, ὥστε καὶ βλάβην ἔχειν;
ΑΓ.   οὔ φησ' ἐάσειν τόνδε τὸν νεκρὸν ταφῆς
ἄμοιρον, ἀλλὰ πρὸς βίαν θάψειν ἐμοῦ.
ΟΔ.   ἔξεστιν οὖν εἰπόντι τἀληθῆ φίλῳ
σοὶ μηδὲν ἧσσον ἢ πάρος ξυνηρετεῖν;
1330 ΑΓ.   εἴπ'· ἦ γὰρ εἴην οὐκ ἂν εὖ φρονῶν, ἐπεὶ
φίλον σ' ἐγὼ μέγιστον Ἀργείων νέμω.
ΟΔ.   ἄκουέ νυν· τὸν ἄνδρα τόνδε πρὸς θεῶν
μὴ τλῇς ἄθαπτον ὧδ' ἀναλγήτως βαλεῖν·

1312   σοῦ τοῦ θ' Hertel: τοῦ σοῦ θ' codd.
1320-1 Ag. trib. plerique, Teuc. L
1320   κλυόντες Kamerbeek: κλύοντες codd.
1323   κλυόντι West: κλύοντι codd.
1324   Ag. trib. rat, Teuc. Lpa
1329   ξυνηρετεῖν Lobeck: -τμεῖν IQᴾᶜ, -εμεῖν GRt
1330   εἴπ'· ἦ γὰρ pat: ἐπεί γ' ἂν L, ηπει γ' ἂν Λ, ἢ που γ' ἂν r

distress, whom you thrust out unburied, and are not ashamed of saying it? Be sure of this, that, if you cast him out, you will cast us out as well, three people lying together with him. For it is better for me to die conspicuously labouring on his behalf than on your wife's behalf, or am I to say your and your brother's wife? Therefore look not to my case, but your own as well. For, if you do me any harm, you will wish one day even to have been a coward rather than bold at my expense.

1310

1315

[*Enter Odysseus*]

Leader	Lord Odysseus, know that your arrival is timely, if you have come not to join in the quarrel but to reconcile it.
Odysseus	What is it, men? For I heard from a distance the sons of Atreus shouting over this brave corpse.
Agam.	Yes, for have we not just been the recipients of the most disgraceful words, lord Odysseus, from this man here?
Odysseus	What kind of words? I can forgive a man who when he is the recipient of insults matches them with insulting words.
Agam.	He did receive shameful insults; for that was the kind of thing he was doing to me.
Odysseus	What was it that he *did* to you, that it resulted in actual injury?
Agam.	He says that he will not allow this corpse to be deprived of burial, but that he will inter him in despite of me.
Odysseus	May a friend speak the truth and remain your partner no less than before?
Agam.	Speak; for otherwise I should not show sense, since I consider you my greatest friend among the Argives.
Odysseus	Then listen. Do not bring yourself, by the gods, so insensitively to cast out this man unburied; and by

1320

1325

1330

116

μηδ' ἡ βία σε μηδαμῶς νικησάτω
1335 τοσόνδε μισεῖν ὥστε τὴν δίκην πατεῖν.
κἀμοὶ γὰρ ἦν ποθ' οὗτος ἔχθιστος στρατοῦ,
ἐξ οὗ 'κράτησα τῶν Ἀχιλλείων ὅπλων,
ἀλλ' αὐτὸν ἔμπας ὄντ' ἐγὼ τοιόνδ' ἐμοὶ
οὔ τἂν ἀτιμάσαιμ' ἄν, ὥστε μὴ λέγειν
1340 ἕν' ἄνδρ' ἰδεῖν ἄριστον Ἀργείων, ὅσοι
Τροίαν ἀφικόμεσθα, πλὴν Ἀχιλλέως.
ὥστ' οὐκ ἂν ἐνδίκως γ' ἀτιμάζοιτό σοι·
οὐ γάρ τι τοῦτον, ἀλλὰ τοὺς θεῶν νόμους
φθείροις ἄν. ἄνδρα δ' οὐ δίκαιον, εἰ θάνοι,
1345 βλάπτειν τὸν ἐσθλόν, οὐδ' ἐὰν μισῶν κυρῇς.
ΑΓ.   σὺ ταῦτ', Ὀδυσσεῦ, τοῦδ' ὑπερμαχεῖς ἐμοί;
ΟΔ.   ἔγωγ'· ἐμίσουν δ', ἡνίκ' ἦν μισεῖν καλόν.
ΑΓ.   οὐ γὰρ θανόντι καὶ προσεμβῆναί σε χρή;
ΟΔ.   μὴ χαῖρ', Ἀτρείδη, κέρδεσιν τοῖς μὴ καλοῖς.
1350 ΑΓ.   τόν τοι τύραννον εὐσεβεῖν οὐ ῥᾴδιον.
ΟΔ.   ἀλλ' εὖ λέγουσι τοῖς φίλοις τιμὰς νέμειν.
ΑΓ.   κλύειν τὸν ἐσθλὸν ἄνδρα χρὴ τῶν ἐν τέλει.
ΟΔ.   παῦσαι· κρατεῖς τοι τῶν φίλων νικώμενος.
ΑΓ.   μέμνησ' ὁποίῳ φωτὶ τὴν χάριν δίδως.
1355 ΟΔ.   ὅδ' ἐχθρὸς ἁνήρ, ἀλλὰ γενναῖός ποτ' ἦν.
ΑΓ.   τί ποτε ποήσεις; ἐχθρὸν ὧδ' αἰδῇ νέκυν;
ΟΔ.   νικᾷ γὰρ ἀρετή με τῆς ἔχθρας πλέον.
ΑΓ.   τοιοίδε μέντοι φῶτες ἔμπληκτοι βροτῶν.
ΟΔ.   ἦ κάρτα πολλοὶ νῦν φίλοι καὖθις πικροί.
1360 ΑΓ.   τοιούσδ' ἐπαινεῖς δῆτα σὺ κτᾶσθαι φίλους;

1339   οὔ τἂν Elmsley: οὐκ ἂν Irp, οὔκουν a, οὐκ ἂν γ' t: οὐκ ἀντατιμήσαιμ'
       Bothe
1357   πλέον C, gl in quibusdam codd.: πολύ cett., Stob., Eust.
1358   βροτῶν IRpt: -οῖς GQa

no means let violence prevail over you into hating him
1335   so much that you trample on justice. For me too he
was once the most hated man in the army, ever since I
became master of Achilles' arms, yet, though that is
the kind of man he was to me, I would not so
dishonour him, as to deny that in him I saw the single
1340   most excellent man of all the Argives, as many of us
as came to Troy, except for Achilles. So it would not
be right for him to be dishonoured by you; for it is not
he, but the laws of the gods, that you would be
1345   destroying. It is not just to harm the good man, if he
should die, even if you happen to hate him.

	Agam.	Do you so champion him, Odysseus, against me?
	Odysseus	I do; but I did hate him, when it was right to hate him.
	Agam.	Should you not also trample on him when he is dead?
	Odysseus	Do not take pleasure, son of Atreus, in an advantage that is not right.
1350	Agam.	It is not easy for the ruler to show piety.
	Odysseus	No, but it is easy to give honour to one's friends when they give good advice.
	Agam.	The good man ought to obey those who are in authority.
	Odysseus	Stop! You exercise authority by yielding to your friends.
	Agam.	Remember the kind of man to whom you give the favour.
1355	Odysseus	The man was my enemy, but he was noble once.
	Agam.	What ever will you do? Do you have such respect for an enemy's corpse?
	Odysseus	Yes, for his excellence prevails with me more than his enmity.
	Agam.	Yet such men are unstable among mortals.
	Odysseus	It is certainly true that many who are now friends turn out later unpleasant.
1360	Agam.	Do you then recommend that one acquire such men as friends?

118

ΟΔ. σκληρὰν ἐπαινεῖν οὐ φιλῶ ψυχὴν ἐγώ.
ΑΓ. ἡμᾶς σὺ δειλοὺς τῇδε θἠμέρᾳ φανεῖς.
ΟΔ. ἄνδρας μὲν οὖν Ἕλλησι πᾶσιν ἐνδίκους.
ΑΓ. ἄνωγας οὖν με τὸν νεκρὸν θάπτειν ἐᾶν;
1365 ΟΔ. ἔγωγε· καὶ γὰρ αὐτὸς ἐνθάδ᾽ ἵξομαι.
ΑΓ. ἦ πάνθ᾽ ὅμοια· πᾶς ἀνὴρ αὑτῷ πονεῖ.
ΟΔ. τῷ γάρ με μᾶλλον εἰκὸς ἢ ᾽μαυτῷ πονεῖν;
ΑΓ. σὸν ἆρα τοὔργον, οὐκ ἐμὸν κεκλήσεται.
ΟΔ. ὧδ᾽ ἢν πόῃς, πανταχῇ χρηστός γ᾽ ἔσῃ.
1370 ΑΓ. ἀλλ᾽ εὖ γε μέντοι τοῦτ᾽ ἐπίστασ᾽, ὡς ἐγὼ
         σοὶ μὲν νέμοιμ᾽ ἂν τῆσδε καὶ μείζω χάριν,
         οὗτος δὲ κἀκεῖ κἀνθάδ᾽ ὢν ἔμοιγ᾽ ὁμῶς
         ἔχθιστος ἔσται. σοὶ δὲ δρᾶν ἔξεσθ᾽ ἃ χρῇς.
ΧΟ. ὅστις σ᾽, Ὀδυσσεῦ, μὴ λέγει γνώμῃ σοφὸν
1375   φῦναι, τοιοῦτον ὄντα, μῶρός ἐστ᾽ ἀνήρ.
ΟΔ. καὶ νῦν γε Τεύκρῳ τἀπὸ τοῦδ᾽ ἀγγέλλομαι,
         ὅσον τότ᾽ ἐχθρὸς ἦ, τοσόνδ᾽ εἶναι φίλος.
         καὶ τὸν θανόντα τόνδε συνθάπτειν θέλω,
         καὶ ξυμπονεῖν καὶ μηδὲν ἐλλείπειν ὅσων
1380   χρὴ τοῖς ἀρίστοις ἀνδράσιν πονεῖν βροτούς.
ΤΕΥ. ἄριστ᾽ Ὀδυσσεῦ, πάντ᾽ ἔχω σ᾽ ἐπαινέσαι
         λόγοισι· καί μ᾽ ἔψευσας ἐλπίδος πολύ.
         τούτῳ γὰρ ὢν ἔχθιστος Ἀργείων ἀνὴρ
         μόνος παρέστης χερσίν, οὐδ᾽ ἔτλης παρὼν
1385   θανόντι τῷδε ζῶν ἐφυβρίσαι μέγα,
         ὡς ὁ στρατηγὸς οὑπιβρόντητος μολὼν
         αὐτός τε χὠ ξύναιμος ἠθελησάτην

1366 πονεῖ] φρονεῖ rO
1367 φρονεῖν L⁵ˡr
1369 ὧδ᾽ F. Polle: ὡς codd.   ἢν Broadhead, *Tragica* (Christchurch 1968) 72: ἂν codd.
1372 ὁμῶς rpa: ὅμως LO, γρ in Xr, t
1373 χρῇς Dindorf: χρή codd.
1379 ὅσων Zcˢˡ: ὅσον cett., ὅσῳ Lˢˡ

	Odysseus	I do not normally recommend an unyielding soul.
	Agam.	You will show us up as weaklings today.
	Odysseus	No, but as men who observe justice in the eyes of all the Greeks.
	Agam.	Do you therefore bid me to allow the corpse to be buried?
1365	Odysseus	I do; for I myself shall also come to that.
	Agam.	The whole world is alike: every man labours for himself.
	Odysseus	For whom is it more natural for me to labour than for myself?
	Agam.	It will then be called your deed, not mine.
	Odysseus	If you act in this way, you will at all events be worthy.
1370	Agam.	Understand this well, however, that although I would assign *you* an even greater favour than this, *he* both in the next world and in this alike will remain my worst enemy. *You* can do what you wish.

[*Exit Agamemnon*]

1375	Leader	If anyone denies, Odysseus, that you are wise in judgement, when you are this kind of person, he is a foolish man.
1380	Odysseus	Next I proclaim to Teucer that as much as once I was his enemy now I am his friend. And I want to join him in burying the dead man here, and to share the labour and to fail in none of all the labours which mortals should perform for men who are the best.
1385	Teucer	Most excellent Odysseus, I can give you only praise when I speak; you have deceived me greatly in my expectation. For, although you were the most hateful of the Argives to this man, you alone stood by him with helping hand, and did not bring yourself, though he was dead and you were alive in his presence, to treat him with great outrage, as did the crazy general who came, he and his brother, and they wanted to cast him out without burial disgraced. So may the father

λωβητὸν αὐτὸν ἐκβαλεῖν ταφῆς ἄτερ.

1390   τοιγάρ σφ' Ὀλύμπου τοῦδ' ὁ πρεσβεύων πατὴρ
μνήμων τ' Ἐρινὺς καὶ τελεσφόρος Δίκη
κακοὺς κακῶς φθείρειαν, ὥσπερ ἤθελον
τὸν ἄνδρα λώβαις ἐκβαλεῖν ἀναξίως.
σὲ δ', ὦ γεραιοῦ σπέρμα Λαέρτου πατρός,
τάφου μὲν ὀκνῶ τοῦδ' ἐπιψαύειν ἐᾶν,

1395   μὴ τῷ θανόντι τοῦτο δυσχερὲς ποιῶ·
τὰ δ' ἄλλα καὶ ξύμπρασσε, κεἴ τινα στρατοῦ
θέλεις κομίζειν, οὐδὲν ἄλγος ἕξομεν.
ἐγὼ δὲ τἄλλα πάντα πορσυνῶ· σὺ δὲ
ἀνὴρ καθ' ἡμᾶς ἐσθλὸς ὢν ἐπίστασο.

1400 ΟΔ. ἀλλ' ἤθελον μέν· εἰ δὲ μή 'στί σοι φίλον
πράσσειν τάδ' ἡμᾶς, εἶμ' ἐπαινέσας τὸ σόν.

ΤΕΥ. ἅλις· ἤδη γὰρ πολὺς ἐκτέταται
χρόνος. ἀλλ' οἱ μὲν κοίλην κάπετον
χερσὶ ταχύνετε, τοὶ δ' ὑψίβατον

1405   τρίποδ' ἀμφίπυρον λουτρῶν ὁσίων
θέσθ' ἐπίκαιρον·
μία δ' ἐκ κλισίας ἀνδρῶν ἴλη
τὸν ὑπασπίδιον κόσμον φερέτω.
παῖ, σὺ δὲ πατρός γ', ὅσον ἰσχύεις,

1410   φιλότητι θιγὼν πλευρὰς σὺν ἐμοὶ
τάσδ' ἐπικούφιζ'· ἔτι γὰρ θερμαὶ
σύριγγες ἄνω φυσῶσι μέλαν
μένος. ἀλλ' ἄγε πᾶς, φίλος ὅστις ἀνὴρ
φησὶ παρεῖναι, σούσθω, βάτω,

1415   τῷδ' ἀνδρὶ πονῶν τῷ πάντ' ἀγαθῷ
†κοὐδενί πω λῴονι θνητῶν
Αἴαντος, ὅτ' ἦν, τόδε φωνῶ.†

ΧΟ. ἦ πολλὰ βροτοῖς ἔστιν ἰδοῦσιν
γνῶναι· πρὶν ἰδεῖν δ' οὐδεὶς μάντις

1420   τῶν μελλόντων ὅ τι πράξει.

1396-7 del. Schneidewin
1398 τἄλλα πάντα] τἀμὰ πάντα Rauchenstein
1404 ταχύνετε Lrpa: -ατε QpZrt
1409 γ' om. p
1417 Αἴαντι r τόδε Blaydes: τότε Lrpa, ποτε p
1419 ἰδεῖν δ' Lat: δ' ἰδεῖν Λrp, ἰδεῖν γ' F

who rules over the sky above us and the Fury who
1390 remembers and Justice who brings accomplishment
destroy the wretches wretchedly, even as they wished
to cast him out unworthily and in disgrace. But as for
you, seed of your aged father Laertes, I shrink from
allowing you to touch his burial, in case I should
1395 offend the dead by doing it. But do join with me in
doing the rest, and if you wish to bring along anyone
from the army I shall not mind. I shall arrange
everything else; but understand that as far as I am
concerned you are a good man.

1400 Odysseus Well, I wanted it; but if you do not welcome my doing
this, I shall accept your word and go.

[*Exit Odysseus*]

Teucer Enough; for much time has already elapsed. Some of
you quickly prepare a hollow trench with your hands,
1405 and others place a high tripod in the middle of the fire
convenient for the holy bath; and let one company of
men bring from the hut the armour which he wore
under his shield. Boy, with all the strength you have,
1410 touch your father lovingly and help me to raise this
frame; for his channels are still warm and gasp up his
dark might. Come everyone, everyone present who
claims to be a friend, let him hurry, let him go,
1415 labouring for this man who was good in all respects.
† And there was no better man than Ajax, when he
was alive; this is what I say. †

Chorus Mortals can understand many things when they have
seen them; but before he sees them no one can predict
1420 how he will fare in the future.

[*Exeunt everybody*]

Tecmessa covering Ajax' corpse. Red figure painting on the tondo of a cup by the Brygos painter (New York Metropolitan Museum L.60.11.35)

Commentary

1-133: Prologue

As in all his surviving plays except *Trachiniae* Sophocles begins his play with dialogue. Its most obvious function is to give the audience the information that it requires at the beginning of the play. So Odysseus is introduced in line 1, and the identity of the goddess is revealed at 14. The setting, in front of Ajax' hut at Troy, is made clear at 3–4. Athena in her opening speech tells us of his 'sword-killer's hands' (10), and Odysseus recounts the slaughter of the animals and the general suspicion that Ajax is responsible. Athena already knows all this, and Sophocles seems to go out of his way at 13 and 36 to draw our attention to the lack of realism. But it should not be exaggerated. Odysseus merely suspects that Ajax is the perpetrator, and it is left to Athena to give a full account, and to explain in particular that she herself inflicted madness on him so that he attacked the animals instead of his enemies. During all this we are kept waiting for the appearance of Ajax himself. We expect it at 71–3, but it is not till Athena repeats her summons (89–90) that he finally emerges from his hut, flushed with triumph, and probably carrying the whip (110, 242) that gave the play its later sub-title, *Mastigophoros*, 'Whip-carrier' (Taplin (1978) 85, with 188 n.7, supposes that what he carries is his sword, but more probably the audience's first sight of the sword is at 646; see Seale 177 n. 10, Heath 168 n.7). Athena plays with him until he returns to his hut to torture the supposed Odysseus, leaving Athena to comment on her treatment of Ajax in a way which evidently does not satisfy Odysseus (118–26), and to draw a moral which raises more problems than it answers for our understanding of the tragedy.

We learn a great deal about the relationships among the three characters. Apart from Heracles at the end of *Phil.*, Athena is the only deity to appear on stage in extant Sophoclean tragedy. Odysseus is revealed from the opening lines as the familiar hero of Homer's *Odyssey*, intelligent and indefatigable in pursuit of his goal, while Ajax is fully recognisable as the mighty warrior of the *Iliad*. The contrast between intelligence and physical might is thus clearly established at the outset, but it is not quite absolute: Ajax is not without brains (119–20). From the very beginning we are meant to admire him (the view of Poe, 29–38, that the prologue is meant to be funny, that it is 'a parody of the tragic situation', is wide of the mark). He appears before us mad, and we look forward with apprehension to his return to sanity and his discovery of his shame. But even in his delusion he is a splendid figure, exulting in his supposed triumph. Paradoxically, this is the real heroic Ajax, and it is important for us to see him so, before he becomes conscious of his disgrace. In the heroic code it is not the attack on his enemies that is shameful, but the fact that he has turned his sword against helpless animals, and failed to secure his vengeance. As early as line 2 the enmity between Ajax and Odysseus is stressed. Athena takes it for granted that the latter will want to do as much harm as possible to his enemy, and Odysseus seems to confirm her assumption at 78. For this essential component of Greek ethical values see Intro. 11. Similarly Ajax' desire to avenge himself on the Atreidae and Odysseus is entirely normal. Athena is the traditional supporter of Odysseus, and Ajax is pathetically deluded in supposing that she is his own ally (91–2n.), but, in her acceptance of the traditional code of helping friends and harming enemies, her values are those of Ajax himself (e.g. 79). It is the human Odysseus who provides the first surprise in the play, when he rejects Athena's invitation to laugh (79–80). At 121–6 he pities Ajax, although he is his enemy, as he reflects on their shared humanity. This remarkable attitude, which is much more attractive than that of the goddess and evidently beyond her understanding foreshadows the final scene of the play (see Intro. 15-16).

The play opens with Athena calling to Odysseus, who must have entered by a side-passage (*eisodos*), and is circling round in front of Ajax' hut, trying to track his enemy, and peering inside the central door. Lines 14–17 indicate that Athena is invisible to Odysseus (but not, despite Kitto, *Greek tragedy* 151, Gellie 5, to the audience), although he can hear her voice. Similarly at Eur. *Hipp.* 1391–3 Hippolytus can smell Artemis' fragrance, but cannot see her. Artemis is probably either on the *mechane*, the crane which was often used for divine appearances at the end of Euripides' plays, or on the *theologeion*, the flat roof of the stage-building (for the nature and use of these acting areas see D.J. Mastronarde, *ClAnt.* 9 (1990) 247–94), and many scholars suppose that the same is true here; see esp. W.M. Calder III, *CPh* 60 (1965) 114–116, and (in answer to W.J. Ziobro, *Class. Folia* 26 (1972) 122–8) *CF* 28 (1974) 59–61. But a prologue is different from a conventional *deus ex machina* at the end of a play. The only real parallel for a divine epiphany to a mortal in a prologue is in Aesch. *Eum.*, where the position of Apollo is equally uncertain (Calder would add Sophocles' lost *Polyxena*). When Ajax enters at 91 there is no suggestion that he cannot see Athena; it is only Odysseus that is invisible to him. The view of Stanford seems preferable, that Athena appears from the beginning at ground level, having followed Odysseus (36–7) by the same *eisodos*. She stands at the side of the stage at some distance from Odysseus. It is no more difficult for the audience to accept her invisibility to Odysseus than it is to believe in Odysseus' invisibility to Ajax. 'It seems...that the emphasis on non-visual means of recognition is a conventional motif when a god is identified by a mortal intimate to whom no explicit profession of identity has been made' (Heath 165). There is probably no need to reason that, since it is early morning (9, 21), it is too dark for Odysseus to see her. As the scene progresses the pretence is gradually dropped, until (perhaps at 36) we forget that she is supposed to be invisible. At the end of the prologue Athena and Odysseus depart probably by different *eisodoi*.

1-3 **for ever...so now:** the second clause presents a specific case of what usually happens (for μέν...καί so used cf. Eur. *Hel.* 734–6, and see Denniston 374; for the tendency of speeches to open with μέν Denniston 383).
  son of Laertes: i.e. Odysseus. Λαρτίου is a metrically convenient form of his father's name found also at 380. Other spellings are used at 101, 1393.
  hunting down...your enemies: the line stresses both the traditional enmity between Ajax and Odysseus and also the enterprising character of the intelligent Odysseus. And it introduces the hunting metaphor which will dominate the prologue: Ajax, who hunted helpless animals, is now in his turn being hunted (Jouanna 168–86). For the close association between hunting-terms and intelligence see M. Detienne and J.-P. Vernant, *Cunning intelligence in Greek culture and society* (tr. New Jersey 1978) 44.

3-4 **at the huts...of the line:** the language of 63 and 65 suggests a building rather than a tent, and it is a building, the *skene*, the very word used here by Sophocles, that the audience sees at the back of the stage. For 'huts' here as a genuine, not (Jebb) a poetic, plural see Scullion 123 n. 129. Ajax' encampment was at the end of the Greek line, the other end being occupied by Achilles' (Hom. *Il.* 8.224–6 = 11.7–9, 10.113). Sophocles may be drawing attention to the 'marginality' of Ajax and his army (Bowie 114, H. Gasti, *QUCC* 40 (1992) 83), but more probably we are to think of him as occupying the place of honour (Jebb).

5-8 As the hunting imagery develops Odysseus changes from the hunter to the hound. For Odysseus as the latter Jouanna (170 n. 1) compares Hom. *Il.* 10.360-4.

all this time: lit. 'for a long time', but only in relative terms. The audience saw Odysseus enter the stage only a few moments before the play began.

measuring: metaphorically, 'gauging with the eye' (cf. Thuc. 3.20.3), as well as 'following the tracks', unlike Aesch. *Cho.* 209, where Electra literally measures Orestes' prints by putting her own feet beside them. For this as a technical term in hunting see Jouanna 169 n. 2.

It is like...your goal: word-order suggests that 'keen-scented' is nom. singular agreeing with 'course', in which case it is transferred from 'bitch' with which it logically belongs (cf. *Ant.* 793). But it could be genitive singular of εὖρις (cf. Aesch. *Ag.* 1093) and agree with 'bitch' (so F. Sommer, *Abh. bay. Ak.* 27 (1948) 88-90). Laconian dogs, for which see D.B. Hull, *Hounds and hunting in ancient Greece* (Chicago and London 1964) 31-3, L.C. Reilly, *JHS* 113 (1993) 160-2, were renowned for their keen scent (see Hull 38). In the compound ἐκφέρει the prefix indicates the completion of the process of carrying; cf. *Tr.* 824, *OC* 1424.

10 **sword-killer's:** this is the first mention of Ajax' sword, the sword with which he will kill himself. The epithet helps to establish at the beginning his status as a warrior, and the sword itself will play a crucial part in the tragedy (Taplin (1978) 85-7, Cohen, Segal (1981) 116-18, Seale 175). Already there is pathos as we reflect on what Ajax has just killed with his sword. His hands are perhaps dripping with blood as well as sweat. On the cup by the Brygos Painter (Intro. 3) the hair of the corpse seems to be wet, perhaps with sweat (Davies (1973) 63).

11-12 **but you should tell me:** the positive 'there is need' has to be understood from the negative expression in the previous clause, for which cf. 852.

13 **you have taken this trouble:** for the periphrasis of ἔθου and object cf. 536, *OT* 134, 1460.

14-16 At [Eur.] *Rhes.* 608-9 Odysseus greets Athena in very similar terms; cf. also *El.* 1225, *Phil.* 234, *OC* 324-5, and, for this kind of address to a 'voice', see Long 123-4. It is particularly appropriate here, because it is only by her voice that Ajax recognises Athena. 'Dearest' contrasts with 'enemies' at 2. The alliteration of φ and θ in 14 is striking, but, as often, it is hard to tell whether it is intended by the poet.

how easily...your utterance: lit., 'how easily recognisable do I hear your utterance'.

though you are invisible: lit. 'even if however...', the word for 'however', ὅμως, belonging more logically in the principal clause, as at Aesch. *Cho.* 115, etc. R.G.A. Buxton, *JHS* 100 (1980) 22 nn.1 and 2, rightly argues against the view that ἄποπτος here means simply 'seen from afar' or 'dimly seen', an explanation which is found already at *Suda* A 3490, Hesych. A 6566, and more recently in Taplin (1977) 116 n.1, 366 n.1.

16-17 **and grasp it:** a compound of the simple verb used by Athena at 2, again stressing the quickness of Odysseus: no sooner does he hear than he understands. Here too there is alliteration of φ. The largely ornamental comparison of Athena's voice with the trumpet recalls Hom. *Il.* 18.217-21 (the shout of Achilles, with Athena standing by). Paus.

2.21.3 records a temple of Athena 'Trumpet' at Corinth. According to Σ *Il.* 18.219 (b) the trumpet was invented for the Etruscans by Athena, and the Etruscan trumpet is often mentioned: e.g. Aesch. *Eum.* 567, Eur. *Heracl.* 830. κώδων is strictly the bell-shaped mouth of the trumpet.

18-19   an enemy: the phrase confirms Athena's words at 2, and contrasts with 14, and it is effectively separated from 'Ajax the bearer of the shield', which ends the sentence.

I circle round: lit, 'I circle a course'. So at Eur. *Or.* 632 Menelaus 'circles his foot'; cf. also Ar. *Birds* 1379. For this movement as a description of hunting-dogs (or, Xen. *Cyn.* 8.3, hunters) which have lost the track cf. Xen. *Cyn.* 4.3, 6.21, and see Jouanna 170–3.

the bearer of the shield: the epithet is not ornamental. We are meant to recall the *Iliad*, in which he is the possessor of the great, tower-like, body-shield, made of seven layers of ox-hide (7.219–20, etc.); cf. 574–6n. and see A.M. Snodgrass, *Arms and armour of the Greeks* (London 1967) 19–20. This kind of shield was already obsolete long before the Trojan War. In *Il.* only Ajax carries it, apart from Hector at 6.117–18 and Periphetes at 15.645-6. Even more than his sword (10), which will turn into a symbol of his destructive madness and tragedy, his shield symbolises his status as a warrior and hero and as the protector of his people; see Segal (1981) 116.

20   he, none other: the 'polarisation' of expression, with the same idea stated both positively and negatively, is very common in Greek. The hunting metaphor continues from 5–6.

I have long been tracking: Greek uses the present tense as the tracking is still continuing.

21-2   he has performed: a periphrastic perfect, formed, as in English, by the present of the verb 'to have' and the aorist participle. It is fairly common in Sophocles. The verb governs a double object, 'us' and 'deed', as in the common ἀγαθὸν ποιεῖν τινά, 'do good to someone'.

inconceivable: cf. *El.* 864, 1315. But the adjective could also be translated as 'unintelligible', or even as 'aimless', Ajax having missed his target (Ferguson 13).

if indeed he *has* done this: Odysseus is not yet sure, and finds it hard to believe, that Ajax is the culprit. Musgrave's γ' ὅδε for τάδε, 'if at any rate it is he who has done it', is attractive but probably unnecessary.

23   are perplexed: lit., 'wander', 'roam'. The verb, which seems to be used only here in this metaphorical sense, suits the random movements of Odysseus at the beginning of the play. For the polarisation of expression see 20n.

24   undertake: lit. 'yoke myself to'. Such yoking metaphors are common in Greek; cf. 123.

25-6   for refers back to 21–2 (see Denniston 63). **destroyed and killed:** the two participles are virtually synonymous.

27   by human hand: the Greek says simply 'by hand'. This kind of expression, like 'on foot' with verbs of motion, is often used redundantly with any verb that describes a manual operation. But here it stresses the fact that the animals did not die naturally, or by wild animals; see Denniston-Page on Aesch. *Ag.* 1495-6. For this stress on the work of Ajax' hand cf. 10, 40, 43, 50, 56–7, 219, and see Cohen 26, Renehan 341. Lloyd-Jones and Wilson, less well, think that the sense may be rather 'that the killings could not have been the work of an enemy shooting projectiles from some way off'.

together with...the flocks: Ajax has killed the shepherds and herdsmen (not, as *Suda* E 2616 says, the sheepdogs) as well as their charges. Little will be made of this later in the play (but cf. 232). The comitative dative, 'overseers and all', is common in this type of expression; cf. αὐτοῖς τοῖς ἀνδράσι, 'crew and all'. For 'overseers' cf. *OT* 1028 ποιμνίοις ἐπεστάτουν, Pl. *Laws* 906a. ποίμνια are usually flocks of sheep as distinct from goats or herds of cattle (cf. Hdt. 1.126.2), but here they evidently include cattle.

28 **attributes:** for this use of τρέπω (lit. 'turns') cf. Isaeus 8.41, Pl. *Ep.* 3.315e. On the choice between this reading and νέμει, 'assigns', see Dawe 123–4. P.E. Easterling, *CQ* 17 (1967) 60, prefers the view that τρέπει is an explanatory gloss.

29 **all by himself:** the detail is not very significant in itself, but the Sophoclean hero regularly feels that he is alone, cut off from his society, and the idea will become important for our understanding of Ajax' tragedy; cf. 47, 294, 461, 467, 614, 1276, 1283, and see Knox (1964) 32–3, (1979) 144 with n. 100.

30 **leaping over the plain:** for the alliteration in πηδῶντα πεδία see 14–16n. The accusative is that of the ground traversed, without preposition. The metrical resolution in the second foot perhaps echoes the sense.
with freshly-sprinkled sword: see 10n. By now we know why Ajax' sword is sprinkled with blood, and it is already turning into a symbol of his shame. The same phrase at 828 will describe the sword stained with his own blood. The eye-witness saw him, not performing the deed, but only returning after it.

31 **informed me and revealed it to me:** a historic present (cf. 25) and aorist are combined; cf. *Ant.* 406.
to me in the Greek comes emphatically at the beginning of the sentence, and is opposed to 'everyone' at 28.

32 The hunting language picks up 6, 20, and perhaps continues with 'I identify (lit. 'mark for myself') some of the signs', or 'I partly (τὰ μέν) identify the tracks'; cf. Xen. *Cyn.* 6.22 (of hounds following tracks), Soph. *Ichn.* fr. 314.106, and see Jouanna 174 n.1. We may suppose that Odysseus' difficulty is caused by the early morning darkness, as well perhaps as by Ajax' irregular course.

33 **I am confused:** lit. 'I have been struck out of myself' or 'thrown off course', here specifically off the track, a verb commonly used (8 times in Sophocles) to express mental shock or disturbance.
where he is: for the omission of 'is' in the Greek cf. *OC* 1218. For ὅπου most MSS read ὅτου, 'whose they [the tracks] are' (for a defence of this reading see Ch. Josserand, in *Mélanges Émile Boisacq* II (Brussels 1938) 5–10). But, where he can see them, Odysseus knows that the human, as opposed to the animal, tracks belong to Ajax. His problem, as it will be later for his friends the chorus (cf. 890), is to find where Ajax is now (cf. 6–7). It is true that Athena has already answered the question (9), but the present tense, like all the others in Odysseus' narrative, is historic (Jouanna 180). For the superiority of ὅπου see Dawe 124–6, who, however, takes the tracks as the subject, Ferrari 21–2, Jouanna 175–81. For ὅπου at line-end cf. 103, 890, *OT* 926, *Ant.* 318.

34 **at the right time:** as at 1316 the internal accusative is used adverbially (= πρὸς or ἐς καιρόν 1168; cf. Eur. *Hel.* 479, fr. 495.9, and see Moorhouse 42.
past: lit. 'as to the former things indeed'. The combination of τε and οὖν, the latter with strengthening force, seems to be unique; see Denniston 420.

35 **by your hand:** see 27n. Dawe prefers the variant φρενί. There is a converse error at 46. At Hom. *Il.* 10.278–80 Odysseus similarly acknowledges Athena's constant support; cf. also *Od.* 20.47–8.

36-50 This kind of line-by-line dialogue, stichomythia, in which each speaker picks up the thought and often the syntactic construction of the previous speaker, is often employed, as here, to present a rapid series of questions and answers.

36 **a while ago:** see 5–8n.

38 **Dear mistress:** a human being is so addressed at *Ant.* 1192, *Tr.* 429, 472, but δέσποινα itself is regularly used in tragedy of a goddess (e.g. *El.* 626).

am I really: for ἦ καί introducing an eager question see Denniston 285, and cf. 44, 48, 97.

to good effect: lit. 'with a view to advantage'; cf. *OT* 325. καιρόν has already been used at 34, but in a different sense. The Greek ear was evidently insensitive to such repetitions.

39 **Yes:** lit. 'since', affirming Odysseus' question, and at the same time giving the reason for doing so. Others take ὡς as 'that', and understand an imperative 'know' in front of it.

you should know that: σοι is an 'ethic' dative, marking the interest of the person addressed.

40 **put forth his hand:** ἤξεν is probably transitive (contrast 32 and cf. Eur. *Hec.* 1071). It implies rapid motion. But Bergk's ἤμαξεν, 'made bloody', deserves consideration (cf. 453). For 'hand' at the end of the line cf. 35n.

so irrational: δυσλόγιστον may be either an adverb or an adjective agreeing proleptically with χέρα. Less well we could take it with 'for what purpose' and translate 'unintelligible'; cf. 21–2n.

41 **Anger overwhelmed him:** lit. 'being weighed down by anger. For the association of 'heaviness' with anger cf. 1017, *OT* 673, 781.

because of Achilles' armour: the genitive of cause is common after a verb expressing emotion; cf. *El.* 1027, *Ant.* 1177. It probably explains the whole phrase 'oppressed with anger', rather than 'anger' alone.

42 **on the flocks:** emphatic by position (as opposed to men).

with this onslaught: an internal or adverbial accusative, lit. 'as to this going'; cf. *Tr.* 339, and see H. Lloyd-Jones, *SIFC* 87 (1994) 140–2. There is no significance in the repetition of βάσιν from 8 and 19; see 38n.

43 **with your:** answering 'on the flocks' at 42.

staining his hand: it is impossible to tell whether the jingle of sounds in χεῖρα χραίνεσθαι is a conscious effect.

45 **accomplished it:** for the middle (Dain, Kamerbeek) cf. *OT* 287. But the active ἐξέπραξεν, the reading of most MSS, is commoner in tragedy, and is preferred here by Pearson and Dawe (see also Fraenkel 4).

46 Lit. 'with what kinds of darings these', referring to the deeds of daring that he planned (44). For the plural cf. 1392. For the combination of 'what kind' with 'these' cf. *Phil.* 1204.

47 The darkness is appropriate to the stealth with which Ajax set out. For his solitariness see 29n. It is paradoxical that to recover his honour Ajax has had to act stealthily and in the dark, adopting the methods usually associated with his enemy Odysseus (as in Hom.

Il. 10). But Segal (1981) 124 goes too far in describing this line as setting forth 'the total negation of heroism as Ajax has understood it in the past' (see also Bowie 114, Bradshaw 117).

50 Then how: πῶς, as often, introduces a surprised question.

eager for blood: an ancient reading διψῶσαν, 'thirsty' (cf. fr. adesp. 96, Lycophr. 1171), gives equally good sense, but it looks like an editorial explanation of μαιμῶσυν. For H's μαργῆσαν cf. Eur. *Hec.* 1128, *HF* 1005. The genitive φόνου ('blood') could go equally well with 'stayed' (from bloodshed; cf. Eur. *HF* 1005), and is perhaps intended to be taken with both.

51-2 With this punctuation the joy is that which Ajax would have had in killing his enemies. With no comma after βαλοῦσα others render, 'casting on his eyes the grievous fancies of incurable joy', the joy now being that which he experiences in his present madness. But the definite article with 'joy' indicates that it refers to that which has already been mentioned at 50; see Winnington-Ingram, *BICS* 26 (1979) 1–2.

grievous imaginations: despite LSJ s.v. γνώμη III b 4, it is only the context, not the meaning of the word itself, that shows that these convictions or opinions were false. They are 'grievous', lit. 'hard to bear', because of their consequences. Alternatively the adjective is active in force (so Kamerbeek, *Mnem.* 3 (1950) 16–17, Coray 261), 'misleading', the opposite of ἐπίφορος at Aesch. *Cho.* 813.

incurable joy: this is almost an oxymoron. The adjective naturally accompanies such nouns as 'pain' (Hom. *Il.* 5.394) or 'anger' (*Il.* 15.217). Here Ajax' joy is itself thought of as a disease which would have been incurable. LSJ lose this by giving a dubious active sense, 'damaging beyond remedy, pernicious'.

53-4 Here (contrast 27n., 42) the cattle are evidently distinguished from the 'flocks' of sheep. The cattle have not yet been divided up among the victors (for this process cf. Hom. *Il.* 1.124–5). So Ajax has tried to attack the Greeks indiscriminately, not just the sons of Atreus; see V.J. Rosivach, *CW* 69 (1975) 201–2. 'Mixed' probably means the same as 'undivided'. Kamerbeek supposes rather that it means that there are various kinds of cattle, not just oxen.

booty...guarded: lit. 'the watching over of the herdsmen [subjective genitive] consisting in the booty [defining genitive]'. For this highly ornate periphrasis, 'one in a series of elevated expressions' (cf. 55, 64), see Long 96–7.

55-6 and slaughtered...spines: a highly compressed phrase, lit. 'and hewed the many horned bloodshed...', i.e. 'he was causing bloodshed by hewing many horned cattle'. The presence of the epithet 'many horned' ('many beasts with horns', not 'beasts with many horns'), makes the phrase even more difficult than ἕλκος τυφλωθέν at *Ant.* 972–3, where 'a blinded wound' means 'a wound inflicted by blinding'; cf. also Eur. *Supp.* 1205. With 'all around him' we picture Ajax standing in the middle of the carnage laying about him.

cutting through their spines: cf. 299. The same verb is applied at Aesch. *Pers.* 426 to the killing of the Persians at Salamis. From 55–7 the alliteration of κ and χ echoes the harshness of what is being described.

56-8 and he thought at times: ἔσθ' ὅτε is answered by ὅτ' ἄλλοτ(ε), 'at other times', (sc. ἔστι δέ) at 58. The infinitive κτείνειν has to be understood with this clause too. Broadhead's ἐμπίτνειν (-εῖν Kayser; two MSS have ἐμπίπτειν), infinitive, produces easier sense, but the compound usually governs a dative. The μέν after κἀδόκει is probably not misplaced (Jebb), for ἔστι μὲν ὅτε, but rather it introduces an implied antithesis between what Ajax thought and the reality of the situation (see Denniston 382). In fact it is he himself who is in the power of Athena.

the two sons of Atreus: Σ observes that the treatment of Odysseus is reserved for later.

with his own hand: the word can mean also 'suicide' ('killing oneself') or 'murderer'.

59   **with attacks of madness:** the phrase may go with either 'urged on' or 'in his frenzied movement'.

60   **and threw:** in the Greek the two verbs, 'I urged, I threw', are juxtaposed without a conjunction. The asyndeton creates an effect of vehemence and rapidity; cf. *El.* 719, Aesch. *Pers.* 426, *Cho.* 289.

into evil hunting-nets: Ajax, who set out to hunt his enemies, has now himself fallen into the hunters' nets; see 1–3n.

61   **this killing:** φόνου is preferable to πόνου ('labour') in that it picks up 50, 55 and rounds off the description of the killing before we move on to the torture of the still living animals; see Ferrari 22–3.

62   **the surviving cattle:** lit. 'the living ones of the cattle' (partitive genitive).

64   The language picks up 55–7, where Ajax' delusion was introduced in the context of the killing. Here it refers to the torture. 'Fair-horned prey' is more than a circumlocution for 'animals'. ἄγραν, 'prey', is a technical hunting term, and the epithet defines the nature of this particular prey. Ajax' metaphorical hunting of his human enemies has turned into a literal hunting of domestic animals, as a result of which he is now the victim of the hunt.

66–7   **to you too:** Athena proposes to share the spectacle with Odysseus.

in full view: 'so that it is clear' (cf. 81, 229), the adjective used proleptically. Odysseus is then to report it to the rest of the army, so that the whole world will know what Ajax has done. His shame arises not from his attempted attack on his enemies, nor even from his madness, but from his failure to take vengeance, from his display of heroism against helpless animals, and from the knowledge that everyone is laughing at his failure; see Intro. 12.

68–9   **do not expect any mishap:** or perhaps (Renehan 341–2) 'do not take it [the waiting] to be a misfortune'. With this punctuation the phrase is in parenthesis. The postponement of 'the man', the object of 'wait for', is awkward, and we cannot rule out the removal of the comma after δέχου, taking συμφοράν as predicative, 'do not expect the (coming of the) man as a calamity', with the verb used in both a literal and an intellectual sense (see A.A. Long, *MH* 21 (1964) 228–31). For a man described as a συμφορά cf. Aeschines *Ctes.* 253, also Dinarchus 1.65. But the expression here would be rather odd. For a satisfactory defence of 68–70 against their deletion, as inconsistent with 83–5, by E. Reichard and by Fraenkel (1977) 5, *Kleine Beiträge* (Rome 1964) I 409–13, see Long, Dawe 127–8, Ferrari 23–4.

69–70 **I shall turn away...and prevent:** lit. 'I shall prevent the beams turned away [proleptic]...'.

the beams of his eyes: the same expression is used at Eur. *HF* 132 (cf. *Phoen.* 1564). At *Andr.* 1180, *Rhes.* 737 αὐγαί by itself means 'eyes'.

from seeing: a simple infinitive, as regularly after κωλύω, 'I prevent'. With other verbs of preventing μή usually precedes the infinitive, but cf. *OT.* 129, etc.

your face: or perhaps 'your looking at him' (see Long 68–9 n. 230).

71 **you there:** a colloquial and peremptory use of the nominative of the pronoun, which occurs 46 times in Aristophanes, but rarely in tragedy (seven times in Sophocles; cf. 89, 1047); see P.T. Stevens, *CQ* 39 (1945) 102.

72 **pulling back:** lit. 'straightening out', i.e. to be tied so that the torture can begin. ἀποστρέφω, 'twist back', is similarly used at *OT* 1154, Hom. *Od*. 22.172, 190. It is presumably the front legs of the animals that Ajax mistakes for his enemies' arms.

74-90 The stichomythia keeps us in suspense as we wait for Ajax to emerge from his hut. Odysseus' reluctance to see his enemy mad stems at this stage from simple fear. It is not that we are to think of him as a coward. Rather, his fear is a measure of Ajax' greatness. So mighty a warrior is he that even Odysseus is afraid. Already Sophocles suggests that the judgement of the arms was unfair (see Perrotta 75–6): Ajax is the greater hero.

75 'The first question with οὐ equals an order, the second adds a further negative μή to οὐ and this produces a prohibition instead of an order' (Moorhouse 338); cf. *OT* 637–8, *Tr.* 1183. To 'incur cowardice' means to incur a reputation for it; cf. *Ant*. 924, Eur. *IT* 676. ἀρῇ is 2nd person future indicative of ἄρνυμαι. Most MSS have ἀρεῖς or ἄρῃς, from ἀείρω, but the initial α in that verb is long, which is impossible here.

76 **Please no:** strictly speaking, an imperative has to be understood.
be content...that he: Greek often prefers the personal construction, 'let him be enough...staying'; cf. *Ant*. 547, and see 326n.

77 **In case what may happen:** a fear or purpose clause governed by the verb of 76; cf. Eur. *Supp*. 544.
Was he not a man before: 'man' probably implies 'hero' (see March 12, and cf. 1238, *OC* 393, and the antithesis between ἄνδρες and ἄνθρωποι at Hdt. 7.210.2). Ajax was already a hero before his madness, so he is no more fearsome now that he is mad. The word is used some 80 times in the play, far more often than in any other Sophoclean tragedy (next is *OT* with some 60 occurrences), and nearly half of the occurrences refer to Ajax himself. The question of what it means to call Ajax a 'man' will become increasingly important (see 1236n.). Others, less well, understand 'man' as opposed to god: Ajax was only a man before, and he is certainly not a god now. Dawe and Lloyd-Jones and Wilson, after Brunck, place dots or a dash at the end of the line: Odysseus interrupts and completes Athena's sentence for her. But with this kind of aposiopesis in stichomythia the first speaker usually gives a clearer indication of how the sentence is to continue.

78 Odysseus refers to himself as 'this man' (cf. *Ant*. 1034, *Phil*. 1036), the repetition of the word marking the importance of the relationship between the two 'men'.

79 For οὔκουν (all the MSS have οὐκοῦν) 'in questions, usually at the opening of an answer', and especially in drama, see Denniston 431–2. Athena's question is in keeping with the code of helping friends and harming enemies (see Intro. 11). Any Greek would welcome the chance to triumph over the latter. Conversely, the Sophoclean hero fears more than anything else the laughter of his enemies (see Knox (1964) 30–1). To him it is a form of *hybris*; cf. 153, 198, 367, *Ant*. 482–3, and see Blundell 62. Athena is therefore in effect inviting Odysseus to commit *hybris* against Ajax (quite untenable is the view of Jebb and others that the goddess is merely testing her favourite and does not really want him to laugh). This is less surprising behaviour for a goddess when we remember that divine and human standards are the same. Athena merely accepts without question the traditional ethical code. Much more startling is Odysseus' rejection of the opportunity to laugh at his enemy. Already the values of the human being are beginning to seem more enlightened than those of the goddess. But the point concerns, not so much the conduct of the goddess, as her view of how the human Odysseus should conduct himself.

80   Odysseus repeats the thought of 76, but this time ἀρκεῖ is impersonal, 'it is enough for me'. The μέν after 'for me' marks an implied antithesis with others who might feel differently.

81   **in full view:** cf. 66.

82   **kept out of his way or shrunk from him:** lit. 'stood out of his way with shrinking'. The intransitive verb (for which cf. 672) rarely governs a direct object, but cf. Dem. 18.319, 20.10.

83   οὐ μή + aorist subjunctive expresses a strong negative future statement.

84   That is, 'if he has not lost his sight'. γε emphasises ὀφθαλμοῖς: he may be mad, but at least he can still see.

85   Ajax will not actually be blinded. He will merely be unable to see Odysseus.

86   **Well:** μέντἄν = μέντοι ἄν by crasis.

87   **Be quiet then, stand there:** lit. 'be quiet standing'.
     just as you are: lit. 'as you happen being'.

88   **I'll stay:** lit. 'I would stay'. For ἄν + first person optative expressing an intention see W.K. Pritchett, *AJPh* 76 (1955) 13–15, Moorhouse 230. Here, though not always, it seems to convey a sense of reluctance ('I must stay'); cf. *Ant.* 1108.
     I could have wished: as at *Phil.* 427, 1239, 1278, an unfulfilled potential for past time, unfulfilled because the circumstances are now such as to make pointless the expression of the wish; see Goodwin § 245.
     to be safely out of the way: lit. 'to happen being outside', with ὢν τυχεῖν being much the same as κυρεῖς ἔχων at 87. With 'outside' we have to understand 'trouble' or the like (cf. *Phil.* 504). At this point Odysseus probably withdraws to the end of the stage, where he is invisible to Ajax.

89   Cf. 71. Athena returns to her purpose before the stichomythia interrupted it.

90   **your ally:** Athena may have stood beside Ajax in the night claiming to be helping him (Fraenkel 6), but we know (despite Adams 97–8, for whom she really is the ally of Ajax, and has proved it by diverting his sword from his enemies), that she is really the ally of Odysseus, not Ajax. This deceitful word provides the cue for the entry of the deluded hero, and it foreshadows 774–5 where we learn that Ajax angered Athena by rejecting her alliance.

91-117   The exchange between Ajax and Athena takes the form of a stichomythia, for the most part single-line, but introduced by three lines from Ajax and two from Athena, and ending with three couplets. Until 109 Athena asks eager questions for Ajax to answer, giving the impression that he is the dominant partner. In this delusion he is confirmed when he returns inside his hut at 117 having had the last word in the dialogue.

91-2   The language is strikingly similar to that with which Odysseus greeted Athena at 14–15. Each man believes that he is the favourite of the goddess, but we know that one is deluded. Poe 29 may be right to find subtle condescension in 'how well...my side', but there is no such tone at Hom. *Il.*10.278–9, where Odysseus thanks Athena because she has always stood by his side in all his troubles.
     daughter of Zeus: Athena was born fully armed from the head of Zeus.

92-3 I shall honour you: for this metaphorical sense of στέφω cf. *Ant.* 431, *El.* 53, 441, 458, Σ *OT* 3. But here the word may refer more literally to the 'wreathing' of Athena's statue.

with golden spoils: i.e. with offerings made from the proceeds of the spoils.

in gratitude for this hunt: the tragic irony is clear. Ajax envisages a metaphorical hunt of human beings. He does not know that it has turned into a literal hunt of animals, or that Athena derives her honour from the fact that he is the victim in her and Odysseus' hunt (see Jouanna 185).

95   did you dye your sword: less well 'did you dip', with which we would expect πρός + accusative rather than dative. For the verb in this context cf. [Aesch.] *PV* 863, Eur. *Ph.* 1578, and, rather differently, Aesch. *Cho.* 1011. ἔγχος, properly a spear, is often extended in poetry to weapons in general, and esp. to a sword; cf. 287. For Ajax' sword see 10n.

96   I can freely boast of it: lit. 'boasting is possible', =κομπεῖν πάρεστι. Almost the first word we hear from Ajax is a boast.

I don't deny that I did it: for the polarisation of expression see 20n. The last four words occur in the same position at *Ant.* 443. With τὸ μή sc. βάψαι, 'to have dyed it'.

97   Did you really: see 38n. **turn your armed hand:** a difficult expression. ᾔχμασας is aorist indicative of αἰχμάζω, which, being derived from αἰχμή, the point of a spear and hence the spear itself, means 'act the warrior' at Aesch. *Pers.* 756 (cf. Soph. *Tr.* 355). Here it seems to mean 'arm your hand with a sword'. But the word may be corrupt. Reiske proposed ᾔμαξας, 'made bloody' (cf. 40n., Σ 97a), but the corruption into the rarer word would be strange.

98   From the very beginning it is of his honour that Ajax is most conscious. But again he is deluded. Before long we shall see the sons of Atreus making every effort to dishonour him. Whether they will succeed is the main issue in the second part of the play.

99   I understand your word: the instantaneous aorist, according to the usual explanation, refers to the moment ago when Ajax spoke the word; cf. 536, 693, *El.* 1479, Aesch. *Cho.* 887. For Moorhouse 195 it arises rather 'from the punctual aspect' of the aorist, with no reference to past time. 'Word' has to be supplied with 'your' from the context.

100   now: emphatic. Ajax enjoys a bitter and sarcastic taunt.

my arms: i.e. the armour of Achilles, which, as Σ remarks, Ajax considers to be his own.

101   well then: for this colloquial formula of transition see P.T. Stevens, *CQ* 39 (1945) 102. Athena moves the conversation from the supposedly dead Atreidae to the still living Odysseus. For this progressive use of γάρ, when a speaker 'having been satisfied on one subject, wishes to learn something further', see Denniston 81–5, and cf. 983.

102   Lit. 'where of fortune does he stand for you?', with τύχης a partitive genitive (cf. 314, 386), and σοι an ethic dative (see 39n.).

103   Ajax' first reaction to the name of his enemy is entirely predictable. κίναδος is said by Σ Theocr. 5.25 (cf. *Etym. Magn.* 514.13) to be a Sicilian word for a fox. Attic writers use it only of men. The Greeks shared our modern idea of the fox's cunning; cf. Pind. *Py.* 2.77, *Isth.* 4.47, Ar. *Clouds* 448 (with Σ), *Birds* 430. Ajax' abuse is appropriate to the traditional picture of the clever Odysseus, especially as we see him in those plays (*Phil.*, Eur. *Hec.*) in which that cleverness is presented as a vice. It is ironical that it will turn out in this play to be *in*appropriate. That Ajax chooses a neuter word for fox perhaps

adds to the insult. τοὐπίτριπτον (i.e. τὸ ἐπίτριπτον) occurs only here in tragedy, but it is an epithet of κίναδος also at Andoc. 1.99 (cf. Ar. *Clouds* 447 περίτριμμα, immediately before κίναδος at 448). It comes from ἐπιτρίβω, and means probably 'ground down', 'smooth', i.e. 'practised in villainy'. Ajax will indulge in similar abuse at 381. The whole expression, emphatic at the beginning of the sentence, is the object of ἐξήρου, which governs also the indirect question 'where <he is>'; cf. οἶδά σε ὅστις εἶ, 'I know who you are'. This is not quite what Athena asked. Ajax takes her question more literally, and Athena lets his misunderstanding pass.

104 I am <asking you>: i.e. 'yes'. The noun ἐνστάτην, 'one who stands in the way', is found only here and at Ael. frr. 23, 248, the corresponding verb at Thuc. 3.23.1, 8.69.2.

105-6 mistress: another parallel with the exchange between Odysseus and Athena (38n.).
  most welcome: the same word as that translated 'sweetest' at 79. It is Ajax, not Odysseus, who shares the values there expounded by Athena. For the jingles δέσποινα and δεσμώτης, θακεῖ and θανεῖν see 43n. Perhaps (Stanford) the alliteration can be spoken with fierce relish, but one may suspect word play for its own sake. The dramatic irony is obvious: while Ajax says that Odysseus is sitting inside, the audience can see him standing at the end of the stage.

107-10 Athena's temporal clause depends on 'I do not want him to die' in 106, while Ajax picks up the same words at 108, but is interrupted by Athena before he can complete the sentence. It is usually said that the exigencies of strict stichomythia make this kind of interruption necessary. But at 105–6 Sophocles gives two lines to a single speaker. Finally at 110, when Ajax resumes his sentence, 'I do not want him to die...until he dies' is illogical, but not excessively so: the emphasis is on the preceding participial phrase, so that the sense is 'until he is whipped (before he dies)'; see Moorhouse 254, 298–9.

108 pillar of my house: ἑρκείου is the adjective from τὸ ἕρκος, the enclosure of the courtyard of a Homeric house, and hence the 'courtyard' itself. Zeus is called ἑρκεῖος 'patron of the household', because he has his altar in the courtyard. So here the phrase means simply 'domestic building'. As Lloyd-Jones and Wilson remark, the sense 'roof' for στέγη is not certainly attested for tragedy. Again (see 3–4n.) Sophocles envisages a house rather than a tent or hut.

111 Pray do not...: Denniston 276 shows that μὴ δῆτα is often used in a passionate negative command or wish. But here Athena is only pretending. The almost mechanical repetition of the language of 109 suggests the casual way in which she plays with Ajax.

112 Ajax somewhat arrogantly presumes to give orders to Athena. 'I bid to fare well' is often an idiomatic way of saying 'I dismiss from my mind'. But here Ajax means simply that he is prepared to let Athena 'fare well', i.e. have her own way, in everything else, except in the punishment of Odysseus, the only thing that matters to him. The accusative and infinitive after ἐφίεμαι = 'command' has, however, been suspected by some scholars: σ' cannot be taken as elided σοι (see 190–1n.).

113 this, and no other: for the polarisation cf. the similar 20 (n.), *OC* 908.

114 Very well then: δ' οὖν 'is often used in the dialogue of drama...to denote that the speaker waives any objection that he has, or might be supposed to have, to something being done, or contemplated, by another person...The tone is usually defiant or contemptuous' (Denniston 466); cf. 961.
  since it...like this: the noun τέρψις behaves like a predicative adjective, 'pleasing' (see Long 74), and 'this' is attracted from the neuter into the case of the noun. However,

the epexegetic articular infinitive τὸ δρᾶν, 'namely to do it', is awkward, and the text has been suspected.

115 take action: lit.' 'use your hand' (cf. 1384n., Hdt. 9.72.2). For the jingle χρῶ χειρί (also χωρῶ 116) see 105–6n.

spare none of the things you plan: ὧνπερ = ἐκείνων ἅ. Euripides uses a very similar turn of phrase at *Med.* 401.

116-17 I am off to work: whether sane or mad Ajax is the man of action.

but this I bid you: the same verb as at 112. δέ is postponed for purely metrical reasons.

an ally: σύμμαχον picks up 90, while παρεστάναι, 'stand beside me', echoes παρέστης 92. Thus the whole encounter between Ajax and Athena, and the presentation of his madness, is framed by his delusion that the goddess is his ally. These are his last words in the scene. **of this kind** marks the tragic irony. Athena will always be 'this kind' of ally to Ajax, i.e. not an ally at all.

118-20 Athena's initial comment to Odysseus has nothing to do with Ajax' immorality or wickedness. It may seem surprising that she praises him for his good qualities, incidentally revealing to us that Ajax is not just physically strong; he can think too, at least in a practical way (see Intro. 1). But Athena's concern is not really to praise her enemy. She is thinking in conventional tragic terms (cf. Arist. *Poet.* ch. 13) of the prosperous man who falls. Her concern is not with morality, but with the power of the gods, who are strong enough to destroy even such a man as Ajax.

Do you see...of the gods: for the structure of the sentence see 103n.

with greater prudence: a rare adjective, which occurs in the positive at Aesch. *Supp.* 969, Hdt. 3.36.1.

than this man: whatever we may make of 77 (n.), here there does seem to be a contrast with 'gods' in the previous line.

what had to be done: lit. 'the timely things'; cf. 34, 38.

121-6 Odysseus takes seriously Athena's insincere, or at least grudging, praise of Ajax, and in effect once more declines to share her triumph over his enemy. But at 74–90 Odysseus' reluctance was due largely to his fear of Ajax. Here he shows a more enlightened and attractive understanding that Ajax is a human being like himself, and so he pities him out of common humanity. Athena's opponent Ajax shares her values (105–6n.), while her favourite Odysseus rejects them and identifies himself with the goddess' human victim even though he is his enemy.

121 I know: μέν after ἐγώ ('I') implies the antithesis, 'whatever may be the case with other people'.

122 in his wretchedness...my enemy: the line is framed by the two compound adjectives, each beginning with δυσ-. The first has already been used by Athena of Odysseus, as she played maliciously with Ajax (109, 111). Odysseus' application of it in all seriousness to Ajax looks almost like a tacit rebuke of the goddess.

123 For the yoking metaphor cf. 24n., and for its use in this context see Padel 129. The double compound is found only here before Plutarch. The idea is perhaps that Ajax and delusion are like two horses or oxen yoked together in a chariot or carriage so as to be inseparable. But Barrett (on Eur. *Hipp.* 1389–90) may be right that in such συν-compounds of ζεύγνυμι the "yoke" metaphor...has ceased to be felt exactly, so that ζεύγνυμι has become merely "fasten inescapably" and συζεύγνυμι merely a strengthened form of that'. ἄτη, a characteristic tragic word, often means 'ruin', but 'delusion' is more appropriate to the present context, in which it is this delusion that will lead to Ajax' ruin.

124 The formulation of this idea may seem selfish, but what is remarkable is that it is in an enemy that Odysseus can see himself; see also 1365–7n., and cf. *OC* 567–8, ἔξοιδ' ἀνὴρ ὢν χὤτι τῆς εἰς αὔριον | οὐδὲν πλέον μοι σοῦ μέτεστιν ἡμέρας, 'I know that I am a man, and that I have no greater share than you in tomorrow'. At Hdt. 1.86.6 Cyrus similarly recognises a common humanity with his enemy Croesus.

125-6 The thought is not original (for parallel passages see Heath 158 n.74), but it is beautifully expressed. For the language cf. esp. *Phil.* 946, fr. 659.6, Pind. *Py.* 8.95-6, fr. 131b 2 αἰῶνος εἴδωλον, Aesch. *Ag.* 839 εἴδωλον σκιᾶς, fr. 399, Com. adesp. fr. 692 K.

127-33 Athena's closing lines have all too often been interpreted as containing the moral of the play: *hybris* leads to a fall (see Intro. 12-14). In fact she does not use the word *hybris*, and nowhere in the play does it describe Ajax' attitude to the gods. Athena warns Odysseus in conventional terms against using overweening language to the gods, and against arrogant behaviour in general, and she declares that the gods love those who are σώφρων, 'sound-minded'. It is true that ὑπέρκοπος and ὑπέρκομπος are frequently associated with *hybris* (e.g. Aesch. *Pers.* 827, *Ag.* 468), and that σωφροσύνη is often thought of as its opposite (Fisher 111-13, 245). Moreover, the speaking of boastful words is certainly characteristic of Ajax as we have just seen him (96n.), and he is clearly anything but σώφρων. The idea that an excess of power or wealth (130) may lead to *hybris* is a very common one (Fisher 102-4, 213, 276). Nevertheless, for various reasons, we should beware of accepting Athena's interpretation without question (for doubts about the moral see Whitman 69–70, Rosenmeyer 172–3, Goldhill 194, 'Athene's statement is emphatically expressed in the very terms which the play puts in doubt'). (1) The quality for which Athena condemns Ajax is the one that Sophocles intends us to admire in him (see Kirkwood 32). The Sophoclean hero is never σώφρων, but excessive in everything that he/she does. It is the ordinary, little people who advocate σωφροσύνη, like the unattractive Menelaus at 1071–86, and we may well feel dissatisfied with an interpretation of the play that puts Athena and Menelaus together as representatives of Sophoclean wisdom. (2) At 79 we have heard Athena inviting Odysseus to commit what is in effect *hybris* (see also 955–60n.), and it seems only a short step to the four Euripidean passages in which a god is said to commit *hybris* against a mortal (*Hipp.* 446, *Ion* 506, *Ba.* 9, 616; see Fisher 413–14, 447). It ill becomes Athena now to state piously that it is the σώφρονες whom the gods love. By σωφροσύνη she seems to mean little more than submission to her power (cf. 1071 and see Blundell 88 n.144). Odysseus has already displayed σωφροσύνη, but (despite Jebb xli, Fisher 324), it is not what Athena means by it, and she shows no understanding of his attitude. (3) Her words leave undefined the nature of Ajax' offence against her. Vague talk of arrogant words and behaviour does not explain why her anger against him has erupted on this particular occasion, and the conventional reference to riches is no more applicable to him (or to Odysseus) than to any other Homeric character (for a different view see Tyler 29 n.17). Nowhere in the play are we told that she was angry because he wanted to attack his enemies; see Intro. 11. Her last word is κακούς, but how this applies to Ajax is left unclear (see 132–3n.). (4) Athena's words are not even self-consistent. The 'moral' that the gods love the good and punish the evil is undercut by 131–2, where we learn that *all* human life is subject to falling and rising. This theory of inevitable alternation, for

good and bad alike, is quite different from the untragic (and untrue) view that good
people enjoy unbroken prosperity, and only the wicked suffer.

129 nor be puffed up with self-importance: lit. 'nor take upon yourself any bulk', where
ἄρῃ (aorist subjunctive middle of αἴρω, from ἠράμην; contrast 75) suits both the literal
sense of ὄγκος and its metaphorical idea of self-exaltation.

130 the depth of your great wealth: lit. 'long' wealth, which combines a little awkwardly
with 'depth'. But μακρός can be used to indicate any dimension of size. Pindar applies
it to prosperity at *Py.* 2.26. For 'depth of wealth' cf. Pind. *Ol.* 13.62, and the adjective
βαθύπλουτος.

131-2 This notion of alternation, expressed here in the language of weighing in the scales (cf.
Hom. *Il.* 19.223), that all human life is subject to changes of fortune, is widespread in
Greek thought; cf. 125–6, *Ant.* 1158–60, *Tr.* 131–5, fr. 576, 646, Archil. fr. 130,
Theogn. 441, Mimn. 2.15–16, Sol. fr.14, Simon. 16, 18 *PMG*, Eur. *Ion* 969. The idea
can be traced back to Hom. *Il.* 24.527ff., where Achilles explains to Priam that there are
two jars on Zeus' floor, from which he dispenses his gifts to men, one full of good
things, the other of bad. Some receive entirely evil gifts, no one entirely good. The most
for which one can hope is an alternation between good and evil. Suffering is thus a
necessary part of the human condition, and the gods alone are spared it. Here Sophocles
is less pessimistic than Homer, in that no one is said to suffer uninterrupted misery.
And, just as one day can bring a man down, so it can restore. The alternation from
misery to happiness is of less concern to tragedy, but theoretically it is possible (cf.
Theogn. 355ff., Pind. *Ol.* 2.15ff.), and this notion (despite K. Reinhardt, *Hermes* 78
(1943) 111–12, for whom the first part of the antithesis is expanded by the statement of
its opposite, but only the former is important) will become important later in the play.
The stress on 'a day' (i.e. one day) is obviously relevant to the tragedy of a man who
falls so quickly (cf. *OT* 438, *El.* 1149, Aesch. *Pers.* 431), but Sophocles hints also that
that his fortunes could equally quickly be restored, if only he were a different kind of
man. At the end of the play Ajax will in fact be restored to honour through his burial
(see March 22–4).

132-3 The chiastic arrangement puts 'the sound-minded' emphatically at the beginning of the
sentence, and 'the wicked' at the end. Neither word is easy to translate. σωφροσύνη can
mean self-control, discipline, temperance, prudence, modesty, chastity. In fifth-century
Athens it was appropriated as a political virtue by the oligarchs. In antithesis with
σώφρονας Athena appears to give a moral sense to κακούς (see Heath 169 n. 8; Adkins
172 describes this as 'a remarkable change of linguistic usage'). But the audience has
been given no reason to accept Athena's evaluation, and the word may still suggest the
old Homeric distinction between the ἀγαθοί or ἐσθλοί, not the good in a moral sense, but
the heroes, and on the other hand the κακοί, those who are of lower birth and status,
cowardly, of no account. So it is the status of Ajax as a hero that is called into question.
And the end of the play will show us that Athena is in fact wrong if she means to deny
him that status here. The question leads naturally into the parodos of the chorus.

134-200: Parodos
The parodos, or entrance-song, is divided into two sections: (1) 134–71, declaimed in
recitative anapaests, probably by the whole chorus of fifteen, not by its leader alone, as it
marches up the side-passage into the orchestra; (2) 172–200, fully sung in lyric metres by the

chorus now in position in the orchestra. For this kind of two-fold parodos cf. Aesch. *Pers.*, *Supp.*, *Ag.*, but only here is it found in Sophocles; see H.W. Schmidt, in Jens 11–12. The chorus consists of Ajax' loyal followers, the crew of his ship (cf. 565) and his fellow-soldiers, as is indicated by the theme of the anapaests, though only at 201 is their role specifically indicated. In the prologue we saw Ajax in the presence of his enemies, but now we see him through the eyes of his friends. The chorus speculates about the rumour that has already reached it, that Ajax has attacked the animals. As in the prologue Odysseus had heard a rumour which was then confirmed by Athena, so here for the chorus it will shortly be confirmed by Tecmessa. In (1) it is reluctant to believe the rumour, attributing it to the malice of Odysseus, but in (2) it seems more ready to accept its truth, and speculates as to which god made Ajax do what he would never have done on his own initiative. We know its guesses to be wrong, but they still contain enough truth to be interesting (the parodos of Eur. *Hipp.* is very similar, and in both plays the chorus addresses the offstage character; see Schmidt, in Jens 13, 40–1).

The principal unifying factor of the composition as a whole is the chorus's concentration on the greatness of Ajax and his heroic status. It was this that Athena called into question at the end of the prologue. The chorus makes us see a very different figure. It is no accident that four times (154, 158, 160–1, 169) it describes him, either directly or by implication, as μέγας, 'great' (Winnington-Ingram 22 n.35 notes that the word occurs 36 times in the play, far more often than in any other play of Sophocles, 13 times between 139 and 241). The many epic words reinforce the impression of Ajax as a Homeric hero. The two bird-similes which frame (1) set Ajax apart in isolation both from the ordinary people who support him and from his enemies. But, since the rumour if true must mean a loss of honour for Ajax, the most important thing in a hero's life, the chorus is naturally worried. The idea appears already in (1), at 137–8, 142–3, but becomes a dominant theme in (2), at 173–4, 186, 191. The disgrace of Ajax is marked by the triumph and laughter of his enemies, which they vividly picture in both (1) and (2), at 151–3 and 196–9. It is here in the parodos that the word *hybris* makes its first and second appearances, applied not to Ajax but to his enemies. Already it is becoming apparent that the play will have no simple moral. The chorus's suspicions about the *hybris* of the Atreidae will be fully justified, but with Odysseus the case is more complicated. It is doubtless true that he has helped to spread the rumour (148–51, 189), but we have already seen him (79n.) declining to commit the kind of *hybris* here envisaged by the chorus.

Finally in the epode the chorus calls on Ajax to stir himself from his inactivity, and to come out of his hut, not as Athena did to mock him, but to dispel the rumour. The audience expects his entry, but Sophocles will surprise us by bringing out Tecmessa instead.

The lyric part of the parodos consists of a metrically responding strophe and antistrophe, in largely dactylo-epitrite metre, which is appropriate to a song about a hero (Scott 72), followed by a non-responding epode in Aeolic metre.

134-5 Son of Telamon: this Homeric patronymic adjective is regularly found at line-end in the formula Τελαμώνιος Αἴας. From the very beginning of the parodos Ajax is presented to us as the traditional hero. At 462–6 he will be ashamed to face Telamon, as having brought disgrace upon his father (see Davidson (1975) 175 n. 10). Some scholars believe that the adjective originally described Ajax as the possessor of the famous 'shield-strap' (τελαμών), and only later came to be the patronymic, with Telamon himself owing his existence to his son's formulaic epithet; see M. Sulzberger, *REG* 39

(1926) 414, W. Whallon, *YClS* 19 (1966) 27–8. For the apostrophizing of an offstage character in a choral ode see Taplin (1977) 281. It serves to build up the tension as we wait for Ajax' reappearance.

sea-girt...beside the sea: the two Homeric epithets are not very different in sense. The latter is used of islands at *Hy. Apollo* 32, Aesch. *Pers* 886, of Salamis at *A.P.* 9.288. Most MSS make both adjectives agree with Salamis, but they are better divided between the two nouns. The Greek says literally, 'having the near the sea base consisting of sea-girt Salamis'. For the language cf. 859–60. The chorus rouses our sympathy for Ajax by picturing him in peace-time in his island home. So Homer often contrasts the home-life of a warrior with his death in battle.

136-8 The theme of alternating fortunes picks up 131–2 (n.).

when you prosper I rejoice over it: the anaphora of σὲ μέν...σὲ δ(έ) serves to bring out the chorus's preoccupation with Ajax. We might expect a dative after ἐπιχαίρω, but for an accusative 'used with a supplementary participle to indicate the source of feeling' (Moorhouse 36) cf. *Phil.* 1314 and see Barrett on Eur. *Hipp.* 1338–41.

whenever introduces an indefinite generalisation which leads to the specific case at 141 ('so now too'). Apparently Ajax has been in trouble before; see A.G Laird, *CQ* 16 (1922) 43–4 (against the attempt of A.C. Pearson, *AJPh* 33 (1912) 427–8, to take ὅταν as causal, 'so now that').

the stroke...the Danaans: misfortunes may be attributed to the gods or to human malevolence, or to both at the same time. So the chorus will veer between blaming a god and his enemies for Ajax' troubles. For the stroke of Zeus, an idea probably suggested by his thunderbolt or lightning conceived as a whip, see Janko on Hom. *Il.* 13.812–16, and cf. 279 below, fr. 961, Aesch. *Ag.* 367. ζαμενής, 'violent', is first found at *Hy. Herm.* 307, but occurs only here in tragedy.

slanderously: a predicative adjective, 'speaking ill', the verbal element of which is the same word as at 67, where Athena invited Odysseus to spread just such a slander.

140 like the eye of a winged dove: a shorthand way of saying 'like a winged dove with fear showing in its eyes'. As early as Homer the dove is the symbol of a frightened creature (*Il.* 21.493, 22.139–42; cf. Aesch. *Sept.* 294, *Supp.* 223–6, Eur. *Andr.* 1140). The chorus sympathises with Ajax but does not have his heroic temperament. The winged dove and the chorus's fear are bound together by the alliteration of π.

141 in the course...past: genitive of time within which. Kamerbeek follows Jebb in taking the phrase with 'you have gone over etc.', on the grounds that the rumours began only at midnight. But the timing is hardly as precise as this; see 148n.

142-3 The dove-simile probably continues, with the clamour of the rumour being thought of as the noise that frightens the doves.

assails us: lit. 'takes possession of us'. **to our discredit:** if Ajax is to lose his reputation (κλέος), the chorus as his followers must do so too. But its concern for its own reputation is important only in that it points to his much greater loss.

143-4 that you have gone over: accusative and infinitive of indirect statement after 'great clamour assails us'.

which abounds in horses: the ornamental adjective, which occurs only here, must derive from ἵππος and μαίνομαι, 'mad with horses'; see Pearson on fr. 652 καρπομανής. For the incongruous combination of ideas Σ and *Suda* l 571 record various implausible explanations, e.g. that the adjective goes with 'you' (Ajax). But 'where horses run wild' is not impossible, and is accepted by Campbell and Stanford.

145 cattle and booty: a hendiadys, more logically 'the cattle that formed the booty'. Less probably the 'booty' refers to the sheep (so Stanford; cf. 53–4).

146 captured by their spear: cf. 894.

still remained to be divided: cf. 53–4. The variant reading κοινή, 'common', which appears as a gloss in some MSS, is favoured by West 109, but it looks like an attempt to explain λοιπή (see P.E. Easterling, *CQ* 17 (1967) 58). The absence of diaeresis in the middle of the anapaestic dimeter is unusual, but cf. *El.* 94, *Tr.* 1276, *Phil.* 1470.

147 with your flashing sword: the phrase is Homeric: *Il.* 4.485 (in a passage featuring Ajax; see Garner 55), 7.473, 20.372, *Od* 1.184; see also 221n. The epithet focuses our attention on Ajax' sword (Stanford (1978) 191), or lit. 'iron', Sophocles forgetting or ignoring the fact that in the Mycenean Age weapons were of bronze.

148 whispering: the onomatopoea in ψιθύρους is strengthened by the sigmatism of the whole line (see Davidson 168).

fabricates: the word is frequently used in prose of deceitful fabrication; cf. also [Aesch.] *PV* 1030. It is idle to enquire whether Odysseus had time to spread these rumours between the end of the prologue and the beginning of the parodos. They had already begun to spread during the night (28; see Burton 10), and there is no reason why Odysseus should not be supposed by the chorus to have had a hand in it then.

151 plausibly: neuter plural of the adjective: either 'easy to convince people of' (LSJ) or 'easily believed'. Odysseus' gift for clever and persuasive speech goes right back to Homer.

153 arrogantly mocking: lit. 'committing *hybris* against'. This is the first time in the play that the word has been used, and it is significant that it is in the context of the behaviour, not of Ajax, but of his enemies. For the dative after the verb in the sense of enjoying a triumph cf. Hdt. 1.212.3. But 'your distress' goes equally well with 'enjoys', and should perhaps be taken with both.

154-7 The larger the target the easier it is to hit with an arrow or other missile. So it is easier to attack a great man like Ajax than it would be to attack small men like the chorus. It is great men who are envied (157), so that, while from one point of view the envy of others is undesirable, from another it is to be welcomed as a sign of one's prosperity; cf. Hes. *Op.*193–6, Aesch. *Ag.* 939, Hdt. 3.52.5, 'it is better to be envied than pitied'. The idea is a commonplace in Pindar, e.g. *Py.* 1.85, 11.29–30, *Nem.* 8.21–2 (quoted by Σ); see Heath 175.

154-5 one who...someone: the presence of τις, 'someone', in the next clause makes it easier to understand τις as subj. of ἱείς and ἁμάρτοι; cf. Aesch. *A g.* 71 and see Pearson on fr. 951. ἁμάρτοις, 'you would not miss',which is easier in itself, would be confusing after '*your* distress' (see Pearson (1922) 20), and is probably a deliberate correction.

at great souls: the genitive is normal after verbs of aiming at a mark. For the double ἄν in 155–6, where the main verb is preceded by a dependent participle, itself hypothetical, see Fraenkel on Aesch. *Ag.* 1048.

157 who *has*: sc. 'success' or 'power'; cf. Eur. *Alc.* 57, *Supp.* 240, Ar. *Plut.* 596.

envy creeps: in tragedy ἕρπω can mean simply 'go' (cf. 287, 543), but here the full sense of surreptitious creeping is clearly appropriate.

159 defensive tower: lit. 'a defence consisting in a tower' (defining genitive). Jebb, less well, understood 'a protection for a tower', i.e. the city-walls. We may remember that Ajax in the *Iliad* carries a tower-like shield, and is himself described as a tower for the Greeks at *Od.* 11.556. For the metaphor cf. also *OT* 1201, Alc. fr. 112.10 L-P, Eur. *Med.* 390.

160-1 The chorus try to persuade themselves that, just as the small men need the great, so great men themselves depend on the assistance of the small. The service is reciprocal. Sophocles may have in mind a wall in which the gaps in the large stones are filled with smaller ones; cf. Pl. *Laws* 902d-e, and see J.W. Donaldson, *The new Cratylus* (3rd edn. London 1859) 684–5. Ajax, in his isolation as a tragic hero (29n.) will never really acknowledge any such dependence on the ordinary people in his life, so that in a sense 162-3 applies to him as much as to his enemies (see M. Davis, in J.P. Euben (ed.), *Greek tragedy and political theory* (California 1986) 150). Yet the restitution of his status as a hero will depend on the efforts of the 'small' Teucer and of Odysseus, who, though not a small man, is cast in a very different mould from that of Ajax.

might best be kept upright: the single verb does duty for both clauses. Often it describes a ship keeping a steady course (so Jebb here). But the notion of keeping upright follows on better from the metaphor of the tower.

163 to teach...in advance: not (Jebb) 'gradually', but 'beforehand', so that they will know it when the need arises. The fool learns only *after* he has suffered the consequences of his folly; cf. *OT* 403, Hom. *Il.* 17.32, 20.198, West on Hes. *Op.* 218, Aesch. *Ag.* 177, 250. Theogn. 430–1 complains about the impossibility of teaching the foolish man to be sensible.

these maxims: lit. 'views (judgements) about these things'.

164 clamour is raised against you: θορυβέω is nowhere else used in the passive in quite this way. But cf. Arist. *Rhet.* 1356b 24 θορυβοῦνται δὲ μᾶλλον οἱ ἐνθυμηματικοί, Isocr. 12.233. The verb picks up the noun at 142, which was preceded by the bird-image, while here the verb leads to the chattering of the birds in the second image that follows in the next sentence.

167-8 For indeed: the combination of ἀλλά and γάρ is apparently elliptical, 'but <I can do nothing> for'.

from your sight: the terrifying 'eye' (ὄμμα) of Ajax contrasts with the timid eye of the chorus/dove at 140.

they chatter: the verb is used in general of any clattering noise, of the chatter of birds also at Arist. *HA* 632b 17.

like: ἅτε introduces a comparison only here in Sophocles.

of birds: the same word, lit. 'winged ones', as at 140.

169-71 but: δ(έ) (Dawes) is required by both sense and metre. It is omitted by all MSS, no doubt because of its postponement to third position in the sentence.

shrink in fear: the idea of cowering is suggested by the prefix ὑπο-, 'under'.

the great vulture: vultures, unlike eagles (ἀετοί) do not in fact attack small birds, but eat only carrion. Some have therefore supposed that the αἰγυπιός is an eagle rather than a vulture (cf. Hesych. A 1740 and 1741), while others (e.g. J. Macl. Boraston, *JHS* 31 (1911) 229–32) take it to be the lammergeyer or bearded vulture, which is not a true vulture and is said to capture living prey; see M. Detienne, *The gardens of Adonis* (tr. J. Lloyd, Hassocks 1977), 27, and cf. Ael. 2.46 (J. Pollard, however, *Birds in Greek life* *and myth* (London 1977) 79–80, reports that it does not attack living prey). Most probably the Greeks made no clear distinction between vultures and eagles (so D'Arcy W. Thompson, *A glossary of Greek birds* (2nd edn. Oxford 1936) 25–6, Easterling (1987) 54–9). Sophocles may have in mind the simile at Hom. *Od.* 22.302, where αἰγυπιοί attack the other birds (cf. *Il.* 17.460), and/or Alcaeus Incert. 10 L-P, where birds cower down at the *sudden* appearance of an eagle (cf. Bacchyl. 5.16–23). Cf. also *Il.* 16.583 and the passages cited at 140n. The Alcaeus passage supports the taking of 'suddenly' with 'appear' rather than with 'cower down'.

cower...in silence: so great and terrifying is Ajax that the effect of his mere appearance would, the chorus hopes, be sufficient to silence the clamour of 164, as the appearance of the vulture silences the bird-chatter of 168. Cf. the reaction of the heroes to Medea's prophecy at Pind. *Py.* 4.57, also Hom. *Od.* 8.190. It is with the silencing of his enemies that the anapaestic section ends.

172 **Was it then:** for interrogative ἦ ῥα, an epic combination, see Denniston 284, and cf. 955 (affirmative).

Artemis Tauropolos: the chorus's first guess is that Ajax' madness has been caused by the goddess whose cult was practised in Amphipolis, in Asia Minor, and especially at Halae Araphenides on the east coast of Attica, where her statue was brought by Orestes from the Tauric Chersonese (Eur. *IT* 1449ff.). The guess is wrong, but the associations that it raises in our minds with Artemis serve to stress the nature of what Ajax has in fact done. She is often associated with madness (H. Lloyd-Jones, *JHS* 103 (1983) 96–7, 99); Ajax has slaughtered animals, including bulls, and Artemis is the Mistress of Animals, her title Tauropolos suggesting bulls in particular (for evidence from coins see Burton 13); he has hunted the animals and has himself been hunted by Odysseus, and Artemis both delights in hunting and is dangerous to male hunters (e.g. Actaeon, Orion). The cult of Artemis in the Tauric Chersonese was associated with human sacrifice, for which in Attica an animal was substituted. So Ajax has killed animals as a kind of substitute for the human beings whom he had intended to kill. The feminine ending Ταυροπόλα is unusual, but not unparalleled, in a compound epithet.

173-4 The chorus break off to apostrophise in parenthesis the rumour which is uppermost in their minds (cf. *OT* 151–8). As at 142–3n. they sing of their own shame, but are really thinking of that of Ajax.

175 **herds of cattle:** ἀγελαίας is an adjective, from ἀγέλη, 'herd', agreeing with βοῦς. The phrase is Homeric (e.g. *Il.* 23.846).

the property of all the people: referring probably to the still undivided spoil of 53–4n.

176 **perhaps:** for ἦ repeating the same particle at 172 see Denniston 281. 'The hesitation implied by που imposes a slight check on the certainty implied by ἦ' (Denniston 286).

some victory...profit: the MSS have ἀκάρπωτον (accusative) agreeing with χάριν, but Dawe 133 shows that in the passages cited by editors as parallel χάριν is always an internal accusative with the verb, which is not the case here. The genitive is therefore to be restored.

177-8 The suggestion of 176 is divided into two alternatives: Ajax has cheated Artemis either of her share of the spoils of war (cf. 92–3) or of her share in the trophies of the hunt. But the text is uncertain. For ἦ followed by εἴτε see Denniston 507. But ἦ ῥα is unparalleled in classical Greek. Lloyd-Jones and Wilson print Hermann's ἦρα, accusative singular of a noun (see Janko on Hom. *Il.* 14.130–2, Russo on *Od.* 18.56) that means the same, and would be supposedly used in the same way, as χάριν 176: 'because of her glorious spoils or because she was cheated etc.'. But the word occurs nowhere else in tragedy, and (see P.E. Easterling, *JHS* 114 (1994) 188) its juxtaposition with the synonymous χάριν is unattractive. Rather, the participle 'being cheated' governs the genitive 'of her glorious spoils' (cf. 1382).

because of...no gifts: the dative is best taken as causal, parallel with the participle 'being cheated'. For the idea that a god might take offence at being denied a sacrifice cf. e.g. Artemis at Hom. *Il.* 9.533–40. *Elaphebolos* ('Shooting deer') is an epic title of Artemis (*Hy. Art* 27.2, Soph. *Tr.* 213; cf. Call. *Hy. Art.* 262), and at Athens a festival called the *Elaphebolia* was celebrated in her honour in *Elaphebolion*, the ninth month of the year; see L. Deubner, *Attische Feste* (Berlin 1932) 209–10. Before the expedition sailed to Troy Agamemnon incurred Artemis' anger because, having killed a stag while hunting, he boasted that he was a better hunter than the goddess (*Cypria* p. 32.55–8 Davies, Soph. *El.* 566–72).

179-81 The chorus's second guess is that Ares, the war-god, is responsible for Ajax' madness. Again the guess is wrong, but the association of Ares with the great warrior is appropriate enough, and the suggestion that Ajax may not have acknowledged the god's help in battle foreshadows Calchas' later explanation of Athena's anger (770–7). Here too the text is uncertain. Σ (cf. *Suda* E 1498) explains the ἤ ('or') of the MSS by supposing that the god with bronze breastplate is Ares (cf. Hom. *Il.* 5.704), while Enyalios is a different god. But the epithet is hardly sufficient by itself to identify Ares, and, whether or not Ares and Enyalios were originally one and the same war-god, in classical literature, as in Homer, Enyalios is almost always a title of Ares; see W. Burkert, *Greek religion* 43–4, 120, 171, J. Chadwick, *Documents in Mycenaean Greek* (2nd edn. Cambridge 1973) 208. According to Plut. *Sol.* 9 Solon erected a temple of Enyalios on Salamis. The best of many emendations is Reiske's σοί, 'against you', balancing σε at 172 (see J.M. Bremer and A.M. van Erp Taalman Kip, *Mnem.* 47 (1994) 236–7), μομφὰν ἔχων being equivalent to μεμφόμενος, 'blaming', + dative (cf. Pind. *Isth.* 4.39, Eur. *Or.* 1069). For the causal genitive after it ('at your partnership in battle') cf. Hom. *Il.* 1.65, Aesch. *Sept.* 652. The phrase may be modelled on *Il.* 18.309 where ξυνὸς 'Ενυάλιος means 'War is alike (i.e. evenly-balanced) for all' (cf. also Eur. *Phoen.* 1572).

punish the outrage: another epic phrase: *Il.* 19.208, *Od.* 20.169.

182-3 For: the sequence of thought is clear: '(some god must have driven you mad) *for* it was not of your own will that you did it'. γάρ should therefore not be emended to turn it into an unfulfilled past condition, 'you would not have done it' (so Dawe 133–4, reading τἄν = τοι ἄν).

you went astray: lit. 'you went to the left', that being thought of as the unlucky side, as in 'sinister'; cf. Hom. *Od.* 20.242.

son of Telamon: see 134–5n.

184 and fell upon the flocks: this explains the manner in which Ajax went astray.

185 for...from the gods: the sentence does not give the reason for the previous 'for' clause, but restates its argument in positive form, so that both 'for' clauses together give the reason for the statement in the strophe, that some god must have driven Ajax mad. For this sequence of successive γάρ's with the same reference see Denniston 64–5. At the same time the present sentence amounts to a restatement of the strophe, so that the whole

COMMENTARY

sequence has an ABA pattern that is characteristic of Sophocles: divine madness – not Ajax' own initiative – divine madness; cf. *Ant.* 465–8. The optative + ἄν is best explained as expressing 'what may hereafter prove to be true' (Goodwin § 238; differently Moorhouse 231); cf. *El.* 1450, *OT* 1182, Hdt. 1.2, Thuc. 1.9.4.

185-6 but may Zeus...Argives: the chorus returns to the rumour (φάτις) of 173. Having assumed from that point onwards that it is true, it now expresses the wish that the gods may avert it, i.e. make it untrue. The wish is natural but somewhat illogical; if Ajax has done what he is said to have done, the gods can neither stop the rumour nor make it untrue; they can only mitigate its consequences. But the chorus means in effect, 'let us hope that it is untrue'. Zeus is named as the supreme god, Phoebus (Apollo) because he is the Healer, who concerns himself with matters of pollution and purification. Calchas similarly calls on him at *Aesch. Ag.* 146. For the contorted word-order see Kühner-Gerth II 600. V. Liapis points out to me that 'rumour', postponed to the end of the sentence, comes as a surprise. We might expect the 'evil' object of 'avert' to be the sickness just mentioned. But the human rumour and the divinely-sent sickness are alike presented as causing Ajax' disgrace.

187-9 Now the chorus tries to take comfort from the assurance of the anapaestic section that the rumour is a lie, but by this time it is less certain, as the conditional clause shows. The 'great kings', a sarcastic rather than ornamental description, are Agamemnon and Menelaus, while 'the king...Sisyphus' is Odysseus. Sophocles borrows here from the version according to which his real father is not Laertes but the crafty Sisyphus, having been conceived by Anticleia before she married Laertes; see Aesch. fr. 175 (probably spoken by Ajax to Odysseus), *Suda* Σ 490, and cf. the similar taunt of Philoctetes at *Phil.* 417, 625, fr. 567.

and the king: χὠ (= καὶ ὁ) is Morstadt's necessary emendation of ἤ ('or'). There is no parallel for the genitive, without an accompanying nominative, to describe a particular member *of* a family; see Moorhouse 56–7. But another possibility is Johnson's ἤ παῖς, 'or the son' (so Dawe).

abandoned: from α-privative and σώζω, lit. 'unsaveable'. It is a prosaic word that occurs elsewhere in tragedy only at Aesch. *Ag.* 1597, where it means 'bringing destruction' (LSJ).

are uttering...words: μύθους is governed by both ὑποβαλλόμενοι and κλέπτουσι. The former means 'suggesting' (though the middle usually means 'pretend that someone else's child is one's own'), while the verb, which usually means 'steal', is used here in the more general sense of 'do secretly'; cf. 1137, *El.* 37, Pind. *Nem.* 7.23.

190-1 no longer...no longer: after the repeated μή the MSS wrongly insert μ' ('me'). The accusative makes no sense, and the elision of the dative μ(οι) is not normally permitted in tragedy. The simplest course is to delete it with Blaydes. It was probably inserted to eliminate the hiatus before ἄναξ, for which cf. *OC* 1485.

keep your face...hidden: not (Schwyzer-Debrunner 139) 'keep your eye fixed on the huts'; see Moorhouse 80. ὄμμα is an echo of 167. By merely showing his face Ajax will silence the rumour, as the little birds were silenced at 169–71. For the thought cf. *Tr.* 813–14. Reiske's ἐμμένων, printed by Lloyd-Jones and Wilson, eliminates the echo and is more prosaic.

beside the sea: the epithet is Homeric (*Il.* 2.538, 584), though not with this noun.

bear...rumour: i.e. 'put up with it', 'allow it to go unchallenged'. The chorus has just appealed to Zeus and Apollo to avert the rumour; now it suggests that Ajax can do it himself. ἄρῃ is second singular aorist subjunctive middle of αἴρω; cf. 129n.

192 **rise up:** the adverb ἄνα is used, as frequently in Homer, as the equivalent of an imperative. With the hiatus after it Sophocles follows Homer, who never in this usage elides the second syllable. For the repetition of the negative command (190–1) in positive form cf. 20n. **your seat:** the poetic ἕδρανον is confined in tragedy to lyrics.

193-4 **you have too long been firmly set:** ποτέ seems to be equivalent to παλαί, 'for a long time' (so Σ), as in the combination ἀεί ποτε at 320, *Ant.* 456. Jebb took it with ὅπου, 'wherever', but there is no room for the indefinite when the chorus knows where Ajax is sitting.

in this lengthy...conflict: μακραίωνι, 'lengthy', agrees with σχολᾷ, 'leisure', but is put near the beginning of the clause for emphasis. The relationship between ἀγωνίῳ, 'pertaining to a struggle', and its noun σχολᾷ is not entirely clear. LSJ give 'strenuous rest' as a possible translation. But it is easier to take it as referring to Ajax' refusal to take part in the fighting ever since the award of the arms to Odysseus, a period of perhaps a few days (cf. 1336–7). We may think also of the conflict that will arise from Ajax' 'contentious inactivity' (see Davidson (1976) 129–32).

195 **making...to heaven:** or 'blazing (intransitive as at 1278) with heaven-sent ruin'. For the, no doubt deliberate, ambiguity, in οὐρανίαν cf. *Ant.* 418, Aesch. *Pers.* 573. ἄταν itself could be translated as 'delusion' (see 123n.).

196-7 The metaphor of 195 leads to a related image, but with a different reference. At Hom. *Od.* 15.329 the *hybris* of the suitors, like Ajax' 'ruin' here, reaches heaven. Here the *hybris* of Ajax' enemies spreads like a forest-fire, fanned by the winds. For the metaphor cf. Hom. *Il.* 14.396–7, 15.605–6, 20.490–2. *Hybris* can be 'quenched' like a fire; cf. Heraclit. 22 B 43, Hdt. 5.77.4, Meiggs and Lewis, *A selection of Greek historical inscriptions* (rev. edn. Oxford 1988) no. 15, *Epigrammata graeca* (Page) Simon. III 89–92; also 1057 below. The *hybris* is the same as at 153n. Often *hybris* is thought of as leading to ἄτη, whether 'delusion' or 'ruin', for the person who commits it (e.g. Aesch. *Pers.* 821-2). Here the *hybris* of others is likely to result in ruin (if that is the sense at 195) for Ajax. With this sense δέ ('and') introduces what is in effect a γάρ ('for') clause.

so fearlessly: the neuter plural of the adjective is used adverbially (Lobeck's ἀτάρβηθ' eliminates the hiatus after ἀτάρβητα; cf. 199). The word is more appropriate to the tenor (the *hybris*) of the metaphor than to the vehicle (the forest-fire). Their freedom from fear in Ajax' absence corresponds to that of the birds at 167–71 in the absence of the vulture. **where the winds blow freely:** i.e. to fan the fire. The context makes the meaning of the epithet clear. At fr. 371, Eur. *Andr.* 749, fr. 316.2 it means 'sheltered from the winds'. Hence Davidson (1976) 133–5, implausibly removing any reference to fire, suggests that the idea is that Ajax' enemies indulge in *hybris* in security.

198-9 **while they all mock:** genitive absolute. κακχάζω (or καχάζω) means properly to 'laugh aloud'. Strictly speaking one does not use one's tongue to laugh, but jeering naturally combines laughter and speech. Lloyd-Jones and Wilson (see also A. Turyn, *Studies in the manuscript tradition of the tragedies of Sophocles* (Urbana 1952) 129, Ferrari 24–5) prefer βακχαζόντων, 'while they revel (like Bacchants)', a rarely attested

form which would mean the same as βακχεύω (*Ant.* 136). But it is a pity to eliminate the
laughter that is so regularly associated with *hybris* in this play.

cause you sore pain: neuter plural used adverbially, like ἀτάρβηθ᾽ above. 'You' is not
in the Greek, but is better understood than 'me'. The chorus's feelings are introduced
with ἐμοὶ δ(έ) in the next line.

200 is my constant state: cf. 950. The parodos ends, as it began (136–40) with a reference
to the chorus's own reaction, thus reinforcing our sense of its loyalty to, and sympathy
for, its leader. The technique is similar at Aesch. *Cho.* 75–83. See Davidson (1975)
170–2, who remarks that, while the anapaestic section ended (167–71) on a note of
optimism, the parodos as a whole ends with a picture of a frightened and helpless chorus.

201-347

The long first episode (201–595) is divided into two sections by the entrance of Ajax at 348.
Both sections begin with an emotional *amoibaion*, or epirrhematic passage, in which an actor
and a chorus engage in lyric or semi-lyric dialogue (the term *kommos* is best reserved for a
dirge composed in this fashion; see Arist. *Po.* 1452b 24, Broadhead ed. *Pers.* 310, H. Popp, in
Jens 221–2), before settling into the normal iambic trimeter of dialogue. In this first section
from 201–220 Tecmessa and the chorus respond to each other in anapaests, recitative rather
than lyric in character (despite the Doric α at 202, 208, 234, 257), while from 221–62
Tecmessa continues in anapaests, but the chorus sings a corresponding strophe and
antistrophe. After the iambic dialogue of 263–83 Tecmessa launches into what is in effect a
formal messenger-speech, describing, from her point of view, the events of the previous night
and what has been happening inside the hut.

The chorus has just been praying to the gods to avert the rumour and for Ajax himself to
appear. But it is Tecmessa who emerges from the hut to dispel their hopes, and to confirm that
the rumour is true. So at Aesch. *Ag.* 503 the Herald arrives to confound the chorus's wishful-
thinking that the war may not be over. Tecmessa certainly emerges from the central door of
the *skene*, not (Pickard-Cambridge 109 n.1), from a side-entrance. As the prisoner-of-war and
slave of Ajax (211, 485–91), but also his faithful and loving concubine, she belongs to the
same type as Briseis in the *Iliad*. In the prologue we were introduced to Ajax' suffering
though the eyes of his enemies. Here we see the reaction of his supporters, and our sympathy
for him is built up. This section of the episode has two principal functions: (1) It rounds off
the theme of Ajax' madness, recapitulating the events which are already known to the
audience, but from Tecmessa's point of view and with little actual repetition; 230–2 repeat
26–7, and 233–42 repeat 64–5, but with full detail, and confirm that Ajax has carried out the
intention which he indicated at 108–13 (cf. also 296–301). (2) It also prepares us for the
development of the plot. At 257ff. and 306ff. we learn that Ajax has returned to sanity and
has become aware of what he has done, and we await his appearance in the second section of
the episode. At 326 Tecmessa gives us an ominous hint that he is planning some mischief.
The emphasis on the loving relationship between Tecmessa and Ajax prepares us for the role
which she will play later in the drama. 333–47 provide a bridge between the two sections of
the episode. The offstage cries of Ajax are heard, marking the imminence of his appearance,
and incidentally introducing us to his son Eurysaces and his half-brother Teucer, who will
have important roles later in the play.

201 Crew: lit. 'helpers' (cf. 357). For this word in a military context cf. Aesch. *Pers.* 1024. Tecmessa stresses what we already know, that the chorus is on the side of Ajax.

202 earth-born line of Erechtheus: Erechtheus, a mythical king of Athens, was the son of Earth (Hom. *Il.* 2.547–8, Hdt. 8.55). Salamis is associated with Athens already at *Il.* 2.557–8, a passage which was thought by some in antiquity to be an Athenian interpolation (see most recently M. Finkelberg, *CQ* 38 (1988) 31–41). Certainly since the sixth century it had been incorporated in Athens, and this anachronistic honorific address to the chorus will help to engage the sympathy of the Athenian audience on his behalf; cf. 859–61.

204 so far away: the yearning of Ajax and the chorus for Salamis will become an important theme in the play.

205 The three epithets, in this first utterance of Tecmessa, emphasise and sum up the hard heroic nature of Ajax. For his 'greatness' see 134–200, 154–7nn. It is this quality that his enemies will seek to deny. As for his fierceness and savagery cf. 548, 885, 930, *Ant.* 471, and see Knox (1964) 23–4, 42–3. At 651 Ajax will claim that he has been softened by Tecmessa.

206-7 after falling sick...of turbulence: the adj. θολερός, 'prop. of troubled water' (LSJ), is used metaphorically of words at [Aesch.] *PV* 885, in the context of madness compared, as often, to a storm. Here too it is natural to suppose, with Σ, that the storm is that of Ajax' madness (cf. 185, 269n.). The aorist tense of the participle points ahead to the information (257–9) that Ajax is no longer mad. Less well (but see 331–2n.) the sickness may be the distress which he feels now that his sanity has been restored, or (Rosenmeyer 176–7; cf. Gellie 7–8) it describes his whole state of mind ever since the judgement of the arms.

208-9 The troubles of the previous day (cf. 193–4) were already bad enough. Now the chorus asks what new trouble has supplanted them in the night. But 'of the day' is difficult. ἀμερίας is an adjective, not a noun, and we may perhaps understand with it something like ὥρας, 'time' (see Moorhouse 14 and cf. Hdt. 1.202.1). But a feminine adjective often seems to stand for an unspecified abstract noun (e.g. 1040, Aesch. *Cho.* 775 τροπαίαν κακῶν, 'a change from our misfortunes'). ἠρεμίας, 'rest', 'quietness', is an easy change, but it is doubtful whether the chorus would describe in such terms Ajax' state of mind even before his madness. Dawe 134–5 remarks also that ἠρεμ- words belong rather to the language of fourth-century prose. He himself (after Bruhn) prints a lacuna which would contain the genitive of a feminine noun. For the theme of alternation see 131–2n.

210-11 At the outset Tecmessa's status, and her relationship with Ajax, are made clear to the audience; cf. Achilles' description of his relationship with Briseis at Hom. *Il.* 9.341–3. Here we have only the chorus's word for it, but there is no reason to distrust it. 'Phrygian', as often, means 'Trojan'. The fact that Tecmessa will not be named till 331 suggests that, although she does not appear in extant earlier literature (for art see Intro. 3), she and her parentage were already familiar to Sophocles' audience. Despite Gardiner (1987) 57–8, there seems no good reason why he should puzzle us by inventing a new character without telling us her name. Her father is Teleutas at 331. Here, where the first syllable has to be long, we must either print Τελλεύταντος, with two of the MSS (probably a Byzantine conjecture), accepting the inconsistency with 331, or suppose that the proper name excuses a metrical licence. The latter is perhaps preferable. For similar licence in iambic trimeters cf. e.g. fr. 880 Ἀλφεσίβοιαν. Attempts at emendation have not been successful.

bedmate: lit. 'bed'. For the word thus transferred to the person who shares the bed cf. *Tr.* 27 and 360, Eur. *El.* 481.

212 **impetuous Ajax:** cf. 612–13n., 1213.

shows constant affection: lit. 'bears up having conceived affection for', a common use of ἀνέχω (or -ομαι) + participle. 'You' is probably object of στέρξας, but it could be object of ἀνέχει, 'holds you in honour with affection'; cf. Pind. *Py.* 2.89, Eur. *Hec.* 121–2.

214 **am I to tell:** the deliberative subjunctive after πῶς is more often aorist, as at 1024; see Fraenkel on Aesch. *Ag.* 785.

a tale that is unspeakable: lit. 'an unspeakable word'. The same paradox is found at *OC* 1001, Eur. *Hipp.* 602, Dem. 18.122.

216 **our:** ethic dative of the pronoun, 'for us'. ἡμίν with second syllable short is almost confined in tragedy to Sophocles; cf. 733.

famous: the epithet, like those at 205, 212, serves to build up our picture of Ajax, as his supporters see him. The combination of 'famous' with the verb 'fall into dishonour' raises the question that will dominate the play, that of his status as a hero now that he has been disgraced.

217 **in the night:** instead of an adverb with the verb Sophocles uses an adjective agreeing with Ajax; cf. χθιζός for 'yesterday', ἑσπέριος for 'in the evening'. Davidson (1975) 166 remarks that the choice of word 'associates Ajax himself more directly with darkness'; cf. 47.

218 The emphasis on the horrible scene which the audience can as yet only imagine is reminiscent of the hints in Aesch. *Ag.* of the dark secrets within Agamemnon's palace.

219 **slaughtered...blood:** the two weighty compound epithets frame their noun. The second picks up the dyeing metaphor of 95.

222 **hot-tempered man:** the epithet connects Ajax with his sword (147, where the middle syllable is long, as it usually is). Sometimes treated as interchangeable with αἴθοψ, the alternative reading here, its original meaning seems to have been 'brown'. R.J. Edgeworth, *Glotta* 61 (1983) 31–40, suggests that its metaphorical application to a man (or an animal) derives from the association of 'sunburnt' with strong, manly, vigorous as opposed to fair-skinned, effeminate. Hence perhaps it comes to mean 'blazing', 'shining'; see also K.J. McKay, *Mnem.* 12 (1959) 198–203. Hermann's ἀνέρος for ἀνδρός restores responsion with 246, where, however, the text is uncertain.

225 **the great men of the Danai:** the Danai who are great, not 'the great Danai', as if all the Greeks were great. The chorus is thinking primarily of Agamemnon, Menelaus, and Odysseus, and the epithet is probably used sarcastically, as at 188. Contrast its sincere application of the word to Ajax in the parodos. Some scholars suspect corruption, which is not impossible, given that μέγας occurs immediately below.

226 The chorus returns to the rumour which dominated the parodos; cf. esp. 173 where the same adjective is applied to a different word for 'rumour'.

is increased: i.e. the news grows as it spreads. The poetic form ἀέξει for αὔξει occurs in tragedy only here and at Eur. *Hipp.* 537.

228 **what is coming:** for the verb see 157n., and cf. 1255, [Aesch.] *PV* 127 'everything that comes upon me causes me fear'.

229 **the man will die conspicuously:** this is the first hint to the audience that Ajax will die. The chorus already senses that it is the only possible outcome. But its language is vague, and it may be thinking of execution rather than suicide (see 254–5n.). With 'conspicuously' (the adjective is used proleptically as at 66–7n.; cf. also the adverbs at 81, 1311) it seems to envisage a public death. Ajax' suicide will in fact be private. But the audience may sense another meaning: Ajax by his death will become as celebrated as his homeland (598), i.e. he will be restored to his status as a hero.

230 **with frenzied hand:** for the recurring stress on the hand with which Ajax did the deed cf. 27n. The rare adjective παραπλήκτῳ, 'struck off course', occurs only here in tragedy, but cf. the fifth-century lyric poet Melanippides fr. 4 *PMG*. For the verb παραπλήσσω cf. Ar. *Lys.* 831 etc.; also ἐκπλήσσω 33n.

231 **black:** cf. κελαινός of a spear-point at *Tr.* 856, of a sword at Eur. *Ba.* 628, on which Dodds, comparing μέλαν at Eur. *Hel.* 1656, *Or.* 1472, writes, 'the primary reference is presumably to the colour of the metal [perhaps rather to its leather-bound hilt; see Janko on Hom. *Il.* 15.713–15]…but both words have also the sinister associations of Lat. 'ater', Eng. 'dark', which may have been felt in all these passages'. Contrast the flashing sword of 147.

231-2 **the cattle…herdsmen:** see 27n.

233: **So it was from there:** ἄρ(α) marks Tecmessa's realisation of where the animals came from. Until now she has known only the events inside the hut.

234 **the flock** must include the cattle as well as sheep; cf. 53–4n., 63–4.

235 **of which:** plural, despite singular 'flock' as its antecedent.
   he slaughtered: the syllabic augment is quite often omitted in tragic lyrics but rarely in anapaests; see Page on Eur. *Med.* 1413.

236 **he broke in two:** the verb is used of lions tearing the hide of a bull at Hom. *Il.* 18.582.

237-9 **two white-footed rams:** despite de Romilly, for whom no specific identification is intended, the second ram, whose fate is described at 239–44, is obviously the one taken by Ajax for Odysseus. The first must stand for Agamemnon. We might have expected Menelaus to be included, but the contrasting treatment of only two rams is simpler. It is true that at 57, 97–100 Ajax imagined that he had already killed both Agamemnon and Menelaus, and that the whipping of Odysseus did not come till after Ajax' conversation with Athena. But the inconsistency is trifling. ἀργίπους, 'white-footed' is used by Homer of dogs at *Il.* 24.211, where it probably means 'swift-footed', a sense which is inappropriate to rams. Sophocles borrows the epic epithet, but gives it what may be its original sense; see *Lexicon des frügriechischen Epos* s.v. ἀργιπόδας.

239 **cut off:** lit. 'reaped', harvested'. For the grim metaphor cf. Eur. *Supp.* 717, *A.P.* 9.451 (the cutting out of Philomela's tongue). Jebb pointed out that in a sacrifice the tongue was cut out and offered separately (Hom. *Od.* 3.332, Ar. *Peace* 1060). He himself found no reference here to the custom, but V. Liapis suggests to me that the idea of a corrupted sacrifice (Ajax throws away the tongue instead of offering it) is entirely appropriate.

239-42 This is what Ajax promised to do at 108–10. Tecmessa confirms that his madness has continued for some time since he left the stage.
   a horse's harness: i.e. the rein (cf. Hom. *Il.* 16.475).
   shrill double lash: a μάστιξ, 'whip', is 'whistling' at Hom. *Il.* 11.532, in a passage which, for Garner 55–8, has influenced much of the action and imagery of Sophocles' play. The double μάστιξ at Aesch. *Ag.* 642 is a combination of whip and goad, with a

double point at the end (see Fraenkel, Garvie on *Cho.* 375–9, and cf. *OT* 809). But here (despite Fraenkel) Ajax adapts to his use an ordinary piece of equine equipment. He holds it by the middle, as Jebb explains, and strikes with both ends simultaneously (cf. Σ 241a).

243–4 uttering abuse: lit. 'abusing him as to evil words' (internal accusative); cf. *Ant.* 759.

which a god...taught him: even the abusive language of the heroic, but mad, Ajax has a superhuman quality. So at *OT* 1258–9, says the Messenger, it must have been a god who showed the frantic Oedipus the way to the scene of Jocasta's suicide; cf. also Aesch. *Ag.* 663.

245–56 As in the parodos (142–3, 200nn.) the chorus associates its own position with that of Ajax, and expresses the wish to escape from its plight. This kind of escapist wish is commonly put into the mouth of a Euripidean chorus (see Barrett on *Hipp.* 732–4, Dodds on *Ba.* 402–16); cf. also *OC* 1081–4, fr. 476. Here the chorus's wish anticipates the option considered by Ajax himself at 460–6. But he will reject it. To run away would not be the mark of a hero.

245–7 It is time now: a similar thought is expressed by the chorus in a moment of crisis at *OT* 467–8. For the common ὥρα...ἤδη see Fraenkel, *Beobachtungen zu Aristophanes* (Rome 1962) 28–9. τοι is omitted in some MSS after ἤδη, but it does not look like a scribal interpolation (see Dawe 136–7). To secure responsion with 221 its removal would require the adoption of Triclinius' κάρα for κρᾶτα (so Pearson).

to hide...veil: for the desire to veil the face as a typical reaction to shame see Cairns 292–3, and cf. for example Hom. *Od.* 8.84–5, Eur. *Hipp.* 243–4. The phrase is bound together by the triple alliteration of κ.

to steal away on foot: lit. 'to secure (from ἄρνυμαι; cf. 75n. and contrast Aesch. *Pers.* 481, [Eur.] *Rhes.* 54, 'undertake flight', from αἴρομαι) a theft with our feet', a bold poetic phrase; cf. 187–9n., Eur. *Or.* 1499, *Ion* 1254.

249–50 on the swift rower's bench: lit. 'on the swift bench of rowing'. Either the adjective is attracted from the rowing to the bench, or the bench is a kind of synecdoche for the ship. Both θοός, 'swift', and ποντόπορος, 'sea-going', are Homeric formulaic epithets for ships; cf. also *Phil.* 721.

let...have her way: there is probably no need (with Jebb) to understand something like 'reins' as the object of the verb. It is used absolutely at Eur. fr. 779.7.

251–3 the joint commanders: cf. 390, *Ant.* 145.

are setting in motion: ἐρέσσω, 'row', is quite often thus used metaphorically, e.g. at *Ant.* 158 (of a plan); cf. Aesch. *Sept.* 855. Here the metaphor seems to have been suggested by the literal rowing of 249.

254–5 against us: the chorus identifies itself with Ajax.

death by stoning: lit. 'Ares by stoning'. So at Eur. *Ion* 1240 an adjective meaning 'stoning' (λεύσιμον) is attached to 'ruin' (ἄταν). Ares, the god of war, here represents violent destruction in general. The phrase seems to be both direct object of 'I am afraid' and internal accusative with 'to share pain'. The chorus assumes that Ajax and his followers will be regarded as traitors, stoning being the punishment commonly in drama proposed for such offenders against the community; cf. 728, *Ant.* 36, Aesch. *Ag.* 1616, and earlier Hom. *Il.* 3.57. V.J. Rosivach, *ClAnt* 6 (1987) 232–48, argues that in Athens the punishment was in fact rarely inflicted, and that all the dramatic passages depend on Athenian memory of the fate of Lycides and his family in 479 BC (Hdt. 9.5; at Dem.

18.204 the same story is told of someone called Cyrsilus and set in the period before Salamis), which originally appears to have been an act of mob-violence, and only later came to be seen in Athens as the appropriate punishment for traitors.

256 terrible: lit. 'unapproachable'. Tecmessa's reply at 257 shows that 'fate' refers to Ajax' madness, which has now in fact passed.

257-8 The cessation of Ajax' madness is compared to that of a keen south wind, thus providing some support for the view that the storm of 207 is that of his madness; cf. *Ant.* 929-30, Aesch. *Cho.* 390-2, and, for this idea of madness as 'due to external windlike forces', see Padel 91-2. But the relevance of the lightning (wrongly taken by Kamerbeek as the bright light of the sun) to the simile is unclear, and the text has been suspected. The phrase means literally 'without (apart from) bright lightning'. It is best to understand the lightning as part of the storm, and to take the phrase with 'ceases'. 'It ceases without lightning' means 'the wind drops and the lightning ceases'. Stanford (and others) connects it with 'that has burst forth', on the strength of Thphr. *De signis* 32-3, according to whom lightning in winter or autumn causes a south wind to cease. But more naturally it is the presence, rather than absence, of violent lightning that marks the storm that has now passed; cf. Ibyc. 5.8-9.

259 he has fresh grief: the last time we saw Ajax he was happy but mad. His pain was known only to others. Now we learn that his sanity has returned but his happiness has gone. This will be the theme of the following dialogue between Tecmessa and the chorus-leader. So we are prepared, but kept waiting, for his next appearance.

261 one's own self-made sufferings: cf. *El.* 215.
when no one...inflict them: there is no exact parallel for παραπράσσω meaning 'act as accessory', but cf. παραίτιος (with Garvie on Aesch. *Cho.* 910).

262 intensifies: so LSJ. The nearest parallel seems to be Ar. *Peace* 458 (intransitive 'strain'). The compound verb is often used of 'suggesting' false hopes etc., but it is hard to see the relevance of that idea here.

263 I think he is very fortunate: despite its support for Ajax the chorus does not understand him at all. Jebb took the unexpressed subject of the infinitive to be 'we', but what puzzles the chorus is Tecmessa's statement that Ajax is in greater pain now that he is sane.

264 there will be less talk about it: cf. Eur. *Med.* 541. Jebb's 'the trouble is of less account' (see also Moorhouse 53) is a little too vague. What has worried the chorus all along has been the rumour. Now it hopes that with Ajax' return to sanity the army will lose interest in what he has done in his madness. The thought and the expression are similar to fr. 375. For the general notion that one forgets trouble when it is past cf. also Pind. *Isth.* 8.11-12.

265-7 Tecmessa begins to try to convince the uncomprehending chorus that the situation is now worse than before: for then only his friends were unhappy, but now all are unhappy alike. The implication that in such circumstances it is better to remain insane (cf. Eur. *Ba.* 1260-2, fr. 205) is one that is rejected for herself by Phaedra at Eur. *Hipp.* 247-9 (see Barrett).

267 Lit. 'sharing in common among those who share in common to be pained by association with them', an emphatic way of describing mutual sympathy in suffering.

269 we...suffer: 'we' must be Ajax and his friends together. The sum of pain is greater than it was before. Elsewhere in tragedy ἀτάομαι is used only in the participle, as at 384,

Ant. 17, 314. M.L. West restores a subjunctive form at Aesch. *Ag.* 1656, but see V. di Benedetto, *RIFC* 190 (1992) 151–2.

he is not ill: νοσοῦντος is Hermann's emendation of νοσοῦντες, 'we are not ill'. Hermann was certainly right (see Ferrari 26, Winnington-Ingram 23 n. 41, Holt (1980) 23). The sickness has throughout been that of Ajax' delusion (cf. 59, 185, perhaps 206–7n., 271, 274, 280). The unhappiness of his friends continues (273, 276), and for them there has been no change from sickness.

270 **do you mean:** see 99n.

272 **the troubles...grip:** in the Greek the antecedent ('the troubles') is transferred to the relative clause , 'in which troubles he was gripped'.

273 **his company:** lit. 'by being with us', the participle echoing the same word at 267.

275 **vexed:** lit. 'driven', a metaphor probably from the driving of horses; cf. 504, *Tr.* 1045.

277 The particle ἆρ(α) = ἆρ᾽ οὐ, introducing a question that expects the answer 'yes'. 'ἆρα ostensibly leaves the issue open to the person addressed, and the appeal for confirmation is the more confident because less obviously stressed' (Denniston 46, who however does not include the present instance); cf. 1282.
after: 'arising from'.

278-9 **some blow has come from god:** the same notion as at 185, but here in the more definite indicative. Most MSS have the optative (a corruption from the earlier line), which is impossible after a verb of fearing in primary sequence, and could stand only if we could take it as an independent wish for the future ('I am afraid; may it not be that'; see Moorhouse 291). But the chorus refers to what has already occurred, which rules out also the subjunctive ἥκῃ. For the blow or stroke of a god see 136–8n.
for how can it be otherwise: the Greek says simply 'for how?'
now that his madness has stopped: cf. 263.

281 For ὡς + genitive absolute instead of a participle governed directly by the verb of knowing see Goodwin § 917, Kühner-Gerth II 93. For the expression cf. 904, 981–2, *Ant.* 1179, Aesch. *Ag.* 1393.

282 **swooped:** lit. 'flew'; cf. [Aesch.]. *PV* 644, Eur. *Alc.* 420–1 'this trouble flew upon him'. The image is probably that of a bird of prey swooping on its victim. At 169 Ajax was himself the bird of prey, but now he is the victim.

285 Tecmessa begins her narrative with the explanatory γάρ (Denniston 58–60), which cannot be translated into English.
at dead of night: but in such expressions of time ἄκρος, 'on the edge', usually denotes the beginning or end (see Gow on Theocr. 11.35ff., and cf. Pind. *Py.* 11.10, Hp. *Aph.* 3.18, Σ Nic. *Ther.* 25 and 761), and the reference here may be to the period in which the early night has ended and the lamps are extinguished, so that full night has just begun. Σ explains 'at about the time of first sleep'.

286 **lamps:** strictly 'braziers', which in the Homeric household served for both heating and lighting. **burned:** intransitive as at Pind. *Ol.* 7.48, and perhaps at Aesch. *Cho.* 536 (conjecture). Usually αἴθω is transitive.

286-7 **his two-edged sword:** the fatal sword (10n.) is introduced early in the story. The epithet is Homeric (*Il.* 10.256, *Od.* 16.80) as well as tragic. For ἔγχος, properly a 'spear', see 95n.
to go out: see 157n.

on a futile mission: it is mainly with hindsight that Tecmessa describes it as 'empty', but even at the time it may have seemed to her pointless, as 289–91 go on to explain.

288 What: lit. 'what thing', perhaps a colloquial expression; see P.T. Stevens, *CQ* 31 (1937) 190–1, M. Griffith, *The authenticity of Prometheus Bound* (Cambridge 1977) 198. Tecmessa 'addresses and even "scolds" Ajax with a colloquial familiarity' (Blundell 75).

289-90 unsummoned...messengers: the expression is reminiscent of Aesch. *Cho.* 838; cf. also *Tr.* 391–2, Eur. *Andr.* 562.

on this enterprise: the same noun was used of Odysseus at 2.

292-3 ever-repeated: lit. 'hymned', i.e. harped on again and again (by people in general, rather than by Ajax in particular), as in the liturgical formulas of a hymn. It is difficult to tell whether Ajax' brief sentiment, which certainly has the ring of a proverb (see Pearson on fr. 64.4), would be shared unquestioningly by Sophocles' audience, as representing the normal fifth-century attitude to women. Cf. the views expressed by Pericles in the Funeral Speech at Thuc. 2.45.2, Aesch. *Sept.* 232, Eur. *Heracl.* 476, *Tro.* 654. For silence as an 'adornment' for women cf. Democr. 68 B 274. See in general, K.J. Dover, *Greek popular morality in the time of Plato and Aristotle* (Oxford 1974) 95–102. More probably we are meant to find Ajax' dismissal of Tecmessa brusque. He is not showing her his usual affection (211–12, 808), and the ties are already becoming strained. The line prepares us for his rejection of Tecmessa's advice even when he has returned to sanity. For an unsympathetic view of Ajax' treatment of Tecmessa see Synodinou 101.

294 I stopped: i.e. rebuking him.

alone: see 29n.

295 there: i.e. at the scene of slaughter. Tecmessa knows only of what happened in the hut.

296-7 The lines repeat, but with differences and from Tecmessa's purely human point of view, Athena's narrative at 62–4 (cf. also 233–4). The 'prey with beautiful horns' of that passage has become, if Schneidewin's emendation is correct, a 'fleecy prey'. The MSS in fact give 'fair-horned' here as at 64 (the reading of *P.Oxy.* 2093 is unclear), but the phrase should distinguish a third element, the sheep, from the cattle. For τε, exceptionally, linking only the last two units of a series of three see Denniston 501, Fraenkel on Aesch. *Ag.* 1432–3.

298 cut the throats: or perhaps 'beheaded' (cf. 238–9).

299-300 broke their spines: see 55–6n.

while the rest...like men: cf. 65. Tecmessa has already given a more detailed description of this at 239–44. In tragedy ὥστε, like ὥσπερ, often introduces a comparison.

301-4 Tecmessa gives her impression of the dialogue which we heard in the prologue (91–117) between Ajax and Athena. To Tecmessa, looking from inside the hut, it seemed that he was talking to a shadow.

302 dragging out his words: the word conveys the effort with which Ajax spoke in his excited violence; cf. the comic poet Thugenides, fr. 4.594 M, Men. fr. 362 Koerte. If Sophocles has a specific metaphor in mind, it is perhaps that of someone pulling up a tree or plant from its roots, as at Ar. *Frogs* 903 (cf. Eust. 679.61). Jebb compares Pl. *Tht.* 180a, where the metaphor derives from pulling arrows from a quiver.

303 with them he laughed loudly: for Ajax' demented laughter see G. Grossmann, *MH* 25 (1968) 65–85, Segal (1981) 134. But the Greek could mean also 'constructing much laughter <for other people>', i.e. 'making himself a laughing-stock', and Sophocles has perhaps deliberately chosen an ambiguous expression. It is the laughter of his enemies that Ajax will dread (367, 454; cf. 989, 1043).

304 at all the violence...on them: with this translation the violence is that which Ajax inflicts (so Jebb, Kamerbeek), and 'how much violence' is an internal accusative after 'avenged'. This phrase too is ambiguous (see Stanford, Blundell 70 n. 49): it could mean 'at all the violence he had punished', the violence now being that of his enemies (so Fisher 313–14). The former interpretation makes better sense of 'against them', while the latter is more in accord with the expected meaning of ἐκτίνομαι. Both meanings may be intended. His enemies have inflicted *hybris* on Ajax (153, 196–7nn.), and now it is his turn to do the same to them. The reciprocal nature of *hybris* is in accord with the principle that it is right to retaliate on one's enemies, though it is rare for the vengeance itself to be described in these terms (see Intro. 13 n. 50, 1087–8n.). Laughter is itself a typical form of *hybris* (79n.). Grammatically the phrase depends on the idea of saying contained in either 'dragged up words' or 'combining much laughter'.

he had gone: for the participle at line-end adding little to the sense cf. *Ant.* 768, *Phil.* 353, and see Moorhouse 253.

305-6 he rushed...into: ἐνάξας, an otherwise unattested compound, is found only in *P.Oxy.* 2093. ἀπάξας, 'rushing out', is impossible in the context, and is probably a corruption from 301, while ἐπ- may be an attempt to correct it.

308-9 a wreck...wreckage: the *figura etymologica* brings out well the reversal in Ajax' situation. He sits in the middle of his victims, now himself the victim. In terms of the imagery of the prologue the hunter has become the hunted. ἐρεισθείς, 'propped up' (found also in *Suda* E 3002), is less well attested and ruins this point. For the 'wreckage' of corpses cf. Eur. fr. 266.2.

the dead sheep's corpses: lit. 'the slaughter pertaining to sheep'. The genitive depends either on 'corpses', or (Moorhouse 53), as a further defining genitive, on 'wreckage'.

310 For συλλαβών, 'gripping', in which the prefix merely reinforces the sense of violence, see LSJ s.v. σύν D I 2, J. Jouanna, in P. Ghiron-Bistagne et al., *Les Perses d' Eschyle* (Montpellier 1993) 95, and cf. Polyb. 15.28.8.

tightly: for ἀπρίξ cf. fr. 354.4, and see Garvie on Aesch. *Cho.* 425–8. For the practice of tearing out the hair in mourning cf. also 634, Eur. *Andr.* 826, 1209.

with his hand is perhaps superfluous after 'with his nails', but Renehan 343 may be right to argue that the single phrase combines two distinct ideas: Ajax seizes his hair with his hands, and tears with his nails.

311 for most of the time: the separation of the definite article from its noun by its governing verb is unusual. It is perhaps made easier by the μέν which follows it.

312 then: after ἔπειτα Greek often omits the δέ which would naturally answer the μέν in the previous clause.

those terrible threats: lit. 'the terrible threats'. As often (see Jebb's Appx. on *Tr.* 476, Moorhouse 144), the article with δεινός has demonstrative force, 'those terrible words which I remember so clearly'; cf. 650, 1226, *Ant.* 408.

313 if I should not reveal: sc. 'saying what would happen if...'. The future optative in virtual reported speech in secondary sequence expresses what in the direct speech would be future indicative. Σ 312 remarks on the pathos of a situation in which Ajax has to seek from a woman information about what he has done himself. No longer (cf. 293) is she to keep silent.

314 Dawe and Lloyd-Jones and Wilson follow Nauck in deleting this line, which is flat and superfluous after 313. But it is not easy to see why it should have been interpolated.

the situation in which: lit. 'in what of a situation', with τῷ = τίνι, and the genitive partitive.

315-17 Each of these lines contains a compound verb prefixed with ἐξ (cf. also 304, 320). Sophocles often uses such compounds with intensifying effect at an emotional climax; see E. Tsitsoni, *Untersuchungen der EK- Verbal-Komposita bei Sophokles* (Diss. Munich 1963), esp. 69–70.

broke out...lamentations: lit. 'lamented lamentations', a similar *figura etymologica* to that at 308–9, but this time comprising a cognate accusative, i.e. one in which the noun comes from the same root as the verb which governs it.

319-20 always: see 193–4n.

were the mark of: 'characteristic of', a common use of πρός + genitive; cf. 581, 1071. Intransitive ἔχειν here with the prepositional phrase seems to be equivalent to εἶναι (see Jebb on *OT* 709). Less good is the rendering, 'to have such lamentation <was> the mark of...' (de Romilly).

cowardly: Tecmessa uses the same word as Athena at 133 (132–3n.). Here it means someone without *arete*, someone who is not a hero. Now, therefore, that he is after all uttering such unheroic laments, Ajax' status as a hero is called into question. **dejected:** lit. 'heavy of soul'. The compound adjective occurs only here in literature, but cf. βαρύθυμος, 'heavy of heart', and see G. Zuntz, *CQ* 10 (1960) 39 on Theocr. 1.96.

321-2 without any sound of shrill wailing: lit. 'soundless of shrill wailing', a genitive of separation after the α-privative adjective.

bellowing like a bull: cf. *OT* 1265, *Tr.* 805, 904 (of a woman), Eur. *HF* 869–70. The deep groans which Ajax uttered on previous occasions contrasted with the shrill lamentations that he used to despise. The latter no doubt seemed to him to be characteristic of women (cf. *Tr.* 1074–5), while the comparison with the bull suggests his virility in his normal state. Now he has hunted bulls (297), and has been reduced to the position of a woman. His 'loss of language or bull-like roar...is akin to the madness that marks his total isolation from society. To have lost the ability to communicate by language is itself to be an outcast' (Segal (1981) 53); see also Padel 150–2.

323-5 But now: we return to the present situation after the digression of 318–22.

he lies...the man sits: Tecmessa seems confused about whether Ajax is lying down or sitting (cf. 309). But perhaps the lying is not to be taken literally; it may mean simply 'he has been placed' (cf. 207). At Hom. *Od.* 4.788 Penelope similarly 'lies without eating', Medea at Eur. *Med.* 24. For fasting as a reaction to grief see Richardson on *Hy.Dem.* 47.

fallen down...in the middle of the animals: the expression recalls 55, 184, 300. Here Ajax has literally 'fallen', but the echo once again (see 308–9n.) indicates the reversal of his position.

that his sword has slain: the compound epithet is found only here.

326 it is clear that he wants...: Greek, 'he is clear wanting', the usual personal construction, as at 1225; cf. also 76n., 635.

he wants to do: the desiderative form of δράω will occur again at 585; cf. in a similar context of foreboding Eur. *Med.* 93.

some mischief: Tecmessa's fear is vaguely expressed. She may surmise that he is planning some further attack on his enemies. But for the audience the hint of his suicide is clear.

327 Nauck's bracketing of this rather flat line is accepted by Dawe, Fraenkel 12, Lloyd-Jones and Wilson, and by West 109, who argues persuasively that the fear expressed in 326 is more effective if it is based on Ajax' ominous silence than on the utterances of 327. But, as at 314, certainty is impossible. There is no real inconsistency with 325. That Ajax is sitting quietly need not mean that he is making no sound. And 383 is not really so similar as to suggest the source of the interpolation.

328 **I came out:** aorist passive of στέλλω, 'I send', but often used in the passive without any suggestion of being sent.

329 In response to Tecmessa's appeal to the chorus to enter the hut the chorus may now move towards it (Seale 152). But, as Σ 330a observes, given the conventions of the Greek theatre, it cannot actually enter it. Later in the play it will leave the orchestra, but in no extant tragedy does a chorus pass through the door of the *skene* (at Aesch. *Ag.* 1343–71 it *debates* whether to do so). Here the offstage cries of Ajax will serve immediately to keep the chorus in the orchestra, and to make it clear that Ajax himself will appear to face the chorus and Tecmessa.

330 Cf. Hom. *Il.* 11.793 = 15.404 (where it is Achilles who is to be persuaded), *OC* 1193–4. Tecmessa's words show how little she understands Ajax. A Sophoclean hero is hardly ever *persuaded* by the words of his friends (see Knox (1964) 13–15). But the line prepares us for the attempt which she and the chorus will shortly make.

331-2 **terrible... misfortunes:** the adjective and its noun effectively frame the sentence, with the former emphatically placed between 'Tecmessa' and 'daughter of Teleutas'. Bentley's δεινοῖς gives a smoother construction than δεινά, which would be governed by 'you tell'. The corruption arose from the separation of the adjective from its noun.

driven...frantic: the compound verb occurs only here. Etymologically it should describe someone possessed by Phoebus Apollo (cf. Eur. *Hec.* 827 of Cassandra), but is used here with a more general sense. It is unclear whether the chorus-leader refers simply to Tecmessa's account of Ajax' frenzied lamentations (317–22), or whether he believes, despite 257–9, 263, that he is still really mad. At 337–8 he considers that both alternatives are still open, and decides between them only at 344, after Ajax has begun to speak articulately. All of this creates some uncertainty in the audience's mind as to 'the precise boundary between madness and reason' (Goldhill 185; see also 611n.). But Vandvik's view that Ajax is really mad throughout the play is certainly mistaken (see Hester 247 n.8, Holt (1980) 30 n.3), as is the theory of Biggs 223–7, that the disease began with the award of the arms (which is contradicted by 51–2, 447–56), and that it is a necessary outgrowth of the hero's circumstances in his situation, or (Simpson) that it began with the formulation of the plan to kill the commanders. Holt shows how 'sickness' is used in the play both to describe Ajax' delusion and, after this madness passes, metaphorically to describe his plight. For Holt this means his failure to understand the world as it is, but it is better to take it as the anguish connected with his disgrace.

333 Ajax' cries here and at 336, 339 are *extra metrum* (cf. *El.* 77). The first two are inarticulate groans, while with the third his thoughts focus upon his son. At 342-3 he will become still more coherent, and speak in the normal iambic trimeter metre.

334-5 worse: lit. 'more'; either 'he will be more frantic', or 'he will be frantic with more terrible misfortunes'.

did you not hear: the verb governs both 'this cry of Ajax' and the indirect question, 'what kind of cry he utters'; cf. 785.

337-8 Again (269n.) Ajax' madness is seen as a disease.

which are...state: lit. 'being present with the former diseases which accompany him'. The rather odd expression serves to emphasise the close relationship between Ajax and his condition; he cannot get away from what he has done. At *OT* 303 the city of Thebes 'keeps company with disease'; cf. *El.* 599-600, Hom. *Od.* 7.270. Here there is something to be said for Blaydes' παροῦσι...ξυνών (also Dawe 139), '(Ajax) keeping company with the former diseases that are still there'. But for παρών at line end cf. 1131, 1156, 1384, and see Moorhouse 253.

339-41 This is the first reference in the play to Eurysaces, whose name derives from the great shield of his father (18-19, 574-6nn.). His absence from the hut will be explained at 531-6. Lloyd-Jones and Wilson follow Campbell and Σ (also Fraenkel 12-13) in supposing that Ajax is calling for Teucer, and that Tecmessa misunderstands him until he explains his meaning at 342. But, even if Ajax is the older brother, παῖ = Teucer, without further specification, would confuse the audience as much as Tecmessa, and it is hard to see what purpose is gained by this (see Renehan 344). Rather, here and at 342 Sophocles prepares us for the later appearance of both characters, though only Teucer is specifically summoned to come. We shall see Eurysaces before we see Teucer. Tecmessa's abrupt questions show her to be distraught.

342-3 Sophocles explains why Teucer has not been present to help Ajax in his need. At 720 we learn that he has gone to Mysia; cf. also 564. It is ironical that Teucer has been collecting booty, while Ajax has been slaughtering that which has already been won.

344 See 331-2n.

open the door: the Greek says simply 'open', with no object expressed; cf. Aesch. *Cho.* 877, and see D. Bain, *Masters, servants and orders in Greek tragedy* (Manchester 1981) 63 n. 15. The command is vaguely addressed to those inside the hut.

345 a sense of shame: αἰδώς is the sense of respect for others' feelings which inhibits one from doing what might hurt or offend them; see Cairns 230 on this passage. The chorus-leader's hope, that the presence of his friends will cause Ajax to restrain himself, is as unlikely to be fulfilled as the hope of Tecmessa at 330. His respect for his friends will be far outweighed by his sense that he has lost his honour. But again the line prepares us for the attempt that the chorus will make.

towards me too: i.e. as well as towards Tecmessa, or (Jebb) 'even towards me' (in self-deprecation). The phrase could, less well, be taken with 'when he looks', a sense which would be better given by Herwerden's ἐμέ (accusative) for ἐμοί.

346-7 The door is opened, and the audience sees Ajax sitting in the midst of the slaughtered animals. Ley 90 suggests that they would be represented by some kind of painting. Most probably the *eccyclema* is used, a moveable platform which is pushed out through the door with the tableau arranged upon it. The alternative view, that we see the scene through the door (so, for example K. Joerden, in Jens 410-12), is unlikely. The interior of the hut would be invisible to a large part of the audience, and for much of the day during the City Dionysia the door would be in shadow; see Garvie Aesch. *Cho.* lii–liii, with literature. Still less probable is the view of Pickard-Cambridge 109 (also Stanford) that only the chorus is supposed to see the scene, and that Ajax remains behind the door until 430. The emphasis on seeing (346; cf. 364) recalls Odysseus' first sight of the mad Ajax (118) and his inability to see Athena in the prologue (see Schlesinger 367).

348-595

The second part of the first episode begins, like the first part, with an *amoibaion* (348–429), between Ajax on the one hand and Tecmessa and the chorus-leader on the other. Ajax sings three strophic pairs, for the most part in emotional dochmiacs and iambics, while Tecmessa and the chorus-leader speak in more restrained iambic trimeters. The lyric section provides a break in the long first episode. The final strophic pair (394–427) is treated by W. Barner, in Jens 302, 315, as a separate monody which develops naturally from the *amoibaion*. In the prologue we saw Ajax mad in the presence of his enemies, while here we see him sane in the presence of his friends. Paradoxically the former was truer to the hero as he really is. Now Ajax is conscious of his fall, filled with shame because he has failed to take vengeance on his enemies and has become a laughing-stock (367, 382), His desire for vengeance is as great as ever (387–90), and he has certainly not learnt *sophrosyne*. But his failure calls into question his status as a hero, and he sees death as the only solution (361, 391), As we have been expecting since 330 (n.), 345, Tecmessa and the chorus-leader try to comfort him and to make him see sense, but, like all Sophoclean heroes, he is impervious to advice. He begins by appealing to his fellow-sailors, but at 369 he harshly dismisses Tecmessa, and from then on he totally ignores the words and even (except at 406) the presence of his friends. The final long stophic pair is, apart from the iambic couplets that follow each stanza, unbroken by interruptions from Tecmessa or the chorus. In the final antistrophe (412–27) Ajax' isolation is marked by the pathetic appeal, no longer to his friends, but to his environment, just as Philoctetes (*Phil.* 936–62) addresses the landscape which has made him what he is, because (938) he has no one else to whom he can speak (cf. also *Phil.* 1081–94, 1452–68, *OT* 1391–9, [Aesch.] *PV* 88–92, and see Knox (1964) 33–4).

At 430 Ajax becomes calmer, as he returns to the iambic trimeter of dialogue. The rest of the episode develops the themes already stated in the *amoibaion*. In the long speech at 430–80 Ajax continues to ignore his friends (see Reinhardt 19). He contemplates his disgrace and systematically analyses the possibilities that are open to him, concluding that death alone is tolerable. In her answering speech (485–524) Tecmessa appeals passionately to his sense of honour and to the sense of respect and responsibility which the noble man should feel towards his dependants. But in the stichomythia at 525–44 Ajax merely calls for his son, whose appearance was prepared at 339. His second long speech (545–82) shows that he has taken note of what Tecmessa has said about his responsibility to his dependants, but that he is still resolved on death. Her appeal has failed, and he has not been softened (594) or persuaded by the words of his friends (330). As he goes back into his hut, accompanied by Tecmessa and the child, the audience fears the worst.

349-50 you who alone...my friends: Blundell 72 n. 62 remarks that only here and at 406 does Ajax call another character φίλος. But, even as he acknowledges the loyalty of the chorus, he contrives by the repetition of 'alone' to convey the impression of his isolation (cf. *OT* 1321–3 and see H. Popp, in Jens 256).

your loyalty: νόμος often means 'law', but is used here in the more generalised sense of established custom, viz. the principle of loyalty to one's friends.

351-3 see: the verb governs both the pronoun 'me' and the indirect question introduced by 'what'; see 334–5n.

what a wave...of blood: the metaphor of the storm picks up 206–7 and 257–8, and is appropriate to a context in which Ajax has addressed the chorus as sailors. The wave is the wave of trouble (not, Jebb, bloodshed), and the storm of blood is the killing of the animals which has caused it. The idea of a wave running round and encircling one is slightly odd, but Ajax feels hemmed in by his troubles. For the association of κῦμα, 'wave', and ζάλη, 'storm', cf. Aesch. *Ag.* 665.

354-5 The lines are addressed to Tecmessa. Ajax is no longer mad, but he is certainly not behaving rationally (see 331–2n., Winnington-Ingram 26 n. 49). For ἀφροντίστως to describe a lack of deliberation cf. *Tr.* 366 and see Coray 191–2 (she takes τοὔργον, 'the deed' as subject of ἔχει).

357 The circumlocution, which is similar to, but more elaborate than, that of Tecmessa at 201, is not (despite Long 111, comparing 872) purely ornamental. The notion that his men have helped him before may suggest that they are likely to do so now.

358 (you people)...who: the relative pronoun is masculine despite the neuter antecedent.
rapidly plied: lit. 'whirled', but the verb may be applied to any rapid motion.
at sea: the MSS have ἁλίαν with a feminine termination, but a short final syllable is required by the metre, and Sophocles must be treating the adjective as one with only two terminations, as does Euripides in the same phrase at *Heracl.* 82.

359 you and you alone: lit. 'you indeed you indeed alone'. The effect of the repetition is similar to that at 349 (cf. *Phil.* 1095). For the thought cf. *OT* 1321.

360 of those who care for me: lit. 'of my shepherds' (see Σ, *Suda* Π 3088). Jebb objected that the phrase 'would suggest rather the idea of chieftainship', as in the Homeric 'shepherd of the people'. But Sophocles may have used it here with a different implication. That Ajax has himself killed the literal shepherds or herdsmen (27, 232) adds a certain pathos to his appeal. Sophocles may have had in mind also Aesch. *Supp.* 767, where, however, the 'shepherds of ships' are those who command them; cf. also Soph. fr. 432.10 and ποιμαίνω in the passages cited by Lloyd-Jones and Wilson, *Sophoclea* 17–18. But the text may be corrupt. The words, as V. Liapis points out to me, ought to imply that Ajax has other 'shepherds' who are not helping him, but who are they? (hardly, Stanford, the captains of his other ships). Jebb, Pearson, and Dawe accept Reiske's πημονάν, 'to help me against trouble', but the corruption is hard to explain.

361 The Greek says merely 'slaughter me with', which seems to mean 'join me in slaughtering myself', i.e. 'help me commit suicide'. But the sense 'kill me with the cattle' is not impossible. Indeed the prefix could be merely intensive (so Heath 178 n. 24; see 310n.). Anyway, Ajax for the first time expresses clearly his desire to die. At 326 it was only hinted at.

362-3 Don't speak ill-omened words: more precisely, 'speak words of good omen', which often amounts, as in a religious ritual, to 'hush, do not speak at all'; cf. *El.* 1211. Such is the power of the spoken word that Ajax' talk of death is enough to alarm the chorus; cf. Aesch. *Ag.* 1247.

treat evil with an evil cure: the idea is perhaps proverbial; cf. fr. 77, Aesch. fr. 349, Hdt. 3.53.4, Thuc. 5.65.2, Pl. *Prot.* 340e.

the misery of your ruin: the genitive may be either possessive or defining. For the chorus-leader the suicide of Ajax would only make matters worse. He himself will see things differently.

364-7 Two lines describe the hero as he was, one (366), in abrupt asyndeton, the depth of his disgrace. 'Among the foe' is balanced by 'among unfearing beasts'. The shame for Ajax consists, not in having tried to attack his enemies, but in turning his hand against helpless and unsuspecting animals. But ἀφόβοις could also mean 'who cause no fear', i.e. 'harmless' (unlike his enemies). Both senses provide a poignant contrast with 'terrible'. The result is expressed in 367. For laughter as a form of *hybris* see 79n. He who tried to inflict it on them has now become its victim, and he who laughed is now the victim of their laughter; hence the ambiguities at 304n. There is a still deeper irony, of which Ajax himself is unconscious: Odysseus has not laughed. Ajax takes it for granted that his enemies will behave as he would himself; it is Odysseus who is different.

fearless in battle: lit. 'of battle', an objective genitive. The same phrase occurs at [Aesch.] *PV* 416. The MSS have μάχαις, with δαΐοις (or -αις, agreeing with it), 'in destructive battles' (cf. Hom. *Il.* 7.119), which spoils the antithesis with 'among unfearing beasts'.

in my hands: see 27n. 367 = 382, though iambic trimeter in form, is certainly sung, not spoken; see Popp, in Jens 233–4.

369 Away with you: lit. 'won't you <go> away?' Cf. the similar expression, but with no ellipse of the verb, at *OT* 676; also *OT* 430–1.

take yourself...pastures: a literal translation is impossible. The Greek says 'go off back again as to your foot [internal accusative] to pasture'. For the superfluous mention of the foot see 27n., Denniston on Eur. *El.* 94. It occurs with the uncompounded νέμω at Pind. *Nem.* 6.15. The metaphor of pasture (cf. *El.* 1384) may suggest Ajax' preoccupation with the animals that he has killed. Unlike 367, the iambic trimeter at 369 = 384 may be spoken to form a pair with Tecmessa's trimeter (so Burton 21).

370 Cf. 430–3n., where Ajax will play upon the etymology of his name.

371 Oh...yield: for ὦ followed by an imperative, or adjuration and imperative, cf. 91 and see Fraenkel on Aesch. *Ag.* 22, Moorhouse 32.

yield...come to your senses: both ideas regularly recur in Sophocles in the context of a vain attack on the hero's resolution (see Knox (1964) 13, 15–17). Ajax is now sane (cf. 82, 273, 344), but he has not come to his senses. The line was assigned by K.O. Müller to Tecmessa, but by the MSS and Σ to the chorus-leader. One might indeed suppose that Tecmessa, having been dismissed at 369, should say no more. But symmetry with the antistrophe suggests that the same speaker should deliver both 368 and 371 (= 383 and 386 chorus; see A.S. McDevitt, *RhM* 124 (1981) 22–3, Scott 284 n.181), while the chorus's closing couplet at 377–8 corresponds with Tecmessa's at 392–3. It is effective that Tecmessa should deliver the appeal when Ajax has just told her that he is not disposed to listen.

372-6 from these hands: the genitive of the dual is Triclinius' correction of the dative plural (χερσὶ μέν), which does not correspond with his, probably correct, reading at 387. Those who keep προπάτωρ there have to print here Hermann's χερὶ μέν, 'with my hand', with μέν out of place as at *Phil.* 279. But the genitive gives better sense (cf. *OC*

838, 906), and the scansion with χεροῖν is more in keeping with the rest of the composition (see Lloyd-Jones and Wilson 18). The thought is similar to that of 364–6, but here the killing of the helpless animals is expanded into three lines, while the single 373 concisely expresses Ajax' failure to behave like the hero described in the two lines at 364–5.

accursed wretches: an *alastor* is most often an avenging spirit, but sometimes, as here, a man who deserves to be pursued by such avengers; cf. Aesch. *Eum.* 236, Men. *Perikeir.* 986 Sandbach (408 Koerte).

fell...upon: cf. 300 and see 323–5n.

with their twisted horns...glorious: the two Homeric epithets are not entirely ornamental, but help to focus attention on Ajax' grotesque choice of victims. The latter is used by Homer of Polyphemus' sheep at *Od.* 9.308, but here it is a mark of Ajax' bitterness. He applies incongruously to the goats the adjective that would more naturally describe his worthy opponents on the battlefield.

377-8 at what is over and done: for this 'fixed formula' see Fraenkel on Aesch. *Ag.* 1379. The chorus-leader's attempt at consolation is unlikely to be any more effective than the English 'it is no use crying over spilt milk'. For the idea that the past cannot be undone cf. *Tr.* 742–3, Simon. fr. 98, Pind. *Ol.* 2.15–17. Jebb and Kamerbeek (see also Moorhouse 312) defend the infinitive of almost all the MSS as a combination of two constructions, ὅπως + future indicative and a consecutive infinitive. But the latter would require the negative μή not οὐχ.

379-82 The enmity between Ajax and Odysseus was established at the beginning of the play. Here Ajax singles him out from his other enemies as the one who will be laughing; for the irony see 364–7n.

you hear everything is the attractive emendation of Lloyd-Jones and Wilson (cf. *OC* 1767, Semon. fr. 7.13; a few MSS have an unmetrical ἁπάντων τ' ἀίων). All of Odysseus' senses are acute. So he was presented at the opening of the play (esp. 1–2, 11; cf. *Phil.* 1013). Most MSS have ἁπάντων τ' ἀεί, giving 'you who are always the instrument (or 'product') of all that is evil (with ἁπάντων neuter; Kamerbeek takes ὄργανον as an adjective 'working'). It is not certain that this reading is wrong; cf. *Phil.* 927–8; also 407–9. For τε coupling the two phrases see Denniston 501. But the pairing of seeing and hearing is more effective.

Laertes: see 1–3n.

filthiest knave: the adjective occurs only here in tragedy, the noun only here and 389 (unless at *Ant.* 320). It is evidently derived from ἀλέω 'grind corn' (not, Campbell, from ἀλάομαι, wander'; cf. Σ): Odysseus is fully ground, i.e. subtle or practised, in his villainy. Cf. the similar abuse at 103, and see Long 114–20 on -μα nouns used in this way.

no doubt: see 176n.

keep on laughing: laughter appeared also in the corresponding line 367. For ἄγω in this sense cf. Eur. *Or.* 182 and see LSJ A IV 3. The phrase suggests prolonged laughter, and perhaps also (Stanford) the idea of a celebration.

383 As at 377–8 the consolation is little more than a commonplace. For the idea that the gods are responsible for the allocation of human success and failure, that their allocation is often arbitrary, and that one must therefore put up with what they send see Garvie on Hom. *Od.* 6.187–90. But the notion of alternation, of a cycle in human affairs, that is implicit in the expression of this idea here, has a bearing on the later development of the plot (see 131–2, 646–7nn.) If now it is Ajax' turn to weep and that of Odysseus to laugh, he should perhaps wait patiently until the cycle comes round again.

384 I wish indeed I could see him, if taken as a complete utterance, is remarkably mild, and hardly justifies the chorus-leader's response at 386. Clearly the latter assumes that Ajax is uttering a threat. Lloyd-Jones and Wilson are therefore probably right to put a dash at the end of the line: Ajax breaks off to lament, and the chorus-leader tries to forestall the continuation of the threat. For 'I wish I could see him' introducing such a threat cf. *Phil.* 1113, Aesch. *Cho.* 267, *PV* 973. The alternative is to suppose that 'see' is corrupt, but no plausible emendation suggests itself. Lloyd-Jones and Wilson suggest ἕλοιμι ('catch' or perhaps 'destroy'), but something stronger is required.

in this state of ruin: see 269n.

386 Do not talk so proud: as the second half of the line shows the chorus-leader means that Ajax is in no position to do so, i.e. to fulfil the threat which he is about to utter; so Gardiner (1987) 62 n. 23, against the view that the warning is against irreverent language that might offend the gods. The Sophoclean hero always does 'talk big'. We have already heard Ajax do so in the prologue (esp. 96, 127–8), and will do so again at 422–3. The chorus-leader (cf. *El.* 830) is asking him to be untrue to his very nature as a hero.

the plight that you are in: lit. 'where you are of evil', a partitive genitive as at 102n.; cf. *OT* 367, 413.

387 father of my ancestors: πάτερ is the reading of Triclinius, which he claims to have found in a MS. Ajax' grandfather, Aeacus, was the son of Zeus (cf. Hom. *Il.* 21.189). Most MSS have προπάτωρ, 'forefather', which would be inaccurate.

388-91 how might I...? introduces what is in effect a wish; see Fraenkel on Aesch. *Ag.* 622. Ajax' desire for revenge remains implacable, and embraces both Odysseus, 'the hateful knave', and the sons of Atreus. For this common type of wish, in which all the emphasis is on the participle, 'may I...before I die', see Garvie on Aesch. *Cho.* 438, Moorhouse 213, 252–3, and cf. esp. Aesch. *Ag.* 1610–11, Eur. *El.* 281. But Ajax' wish for death is not merely rhetorical. Suicide is perhaps already in his mind.

wiliest: the word, which is applied to foxes at Ar. *Lys.* 1268, is consistent with Odysseus' reputation in antiquity, and with his description at 103.

knave: see 379–82n.

jointly reigning: cf. 251, Aesch. *Ag.* 43.

392-3 for me as well: 'for me' depends on 'pray', not on ὁμοῦ, along with'; see A. Corlu, *Recherches sur les mots relatifs à l'idée de prière, d'Homère aux tragiques*(Paris 1966) 100 n. 1. Like the chorus Tecmessa is completely bound up with Ajax. It is all the more pathetic that he ignores her, and rejects the few people who are on his side. At *Ant.* 548 Ismene similarly says that she cannot envisage life without Antigone, when her appeal to die with her is harshly rejected by her sister.

394-5 The oxymoron is striking. The darkness of death and of the underworld (cf. *OC* 1389–90, Eur. *Hec.* 1–2) has turned into the only light that Ajax can now envisage, and so he longs to die. At the end of *OT* Oedipus, unable any longer to face the light of day, chooses the darkness of blindness. Contrast Hom *Il.* 17.645–7, where Ajax prays to Zeus that he may die not in darkness but in the light. See Stanford (1978) 189–97, for whom the language of the whole play is orchestrated in terms of a crescendo and diminuendo of 'light-and-darkness imagery' (190).

396-7 take me, take me to live with you: cf. 517, *Tr.* 282, 1161. For the repetition see 359n.

397-400 to look...to: for βλέπω in this kind of context cf. 514, *El.* 888, 954, 958-9, *Ant.* 922-3, in all of which, however, the preposition 'to' makes the sense clearer.
of gods or...for a day: for the antithesis cf. *Ant.* 787-90.

403 tortures me to my destruction: the alternation in Ajax' fortunes is marked by the repetition of the verb of 65, 111, 300. Both Athena and Ajax torture their victims. The adjective ὀλέθριον is proleptic. The words can be made to correspond precisely (⌣⌣⌣⌣ – – –) with 420 by printing ἐύφρονες there instead of εὔφρονες (–⌣⌣ – – –, dodrans A, a form of dochmiac). But the epic form is dubious for Sophocles (in epic ἐύ is always ⌣–), as is the resolution in the initial anceps of the dochmiac; see Lloyd-Jones and Wilson 19, Renehan 344-6). ὀλέθριον may therefore be corrupt.

403-4 The questions foreshadow 457-80, in which Ajax will analyse more rationally the courses that are open to him; cf. also 1006.

405-6 Despite numerous attempts at emendation no convincing solution has yet been proposed for the problems of text, colometry, and interpretation. For discussion see T.C.W. Stinton, *JHS* 97 (1977) 127-8 (= *Collected papers on Greek tragedy* (Oxford 1990) 271-3). The lines as transmitted do not correspond with the antistrophe, where the colometry and the scansion of Τροία are themselves uncertain. 'These things' in 405 is supposed by Jebb and others to mean Ajax' past glories, and 'creatures' has to be understood with 'along with such'. Ajax' reputation has perished along with the death of the animals. But the expression is remarkably obscure. Better is Pearson's (after Lobeck) τίσις δ' ἐμοῦ πέλας, 'and if vengeance is near me'. Stinton objects that 'it is dishonour, not vengeance, that Ajax dreads', but the vengeance that he has in mind would itself be dishonourable. However, the sense awkwardly anticipates 408-9, from which it is separated by the reference to the foolish hunt. And 'near me' looks suspiciously like an explanatory gloss on 'along with'. Lloyd-Jones and Wilson suppose a lacuna of – ⌣ – before 'my friends', read μέγα for μέγ' at 423 (with *brevis in longo*), and print Τρωία trisyllabic at 424. But the problem of sense remains.

407 Ajax now tacitly accepts the judgement of Tecmessa at 286-7n.
I have got involved in: for this sense of πρόσκειμαι cf. *El.* 240, 1040, Eur. fr. 418 N, LSJ II 1.

408-9 Ajax expects the vengeance not only of his principal enemies but of the whole Greek army, which he tried indiscriminately to attack (53-4n.). He is rejected by the whole community which he has himself rejected (see Intro. 14).
brandish: lit. 'brandish in both hands': each soldier wields his sword with two hands for greater force (so LSJ); cf. Eur. *Tro.* 1102 where Zeus thus holds the lightning. Alternatively the reference might be to spears, rather than swords, one held in each hand in the normal Homeric manner. Σ gives both interpretations (cf. *Suda* Δ 1256).

410-11 that...utter such words: accusative and infinitive of exclamation. For the thought cf. 317-18. **sound:** in the sense of 'useful'. One might have expected Tecmessa to use a stronger word.

412-13 Ajax selects three features of his environment at Troy.
paths of the roaring sea: i.e. the Hellespont. Aeschylus uses the same phrase at *Pers.* 367. It is hard to see any special relevance in the caves, but caves appear in a similar description at fr. 549 (cf. Eur. *IT* 107, 262). The pasture picks up the metaphor of 369,

and again suggests Ajax' preoccupation with the cattle. For the emotional effect of such apostrophes to nature in classical poetry in general see A.P. Wagener, *TAPhA* 62 (1931) 78–100.

414 **for long...too long:** the repetition balances that in the corresponding position in the strophe; cf. 879 = 925, and see A.H. Coxon, *CR* 61 (1947) 70–1.

416 **but no longer...detain me:** the verb is omitted in the Greek, and has to be understood from 415; cf. 257.

418 Scamander was one of the two important rivers at Troy.

420 **kindly to the Argives:** i.e. to all the other Greeks. In his isolation Ajax sees the Trojan landscape, even as he appeals to it, as hostile to himself and therefore on the side of his enemies (cf. 457–9, 859–63nn.). We are not to think of Hom. *Il.* 21, where Scamander is by no means kindly to Achilles (see Renehan 345). The idea of Σ (also Jebb and Stanford) that the river is kindly to all the Greeks, including himself, because it has supplied their drinking-water, would be intolerably flat. Lloyd-Jones and Wilson emend εὔφρονες to κακόφρονες, 'malevolent to', which provides exact responsion with 403 (n.), but this spoils the point of Ajax' conscious separation from the other Greeks.

421-2 Ajax hints strongly that he means to die. For οὐ μή + aorist subjunctive see 83n.

422-3 **I shall boast:** a similar expression to that at 386, but here with reference to a boast, not a threat. Ajax ignores the chorus-leader's advice there.

423-6 Normally (see Intro. 1) Ajax was reckoned as the best fighter *after Achilles* (cf. 1341). Here, with his 'big word', he claims to be the best without exception, his boast recalling that of Achilles himself at Hom. *Il.* 18.105–6. Heath 179 n. 27 (see also Rose 83 n. 27) is right to protest against the view of Winnington-Ingram 14–15 that this is a sign of megalomania. Such boasting is normal for an epic hero; cf. *Tr.* 811–12. For the text see 405–6n.

426-7 **I lie...prostrate:** but the variant πρόκειται ('he lies...') could be correct: from 421 Ajax describes himself in the 3rd person. The verb is regularly applied to corpses laid out for mourning before burial; e.g. 1059, *Ant.* 1101, Aesch. *Sept.* 964. Ajax thinks of his present situation as equivalent to death. But the choice of word is sinister in the light of what will happen later: we shall see his corpse laid out, but his enemies will forbid its burial.

in dishonour: so Achilles complains at Hom. *Il.* 1.412 that Agamemnon has failed to honour 'the best of the Achaeans'.

428-9 The chorus-leader acknowledges that his words can have no effect on Ajax, and so the amoibaion ends.

I can't...but I do not know: the same verb (lit. 'I do not have') governs both an infinitive and an indirect question with a deliberative subjunctive (cf. *Ant.* 270–2).

430-80 In this, his first full-scale speech, Ajax, after the emotional lyrics, analyses the situation rationally. He has turned out to be a lesser man than his father, he has turned his hand against the helpless animals, and he has incurred the laughter of his enemies. From 457 he considers three possible courses of conduct, and rejects the first two. He could go home, but would find it impossible to face his father. He could rush alone against the Trojans and restore his honour by dying in a duel, but that would only help his enemies. Only suicide remains for him. The noble man, if he cannot live well, should die well (479–80). Ajax does not even consider the possibility that he might just do nothing and wait for his fortunes to change (see 474n.). For him that would be to rely on empty hopes (478). The rhetorical structure of the speech is simple but effective. The difference between himself and Telamon is clearly marked by μέν and δέ at 434 and 437. Twice, after speculating on what might have been, he brings us back with νῦν δέ ('but as things are') to the present unhappy reality (445 and 450). The second part of the speech begins with the blunt deliberative question of 457, sandwiched between two longer questions, the second of which is made emphatic by the three verbs of hating, the first two of them juxtaposed. The two rejected options are presented at some length, before each is scornfully dismissed in less than a line. The first rejection follows on inevitably from the rhetorical question of 463–5, the second from the impossibility of helping enemies (see Intro. 11). Finally Ajax makes his choice in the simple but memorable couplet that ends his speech, with χρή ('should') providing the answer to the question of 457. We feel that he has made the right decision.

430-3 At 370 Ajax has already said *aiai*, 'alas'. Now he relates the exclamation to the etymology of his name, *Aias*. This is no frigid conceit, but springs from the common Greek notion that a name is not a matter of convention but belongs naturally to its bearer, and provides a clue to his character or destiny; see Pl. *Crat.* 435d, Garvie, *Aeschylus' Supplices: play and trilogy* (Cambridge 1969) 71–2. For examples cf. fr. 965, Hom. *Od.* 19.406–9, Aesch. *Sept.* 577–8, 829–30, Eur. *Ba.* 367, 508. Pind. *Isth.* 6.53 derives Ajax' name from *aietos*, 'eagle' (cf. Hes. fr. 250, Apollod. 3.12.7). The present etymology, which appears here for the first time, corresponds with the supposed marking AI on the petals of the *hyacinthus* flower (first attested in literature at Euphorion fr. 40 Powell (third century BC); see Gow on Theocr. 10.28). In a fourth-century Etruscan stamnos (J.D. Beazley, *Etruscan vase-painting* (Oxford 1947) Pl. 11.4, *LIMC* I 1.329) Ajax, about to commit suicide, stands beside Tecmessa, and at his feet is shown a plant on whose stem *Aivas* is written. M.R. Halleran, *Mnem.* 45 (1992) 358–9, argues that Ajax' rhetorical question is modelled on the similar etymologising at Aesch. *Ag.* 681–2 (note τίς ποτ'...ὧδ' in both passages). Where such significant names are being discussed the adjective ἐπώνυμος, 'called after', regularly occurs (cf. 574). Lloyd-Jones and Wilson may be right to accept Morstadt's deletion of 433. 'Twice' may well seem sufficient (cf. 940), and 'thrice' (for which cf. *Phil.* 1238) only weakens the pun, as does the flat repetition of 'misfortunes', while the relative pronoun of 434 follows better after the 'I' at the end of 432. The caesura too before γάρ, though not unparalleled, is unsatisfactory. But, as at 314, it is hard to see why the line should have been interpolated, unless (Fraenkel 13) the line was inserted by a fourth-century producer who wished to shorten the speech by omitting 434–56.

434-6 Telamon took part in Heracles' expedition against Troy, when it was ruled by Laomedon, Priam's father. Laomedon was killed, and Heracles gave to Telamon Hesione, Laomedon's daughter, to be his wife; see Apollod. 3.12.7, Diod. Sic. 4.32. She is the mother of Ajax' half-brother Teucer. For Telamon as 'the focus of Ajax's sense of public disgrace' see Heath 180–1.

won...for excellence: cf. 1300. So at Hom. *Il.* 6.208 Glaucus explains the aim of every hero as 'always to be the best and to be superior to others'. The prize may be Hesione, but more probably it is metaphorical, his reputation in general.

the land of Ida: i.e. Troy, Ida being the mountain there.

437 **his son:** Campbell notes that the emphatic παῖς effectively bisects the line.

439   who performed...hand: lit. 'having defended (sc. the Greeks; cf. 360) as to [internal accusative] no less deeds of my hand'. For the semantic development of ἀρκεῖν see M. Lynn-George, *Colby Quarterly* 29 (1993) 215–18. Originally meaning 'ward off', 'protect (from hostile forces)', it comes to mean 'furnish at need' or 'suffice'; cf. 76, 535, 590, 727.

440   perish: Ajax probably uses the word metaphorically, but his choice is ominous, in view of our expectation of his suicide (for a similar effect cf. Eur. *Hipp.* 419).

   so dishonoured: the phrase contrasts with Telamon's glory at 436 and also picks up the same adjective at 426–7.

441   And yet...I understand: the expression of the afterthought is similar at *El.* 332, *OT* 1455.

442-6   This is the first reference in the play to the award of the arms of Achilles to Odysseus. Ajax clearly believes that it was unfair, and that Achilles himself would have agreed, but whether Sophocles shares his opinion is never made clear; see Intro. 5, 1135n.

443   the victory for excellence: for κράτος in this sense cf. 768, *El.* 85, 476, Pind. *Isth.* 8.5.

444   seized: instead of 'received' Ajax chooses a 'loaded' word, which suggests that Odysseus *stole* the arms.

445-6   have procured them for: πράσσω often means 'transact business' (LSJ III 5), and seems to be applied particularly to any kind of secret or underhand transaction (LSJ III 6 b): e.g. *OT* 124–5, of intrigue by bribery. But it is hard to find an exact parallel for the expression here (the nearest is perhaps Plut. *Pomp.* 51, quoted by Jebb, πράττειν μὲν ἑαυτοῖς...ἡγεμονίας, 'to procure for themselves commands'), and one should not rule out Hartung's ἔπρασαν, 'sold', though the aorist of πέρνημι does not occur elsewhere in tragedy; cf. *Phil.* 978, Aesch. *Cho.* 132 (where the MS confuses the verb with πράσσω), and see Dawe 140.

   a villain: lit. 'one who is prepared to do anything'. i.e. 'to stop at nothing'. The three-word description is almost identical with Aesch. *Sept.* 671, but with παντουργῷ substituted for παντόλμῳ. Athena expressed the same idea in more complimentary terms at 2.

   my triumphs: lit. 'the triumphs of this man', a common way of referring to oneself. For κράτη with this sense cf. *El.* 689.

447-9   We move from Ajax' earlier to his present disgrace. If he had avenged himself on the sons of Atreus they would not have lived to treat anyone else in the way that they have treated him.

   If these eyes...judgement: the primary meaning is that in his madness Ajax was unable to see or think straight (cf. 51–2, *OT* 528–9), but we are to think also of the wide-open eyes which roll in pain or madness; see Page on Eur. *Med.* 1174–5, and, for διάστροφος of the eyes in such a context, cf. *Tr.* 794, Eur. *HF* 868, *Ba.* 1122, 1166, Hp. *Morb. sacr.* VI p. 372 and 374 L, of the φρένες, 'mind', [Aesch.] *PV* 673.

   parted company from my intention: lit. 'rushed away from', a rather odd expression, which may be corrupt.

   procured by voting: this is perhaps the force of the active. Normally the middle ψηφίζομαι is used of voting oneself. 1136 implies that the sons of Atreus did not vote themselves.

450-2 while...against them: ἐπευθύνοντ᾽, 'directing', gives better sense than ἐπεντύνοντ᾽, 'preparing'. The time for preparation was past; cf. 49. See Pearson (1922) 22–3, and for the verb cf. *Phil.* 1059.

Gorgon-eyed: Ajax chooses a more sinister epithet than the epic γλαυκῶπις, for which see Garvie on Hom. *Od.* 6.13 (but also more recently W. Pötscher, *Philol.* 141 (1997) 3–20); cf. fr. 844.2. De Romilly suggests that Sophocles may have had in mind Pheidias' statue of Athena Parthenos with its Gorgoneion. The face of the Gorgon Medusa turned to stone anyone who looked at it. The Erinyes who inflict madness on Orestes appear to him like Gorgons at Aesch. *Cho.* 1048 (cf. *Eum.* 48), and at Eur. *HF* 868 the eyes of the mad Heracles are described as both 'rolling' (see previous note) and 'Gorgon-eyed'.

unconquerable: or 'unwedded' (Σ, *Suda* A 428).

the disease of madness: cf. 59 and see 269n.

453 I bloodied my hands: cf. 43; also 40, 97nn.

454 The two long compound verbs give weight to the line. For the laughter of one's enemies see 79, 364–7n.

455-6 For the thought cf. *El.* 696–7. So at Hom. *Il.* 16.843–50 the dying Patroclus declares that Hector would never have defeated him if he had not been helped by Zeus and Apollo. Homeric heroes commonly attribute their failures to divine intervention. But other people rarely seem to accept this kind of excuse, and here it is clear that Ajax himself does not really believe that it lessens the shame of killing the animals.

not with *my* consent: for ἑκών treated as a participle see Goodwin § 875.3, Kühner-Gerth II 102.

the coward: lit. 'the bad man'. The word is that used by Athena at 132–3 (n.) (see also 319–20n.), with reference to Ajax himself. He tacitly rejects her evaluation, and by the end of the play it will be established that he is right to do so, but wrong to describe Odysseus as a κακός.

457-9 See 403–4n. 'What am I to do?' is the characteristic cry of the tragic hero. Ajax' thoughts turn to the future: how can he prove that he is not a κακός? That he is hated by both Athena and the Greek army we know to be true (cf. 401–9). For his feeling that even his environment is against him see 420n. In his isolation he totally ignores the support of Tecmessa and the chorus. 459 is the only line in the play with resolution in the fifth foot. Out of sixteen cases in Sophocles (8 of them involving proper names) *Ant.* with 5 has the largest number. From here to 467 there are no fewer than 6 resolutions (9 in the whole speech), perhaps suggesting the passion that is concealed beneath Ajax' rational discourse.

461 the sons of Atreus all alone: from the point of view of Ajax, still conscious of his own worth, it is his enemies who will be isolated by his departure.

462-5 The answer to the two rhetorical questions is already implied at 434–40. Ajax, whose eye so terrified his enemies (167), and which he kept hidden in his hut at 190–1, is now ashamed to show it to his father, and the latter will not bear to look at him. For his inability to face his father, 'a typical *aidos*-reaction', see Cairns 231, also 434–6n., and cf. *OT* 1371–2, *Phil.* 110, Hdt. 1.37.2, also 1290n. The 'glory' of 465 picks up the same word at 436. For the metaphorical 'garland of glory' cf. Eur. *Supp.* 315.

466 well then: for ἀλλὰ δῆτα in a question following a rejected suggestion see Denniston 273.

467 in duels: lit. 'alone with them alone'; cf. 1283, Eur. *Med.* 513. Ajax seems to envisage a series of duels. The language again suggests his sense of isolation from the other Greeks.

470-1 I must seek some...enterprise: Ajax' idea of the proper behaviour of a hero connects him with Odysseus himself at the beginning of the play (2).

such...that from it I shall: for the final-consecutive use of the relative pronoun, with negative μή, cf. 659, 1166, 1261, and see Moorhouse 274–5.

472 his son: lit. 'being born from him', the idea being that Ajax has inherited his father's character (see Garvie on Aesch. *Cho.* 420–2).

a coward: lit. 'without guts', a very rare word. Often the σπλάγχνα are the seat of the affections (e.g. 995) rather than of courage; but cf. Aesch. *Sept.* 237, Eur. *Hipp.* 424, etc.

473 For the idea that it is shameful or foolish to cling to life cf. e.g. *Ant.* 461–6, *OT* 518–19, *OC* 1211–14, Hom. *Il.* 15.511, Aesch. *Sept.* 683–5, Eur. *Hec.* 373–8, Pl. *Phaedo* 117a. For this and other kinds of folk-wisdom relating to the choice of life or death see Heath 161, also Intro. 9–10.

474 Ajax is unable to envisage the possibility that his fortunes may change for the better. For the view that for some people misery is uninterrupted see 131–2n.

475-6 Ajax seems to mean that an extension of life does not improve its quality, but the exact sense is obscure and the text is probably corrupt. Jebb supposed a metaphor from moving back the pieces in a game of draughts (LSJ s.v. ἀνατίθημι B 2; cf. the middle use at Antipho Soph. 87 B 52 D-K), while Kamerbeek thinks of a race. For προστίθημι of handing someone over to death cf. Eur. *Hec.* 368, *IA* 540. It is easy to imagine that the successive days of one's life are bringing one ever nearer to death, or, alternatively, that each day represents a postponement of death. But the combination of the two ideas is difficult, as is the active use of ἀνατίθημι and the genitive of separation after it. No convincing emendation has yet been proposed.

477-8 I would not...valuation: for a more colloquial form of this kind of expression see Fraenkel on Aesch. *Ag.* 275. In Greek thought hope is regularly deceitful or, at best, ambivalent; cf. Hes. *Op.* 96–9, 500, Semon. fr. 1.6–7, Thuc. 3.45.5, 5.103, 6.24.3. The ambivalence is clear at *Ant.* 615–17. For 'empty hopes' cf. also *El.* 1460. For 'warm' (the heart etc.) as a description of an emotional experience see Garvie on Aesch. *Cho.* 629–30, 1004.

479 to die well: the tense is perfect, strictly 'to be dead'. Ajax thinks not so much of the manner of his death as of his reputation after he is dead.

480 you have heard my whole account: i.e. 'that is all I have to say'. Ajax brusquely acknowledges the presence of the chorus and indicates that there is no room for further debate. For this kind of formulaic conclusion cf. *Tr.* 876, *Phil.* 241, 1240, Fraenkel on Aesch. *Ag.* 582.

481-4 The chorus-leader's intervention serves mainly to allow the audience to relax between the two speeches. After 480 his perfunctory attempt to persuade Ajax to change his attitude and yield to his friends is clearly futile. Gardiner (1987) 63 remarks on the ironic reversal of roles for Ajax: at Hom. *Il.* 9. 630–2 it was he who complained that Achilles was deaf to the persuasion of his friends. However, the chorus-leader's words prepare us for the more serious attempt that Tecmessa is about to make. Later still (1353) Odysseus will use the argument successfully against Agamemnon.

a false speech: i.e. one not true to his character, as the polarisation of expression makes clear. The adjective means lit. 'substituted' (for the real thing); cf. *OC* 794; also 187–9n., *Suda* Υ 455 and 456, Eust. 106.7.

thoughts: the word is used by Sophocles especially of anxious thoughts, while γνώμη expresses the will or intention of Ajax; cf. 744.

485-524 Tecmessa's speech (and Ajax' reply to it) is closely modelled on Andromache's appeal to Hector to stay inside Troy at Hom. *Il.* 6.407–39 and on his reply at 440–65 (cf. also 22.477–515); see Kirkwood (1965) 56–9, Easterling (1984), Sorum 369–71, Goldhill 186–7, Poe 45–9, Garner 51–2, Zanker (W.E. Brown finds throughout the play an underlying contrast between Ajax and Hector). Most of these writers rightly insist that the differences are as important as the similarities; 'the whole situation has been thoroughly re-thought and the model transformed without losing its recognisability' (Easterling 2). Ajax rejects the ties for which Hector fought.

For Tecmessa's affectionate relationship with Ajax see 201–347, 212nn. Her speech is marked both by intense pathos and by the persuasiveness of its arguments. She begins fairly flatly with the generalisation of 485–6, which she then illustrates by citing the example of her own unhappy change of fortune (487–91). But she does not presume to point the moral. Instead she appeals to him to consider her reputation and not to leave her to be insulted by his enemies (492–5), an argument which ought to weigh heavily with Ajax, or to become the slave of one of them (496–504). His son too will become a slave (499), and we know that Eurysaces is already in Ajax' mind (339). This will lead to shame for Ajax (505), something which she knows he will want to avoid (cf. 473). Tecmessa's argument that he should show respect for his father (506–7) attempts to answer 434–40, 462–6. He should pity his mother too and his soon to be orphaned son (507–13), and finally Tecmessa returns, with ever increasing pathos, to where she began, her own situation, and begs him to remember the pleasure she has brought him. In the last line she opposes her idea of the duty of the 'noble man' to that of Ajax himself at the end of his speech (479–80). 'Ajax' case for dying and Tecmessa's case for living rest on conflicting ideas of εὐγένεια' (Holt (1981) 279.

Tecmessa' concentration on disgrace and nobility is well calculated to appeal to Ajax (see Winnington-Ingram 19, 29–30, Easterling 2–4, Heath 181–2, Cairns 231–4). By heroic standards it would indeed be shameful to allow his dependants to be insulted or to suffer. A sense of respect for others (αἰδώς) is also expected of the hero. The term spans both the competitive and the co-operative values, and 'Tecmessa's appeals to self- and other-regarding impulses are thus virtually inseparable' (Cairns 233). However, for Ajax the potential insult to his concubine and the grief of his family are much less disgraceful than his present failure and the laughter of his enemies. And, as far as gratitude is concerned, that is one of the 'quieter' virtues, and contributes nothing to his *arete*, (unless, Cairns 233, the implication is that 'reciprocity [of a kindness] is an imperative which it is discreditable to ignore'; see also Blundell 86). Tecmessa's 'persuasive definition' (Winnington-Ingram 29; for the term see Adkins 38–40), her attempt to substitute her own notion of 'nobility', is after all unlikely to succeed.

Like Ajax himself (430–80n.) Tecmessa knows the rhetorical effect of varying the length of her sentences. At 489 the short, pathetic 'but now' (cf. 445, 450), and the following short sentence, which ends emphatically before the caesura with the reference to Ajax' hand, are sandwiched between two longer sentences. The increase in emotion is marked at 501, when the first metrical resolution expresses the scorn of Ajax' enemies (the only other resolutions are at 506 and 517; contrast 457–9n.), and by the emphatic 'of Ajax' before punctuation at the beginning of 502 (cf. 'except for you' in the same position at 515). The anaphora at 506–7, 'feel shame...feel shame', followed by the variation 'pity' (510) recalls the structure of 458–9; cf. also the double question at 518–9. Much pathos is created by the constant repetition of the pronouns 'I' (x 11) and 'you' (x 9) and the possessive adjective 'your' (x 9), often at emphatic positions in the sentence. By combining them in the same line or sentence she tries to create an impression that they are united in their interests (esp. 493, 515, 518–19).

485-6 the fortune...upon them: cf. 803 (the same phrase). Tecmessa is not thinking in metaphysical terms either of Fate or of Chance as controlling human affairs. In Greek thought ἀνάγκη, 'necessity', may refer to any constraint imposed on one either by circumstances or by other people. For Tecmessa it is the constraint of slavery (cf. Hom. *Il.* 6.458 Andromache, Aesch. *Ag.* 1042, 1071 Cassandra). At 489–90 she will attribute responsibility for this jointly to the gods and to Ajax. For the related idea that there is no stronger force than Necessity cf. Eur. *Alc.* 965–6, *Hel.* 514.

487-9 A similar change of fortunes is lamented by Polyxena at Eur. *Hec.* 349–57, with the first half of 357 = the first half of 489 here. Like Ajax himself (474n.) Tecmessa does not consider the possibility that her fortunes may alternate again for the better. The moral which she is too modest to draw is that this is what life is like, and one must just endure it, as she herself is doing. But the *sophrosyne* (see 132–3n.) which she is in effect advocating is not something that the Sophoclean hero ever practises.

mighty in wealth: cf. Pind. *Isth.* 3.2, Eur. *El.* 939 for the expression. Here 'in' is instrumental in force.

if any Phrygian was: in the Greek 'was' is omitted, and 'any' is attracted into the genitive case of 'father'; cf. *OC* 734, Ar. *Plut.* 655, Thuc. 7.21.5.

489-90 I suppose: the hesitation is a mark of Tecmessa's modesty. Ajax is obviously responsible for her enslavement, but she cannot be sure that it was also the will of the gods.

to your hand: i.e. 'to you'. We may think of what Ajax' hands have done more recently (366 etc.).

490-3 At Eur. *Hec.* 824–32 Hecuba will similarly, but with greater emphasis on its sexual element, appeal to the relationship between Agamemnon and his concubine Cassandra, Hecuba's daughter.

the god of our hearth: the title, like Zeus *herkeios* (108n.), indicates that Zeus presides over the unity of the household. For the association of the hearth, the most sacred place in the house, with supplication see J. Gould, *JHS* 93 (1973) 97–8, and cf. Hom. *Od.* 7.153–4, 14.159, Thuc. 1.136.3 and Plut. *Them.* 24.3, A.R. 4.693–4.

by your bed: Σ compares Hom. *Il.* 15.39, where Hera swears an oath to Zeus by their marriage-bed.

you and I were united: cf., with the same sexual implication, Eur. *Andr.* 1245.

494 painful talk: in the parodos the chorus was upset by what his enemies were saying about Ajax. Now Tecmessa tries to make him feel the same way about herself, his dependant.

495 hand me on to be...possession: the adjective is proleptic. For the verb cf. 1297. Most MSS have ἀφείς ('abandon', 'let me go'), instead of ἐφείς, a corruption probably from ἀφῆς in 496.

496-7 on the day you die: most MSS have 'if you die', with εἰ + subj. (without ἄν), a Homeric form of future conditional which is occasionally found in tragedy (Goodwin § 454). The variant readings all result from attempts to restore normal Attic usage. Bothe's ᾗ, the relative pronoun, pointing forward to its antecedent 'on that day', is a considerable improvement, but it cannot be considered certain. **and having died:** the repetition of the key idea of Ajax' death serves to stress the connection between it and the fate of Tecmessa herself, as do the emphatic pronouns 'you' and 'I too'.

498 violently seized: Aeschylus uses the same expression at *Pers.* 195; cf. also *Phil.* 644, Lys. 3.46, 12.96.

499 with your son: the brief reference to Eurysaces prepares us for the fuller development of his situation at 510–13. So Andromache at Hom. *Il.* 6.408 couples Astyanax with herself in her appeal to Hector. 'Your' is emphatic: Ajax is reminded that his son depends on him; cf. 506, 510.

the life of a slave: τροφή means strictly 'nurture', but comes to mean 'life-style' in general. At *Il.* 6.454–65 Hector pictures in greater detail the life of slavery that Andromache will lead after he is dead and Troy has fallen (cf. also *Od.* 8.526–9). Tecmessa, unlike Andromache, has already been reduced to the status of a slave (489), but she distinguishes between her present state, with which she is now content, and the harsh slavery to which she can look forward. So at *Il.* 1.348 Briseis is unwilling to leave Achilles for her new master Agamemnon.

500-4 Similarly at *Il.* 6.459–62 Hector imagines someone saying, this was the wife of Hector, who was best of the horse-taming Trojans at fighting, when they were fighting around Troy'. Both Sophocles and Homer frame the direct speech with the statement that 'someone will say' (for this motif in *Il.* and later see J.R. Wilson, *ICS* 4 (1979) 1–15, I.J.F. de Jong, *Eranos* 85 (1987) 69–84), with 504 being a translation into iambic metre of Homer's ὥς ποτέ τις ἐρέει. But the note of sympathy which is present in the Homeric passage, where the husband is the speaker, is missing from the Sophoclean. Tecmessa, whose concern is to shame Ajax, turns it into a sarcastic saying by one of his enemies, with 'bedfellow' replacing the 'wife' of the Homeric passage. Tecmessa, though a model of *sophrosyne* (487–9n.), faces a tragic fate. Athena's claim at 132–3 seems, at least in her case, to be untrue.

attack me...with these words: cf. 724–5, 1244.

who became: it is doubtful whether the aorist can simply refer to the past *period* of Ajax' pre-eminence (so Jebb). Blaydes' ἴσχυε (imperfect) is worth considering.

instead of...so envied: more lit. 'what a life...in exchange for how great envy', with two balancing exclamations; cf. 557, 923, *El.* 751, *Tr.* 994.

endures: lit. 'nourishes', a perhaps fortuitous echo of 499. But the word is appropriate in a speech which is so much concerned with the nurture of Eurysaces (511). For the verb thus used of 'keeping' something unpleasant cf. *Phil.* 795; more generally *OT* 356, *Tr.* 817.

504-5 drive: i.e. 'harass' (cf. 275, 756), or perhaps (LSJ s.v. ἐλαύνω II) 'strike' (cf. 137). The same verb is used with the same subject, *daimon,* 'a god', or unspecified supernatural power (cf. 534n.) at *OC* 1750. Tecmessa is prepared to accept for herself what destiny or the gods may send (cf. 489). Her concern is only to persuade Ajax of the disgrace that it will entail for him. For shame felt at something suffered by a member of one's family see Adkins 167. At *Il.* 6.462–5 Hector's conclusion is naturally different. He says nothing about disgrace, but concentrates on Andromache's pain, and hopes to die before he hears her cries as she is led off into slavery.

506-7 feel shame: Tecmessa appeals to the *aidos* which in Hector's case *prevented* him from accepting Andromache's appeal (*Il.* 6.442): he could not face his fellow-Trojans if now he behaved like a coward. So we may surmise that for Ajax too what people will say about his present failure will weigh more heavily than what they will say if he fails to respect his family. A further irony is that Ajax is the recipient of the very advice which he gave to the inexorable Achilles at *Il.* 9.640 (see Garner 58–9). For the plight of aged parents with no son to look after them cf. *Il.* 5.152–8, 24.486–92, Hes. *Th.* 603–7.

before your mother too: the participle ('abandoning') has to be understood in the Greek with 'your mother'. Tecmessa seems to take it for granted that Ajax is already abandoning his parents, and that her appeal will therefore be unsuccessful. For a shift in the use of the verb (and αἰσχύνομαι) in Sophocles, from the inhibiting of a contemplated action to a subjective concern with one that one has already begun, see Cairns 264.

508 has...for her portion: a metaphor from holding an allotment of land. For the defining genitive after the compound adjective which includes a noun as its base see Moorhouse 54.

509 prays: ἀράομαι in tragedy more often means 'curse', but is found occasionally in the Homeric sense of 'pray': e.g. *Tr.* 48, *OC* 1445; see A. Corlu, *Recherches sur les mots relatifs à l' idée de prière, d' Homère aux tragiques* (Paris 1966) 259–60.

510-13 At *Il.* 6.432 Andromache more briefly imagines Astyanax as an orphan. She will develop the theme more fully in her lament after Hector's death (*Il.* 22.484–506).

youthful nurture: cf. 499, 503. Tecmessa and Eurysaces will be united in the misery of their future lives. For the expression cf. *OT* 1, *OC* 345–6.

he is to pass his life: the verb implies a long period of endurance; cf. [Eur.] *Rhes.* 982, Hdt. 3.40.2, Hesych. Δ 1871.

apart from you: lit. 'alone from you'; cf. *OC* 1250, Eur. *Med.* 52. Ajax, who is so conscious of his own isolation (349–50n., 467), should understand this argument.

unfriendly guardians: ὀρφανιστής occurs only here in literature, but it is found in an inscription as a title of officials at Selymbria (*BCH* 36 (1912) 549); cf. also *Suda* O 652, Eust. 533.33). In 'not friendly' the negative μή, not οὐ (cf. 1242), is best taken as generic (Jebb). Tecmessa is thinking of guardians in general, who are proverbially harsh to orphans; see also Moorhouse 322.

think how: the clause is probably governed by 'pity' (510), and the 'if...guardians' clause is subordinate to it: 'pity your son, how great..., if robbed etc'.

514-19 At *Il.* 6.411–30 Andromache, at much greater length, says that she no longer has a father and mother. Achilles has killed the former, and all seven of her brothers, while her mother has died naturally (cf. also Briseis at 19.291–7). Therefore Hector is for her her father, mother, and brother, as well as husband (cf. Aesch. *Cho.* 238–43, Eur. *Alc.* 646–7, *Hec.* 280–1, *Heracl.* 229–30, Xen. *An.* 1.3.6). Tecmessa's situation is different in that it is Ajax himself who has destroyed her country. But Sophocles does not overdo the pathos by making him her father's killer. He, like her mother and the mother of Andromache, has apparently died naturally. The only author who identifies his killer is

Dict. Cret. *Bell.Tr.* 2.18 (probably first century AD), and there it is Ajax himself. But after the statement that it was Ajax who destroyed Tecmessa's country ἄλλη implies that Ajax had nothing to do with the death of her parents.

514-15 to look to: cf. 397–400n. Greek uses a deliberative subjunctive. For the lengthening of the short final syllable before βλ cf. *El.* 301, *Phil.* 622. This sentence is effectively framed by the emphatic pronouns 'I' and 'you', stressing the relationship between the two.

annihilated: lit. 'made unseen'.

517 dwell in death: proleptic, 'so as to be dwellers'. The phrase is a kind of oxymoron, dwelling normally suggesting living, but here their home is in Hades; cf. 396. For the adjective 'in death' cf. *OT* 959, *Phil.* 819.

518 I...you: see 514–15n.

519 all: for πᾶσα thus used cf. 275.

520 even me: Tecmessa modestly and humbly subordinates herself to Ajax' parents and his son.

520-1 a man: the word seems emphatic at the beginning of the sentence. Tecmessa probably means 'a true man' (see 77n.). She substitutes for 473 her own definition of how a man should behave, and goes on to clarify her meaning at 524. The optative in the protasis of the conditional sentence is often found when the verb of the principal clause in primary sequence denotes obligation, propriety, or possibility, etc.; see Goodwin § 555, and cf. 1159, 1344, *Ant.* 666. It is equivalent to 'one would rightly...if...'. Here the tentative optative, combined with που, 'perhaps', is characteristic of the modest Tecmessa in this speech. So is the euphemism, 'some pleasure', with which she refers to their sexual relationship (cf. 1204, Mimn. 1.1, V. *Aen.* 4.317–18).

522 kindness...kindness: χάρις has a wide range of meanings. Here it may include the idea of sexual favour (cf. Eur. *Hel.* 1397), as well as the gratitude that such kindness or favour is expected to produce (cf. Eur. *Hec.* 829–30). For the reciprocity of χάρις cf. *OC* 779, Eur. *Hel.* 1234, and see Blundell 33–4 and, on 'the mutual *charis* of sexual gratification' in a successful marriage, 46.

523-4 The lines repeat, but in negative form, the sense of the positive 520–1. For the polarisation see 20n. For failure to reciprocate *charis* as a mark of the bad man cf. Thgn. 101–12.

no longer be reckoned as: lit. 'no longer become'. The expression is odd, and is perhaps corrupt. At 1266–9 (n.) Teucer will use similar arguments against Agamemnon on Ajax' behalf.

525-44 In this bridge-passage Sophocles keeps us in suspense as to whether Ajax will accept Tecmessa's arguments. We may be encouraged that, invited by the chorus-leader to pity her and to praise her speech, he does not reject them outright. But his readiness to approve of her (in the third person), *provided* she does what she is told is ominous in the light of 292–3. At 536 he praises what she has done, but he does not mention her speech at all. The passage prepares us also for the appearance of Eurysaces (already foreshadowed at 339) and Ajax' address to his son. The length of the stichomythia, combined with Ajax' impatience (540, 543) serves to strengthen the impatience also of the audience.

527 at least from me: for γοῦν with a pronoun see Denniston 453–4. Ajax cannot speak for others, and no doubt does not care about their views.

529 As always Tecmessa is compliant.

530 my son: the possessive pronoun is emphatic as at 499n. 'your son'.

531 I let him go away: more precisely 'I set him free', with the unstated implication 'from danger'.

because I was afraid: 'because of fears', dative of cause (cf. Aesch. *Ag.* 50). With great delicacy Tecmessa uses a generalising plural, and does not specify the nature of her fear, until she is questioned by Ajax (532–3). Until 541 Tecmessa, despite 529, is in no hurry to carry out Ajax' instruction; see Heath 183 n. 32.

533 For the hesitant που, 'perhaps', see 520–1n.

534 The tone is bitter. δαίμων here, as often (e.g. *OT* 1194, *Tr.* 910, *El.* 1306; see 504–5n.), is the power that controls the destiny of each individual person. If in his madness Ajax had killed his beloved son, that would have been consistent with everything that has happened to him. For the genitive after πρέπον see Moorhouse 52, who (like Friis Johansen-Whittle on Aesch. *Supp.* 458) takes it as by analogy with ἄξιον, 'worthy'. The genitive is sometimes found after adjectives denoting likeness (see Bond on Eur. *HF* 131). But after πρέπει the genitive, instead of dative, is very rare; cf. Pl. *Menex.* 239c, *Plt.* 271e). It seems better to accept the abnormality here than to spoil the simple trenchancy of the line by repunctuation or emendation.

535 well anyway: Tecmessa brings Ajax back to the main point. For ἀλλ' οὖν so used see Denniston 443–4.

to ward off: see 439n.

536 I approve: for the 'instantaneous aorist' see 99n.

537 even in the present situation: lit. 'as a result of this', i.e. 'as things now stand'; cf. 823, Eur. *Andr.* 1184 etc. For Tecmessa's readiness to help, but also for her reluctance, cf. 529, 531n. She seems to hope that Ajax has forgotten his instruction that the child should be fetched (see Holt (1981) 280). For ὡς with a sense of limitation cf. 395 and see Moorhouse 305. The line is very similar to *Ant.* 552.

538 face to face: cf. 66, 81, 229.

539 Certainly: καὶ μήν expresses 'agreement or consent, or a generally favourable reaction to the words of the previous speaker' (Denniston 353–4); cf. 990. Alternatively, we might take καὶ μήν as introducing the new arrival. But 540 shows that, for Ajax at least, Eurysaces is not yet arriving, and the conventional entrance-formula will not be used until 544 (n.).

540 For negative or interrogative μέλλω = 'delay', 'put off', + μὴ οὐ + infinitive see LSJ s.v. III, Moorhouse 328–9, and cf. [Aesch.] *PV* 627.

542 lead him by the hand: cf. 27n., 35.

543 coming: see 157n.

fail to hear: lit. 'be left behind by'; see LSJ s.v λείπω B II 4, and cf. Eur. *Or.* 1041, 1085, *Hel.* 1246.

544 here comes: both καὶ δή (more often καὶ μήν; see Denniston 251) and the deictic ὅδε regularly mark the arrival of a new character on stage. The child, accompanied by a servant, enters probably by the *eisodos*, not from the hut, from which he had been sent away (531), and not from a side door in the *skene*, representing an adjacent room in Ajax' hut (Kamerbeek) or (D.J. Mastronarde, *ClAnt* 9 (1990) 278) a separate hut; see 594–5n.

545-82 Ajax' moving farewell to his son again recalls Hom. *Il.* 6.466–84, but it is not lightened by the smiles of the loving parents in that passage (6.471, 484). We have been waiting for Ajax' reaction to Tecmessa's speech, but he makes no direct reference to it. Nevertheless (despite Reinhardt 21–2, for whom not a syllable of her speech has reached her husband's ears), he has clearly noted her arguments that he has a duty to care for both his parents and his son (see Cairns 234). He answers both by entrusting the latter to the care of Teucer and the chorus, and by appointing his son to look after his grandparents in their old age. It is pleasing that their future is assured, but horrifying that Ajax has so easily disposed of the only reasons for him to stay alive. He totally (unless at 559) ignores Tecmessa's appeal that he should show her gratitude. For the audience the only hope is that Teucer may arrive in time to prevent the suicide. But again our feelings are mixed: we want Ajax to remain true to himself, and suicide seems indeed to be the only solution. After making arrangements for the disposal of his armour, Ajax ends his speech with a series of short clauses (578–82) which characterise him as the man of action whose mind is firmly fixed. The final metaphor from surgery is sufficient to fill his listeners, and the audience, with dread.

545-7 lift him ...here: the words may suggest that Ajax is on a higher level than Tecmessa, i.e. on the *eccyclema* (so N.C. Hourmouziades, *Production and imagination in Euripides* (Athens 1965) 102). Sophocles perhaps has in mind Hom. *Il.* 6.467–70, where the little Astyanax *was* frightened (cf. ταρβήσας 469 with ταρβήσει here) by the horse-hair plume on his father's helmet, and Hector takes the helmet off to quieten his fear (see Easterling 4–5, Goldhill 187). Ajax, however, expects his son already to be as brave as himself. It is almost as if he were standing among, not the slaughtered animals, but his enemies on the battlefield; for this pathetic dissonance see Reinhardt 22, Sorum 368, who remarks that Eurysaces is to establish his parentage by looking at the blood which shows his father's shame.

this: of the variant readings τοῦτόν γε is the simplest and most satisfactory. Despite Dawe 143–4 που in this position can hardly go with ταρβήσει.

newly-slaughtered: cf. 898.

rightly: for the adverb, equivalent to 'truly', in this sort of context see Pearson on fr. dub. 1119 (where Priscian is perhaps quoting in error from our passage).

his inheritance: lit. 'as to (internal accusative) the things that come from his father'.

548-9 broken in like a young horse: the same verb is used literally at [Eur.] *Rhes.* 187. For a compound verb consisting of a nominal and a verbal stem used transitively see Moorhouse 38. Young people, but more often girls than boys, are regularly thought of as young horses, but here the metaphor involves a paradox: a horse is broken in to tame it, whereas Eurysaces is to be trained in savagery. For this quality in Ajax himself cf. 205n. He is aware of his own character. The paradox is strengthened by the incongruity of 'savage ways', lit. 'savage laws', in which the noun suggests civilised society, the opposite of savagery (see Segal (1981) 129, Goldhill 187), and, as V. Liapis points out to me, the usual sophistic *antithesis* with 'nature' (φύσις); see also M. Davis, in J.P. Euben (ed.), *Greek tragedy and political theory* (California 1986) 152.

550-1 in other respects like him: at Hom. *Il.* 6.479–80 Hector more modestly hopes that his son will be said to be 'far better than his father'. Ajax typically is unwilling to go that far, and false modesty would be out of place (see March 15–16). But his concern corresponds with his reluctance to face his own father now that he has been dishonoured

(434–40, 462–6). Aeneas' prayer for his son Ascanius is similar at V. *Aen.* 12.435–6; cf. also Dion. Hal. 8.41.3, Accius *Armorum iudicium* fr.9 Dangel.

bad: probably with the implication 'cowardly'. As at 455–6 (n.) Ajax is in no doubt that he himself is not a κακός.

552-5 For the notion that it is better to be unaware of one's troubles cf. 265–7n., Eur. *IA* 677. For the unawareness, and consequent happiness, of the young child cf. *Tr.* 144–52, *OC* 1229–30, fr. 583, Eur. *Med.* 48. Iphigenia takes a different line at Eur. *IA* 1243–4. After 'aware of nothing' all the MSS, together with *Suda* Z 61 and K 425, insert line 554a, 'for to be unaware is very much a painless trouble', i.e. 'ignorance is bliss'. Stob. 4.24.54 omits it in his quotation of the passage. Though defended by Kamerbeek, it is intolerable after 554. A copyist must have noted it in the margin as a parallel line from some other play, and it has been incorporated in the text, perhaps (Dawe) expelling a genuine line.

until you learn: for ἕως + subjunctive without ἄν in a future temporal clause in tragedy see Goodwin § 620, Moorhouse 296–7, and cf. 1183.

pleasure and pain: the alternation which is the lot of mankind (131–2, 383nn.).

556-7 The implication is that Eurysaces will take vengeance on his father's enemies, the vengeance which he has failed to take himself. Ajax' idea of the 'nurture' of his son is very different from that of Tecmessa (499, 503, 511). Creon at *Ant.* 641–4 also believes that the first duty of a son is to requite his father's enemies and to honour his friends.

you must show: Sophocles oddly, as at *Phil.* 54–5 (cf. Cratin. fr. 115 *PCG),* combines two constructions, δεῖ + accusative and infinitive and the hortatory ὅπως + future indicative; see Goodwin § 360, Moorhouse 308.

what sort...what sort: both the language and the thought pick up 503.

558-9 The mood suddenly changes. Ajax' attitude softens a little as he thinks of the childish innocence of Eurysaces. At 548–9 he wanted him to become savage as quickly as possible. Now he is prepared to allow him a little while to enjoy his childhood.

be fed by light breezes: in contrast with the storm of Ajax' madness (207, 257–8). For the metaphorical 'feeding' cf. Aesch. *Cho.* 26, Eur. *Ba.* 617, and esp. *Tr.* 144 (cited at 552–5n.), Pl. *Rep.* 401c, *Suda* K 2199.   For this idea of wind or breath 'nourishing' see Padel 97–8.

nurturing your young soul: Sophocles is probably thinking of the description of the young Astyanax as ἀταλάφρων (probably 'tender-minded') at Hom. *Il.* 6.400. West, on Hes. *Op.* 131 takes 'in your soul' with 'be fed', and translates ἀτάλλων as 'playing' (cf. Hom. *Il.* 13.27). P. Chantraine, *Dictionnaire étymologique de la langue grecque* (Paris 1968) s.v. ἀταλός, shows that all of the occurrences can be related to a child who either plays or is nourished; see also C. Moussy, in *Mélanges P. Chantraine* (Paris 1972) 157–68.

a joy to your mother here: this, an adaptation of *Il.* 6.481 (cf. also Eur. *Ion* 1379), is the only momentary sign of tenderness for Tecmessa in this speech. Only here does Ajax make any attempt to counter her prediction of unrelieved misery for herself; see Blundell 79 n. 94, but cf. later 651–3. The phrase is in apposition with the whole of the preceding clause.

560-1 The mood changes again as Ajax thinks of the *hybris* which his enemies will want to inflict on Eurysaces, as they have inflicted it on himself, and as they will try to inflict it later in the play (cf. λωβητόν 1388, λώβαις 1392). For οὐ μή + aorist subjunctive cf. 83n., 421.

562-4 We have been expecting the appearance of Teucer since 342–3. Ajax dispels Tecmessa's fear of an unfriendly guardian for his son (511–12, with τροφῆς, 'nurture', in both passages). At the same time Sophocles prepares us for the part that Teucer will play later, as the representative of Ajax himself in the quarrel with Menelaus and Agamemnon.

the resolute...nurture: or 'a guardian unhesitating in his care'.

even if...our enemies: for Teucer's absence cf. 343, 720–1. His affinity with his half-brother is underlined by the hunting metaphor. Both share the same pursuit, but for Ajax it has ended in disgrace.

565 **bearers...people:** the chorus are both warriors and sailors. The second part of the formal address recalls 349 and 357, while the first provides a neat introduction to the theme of Ajax' own armour, in particular his shield, that will be developed at 572–7. For the nominative adjective with a probably nominative noun in apposition with a vocative expression see Moorhouse 23 and cf. Aesch. *Eum.* 681.

567 For a ὅπως clause (+ subjunctive or future indicative) after a verb of commanding see Goodwin § 355.

569 **show him...mother:** the language is similar to *Hy. Aphr.* 134; cf. also *Phil.* 492.

Eriboea I mean: the dative is treated as in apposition with 'mother'; cf. Aesch. fr. 175, Dem. 19.152. Sometimes in such expressions Greek uses an accusative directly governed by 'I mean'. Ajax makes it clear that he is not referring to Teucer's mother Hermione. Ajax' mother is Eriboea also at Pind. *Isth.* 6.45, but Periboea at Apollod. 3.12.7, Paus. 1.42.2. Both 569 and 575 contain two metrical resolutions. The only other such lines in the play are 854, 1302. There are resolutions in this speech also at 562, 565, and, if not an interpolation, 571; see 457–9n.

570 **tend...old age:** for this obligation towards one's parents cf. Eur. *Alc.* 663, *Med.* 1033.

571 **until...god below:** with οὗ sc. χρόνου, 'time'. For the omission of ἄν see 552–5n. But μέχρις οὗ, 'until', is not a tragic expression, and the normal Attic form μέχρι is equally untragic. It is also difficult to see why Sophocles permitted himself a 'first-foot anapaest' with division after the second short, when he could easily have avoided it. The choice lies between (1) emendation and (2) deletion of the line. (1) Pearson ((1922) 23–4) and Dawe (102, 144–5) accept Hermann's ἔστ' ἄν, an expression obsolete in later Greek, and so likely to be glossed. Triclinius and *Suda* Γ 250 have μέχρις ἄν. (2) Lloyd-Jones and Wilson follow Elmsley and Jebb in deletion. The line may have been composed to tone down the seeming exaggeration of 'for ever'. Although the recesses of Hades are poetic enough (cf. Anacr. fr. 50.10 *PMG*, [Aesch.] *PV* 433, Eur. *Hcld.* 218, *HF* 607, and see R. Seaford, *CQ* 25 (1975) 204), the line adds nothing to the sense. Renehan 346 adds that its author took care over the repetition of sounds within the line, so that either μέχρις οὗ must be kept, or the line must go. On the whole (2) seems the right solution.

572-3 Ajax envisages the kind of competition for his armour which he lost in the case of Achilles' (cf. the language at Hom. *Od.* 11.546). ἀγωνάρχης, 'umpire', 'ruler of a contest' (cf. ἀγωνοθέτης) occurs at *IG* 17.1817 as the title of a magistrate at Thespiae (cf. also Σ Hom. *Il.* 24.1b).

my destroyer: after article + noun the attributive adjective ('my') should be preceded by a second definite article. The only real parallel for the anomaly is Eur. *Hipp.* 683, Ζεύς...ὁ γεννήτωρ ἐμός, 'Zeus my ancestor', where emendation is probably correct (cf. also [Theocr.] 27.59). It can be defended here only by supposing that it is equivalent to a relative clause with participle and object, ὁ λυμαινόμενος ἐμέ ('the one who is destroying me'), the article being used with demonstrative force; so Fraenkel 17–18, Kamerbeek, Moorhouse 152–3.

574-6 the very thing...name: so, reading τοὐπώνυμον, Fraenkel, *MH* 24 (1967) 84–5, (1977) 18, and Lloyd-Jones and Wilson. The emphatic αὐτό cannot mean simply 'this (shield)'. Jackson 232–3 took it to refer back to a mention of the shield in his supposed lacuna after μήθ' in 573. Rather it points forward, marking the contrast between the shield and the other weapons (577). For the great shield of Ajax, from which Eurysaces takes his name, 'Broad-shield', see 18–19, for the significant name 430–3n. In bequeathing it to his son Ajax makes it clear that he intends to die, and that the boy is to be his heir. It is unlikely that the shield is seen by the audience. Ajax cannot have been carrying it from the beginning, and there is no indication that it is brought on now. In any case it is too large for the child to carry (see Seale 157, Heath 183 n. 36).

well-stitched loop: the Mycenaean body-shield was carried by a leather strap ('telamon'; see 134–5n.), which passed over the left shoulder, while the later small round Mycenæan shield probably had a central grip. Sophocles here thinks anachronistically (cf. Eust. 995.19) of the hoplite shield which had a bronze strip (*porpax*), sometimes running across the whole diameter of the shield, its centre forming a loop, through which the arm was passed for the hand to grip a leather handle (*antilabe*) at the edge of the shield. See A.M. Snodgrass, *Early Greek armour and weapons* (Edinburgh 1964) 61–5, *Arms and armour of the Greeks* (London 1967) 20, 44, 53, 95, P. Ducrey, *Warfare in ancient Greece* (tr. J. Lloyd, New York 1986) 47–50. 'Well-stitched' may refer either to the attachment of the metal *porpax* to the body of the shield, or to its decoration (see Gow on Theocr. 25.265).

577 buried along with me: again it is clear that Ajax intends to die. So at Hom. *Il.* 6.418 a warrior's arms are burned along with his body. The future perfect tense ('will be buried and stay buried') reflects a confidence that the second part of the play will be required to justify. Teucer will use the same form at 1141. Ajax' orders will be carried out at 1407–8.

578 take this child: Ajax addresses Tecmessa.

579-80 make fast the house: we owe to Eustathius (cf. also Σ H^sl, Christodoulou 31) the correct division of the words δῶμα πάκτου.

do not weep...prone to wail: we are perhaps to suppose that Tecmessa is already crying. Ajax' command is in line with 293. Poe 47 rightly contrasts the comforting words of Hector at Hom. *Il.* 6.484–93 when he sees Andromache's tears. The compound adjective could equally well be translated 'prone to pity'. For the commonplace that lamentation and pity are feminine characteristics cf. Eur. *HF* 536, *Med.* 928, *IT* 1054, and see K.J. Dover, *Greek popular morality* (Oxford 1974) 101. The use of the neuter adjective in the predicate may suggest a note of contempt (cf. Eur. *El.* 1035), but it is common enough in a generalisation (see Moorhouse 14).

581 shut the door quickly: Ajax impatiently repeats his order. Tecmessa and the child are probably moving slowly towards the door. The comparative θᾶσσον might mean 'more quickly than you are actually doing' – Stanford), but more probably has no comparative force; cf. *Tr.* 1183 and see MacDowell on Ar. *Wasps* 187.

581-2 **for a wise doctor:** for πρός + genitive see 319–20n. For the comparison cf. fr. 589, *Tr.* 1000–2, for the use of incantations *OC* 1194, Hom. *Od.* 19.457, Aesch. *Eum.* 649. The distinction between those who practise them and the doctor is not always so clearly defined (see N.E. Collinge, *BICS* 9 (1962) 45).

a disease that calls for the knife: only surgery will cure it. For the metaphor see Garvie on Aesch. *Cho.* 539. The audience will think also of the literal sword with which Ajax will kill himself. Dawe prefers the variant τραύματι, 'wound', on the grounds that the language is medical throughout, and that πήματι is less colourful. But it was probably the medical context that led someone to introduce the medical word.

583-95 As at 481–4, 525–6 the chorus-leader is the first to respond. The long first episode then ends with an irregular stichomythia in which Ajax harshly rejects Tecmessa's final attempt at persuasion.

583 **this vehemence of yours:** that displayed by Ajax in the last few lines of his speech.

585 Cf. 326n. It might seem clear enough from 577 (and 479–80) what Ajax plans to do. But he has not said explicitly that he is going to commit suicide, and, even as she fears the worst, Tecmessa clings to the uncertainty.

586 **question:** ἀνακρίνω is commoner than κρίνω in this sense, but cf. *Ant.* 399 καὶ κρῖνε κἀξέλεγχ(ε), 'and question and interrogate her', *Tr.* 195, *El.* 1445.

self-control is good: it is ironical that Ajax here agrees with the view expressed by Athena at 132–3. But it is one thing for him to urge *sophrosyne* upon a woman (cf. also 293), quite another for him to practise it himself. At this stage we merely note the contradiction, but Sophocles is already looking forward to the next episode, in which it will seem that Ajax has genuinely accepted that *sophrosyne* is good.

587 **how I despair:** Tecmessa's *athumia* contrasts with the *prothumia*, 'eagerness', of Ajax. The periphrastic use of γίγνομαι + participle is more emphatic than a simple 'do not betray'; cf. *OT* 957, *Phil.* 773.

589-90 **you vex me too much:** Creon begins a line with the same words at *Ant.* 573, where, as here, there is no difficulty in supplying the missing object 'me'. For the exclamatory γε after the adverb see Denniston 127. ἄγαν γε is a common expression (cf. 983, *Tr.* 896).

to serve the gods: for ἀρκέω cf. 360, 439n. Here there is perhaps some arrogance in the idea that the human Ajax might 'furnish the needs of the gods' rather than (as at *Phil.* 1020) vice versa. Ajax is again conscious of his isolation (see 349–50, 420nn.). He is rejected even by the gods (cf. 457–8; also 398–403), and is therefore no longer under any obligation to them (cf. Aesch. *Sept.* 702–3, V. *Aen.* 11.51–2). For this as a justification for suicide see Yoshitake 148. The emphatic juxtaposition of 'I' and 'the gods', in front of 'that I am, etc.', marks the unhappy relationship between them.

591 **Do not speak ill-omened words:** cf. the same expression at 362. Here Tecmessa is anxious to stop Ajax from making things worse for himself by declaring his enmity to the gods.

keep...listen: lit. 'speak to those who listen', which amounts to 'I am not listening, so you are wasting your breath'. The line seems to be the model for Eur. *HF* 1185. From 591–4 each line of the stichomythia is abruptly divided between the two speakers. The device (*antilabe*), which is not used by Aeschylus, here marks the breakdown of communication in this last dialogue between Ajax and Tecmessa; see Seidensticker, in Jens 201–3, and cf. 981–5.

592 Won't you be persuaded: see 330n. Tecmessa's attempt is doomed to failure. The future middle is quite commonly used in poetry with passive sense.

593 Will you not...as you can: Ajax repeats the urgent command of 579, 581, with 'as quickly as possible' picking up 578. This time it is probably addressed to servants (cf. 344).

594 be softened: Ajax' only sign of softening has been at 558–9 (n.). By now he has returned to the true Ajax of 548–9 (n.).

594-5 These are the last words that Ajax speaks to Tecmessa. As at 592 the futility of her attempt is clear. The Sophoclean hero refuses to be taught. The emphasis on the shutting of the door makes it clear that someone now goes into the hut (despite Welcker, *RhM* 3 (1829) 87–92, for whom Ajax, Tecmessa, and the child all remain on stage). Mother and child might leave, while Ajax remains on stage, to step forward at 646 to announce his apparent change of mind. But his sudden reappearance from the hut at that point is a dramatic effect that few would wish to sacrifice. Many suppose that Ajax alone enters the hut, arguing, not unreasonably, that Ajax has now rejected Tecmessa, and that the effect of his entry at 646 is weakened if Tecmessa follows him out from the hut (see e.g. Sicherl 91 n. 101, Winnington-Ingram 32 n. 65, Poe 58 n. 117, Heath 184 n. 38). More probably all three depart into the hut, and 578–9 mean 'take the child and shut the door <behind you>, and do not stay outside to lament', rather than 'take the child and shut the door <without going in>, and do not lament as you stay outside'. For the audience it seems certain that Ajax will commit suicide inside, in the presence of Tecmessa and the child (so Taplin (1978) 64). We may even find an ambiguity at 546: Ajax is thinking of his own death. The barring of the door is to prevent any intervention from outside. We wait for a shriek from Tecmessa, and Ajax' reappearance at 646 will be totally unexpected. Jebb and Stanford separate Tecmessa and Eurysaces from Ajax by having them enter the hut by a side-door leading to the women's quarters. Whether or not such a side-door existed on the tragic stage has long been debated (see my *Aeschylus Choephori* xlvii–lii). It is to be rejected here. The sense of urgency with which Ajax orders the hut to be shut up makes it clear that this is an important dramatic moment. The eyes of the audience should be on the central door, and it would be distracting if we had to watch two doors, not knowing to which Ajax is referring. For a single door in *Aj.* see most recently Scullion 93 n. 12, 115. If, as seems probable, Ajax is still on the *eccyclema*, it is now withdrawn through the central door, and Tecmessa and the child walk in behind it. These stage-arrangements have been accepted by some scholars, but for the wrong reasons. Fraenkel, *MH* 24 (1967) 80 (see also Burton 26), argued that Ajax' change of mind at 646–92 presupposes a conversation between Ajax and Tecmessa inside the hut. But it is contrary to tragic convention that we should be required to speculate about what two characters say to each other offstage. Similarly, it is futile to speculate (with Cohen) about the thought-processes of Ajax inside the hut.

596-645: First Stasimon

The long first episode ended with Ajax impervious to Tecmessa's pleas, and clearly intending suicide. In this ode Sophocles turns the audience's thoughts away from that intention. Only at 635 does the chorus allude, in an unspecific way, to the death of Ajax. The ode deals, not with the future, but with the past and present, picking up and expressing in lyric terms various themes that have appeared earlier in the play and that will recur in the third stasimon – the joy of life at home contrasted with the chorus's present misery at Troy (str.1; cf. 134–5, 245–56n.), the contrast between Ajax' present state and his former greatness (ant. 1; cf. 205–7, 421–7), the grief of his old mother (str. 2) and father (ant. 2; cf. 506–9, 569–70). We may explain in psychological terms the chorus's failure to allude to the suicide, or to speculate about what Ajax ought to do: it cannot face the future, so it looks back rather to the past. Its lack of understanding isolates still more the hero, who remains alone in his decision. More important, by turning our attention away from the suicide Sophocles prepares for the ambiguities in the next episode, in which Ajax will claim to have changed his mind. And, although it does not understand him, the chorus by its sympathy arouses the sympathy also of the audience.

596-8 The reminder and brief description of Salamis recall the chorus's first address to Ajax at 134–5.

famous Salamis: there is no need to suppose that Sophocles is referring anachronistically to the defeat of the Persians at Salamis in 480 BC. The honorific adjective is regularly applied in tragedy to Athens itself (cf. 861 and see L. Bergson, *L' Épithète ornementale dans Eschyle, Sophocle et Euripide* (Lund 1956) 54, 194–6), and is here extended to the island which for Sophocles' audience belonged to Athens (202n.). It fittingly describes the land which produced the heroic Ajax (cf. 636–8).

beaten by the sea: the epithet is applied to an island at Pind. *Py.* 4.14, a similar one to Salamis at Aesch. *Pers.* 307. At Eur. *Tro.* 800 Salamis is περικύμων, 'surrounded by waves'.

you lie: ναίω usually means 'dwell', but here, as at Hom. *Il.* 2.626 (of islands), *Od.* 7.29, and like ναιετάω in Homer, 'be situated'.

for ever: the permanence of the landscape contrasts with the transience of human life.

conspicuous: rather than (LSJ) 'famous'; cf. 66, 229.

600-7 As in the parodos (see 200n.) the chorus's dwelling upon its own unhappy situation reinforces our sense of its sympathy towards Ajax, and prepares for the theme of the antistrophe that its troubles are greatly increased by its commander's plight.

600 long is the time that: lit. 'it is an ancient time since'; cf. *Phil.* 493.

601-5 It is unlikely that the text of 601 will ever be restored with certainty (Σ's attempts at explaining it are desperate), but the chorus is clearly describing the misery of camping in the open at Troy. So does the Herald at Aesch. *Ag.* 558–62 (see Fraenkel on 560), a passage which Sophocles may have had in mind, and in which λειμώνιαι, 'of the meadows', suggests that some form of that word is sound here too; so also εὐνῶμαι, 'I lie' (Bergk) at 604 answers to εὐναί at *Ag.* 559 (cf. also 1206–10 below). Responsion with 614 requires ∪–∪ – – – – ∪∪–∪– (iambic + glyconic).

keeping...months: 'of the months' is objective genitive after the adjective (cf. *El.* 232, *Tr.* 247); μηνῶν is Hermann's correction of μήλων, 'of sheep', which might be connected with the meadows. But ἀνήριθμος would then be isolated, and the sense 'uncounted', i.e. 'unheeded' (Σ, *Suda* A 2436; cf. Eur. *Ion* 837, *Hel.* 1679) is ruled out by the echo at 646 (cf. 1186 and see Winnington-Ingram 33 n. 66).

worn away by time: 'time' picks up the same word at 600. For the idea cf. *Tr.* 110 (with the same verb τρύχομαι; for similarities between this ode and the parodos of *Tr.*

see D. Korzeniewski, *RhM* 105 (1962) 151–2), Aesch. *Ag.* 197. In Sophocles time, with all its mutability, is often seen as an implacable and destructive factor in human life; cf. 624 and see de Romilly (1968) 87–111. Shortly (646–9) Ajax will talk about the alternations that are associated with time. Here the emphasis is on the slow wearing down by endless years of misery.

606 sad expectation: for the ambivalence of ἐλπίς see 477–8n. Here the word is in itself neutral, and it is the adjective that determines its sense.

607-8 I shall complete the journey: 'the journey' has to be supplied; cf. *Tr.* 657, *OC* 1562, Hom. *Od.* 7.326. Normally in indirect speech, when the subject of the infinitive is the same as that of the main verb, it remains unexpressed. Here Sophocles uses the accusative and infinitive. 'The effect is...to give a certain objectivity' (Jebb on *Tr.* 706); cf. *El.* 471 and see Moorhouse 317.

inexorable Hades the annihilator: the two compound epithets are both ambiguous. The former might mean 'from whom one turns away' (i.e. 'abhorred'), rather than 'who turns away', the latter, with a play on the name Ἅιδης, 'unseen', 'invisible' (cf. Pl. *Phaedo* 81c, *Crat.* 404b), rather than 'who makes unseen'. The chorus fears that it will die at Troy and never return home. The assonance of αι is repeated at 627, 645, 672, but it is perhaps fanciful to connect it with the name of Aias (430–2); see Stanford (1978) 192.

610 a fresh...wrestle with: the translation is an expansion of the single word ἔφεδρος, which, as Σ explains, means someone who sat by in a wrestling contest ready to take on the winner. For the metaphor see *Suda* E 3850, Garvie on Aesch. *Cho.* 866–8. Even if the chorus can conquer all the troubles that it has been describing, it has still to grapple with the present plight of its leader.

611 shares his home with: the adjective suggests a cattle-steading or a sheepfold; so in a non-metaphorical sense at *OT* 1126; cf. also *Phil.* 1168. The pastoral metaphor is perhaps suggested by Ajax' killing of the animals; cf. 369n. Like 'seized by madness' at 216 the expression is 'far more evocative' than a simple adjective 'mad' would be (Long 107).

divine-sent madness: for the chorus's inability to distinguish Ajax' present abnormal mood from the actual madness inflicted on him by Athena see 331–2n. and cf. 635, 638–40. Both are sent by the gods (cf. 185). Though no longer technically mad he is cut off from normal society and no longer himself; see Gellie 232, Goldhill 188–9 (for whom, however, the chorus is thinking of his desire for suicide), Z. Theodorou, *CQ* 43 (1993) 33 n. 9.

612-13 you sent: the chorus is still addressing Salamis (596). The language is reminiscent of Aesch. *Pers.* 137.

impetuous Ares: i.e. 'furious fighting'. The same adjective was used of Ares himself at 212 (n.). The synonymous θοῦρος is a formulaic epithet in *Iliad* for Ares (e.g. 5.30).

614-15 but now: Heath 184 points out that the stanza has an A-B-A structure: after the brief description of Ajax' former glory the chorus returns to the trouble with which the stanza began.

as he feeds his lonely thoughts: lit. 'lonely feeder of his mind'. The sense of isolation (see 29n.) conveyed by the phrase is hardly counterbalanced by the notion that he has friends to sympathise with him. For the pastoral metaphor cf. Aesch. *Supp.* 929, *Ag.*

669, *Eum.* 78, and see 611n. At Aesch. *Supp.* 795 a crag is ολόφρων, 'thinking lonely thoughts'.

616-17 works of his hands...excellence: ἔργα χεροῖν, 'works of his hands', is in effect a single word governing 'of excellence', a genitive of quality; see Fraenkel, *Ag.* II 316, Moorhouse 54. For the idea cf. 439–40, 443.

619-20 have fallen...unfriendly: a powerful emotional effect is created by the repetition of the verb (see 359n., 396, 414) and by the polyptoton of the adjective (the repetition of the same word but in different cases; cf. 267). Jebb and Kamerbeek think that the metaphor is from dice (cf. *Tr.* 62, Eur. *El.* 1101, *Or.* 603). Rather, 'fallen' means into ruin (Stanford).

621-34 March 4 surmises that this picture of Ajax' grieving mother may be based on her role in Aeschylus' *Salaminiai.*

621-5 the days...hoary: lit. 'who is nurtured with an ancient day and with hoary old age'. For the old age of Ajax' mother cf. 508. In Greek thought time personified regularly keeps company with someone for the duration of some action or process; see Garvie on Aesch. *Cho.* 965–6. Here time is thought of as growing along with the mother. So at Aesch. *Ag.* 106 a man's lifetime is born with him (cf. *OT* 1082–3), and at *Eum.* 286, *PV* 981 it grows old; cf. also *OC* 7, Aesch. *Ag.* 894, and see de Romilly 41–9 (46 on this passage). The idea of nurture picks up 499, 503, 511, but here it is transferred to the care of the old. With the dative λευκῷ of the MSS 'nurtured with' governs also 'hoary old age'. But Dawe 146–7 may be right to prefer Schneidewin's nominative λευκά, 'she who is nurtured...and is hoary with old age'; cf. Eur. *HF* 909.

that he is sick: see 611n.

626 that eats his heart: the MSS have φρενομόρως (or -μώρως), a compound which occurs nowhere else and is barely intelligible; see Ferrari 27–8, who remarks that -μορος in compounds must denote either a type of participation or a type of death. Dindorf's emendation is almost certainly correct. β and μ are frequently confused in minuscule script; cf. Aesch. *Cho.* 1068 where παιδοβόροι is corrupted into παιδόμοροι. At Hom. *Il.* 6.202 Bellerophon 'ate out his heart' (θυμὸν κατέδων); cf. θυμοβόρος at *Il.* 7.210 etc.

627-31 sing woe, sing woe is best treated as a parenthetical exclamation. For this cry of lamentation see Fraenkel on Aesch. *Ag.* 121, where, as here and at Eur. *Or.* 1395, the cry is doubled. Aedo(n), or Procne, killed her own child and was turned by the gods into a nightingale, whose cries became a symbol for perpetual lamentation (cf. *El.* 107–9, *Tr.* 963, Hom. *Od.* 19. 518–23). The polarisation provided by the text adopted here (with Reiske's σχήσει, 'will restrain', for ἥσει, 'will utter'), is characteristically Greek, and much more plausible than the MSS reading which makes a *contrast* between Eriboea's lament and that of the nightingale.

high-pitched lamentations: cf. *El.* 243, *Ant.* 423–4.

631-4 and the thud...grey hair: the beating of the breast and the tearing of the hair (310n.) are traditional elements of mourning; see Garvie, Aesch. *Cho.* pp. 54–5 on 22–31, where the language is similar, also *Cho.* 423–8, Soph. *El.* 88–90, Eur. *Andr.* 826–7. After 'the thud...will fall...' (i.e. 'the hands will fall with a thud') 'the tearing of her grey hair' comes in rather loosely, and with a slight zeugma, as a second subject for 'fall'. See Long 77–8.

635 For better hidden in Hades: i.e. 'it is better for him to be hidden in Hades'. For the language cf. *Ant.* 911, Hom. *Il.* 23.244. The personal construction (cf. *OT* 1368) is like the common Greek idiom 'he is clear being good' (cf. 326n.).

from an empty sickness: i.e. 'who is mad' (cf. Ar. *Peace* 95); see 611n. The line has the ring of a generalisation ('it is better to be dead than mad'; cf. Eur. *Hipp.* 248–9), which leads on in the relative clause to the specific case of Ajax. Although the chorus can hardly be expressing approval of his hints that he will kill himself, it is unlikely that it means only that his mother may well lament for him *as if* he were dead, since his condition is worse than that of the dead (Winnington-Ingram 35, Heath 85 n. 39). Here, and only here in the ode, their language does seem to presume his death.

636-7 whose inheritance...the toiling Achaeans: the Chorus shares Ajax' own evaluation of himself (423–6n.; cf. also 502) as the best fighter at Troy. The general sense is not in doubt, but the text is uncertain. Most MSS omit 'the best', while a lost MS collated in the sixteenth century by J. Livineius had ἄριστα, 'best', as an adverb. Triclinius claims to have found the adjective ἄριστος in 'one of the old MSS', and it appears in a later hand also in Zc (see O. Smith, *C&M* 32 (1971–80) 36). The Σ in M records 'ἄριστος is missing'. But the adverb, not the adjective, provides exact correspondence with the strophe.

638-40 the temperament he grew up with: συντρόφοις is a curious echo of 622 (621–5n.). Ajax has been nurtured together with his character, which is therefore his companion (cf. *Phil.* 203). But now that has changed, and he, lit., 'associates with it [his temperament] from outside'; i.e. 'his original temperament is no longer part of his character, no longer his companion' (cf. Eur. *Or.* 354). The phrase provides a fitting prelude to the speech in which Ajax will claim to have indeed been changed.

641-5 Wretched father: the chorus turns to the grief of Ajax' father when he hears the news, thus bringing us back to Ajax' fear of Telamon's reaction at 434ff., 462–5.

grievous...ruin: the same phrase occurs at Aesch. *Eum.* 376; cf. also 51 above.

engendered: the final reference to nurture in the ode is bitter: what Ajax' life has nurtured has turned out to be ruin; cf. 503. For αἰών, 'time', 'life', conceived in this way see Lloyd-Jones, in R.D. Dawe et al. (ed.) *Dionysiaca: nine studies presented to Sir Denys Page* (Cambridge 1978) 52, on Aesch. *Ag.* 105–6 (cf. also *Tr.* 34–5).

the sons of Aeacus: Aeacus was the father of Telamon.

646-92: Second Episode

Ajax is followed by Tecmessa but probably not the child (Camerer 302 remarks that the deictic pronoun (652) shows that Tecmessa is present, but that there is no such pronoun with παῖδα). The second episode is much shorter than the first, consisting, unusually for Sophocles, in a single speech (see Taplin (1977) 108-9). Only his final speech at 815–65 is comparable in its isolation. This is the most controversial part of the play. What is certain is that Ajax' speech comes as a complete surprise. He who has all along refused to yield or make concessions, or to listen to his friends, now declares that he has been softened by Tecmessa's words, and that he is ready to accept the principle of alternation in human affairs, as in the world of nature, and to yield to both the gods and his worst enemies. He has apparently become a model of *sophrosyne*. Two separate but related questions are involved: (1) Has he really abandoned his determination to commit suicide, or are his words intended to deceive? (2) Has he really learnt *sophrosyne*, or is this too a pretence? The dilemma is neatly put by

Gellie 12, 'Ajax cannot change and Ajax cannot lie. If Ajax cannot change, he speaks to deceive; if Ajax cannot lie, he is recording an honest change of heart'.

(1) We may dismiss the view of Welcker, *Kleine Schriften* II 302–22 (see also Ebeling 299) that Ajax, while still intent on suicide, has no intention of deceiving; if the chorus had been more intelligent it would have understood. This takes no account of the many verbal ambiguities, which (despite Sicherl 92, Knox (1979) 136–8), must indicate a conscious attempt to deceive (see Stevens 329, Poe 56). They disprove also the view of Webster 96–9 (also Bowra 39–42, Leinieks 200) that Ajax does not intend to deceive, because he really has abandoned his suicide-plan, having learnt the lesson of *sophrosyne* as preached by Athena at 127–33 (cf. 586). Faced then with the objection that Ajax does in fact kill himself, Bowra (43–4) has to suppose that Athena's anger and 'a fury akin to madness' will return, because he fails to remain in his hut for the day prescribed by Calchas. But this is an impossible interpretation of the later scene, and there is no suggestion in the play that Ajax becomes mad again (see also 807n.). Leinieks' explanation, that in the next episode Ajax loses control over what happens to him, is equally improbable. Tecmessa and the chorus *are* deceived, and it is hard to escape the conclusion that Ajax intends it. The ambiguities of language ensure that the audience does not share its delusion, or at least may retain only a slight hope that Ajax has given up his plan (for the tension this creates see Bergson 45).

Against this view it is argued that such deceit is out of character for the great hero (cf. *Tr.* 453–4, fr. 352). So Achilles at Hom. *Il.* 9.312–13 says that he hates the man who hides one thing in his heart and says something else. In the prologue of *Phil.* Neoptolemus only against his better nature allows himself to be persuaded by Odysseus to employ deceit (cf. also *El.* 59–61). Odysseus in Homer is the prime example of a different kind of hero, and in our play this is not the first time that Ajax has, paradoxically, found it necessary to use the methods associated with, and which he finds so distasteful in, his enemy in order to assert his heroism (see 47n., Scodel 23, Stevens 328, Blundell 83–4). He is in a position where it is the only way of getting what he wants. The view that it is a sign that he is still insane is certainly mistaken (see 331–2, 611nn.); so for N.E. Collinge, *BICS* 9 (1962) 50–1, it is a classic example of a manic-depressive syndrome, while for Vandvik 169–75 (esp. 174–5) his insanity excuses him from the flaw of cunning and dissimulation. A better reason is that of Stanford for whom (142, Appx. D) Ajax wishes, through his apparent recantation, to spare his friends all possible suffering at the hands of his enemies. For other explanations see Kirkwood (1958) 162, Errandonea 21–40, Moore 55–66. Part of the reason is purely dramatic. Ajax is to die alone because the Sophoclean hero is always isolated in his tragedy, and Sophocles wants him to die on stage, and so Tecmessa and the chorus must be removed. Moreover, the delusion of the chorus makes possible the joyous second stasimon, and the whole following sequence of events (see U. Parlavantza-Friedrich, *Täuschungsszenen in den Tragödien des Sophokles* (Berlin 1969) 20, Heath 189). At the same time the ambiguities perhaps leave some element of hope even for the audience. Or rather, our feelings are mixed. We hope that some way can be found of keeping Ajax alive, but would not be happy if he were to compromise.

(2) For many scholars Ajax has in fact learnt *sophrosyne*, and they give different explanations of this surprising change. Stanford 282–3 says that he has theoretically been converted in his mind to *sophrosyne* and in his heart to pity, but his character has not changed, and that is why he is still intent on suicide. It is difficult to see how one can change from *hybris* to *sophrosyne* without any change of character. For other scholars Ajax' conversion is real and complete. For Linforth (10–20, 25) he has learnt no longer to rebel, but now faces his

plight with a controlled emotion. For Simpson he has been transformed from a man of violent action into a man of thought and a speaker of words. Bowra 40 says that 'if the speech is a deception, Ajax dies without having made his peace with god and man', without having learned his lesson. Bowra rejects out of hand the possibility that this is exactly how Sophocles wants him to die. For Taplin (1978) 128–31, and (1979) 122–9 (*contra* Stevens 335–6, Bergson 47) it is only in retrospect that the audience will understand that Ajax has made his peace with the gods. He is talking of the time after his death when he will be rehabilitated. But, if Ajax really changes his mind or even temporarily weakens, he is unlike any other Sophoclean hero known to us, and the audience would be disappointed, not pleased, that he feels forced to grovel to his enemies. Nowhere in the speech does he say that he was wrong to attack them (see von Fritz 251), and in his next speech (815–65) he is as full as ever of hatred and desire for revenge (for an attempt to reconcile the contradiction in terms of the dual role of hero-cult see Seaford 136, 395–402). Here the exaggerated language of 666–7 (n.) is sufficient to indicate that he cannot really mean it.

The real reason for believing that it is not all deceit or bitter sarcasm is the extreme beauty of the language. The principle of alternation (see 131–2, 383nn.) appears here in all its attractiveness, apparently for Ajax and certainly for the audience, the idea that in human life, as in nature, everything must give way to its opposite. It is hard to believe that all of this is expended on a lie. There is too a ring of sincerity in the pity Ajax expresses for his concubine and son (652–3). He does not directly address his hearers until 684, and it is often said (e.g. by Stanford 285, Sicherl 89, Golder 19–23) that until that point the speech is a soliloquy – he is talking to himself. But, as Heath recognises (188), the ambiguous language, which persists throughout the whole speech, indicates that he is conscious of his hearers' presence (cf. the deictic pronoun at 652). Rather, he is talking to himself as well as to them. It is a 'soliloquy that is meant to be overheard, and meant to deceive' (Stevens 329). The best solution is to separate Ajax' intellectual from his emotional response. With his mind he now sees the world as it is (Holt (1980); see 331–2n.), and recognises the attractiveness of *sophrosyne*; cf. the plethora of words indicating intellectual knowledge and learning (666, 667, 677, 678; see Simpson 97, Bergson 46–7). But the Sophoclean hero rarely relies on his intellect. So Ajax, while acknowledging the claims of *sophrosyne*, cannot bring himself emotionally to accept it in his own case. As A. Lesky says (*Greek tragedy* (tr. H.A. Frankfort, London and New York 1965) 102), 'the hero critically surveys modes of possible behaviour which are alien to his nature and to which he cannot become reconciled'. But we should not underestimate the attractiveness of *sophrosyne* which Ajax clearly sees. The whole speech shows us Ajax resisting and overcoming what is now his strongest temptation.

646-7 Long and immeasurable time...hides them again: the idea of the power of time to reveal what is hidden and to destroy, and in general to control events, is typically Sophoclean, as is the notion of alternation, of cycles, in both the natural world and the affairs of men; see de Romilly (1968) 50–1, 94, 98–9, Rosenmeyer 155–98, and cf. esp. *Tr.* 129–35, *OT* 1213, *Phil.* 305–6, *OC* 607–23. Ajax develops, but more attractively, the idea briefly expounded by Athena at 131–2 (cf. also 383). The theme of alternation is finely expressed in the chiasmus, with the two verbs, 'produces' (lit. 'makes to grow', perhaps by analogy from the growth of a seed; cf. Hom. *Il.* 6.147–8) and 'hides', framing the line, which thus begins with growth and ends with death, all the emphasis being on the latter. The rhetorical effect is increased by the alliteration of φ and by the assonance in ἄδηλα...φανέντα. For ἄδηλα cf. Hes. *Op*. 6.

immeasurable time: lit. 'countless'. The same adjective. was used by the chorus at 603 to describe the long months that it had spent at Troy.

648-9 The conventional generalisation is now applied specifically to human affairs. Sophocles may have had in mind Archil. fr. 122.1, χρημάτων ἄελπτον οὐδέν ἐστιν υἱὸ' ἀπώμοτον, 'there is nothing that is beyond expectation or that one may swear to be impossible' (cf. also *Ant*. 388, Thgn. 659, Pind. *Ol*. 13.83, Eur. *Ion* 1510–11, fr. 761), with the speaker going on to illustrate his generalisation from an eclipse of the sun. Garner 229 n. 2 and G. Crane, *CPh* 85 (1990) 89–101, argue that both Archilochus and Sophocles draw on a conventional *topos*: normally the gods are seen as the agents of such unexpected happenings, but Ajax ignores the gods and attributes the shift in his emotions to time.

the terrible oath: Ajax is thinking of oaths in general, not a specific oath sworn by himself to the sons of Atreus or (1113) to Tyndareus (though the article with δεινός often has demonstrative force; see 312n. and cf. 650). But his previous determination is similar in force to an oath. ἁλίσκεται means lit. 'is taken prisoner', and amounts almost to 'is found inadequate'; cf. 1267.

minds which are too strict: the adjective is used by Creon at *Ant*. 475, in the context of Antigone's stubbornness, of iron which shatters because it has been burnt too hard in the fire. The idea thus leads on naturally to the simile which follows.

650 so terribly firm: lit. 'so steadfast as to those terrible things'. For the article with δεινός see previous note. Here the adjective perhaps combines the idea of Ajax' fearsome character (cf. 205, 548–9) with that of 'marvellous'. Cf. the ambiguity at *Ant*. 332–3.

651 like iron dipped in water: the simile goes better with what precedes (hot iron was dipped in cold water to harden it; cf. Hom. *Od*. 9.390–2, Plut. *Mor*. 136a, 433a, 988d, *Suda* E 323) than with what follows, the reference then being to the dipping of iron in oil to soften it. Kamerbeek's interpretation, 'I have been softened like hardened oil', i.e. 'not at all', is far-fetched.

have been softened...speech: Ajax, who earlier despised women (292–3, 525–44nn.), and who refused to be softened (594–5), now claims to have become himself like a woman (cf. Heracles at *Tr*. 1075, Eur. fr. 360.28–9). Critics are divided as to how seriously we are to take this claim. For Easterling 6 (cf. Linforth 15) Ajax means what he says, though he refers only to the words he now utters, not to his impending behaviour. For others, probably rightly, the idea that Ajax has become a woman is itself a sign to the audience that his words are false, or at least that he has softened *only* in his words (so e.g. Knox (1964) 138–9, A.M. Dale, *Collected papers* (Cambridge 1969) 223, Winnington-Ingram 48). Contrast his 'whetted tongue' at 584 (for στόμα in this sense cf. 1110). But στόμα is itself ambiguous. It is often used metaphorically for the 'edge' or 'point' of a weapon, so that we may take it as a metonymy for his warlike might, continuing the simile of an iron weapon, and suggesting the sword which he 'dipped' in the blood of the animals (95, 219; see Cohen 30), and with which he will kill himself.

652-3 I pity her that I should leave her: lit. 'I pity her to leave her'. Despite the ambiguities of 651 one would like to believe that at least Ajax' compassion is sincere, and that it matches that of Odysseus for Ajax himself at 121. Blundell 82 n. 104 and Cairns 234 n. 63 find even this to be part of the deception. And here too there are ambiguities. On the analogy of verbs like αἰσχύνομαι, 'I am ashamed', the infinitive ought to imply that Ajax will therefore *not* leave Tecmessa (with ἀλλά meaning 'well'), whereas a participle would mean that he pitied her *while* leaving her (with ἀλλά adversative, 'but', 'nevertheless'). But, since οἰκτίρω nowhere else governs an infinitive (cf. however ἐλεαίρω at Hom. *Od*. 20.202), Ajax' real meaning is left open. In these lines, which recall Hom. *Il*. 6.432, 22.483-4, 24.725-6, Ajax refers directly to Tecmessa's appeal at 494-504, 510-13; cf. also 525-6. There he refused to show pity, while at 579-80 he perhaps considered it to be womanish.

654-6 bathing-place: we may note that λουτρά is often, and almost always in Sophocles, used for the washing of a corpse before burial; cf. 1405 and see Knox (1979) 134-5.

the meadows by the shore: a meadow was the scene of Ajax' disgrace (144), and, in a corrupt passage, the setting for the chorus's discomfort at 601.

to wash...of the goddess: the defilement which is to be washed off in the sea (like that of the Greeks at Hom. *Il*. 1.314) is primarily the blood of the slaughtered animals, though (Stanford) there may be a reference also to the religious pollution which came from the killing of the herdsmen (27, 232). What Ajax really plans to do is to wash off the disgrace of failure, and to end the anger of Athena once and for all by his death. Despite Jebb xxxviii, Sicherl 95-6, there is no suggestion that he sees his death as some kind of atonement to the goddess, or even (Scodel 20-5) as a reconciliation with the gods. Moore 59 rightly remarks that suicide as a propitiation would be unparalleled, Seidensticker 139 that Ajax does not reconcile himself with the world but leaves it, while Ebeling 300 n. 4 points out that Athena is not included among the gods to whom Ajax will pray in his suicide-speech.

657 an untrodden place: the loneliness and isolation of Ajax are again emphasised.

658-9 For the custom of burying sacrificial or polluted objects see Sicherl 79, Segal (1981) 139. Ajax' sword, first mentioned at 10 as the instrument of his disgrace (see also 18-19, 30nn.) is now to be the instrument of the death that, he hopes, will put an end to that disgrace. What he really means is that he will fix the sword in the ground and fall on it, and that he will hide it in his body (cf. 899). κρύπτω, 'hide', is regularly used in the context of the burial of a corpse (cf. 1040). His body will be the sword's 'grave'. The sword which (95) he dyed with the blood of his supposed enemies he will now dye with his own.

in the ground where...: the partitive genitive 'in the ground' seems to depend equally on both 'digging' and 'where' (see Moorhouse 59-60).

where nobody shall see it: the negative after the relative pronoun is μή because it is equivalent to a purpose clause (cf. 470-1n.).

660 The real meaning is that the sword will finally be buried with him in his grave (577).

keep it down below: cf. *El*. 438. For the idea of darkness and death as keeper or saviour cf. 394-7. For 'below' = in the underworld cf. 865.

661-2 For the first time in the play we learn that the fatal sword was a gift from Ajax' enemy Hector. But the audience will be familiar with the duel in Hom. *Il*. 7, which ended with an exchange of gifts between Ajax and Hector, the former receiving a sword with sheath and baldric, the latter a belt or girdle (7.303-5).

664-5 The theme that enemies' gifts are fatal will be developed more fully, if the lines are genuine, at 1024-39 (cf. also 817-18, *A.P.* 7.152). For Sophocles' version of the story see 1030-31n. That Ajax killed himself with Hector's sword may be his own invention.

But *Od.* 11.543–64 presupposes his suicide, and the weapon is more likely to have been already a part of the tradition. Cf. the empty scabbard and baldric in the painting by the Brygos Painter (Intro. 3). Davies (1973) 66–7 cites also a sixth-century amphora by the Kleophrades Painter (Würzburg 508). For the sword as Hector's gift, and for the common idea that the living is killed by the dead, see H.D.F. Kitto, *Poiesis: structure and thought* (Berkeley and Los Angeles 1966) 179–88, *YClS* 25 (1977) 325–6. At *Od.* 8.401–16 the less serious quarrel between Odysseus and the Phaeacian Euryalus is also brought to an end with the gift of a sword.

the gifts...are no gifts: or perhaps 'the gifts...are evil gifts' (so *Suda* A 519). For this common type of poetic expression, in which the noun is qualified by a cognate α-privative adjective, either a negating or a pejorative sense is often possible; see Garvie on Aesch. *Cho.* 43–6, χάριν ἀχάριτον. For the thought cf. Eur. *Med.* 618, Ar. *Wasps* 1160, Men. *Sent.* 166, and for quotation of the proverb *Corpus Paroemiographorum Graecorum* I 245, II 69.

666-7 These lines, set apart from 668 by asyndeton, come closest to a downright lie. Even more surprising than his apparent readiness to yield (see 371n.) is the language in which he expresses it. σέβειν, 'to reverence', is (despite Taplin (1979) 128) a strong word which is more often applied to gods (= 'worship'; see 713n., Knox (1979) 157 n. 85) than to men or political authority. We might have believed Ajax if he had said that he was going to worship the gods and to yield to the sons of Atreus. But we cannot take him seriously when he says that he is going to worship the latter. Even τοιγάρ, 'therefore' (probably picking up the train of thought before the digression about the sword; see Heath 187), which 'often has a vindictive tone' (A.N. Michelini, *Tradition and dramatic form in the Persians of Aeschylus* (Leiden 1982) 118 n. 55, suggests his bitterness. The two clauses, balanced by μέν and δέ, are parallel, not contrasting, and Kitto (1956) 189–90, is certainly wrong to suppose that Ajax will yield to the gods because he has to, but will not humble himself before his enemies, Errandonea 21–40 that he drops his plan to kill his enemies and chooses instead a humiliating suicide, so as to spare his family from his enemies' revenge. For various other attempts to take the lines as sincere see Jebb xxxvi–xxxvii, Moore 47–8, 59, Sicherl 80–1, March 20. But they are true only in so far as the dead Ajax will no longer be in a position to oppose either his divine or his human enemies; 'in future', which for his hearers means 'for the rest of his life', really in this sense refers to the period after his death. Formally it is the two verbs of knowing/learning that are balanced (for the stress on the intellectual nature of this process see p.186), but in sense the balance is between the gods and the sons of Atreus, while the sentence is so arranged that the two key infinitives, 'yield' and 'reverence', frame 667. The future tenses (cf. 677) suggest that he has not, as yet, learnt *sophrosyne*; see Goldhill 190–1.

668 the rulers: primarily the sons of Atreus, but Ajax may be thinking also of the gods, with ὑπεικτέον picking up εἴκειν (so Ferguson 18–19).

of course one ought: Linwood's τί μήν is a certain emendation of τί μή. For the elliptical expression (lit. 'what else?'), 'practically equivalent to an emphatic affirmative', see Denniston 333, Garvie, *Aeschylus' Supplices: play and trilogy* (Cambridge 1969) 54–5.

669-70 things that are terrible and very strong: the language picks up 649–50, with καρτερώτατα echoing the verb ἐκαρτέρουν. Ajax relates the universe at large to his own situation (for this way of thinking cf. de Romilly 89–92 on *Tr.* 94–140, Eur. *Phoen.* 535–48, *HF* 101–6). For the third time in four lines he uses a part of the verb (ὑπ)εἰκω, 'yield'. Cf. the triple repetition at *Ant.* 713–18, where Haemon similarly draws upon the natural world in his attempt to persuade Creon to yield.

what is held in honour: the Greek says simply 'honours', 'dignities', 'authorities', which in Ajax' case may include the gods (668n.).

670-3 firstly: lit. 'as to this thing on the one hand', an adverbial use of the demonstrative. It is balanced by δέ, 'and', which amounts to 'secondly' at 672 (cf. *OC* 440–1). There is no conjunction because this sentence introduces the explanation of the preceding sentence.

winters which cover the roads with snow: lit. 'snow-trodden winters', the compound adjective being formed from στείβω, 'tread', as at 657.

gives way...withdraws for...: after the triple 'yield' Sophocles now varies the expression, but the general sense is much the same, despite Kitto (see 666–7n.) for whom Ajax will not really 'yield', but will only 'get out of the way of' his enemies (i.e. die), because he has no choice.

eternal: either because each night seems endless (as from αἰεί), or (better) because of the endless recurrence of night (cf. *El.* 1365; the adjective is used of night also at Aesch. *Eum.* 416). Sometimes the word appears to mean 'wearisome' or 'lamentable' (as from αἰαῖ). For its doubtful etymology and meaning see E. Degani, *Helikon* 2 (1962) 37–56, R. Cantarella, in H. Hommel (ed.), *Wege zu Aischylos* (Darmstadt 1974) I 407 n.2, M.S. Silk, *CQ* 33 (1983) 304–5, 314–15.

day with its white horses: cf. Aesch. *Pers.* 386 (also 301), where too day brings light to the earth. In these, as in the following illustrations, the alternation is from bad to good (see 131–2, 383nn.). H. Diller, *Gottheit und Mensch in der Tragödie des Sophokles* (Darmstadt 1963) 5–6, argues that it is a question not of alternation but of the irreconcilability of opposites: where summer or day is, there is no place for winter or night, and for Ajax there is no place in the brightness and warmth of the living. But Ajax does seem to acknowledge, though only theoretically, the possibility that his own situation could improve, that his wintry storm (cf. 207, 257–8) could change to summer, his darkness (394–5) to light. R.A.S. Seaford, *Hermes* 122 (1994) 282–8, finds allusions to the Mysteries in all this, and suggests that it may be connected with the cult of the hero Ajax (see also *Reciprocity* 398–9).

674-6 Again the idea of yielding is expressed in different terms. We have to understand that the terrible (cf. 649, 650, 669) winds have first roused the sea before they abate and thus put it to sleep (gnomic aorist); cf. V. *Aen.* 3.69–70, 5.763, Hor. *Od.* 1.3.16. For this kind of compression of thought see Kühner-Gerth II 569–70. A god or divine power can work both positively and negatively. Ajax' passion will indeed put him to sleep, but it will be the sleep of death. Sleep is the brother of Death at Hom. *Il.* 14.231 etc. The idea that a calm sea is asleep is common: e.g. Simon. 38.22, *A.P.* 9.290; cf. also Hom. *Il.* 5.524, Alcm. 89. For the 'groaning' sea cf. Eur. *HF* 861.

omnipotent Sleep: the metaphorical sleep of 674, which was good and desirable after storm, leads on to literal sleep, which now suggests lack of consciousness, from which it is better to awake. The sleep of death will finally release Ajax (cf. 832), but there will be no release from *it*. Sleep is the 'all-subduer' (πανδαμάτωρ) at Hom. *Il.* 24.5. At *OC* 609 it is time itself which is 'all-conquering'.

releases...hold: the chiastic structure is like that at 647. The idea of releasing, expressed both positively and negatively, frames the two participles that indicate fettering (of sleep also at Hom. *Od.* 23.17) and capturing.

677 After the illustrations drawn from the world of nature Ajax returns to his starting-point (666–7), his own particular case.

678 **I shall:** Brunck's ἔγωγ(ε), with Madvig's punctuation after it, and the verb understood, is the most probable correction of ἐγὼ δ(έ), which would have to be explained as an elliptical use of δέ...γάρ (so Pearson (1922) 24), or as an anacolouthon: the sentence changes direction (so Fraenkel 22, Kamerbeek, West, *BICS* 26 (1979) 2–3). See Ferrari 28–9, and cf. 104, 1347, 1365.

at this late hour I understand: again the intellectual process is stressed, but this time Ajax (contrast 666–7n.) uses the present tense and the first person singular unambiguously of himself, with ἀρτίως, 'recently', suggesting that he has only now come to his understanding.

679-82 The sentiment that enemies can turn into friends, and vice versa, goes back to the sixth-century Bias of Priene (see Arist. *Rhet.* 1389b 23–5, 1395a 26–7, Diog. Laert. 1.5.87), one of the Seven Sages, and is common later (see Jebb's Appx., West (678n.)). The usual moral is that one should not get too involved in friendship, because friends are unreliable, or, less cynically, that one should be careful in one's choice of friends; cf. esp. *OC* 611–23, Isocr. 1.24, Dem. 23.122, Diog. Laert. 1.2.60. Here the antithesis is not expressed symmetrically. After the generalisation in the first part of the sentence (with 'is to be hated' a verbal adjective) Ajax switches to a statement of his own intention with regard to friends. It is the generalisation that he wants his listeners to hear. It is in line with what Odysseus said at 121–6, and will say again at 1359. But it is the second part of the sentence that really concerns Ajax (for the inclusion of a less relevant converse of a proposition see Stevens 334): those who were his friends, and whom he served (439, 616–17), have turned into his enemies. He has already made it clear (665) that for him an enemy is always an enemy (see Blundell 87).

later...not always: the first adverb can also mean 'again', which perhaps suggests that the enemy who will become a friend was once before a friend. The second adverb picks up the same word ('for ever') at 676.

I shall want: for the future D.L. Page, on Eur. *Med.* 259, compares English 'I shall be pleased to accept your invitation'.

683 **the haven of companionship:** so Theognis 113–114 advises one to avoid the friendship of an evil man as being like a poor harbour. There is pathos in the metaphor (one ought to feel safe in harbour), and a suggestion that the only harbour that Ajax will find will be that of Hades (so Kamerbeek); cf. *Ant.* 1284.

684 **it will turn out well:** the real meaning is that Ajax will solve these problems of relationships by his death. The μέν clause sums up all that precedes, while δέ provides the transition to the direct address to Tecmessa.

685-6 That Ajax should ask Tecmessa to pray to the gods is perhaps inconsistent with his attitude at 590 (see Kirkwood 266 n. 23), as is his own prayer in the suicide-speech. But even Ajax is not averse to seeking divine help, when he needs it, in the conventional way; see Perrotta 95, Gellie 21–2.

what my heart desires: Ajax is deliberately vague. What he desires becomes clear to Tecmessa at 967. ἐρᾷ implies a passionate desire, for death also at *Ant.* 220.

may be accomplished right to the end: for Ajax the end will be soon.

687-8 my comrades: the appeal to the chorus's faithfulness is in keeping with 349–50, 357–61, but is somewhat tactless and pathetic after Ajax' own warning (683) about the unreliability of comradeship. The alliteration of τ is striking, but its effect is hard to gauge.

pay...as she does: i.e. 'both of you observe my wishes'.

688-9 if Teucer should come: as at 342–3, 562–4, 567–9 Sophocles prepares us for the second part of the play. Ajax really means that Teucer is to see to his funeral (826–30), but the generalising plural may be taken by his hearers to include Tecmessa and perhaps her son.

690 where I must journey: his hearers take him to mean the beach (654–6), but he really means 'to the underworld'. For πορεύομαι used of this last journey Sicherl 84 n. 65 compares *Ant.* 892, Pl. *Phaedo* 67b, *Menex.* 236d.

691-2 perhaps...soon: ἴσως is best taken as 'perhaps', τάχ(α) as 'soon'. For the combination cf. Thuc. 6.10.4, 34.2, 78.3.

I have been saved: the speech ends emphatically with the most striking ambiguity of all. From the point of view of everyone else in the play this is a lie: Ajax will not be saved at all (cf. 778–9, 812nn.; at *El.* 1229 'saved' is contrasted with 'dead'). But his standards are different, and for him death *is* his salvation, the only means of preserving his *arete* (see Wigodsky 154–8). He has not changed at all since 394–7; cf. also Eur. *IA* 1440 (with Stockert's note).

693-718: Second Stasimon

The Chorus, left alone in the orchestra, and thoroughly deluded by Ajax' apparent change of heart, sings a joyous prayer-hymn, in basically glyconic metre, which contrasts with the gloomy mood of the parodos and the first stasimon. Elsewhere too Sophocles uses a happy ode to make the imminent tragedy seem all the blacker (see J. Rode, in Jens 107): *Ant.* 1115–54, *OT* 1086–1109, *Tr.* 633–62 (cf. also 205–24). The beauty of the language communicates the chorus's joy to the audience, for whom perhaps there is still a glimmer of hope (see p. 185). But the audience does not really share the chorus's delusion, or, at the very least, it is uneasy, so that the predominant effect is one of tragic irony. The ode consists of a single pair of responding stanzas. In the strophe the chorus calls on Pan and Apollo to lead them in the dance, listing, as is normal in a Greek prayer, the titles and attributes of the gods and the places from which they are being summoned. The antistrophe, with many echoes of the preceding episode, gives the reason for its joy: Ajax has changed his mind and all their troubles are now over.

693 I thrill...I soar...with exceeding joy: both verbs are in the 'instantaneous' aorist (see 99n.). The first (for which cf. Aesch. fr. 387, perhaps also of ἔρως) describes the prickling or shuddering of the flesh (or, Stanford, cf. *Suda* E 3967, the bristling of the hair) under strong emotion (often, but not here, of fear), while the second expresses the soaring effect of that emotion, as at *Ant.* 1307, Anacr. fr. 33. *Eros*, 'passion', is most often sexual (for a wider sense cf. *Ant.* 617); what the chorus feels is akin to sexual excitement. The word is perhaps suggested by Ajax' use of the cognate verb at 686, but what he longs for is death, whereas the chorus longs to dance and jump for joy.

694-8 As Stanford says, the repetition of Pan's name (cf. Theocr. 1.123) echoes the beating of dancing feet, as does the second half of the epithet 'snow-beaten'. Pan is invoked as the god of rustic dancing (cf. *Hom. Hy.* 19.20–1, Pind. fr. 99, fr. adesp. 18.3 *PMG*), who is associated with Psyttaleia, the small island off Salamis, the home of Ajax and the chorus (Paus. 1.36.2 records there some wooden images of Pan); cf. Aesch. *Pers.* 448–9, where too he is described as lover of the dance who haunts the shore of the sea. This is probably the meaning of 'sea-wandering' here. At Theocr. 5.14 he is 'god of the seashore', probably a reference to a shrine on the shore (see Gow). Σ here and *Suda* A 1241 (among a variety of explanations) say that he was a fishermen's god; cf. Pind. fr. 98, Opp. *Hal.* 3.15–28, Aesch. 6.11, and see Roscher, *Ausführliches Lexikon der griechischen und römischen Mythologie* (1897–1902) III 1384–5. Many MSS have ἀλίπλακτε, 'beaten by the sea', perhaps a corruption from 597 (where in some MSS the opposite error occurs; cf. [*A.P.*] *P V* 467). It is probably fortuitous that both stasima begin with such similar words; see also 1185–6n.

from Cyllene's...rocky ridge: Mt. Cyllene is in Arcadia, Pan's birthplace and principal home. Cyllene was the birthplace of Pan's father Hermes, but Maenalus of Pan himself.

you lord...to dance: this is better than 'who of the gods arranges dances'. The gods for whom Pan arranges dances are perhaps especially the Nymphs and Graces (cf. *Hom. Hy.* 19.19, Ar. *Thesm.* 978).

698-700 may move in rapid...dances: either 'may move rapidly (ἰάψῃς intransitive) as to dances', or (better) 'may shoot forth (transitive) dances' (Long 91–2); cf. the metaphorical use of the verb at Aesch. *Ag.* 1548.

Mysian and Cnossian: for the first adjective all the MSS have 'Nysian', Nysa being the holy mythical mountain of Dionysus (see Dodds on Eur. *Ba.* 556–9). There is a natural association, through the satyrs, between Pan and the god of all ecstatic experience (cf. *OT* 1104–5, *Hom. Hy.* 19.46–7), and Dionysus has connections with Crete. But 'Mysian' is the reading of a third- or fourth-century papyrus (*P. Oxy.* 1615), which predates all the MSS, and was read also by one of the sources of *Suda* N 619. Mysia was the home of the great Anatolian mother goddess Cybele, who was worshipped in the wild dances of her attendant Corybantes, and who is associated with Pan at Pind. fr. 95 (see L. Lehnus, *L'inno a Pan di Pindaro* (Milan 1979) 95–7) and Ar. *Birds* 745–6 (see Dunbar's note). With 'Cnossian' we are to think partly of the long Cretan tradition of dancing (cf. Hom. *Il.* 18.590–2, Σ Pind. *Py.* 2.69), and partly of the dancing of the Curetes in honour of Rhea the mother of Zeus. For the association of Pan and the Great Mother cf. Pind. *Py.* 3.78. Corybantes and Curetes, Cybele and Rhea, are often identified with each other (see Dodds on Eur. *Ba.* 78–9, 120–34, 126–9). The chorus intends to have a wild and emotional celebration.

which you have taught yourself: at Hom. *Od.* 22.347 the singer Phemius claims to be self-taught. It is unclear whether the reference is to Pan or to the chorus itself.

701 After this line there seems to be a lacuna, ∪ – ∪ – (so Hermann and Lobeck), corresponding with 'and kindle' (τε καὶ φλέγει) at 714. It may (Kamerbeek) have contained τε καὶ and a present infinitive The alternative is to delete those words there, but see 714n.

702-5 Apollo, whose birthplace was on Delos, is also associated with music and dancing, and that is no doubt the main point here, though it is not explicitly made. But he is also concerned with pollution, purification, and healing (185–6n.), and thus comes in appropriately after 654–5. **come over the Icarian sea:** Icaria is an island between Delos and Asia Minor. πελαγέων, 'sea', may be corrupt. The scansion – ᴗᴗ – ᴗ – ᴗᴗ – is unusual (but cf. Eur. *IA* 556). Lloyd-Jones and Wilson 23–4, retaining φατίξαιμ' in 715, suggest κελεύθων, 'paths', which would give – ᴗᴗ – ᴗ – ᴗ – – , a form of hipponactean or a choriambic enneasyllable. But the sense is not affected. See also Renehan 347–9, who objects also to the plural use of πελαγέων.

fully recognisable: i.e. without disguise; cf. 15. There is perhaps a play on Δάλιος and δῆλος. The four ευj-compounds (704, 705, 708–713) all reflect the chorus's sense of euphoria.

706	**Ares has dissolved:** the verb picks up 676. The chorus naturally associates the War-god with the warrior Ajax; see 179–81n., 612–13, also 254–5n. The god who brings destruction gives peace when he ceases to destroy (cf. 674–5). For the idea cf. *Tr.* 653–4.

the dread grief: the phrase is Homeric (e.g. *Il.* 17.83).

from my eyes: the Greek omits the possessive pronoun, and the meaning could be 'from his (Ajax') eyes'; cf. 51–2, 69, 167, 191, 447, 462. For his grief or distress cf. 153. But the main subject of the ode is rather the chorus's relief, and it is the 'sore pain' of 200 that has been removed. No longer does fear show in its eyes (140). Both interpretations are found in Σ. The idea is perhaps that of dissolving a cloud or a mist; cf. Hom. *Il.* 15.668, Aesch. *Sept.* 228, *PV* 145, Eur. *Hipp.* 172.

707-8	**Oh, oh..oh Zeus:** the repetitions in the invocation echo those in the corresponding position in the strophe (694–5). Both here and at 711 αὖ, 'once more', marks the alternation from evil to good, as does πάλιν, 'again', at 711. At 614 αὖ expressed the opposite alternation.

708-10	**the white light can come near:** the language picks up that of Ajax at 672–3. Contrast the darkness of 394–5, and for the symbolism of the white light of day cf. Aesch. *Pers.* 301, *Ag.* 668, and see Pearson on fr. 6, M. Lossau, *Eranos* 92 (1994) 85–92, esp. 88. πάρα = πάρεστι, 'it is possible', and φάος, 'light', is subject of πελάσαι (intransitive), 'come near', which here governs a genitive as at *OT* 1100–1, *Tr.* 17, *Phil.* 1327. A dative is more common, as probably at 889.

the swift ships...the sea: lit. 'the quick, sea-swift ships'. Both adjectives are Homeric formulaic epithets for ships. For the tautology cf. *Od.* 7.34. The chorus thinks of the ships that brought it to Troy (358), and which, it hopes, will take it home again.

711	**has...forgotten his troubles:** in Greek an adjective, '<is> forgetful of troubles', which occurs elsewhere only at *Tr.* 1021. For the idea that forgetfulness heals pain cf. also *Phil.* 877–8. De Romilly (1968) 133 remarks that 'in all the cases where the idea is to be found, it always applies to a short remitment after an acute crisis'.

712	**the rites of the gods:** i.e. the rites of purification of 655–6. In fact Ajax himself will be the victim of the sacrifice, and what will be accomplished will be his death (925–7).

713	**reverencing them:** the chorus picks up Ajax' word at 667, but applies it more conventionally to the worship of the gods.

with the greatest...divine law: this seems to be the meaning of 'with the greatest *eunomia*'. *Eunomia* is more often a political term, associated especially, but not exclusively, with Sparta (it was the title of a poem by Tyrtaeus, according to Arist. *Pol.* 1306b 39, Strabo 8.4.10). The next line, following in asyndeton, suggests that the chorus is thinking not only of Ajax' purification, but more generally of his acceptance (cf. 666–7) of the law of alternation that governs the universe.

714 great time picks up Ajax' 'long (and immeasurable) time' at 646. The two adjectives are virtually synonymous.

extinguishes and kindles: the first verb can also mean 'withers', but paired with the second it must refer to the extinction of a light (cf. Hom. *Il.* 9.212). For the destructive action of time as the mark of the human condition see de Romilly (1968) 95 and cf. *OC* 609. Stobaeus 1.97.18 quotes the line without 'and kindles', and the words, which are in all the MSS and in *Suda* Φ 525, and which pick up 673, are omitted by most modern editors (but not by Kamerbeek or Stanford) to provide correspondence with the strophe (see 701n.). This might be acceptable if we could take μαραίνει to refer to the extinction of Ajax' blazing passion (Winnington-Ingram 43 n. 95) or to the cancellation of the evil in general (Rosenmeyer 161). But the word more naturally describes something unwelcome, so that without the second verb the chorus presents only the alternation from good to evil. This would be odd in an ode which throughout is concerned to stress the alternation from evil to good. Ajax himself (646–7n.) emphasised the alternation from growth to death, but the chorus, misunderstanding his real intention, reverses this. Knox (1979) 159 n. 128 remarks that the double phrase corresponds with 131 as well as 647.

715-18 I would say...impossible: lit. 'I would say that there is nothing that cannot be spoken'. Whether we read φατίξαιμ(ι) (with most MSS) or φατίσαιμ(ι) (with Livineius) depends on the view taken of the metre (see 702–5n.). The former would be a Doric/NW Greek aorist; see Garvie on Aesch. *Cho.* 953–6.

beyond my hopes: i.e. 'unexpectedly'. Again there is a clear echo of Ajax' speech (648).

has been converted: the double compound μετανεγνώσθη occurs only here, and the single compound μεταγιγνώσκω is nowhere else used in the passive. Knox, *GRBS* 7 (1966) 217, suggests that the unusual and awkward expression helps to convey the strain which the change of mind imposed on Ajax.

from his anger: most MSS (and *Suda* M 716) have accusative θυμόν, but the genitive is necessary to balance 'his great quarrels'. The plural, which describes his repeated bouts of anger, is not found again before Plato (unless at *OT* 892 Musgrave), but there is no reason to doubt it; see W. Schadewaldt, *SIFC* 27–8 (1956) 493–4 (= *Hellas und Hesperien* 291–2).

719-865: Third Episode

By the end of the last episode the audience was almost certain that Ajax still meant to kill himself. It no doubt expects the Messenger who now appears to report his death. But Sophocles frustrates our expectation. In a different way he frustrates also the expectation of the chorus that Ajax will reappear as a happy man. The Messenger brings news that Ajax can be saved if he can be kept in his hut for the remainder of the day. But Ajax has already left it, and the effect of the message is to throw the chorus, and Tecmessa on her appearance at 787, into renewed turmoil and anxiety, which contrasts with the joyous mood of the preceding ode.

The first part of the episode ends with Tecmessa and the chorus rushing off in different directions to look for Ajax, leaving stage and orchestra completely empty. This departure of a chorus in the middle of a tragedy (the *metastasis* according to Poll. 4.108, but the term may belong to post-classical tragedy; see Taplin (1977) 375) is unusual, being paralleled in the extant plays only at Eur. *Alc.* (746), *Hel.* (385), *Rhes.* (564), and, the only parallel for this combined with a change of scene, Aesch. *Eum.* (see Taplin 375–81, 384–7; for possible occurrences in lost plays see S. Radt, in *Entretiens Fondation Hardt* 29 (Vandoeuvres-Geneva 1982) 212). The result is that Ajax is truly alone when he kills himself on stage, having entered by an *eisodos*, presumably after a short pause to allow the half-chorus to leave by it. The second part of the episode is devoted entirely to his final speech, most of it delivered with a calm that contrasts with the bustle at the end of the first part. Yet underlying the calm there is strong emotion (see 854–8n.), and in the middle of the speech Ajax utters an impassioned curse against his enemies. In his farewell to his homeland and his present environment of Troy, which have helped to mould him, and to the sunlight that he will never see again, his tone seems to combine bitterness with resignation, and even glad acceptance of death as the only means of preserving his *arete.*

The two parts of the episode are linked by their references to Teucer, whose arrival we have been expecting since 342 (cf. 562–4, 688–9). Ajax' speech, while providing the conclusion of the first part of the play, also serves as a kind of prologue, before the chorus's *epiparodos*, to the second part. Jebb explains that 'Teucer sends a messenger, instead of going himself, probably because he hopes that his mediation with the chiefs may do some good'. But the real reason is that Sophocles wants Teucer's first appearance to be delayed till after Ajax' death. The Messenger's account (719–33) of his hostile reception in the Greek camp establishes his solidarity with Ajax, and prepares for the later part of the play in which he will represent his half-brother against the hostile sons of Atreus. At this stage Tecmessa still hopes that he will be able to save Ajax (804; cf. 778–9, 812nn.). So does Ajax, but for him salvation means the funeral which will restore his heroic status (829–30). Sophocles thus prepares us for the issue that remains unsettled at his death, but will dominate the rest of the play, and it will come as a surprise that it is not after all Teucer but Odysseus who secures his burial.

In his speech at 748–83 the Messenger reports that Athena's anger will last only for this one day, and recalls two occasions (perhaps invented by Sophocles; see Rosenmeyer 182–4. On the other hand Σ 127 reports that on three occasions Ajax displayed irreverence towards the gods, and it is possible that Sophocles has adapted two of these from epic tradition; see F. Dirlmeier, *NJbb* 1 (1938) 308–9, Linforth 5, 21 n. 4) on which he aroused that anger by proudly rejecting divine help. The bearing of this on the tragedy is much disputed. In the prologue the reason for Athena's anger remained unclear (see 127–33n.). For many scholars (e.g. Bowra 30, Winnington-Ingram 40, 61, 318) it is here that all becomes clear: Ajax falls because of his *hybris*, his failure to recognise his limitations and to live in accordance with his status as a human being. Stanford (760–1n.) finds here the main lesson of the whole play. For those who hold this view Calchas is to be taken as speaking with divine authority. For others his judgement is suspect or less significant (e.g. Reinhardt 29–30, Linforth 20–8, Rosenmeyer 182–4; Schlesinger 375–84 tries, too subtly, to distinguish between the divinely inspired prophecy that the anger will last for only one day and the *comments* of Teucer or the messenger, or of Calchas speaking only as a man; see also Wigodsky 150 n. 1). Certainly the simple explanation is to be distrusted. Although Ajax' rejection of Athena's help was obviously foolish, and the sort of behaviour that from Homer onwards was likely to arouse a deity's anger, Sophocles does not use the word *hybris* to describe it. At 838 he blames not Athena but the sons of Atreus for his death. And in any case it seems unlikely that the key to his tragedy lies in two unconnected events that took place before the play began, and that have nothing to do with its action. No doubt they provide some sort of explanation of Athena's hostility to him, the enemy of her favourite Odysseus, whose side she took in the judgement of the arms at Hom. *Od.* 11.547, but their real purpose is to re-establish, after Ajax' apparent change of heart at 646–92, our sense of his pride in his heroic stature (see von Fritz 247, Gellie 210, March 10), and thus to prepare us for his final speech. His rejection of Athena's help is entirely consistent with the real Ajax (cf. 589–90; 766 echoes 96), whom for the last time we are about to see on stage. Paradoxically Ajax is happy to accept Athena's help only when he is mad (91–3). Moreover (Machin 31–59), these conventional offences against a deity help to weaken any disapproval that the audience may feel for Ajax' attack on his enemies, and thus contribute to his rehabilitation.

That we are not to take too seriously Athena's anger is shown also by the fact that it is to last for only one day (see Poe 90–2; there is no reason to suppose, with Bowra 36 (see also Jebb xl–xli) that a merciful Athena is giving Ajax the chance to escape death. This is not the view of Tecmessa or the chorus at 950–4. For Seaford 130 n. 12 the audience will think of the later cult association of Ajax and Athena; see Intro. 6). One purpose of this is to increase the dramatic sense of urgency and to make possible the use of the 'too-late' motif, as in *Ant.* where Creon's change of mind is too late to save Antigone (V. Liapis points out to me that at 190–200 Ajax' salvation depended on his leaving the hut, whereas here it depends on his staying inside). If he had been a different sort of man, he might have been prepared to wait in the expectation that the anger even of the gods does not last for ever, and that tomorrow his troubles may be over (cf. 779 and see 131–2n., Biggs 227). But then he would not have been true to his heroic self, and we have already seen him rejecting the possibility of alternation in his own case. So in his final speech he remains unchanged. He has not learnt *sophrosyne*, and expresses no regret for his attack on his enemies. His desire for vengeance is as keen as ever. The anger of Athena will indeed not last beyond this day, but this is because he will be dead (see Wigodsky, Hester 253, comparing Heracles' realisation of the meaning of the oracle at *Tr.* 1169–72). For the way in which this speech is set apart see 646–92n. (*init.*).

719 Friends: It is made clear at the beginning that the messenger is a supporter of Ajax.

720-1 For Teucer's absence until now cf. 342–3, 564. The Mysians (in historical times located in the south east of the Troad) are allies of the Trojans at Hom. *Il.* 2.858 (see Kirk).

722 was abused: probably historic, rather than a genuine, present tense: the end of the speech shows that the tumult has already subsided. The noun ὁ κῦδος, 'reproach', from which the rare verb κυδάζω must derive, is known only from Σ here and from the lexicographers.

by the whole body of the Argives: Ajax' quarrel is primarily with Agamemnon and Menelaus, but it has involved the whole Greek army; see 53–4n., and cf. 95, 408–9, 440, 458, 1055.

725 without exception: lit. 'there is nobody who not', a common Greek idiom, the phrase being equivalent to πάντες, 'all', so that the verb is naturally plural.

727 would not be strong enough: for this use of ἀρκέω see 439n.

728 For death by stoning as the method of executing traitors see 254–5n. The chorus's fears there are now confirmed. The treatment proposed for Teucer shows how Ajax himself is now regarded by the army, and how difficult his rehabilitation is going to be.

mangled: a metaphor from carding wool; cf. Aesch. *Ag.* 198, fr. 132c.2, Ar. *Ach.* 320.

729-30 in their hands: see 27n..

were unsheathed from: lit. 'were taken through'. The genitive κολεῶν, 'scabbards', may be taken either with 'drawn (from)' or with διεπεραιώθη.

731   as far as it could go: the partitive genitive (cf. Xen. *An.* 1.3.1) is like the genitive after a verb of aiming at; see Moorhouse 59 ('the strife ceases after running towards its extreme point').

732   through...of old men: lit. 'in the reconciliation of the word of old men'. The preposition ἐν is instrumental in force (LSJ III). For the expression cf. Eur. *Supp.* 602. Σ 731a supposes that Sophocles has in mind the conciliatory words of the aged Nestor in Hom. *Il.* 1.

733   pray: lit. 'for us', an ethic dative (cf. 102). For ἡμῖν with second syllable short cf. 216n.

734   to my lord: or possibly, 'to those who are most concerned (in the matter)'; cf. Aesch. *Cho.* 688-90.

735-6 for he has reformed...temper: lit. 'having yoked new plans to his new temper'. For the metaphor cf. 24n. At 640 the chorus lamented that Ajax was no longer being true to his natural temperament. Here the chorus-leader fails to understand that he is in fact unchanged. But for the audience 'new plans' is a sinister phrase. In Greek 'new' often conveys the sense of 'new and therefore bad'. We look ahead to the suicide.

738-9 Too slow...dispatched me: either Teucer was too slow in sending him on his mission or the Messenger was too slow in fulfilling it.

740   Where have you fallen...this duty: lit. either 'what of this duty has been stinted?', or 'what has been found lacking in this duty?' at Aesch. *Pers.* 489, *Cho.* 577 the verb is used in the participle with a genitive of that which is lacking.

742   should not be allowed out: aorist infinitive of παρίημι (cf. Eur. *Supp.* 468). The verb more often means 'allow in', but the reading of most MSS παρήκειν seems to be unparalleled in the sense of 'going out to'. Stanford and Kamerbeek take it to mean 'pass by <those who should be watching it to prevent it>'.

until...should arrive: a few MSS have the optative τύχοι, but the retained subjunctive which is the better attested reading, is equally correct in a temporal clause in secondary sequence, and the omission of ἄν is not uncommon in poetry; cf. 552-5n., and see Moorhouse 298-9. The line makes clear to the audience that Teucer's arrival is imminent.

743-4 I tell you: this sense is conveyed by the particle τοι, which 'brings the point home to the person addressed' (Denniston 548-9).

he has gone: the verb often means 'to be ruined' (see LSJ II 1 b and cf. 896, 1128). The ambiguity, for which cf. Aesch. *Pers.* 1, 13, would not be lost upon the audience.

changed for the better: see 735-6n. Ajax seems to the chorus-leader to have yielded at last to his appeal at 483-4. For the comparative in preference to the better attested superlative see Dawe 150.

**746   According to Arist. Byz., Ἔμμετροι παροιμίαι, fr. 359 Slater, this line became proverbial.

747   do you come: πάρει is a necessary correction. 748 indicates that that it is about the Messenger's, not Calchas', knowledge that the chorus-leader is enquiring.

748   and I was present: the Messenger begins by establishing his credentials; cf. *Ant.* 1192.

749-50 Much stress is laid on the confidential nature of the conversation between Calchas and Teucer. The explanatory γάρ introduces the account of what the Messenger knows.

753-4 to keep...go out freely: the polarisation, with the two infinitives framing the two lines, gives emphasis to the crucial idea.

755 Calchas clearly envisages the survival of Ajax as a real possibility.

756 only for today: the repetition of the same idea as that of 753 is again emphatic. The accusative of duration of time is the papyrus reading, and gives better sense than the dative of the MSS.
drives: cf. 275, 504.

757 said in his speech: for the solemn character of this kind of pleonasm see Fraenkel on Aesch. *Ag.* 205.

758-61 Calchas' words are in harmony with the common fifth-century view that the gods resent excessive human success and prosperity (cf. 1077-8, *Ant.* 613-14). The idea should be distinguished as far as possible (see Fisher 362-3; D.L. Cairns, *JHS* 116 (1996) 17-22, takes a more moral view of divine *phthonos*) from the more moral, and more ancient, belief, that god punishes human beings for *hybris*, outrageous behaviour (see Intro. 12). Excessive prosperity may lead to *hybris* in the case of men whose mind is unsound (Thgn. 153-4, Sol. fr. 6), but it is not in itself *hybris*. At 762-77 the Messenger will relate two specific offences of Ajax, but they are described in terms, not of *hybris*, but of folly (cf. 763, 766 and see Fisher 325; also Whitman 254 n. 23). As early as Homer it is foolish to insult or to challenge a god (e.g. *Il.* 2.594-600, 5.440-2, 24.606-17; cf. Aesch. *Sept.* 425-31, 529-32). So Locrian Ajax at *Od.* 4.503-4, whom Sophocles may have had in mind here, foolishly boasted that he had escaped from the sea despite the will of the gods. Here his greater namesake was foolish to suppose that he could manage without Athena, which was tantamount to putting himself on her divine level. All of this tells strongly in favour of the reading κἀνόητα at 758, rather than κἀνόνητα, 'useless', although the latter is much better attested both in the MSS and in the numerous citations in later writers (e.g. *Suda* A 2556 and T 9; for the idea cf. Isocr. 12.77), and is accepted by most modern editors, the former appearing only in Zc (but it was evidently read by Σʳᵉᶜ 758e, Christodoulou p. 317, where it is glossed by ἄφρονα 'foolish'). 'Too great' certainly applies to Ajax, as to all Sophoclean heroes (cf. *Ant.* 68, and see Knox (1964) 24-5), but 'useless' is quite inappropriate, and not even Athena charged him with that fault (cf. 119-20). For the corruption cf. 1272.

760-1 whenever...does not then think: for the omission of ἄν in the relative clause with the subjunctive (lit. 'whoever', with no specific antecedent) see 552-5n. In many MSS the subjunctive (the reading of *P.Oxy.* 1615) has been changed to the indicative. The thought is a commonplace: e.g. *Ant.* 768, *Tr.* 473, Aesch. *Pers.* 820, *Sept.* 425, Eur. *Alc.* 799. See Pearson on fr. 590.1, Coray 171 n. 3. But it is misleading to describe such a foolish attitude as *hybris* (see Fisher 238, 242-4, 254, 260-1), though it may lead to, or be accompanied by, hybristic acts, as in the case of Idas at A.R. 1.462-92 (on which see Dickie 89-90).

762-3 The Sophoclean hero regularly rejects sensible advice from others.

764-5 A more symmetrical antithesis would balance 'with your spear on the one hand' (μέν) with 'but with the help of god on the other hand' (δέ), or begin each clause with 'win the victory' in anaphora, followed respectively by μέν and δέ. But Sophocles has put 'with your spear' emphatically in front of the whole complex, so that the effect is, 'with your spear (the most important thing to you) by all means wish…, but do not forget to do so with god's help'.

767-9 This antithesis is simpler, with 'the gods' preceding μέν in the first clause, and 'I' preceding δέ in the second. There is a supplementary antithesis between 'together with' at the end of 767 and 'without' at the end of 768.

the nonentity: lit. 'the man who is nothing'. For the variations in this type of expression (masculine or indeclinable neuter, οὐδ- or μηδ-, with or without the article), usually with little distinction of meaning, see Denniston on Eur. *El.* 370, Moorhouse 338–9 (and in *CQ* 15 (1965) 31–40), and cf. 1094, 1114, 1231, 1275.

I shall win: lit. 'draw upon myself', perhaps a metaphor from hauling in a net (cf. Hesych. E 5201, and see Groeneboom on Aesch. *Pers.* 477). For the active, where the middle is expected (cf. Hdt. 3.72.4) see Broadhead on Aesch. *Pers.* 477. **glory,** κλέος, is the goal of every Homeric hero.

770-3 the boast: we have already seen Ajax' propensity to boast at 96.

in the presence of divine Athena: if the text is correct the genitive seems to be governed by 'he replied' (773). For the genitive see Moorhouse 99. But an exact parallel seems to be lacking. At Aesch. *Pers.* 695–6, σέβομαι δ' ἀντία λέξαι | σέθεν ἀρχαίῳ περὶ τάρβει, 'I am too much in awe to speak face to face with you because of my ancient fear of you', σέθεν may depend on τάρβει. Jebb's tentative δ' ἀντίον, 'face to face with', could be correct.

his murderous hand: the adjective is proleptic, 'to turn his hand…and kill'.

a terrible word…spoken: this too is entirely consistent with what we have seen and heard of Ajax: for his 'terrible' words cf. 312 (cf. his 'big' words at 386n., and Athena's warning at 127–8), for the adjective as characteristic of Ajax 650n. For 'that should never have been spoken' cf. 214.

774-5 the rest…but where I…: again the key words stand at the beginning of their respective clauses, but this time there is no μέν. Ajax sets himself apart from the entire Greek army.

break in: West's εἰσρήξει (113), though the compound is not otherwise attested until much later Greek, gives the best sense: the enemy will not break in, i.e. through. All the MSS have ἐκρήξει, 'will burst out', which ought to mean that there will be no battle at all near Ajax, which is clearly inappropriate.

776-7 with such words: summarising Ajax' second offence, as the first was summarised at 770.

intolerant: 'not putting up with', or possibly 'intolerable', 'not to be put up with'. For the ambiguity see Ferguson 20.

778-9 if indeed he is still alive today: the phrase is in antithesis with 783, 'that man no longer lives'. Cf. 756, but there is no mention here of the necessity to keep Ajax in his hut, so that the words hold out some hope that there may still be time to save him, thus preparing us for the frantic effort of Tecmessa and the chorus. But, after what we have just heard of Ajax' attitude to, and rejection of, Athena's help (the same phrase at 765), the notion that god may help them is grimly ironical. For Ajax' own very different notion of salvation see 691–2n.

780 So much the prophet spoke: the whole account of Calchas' speech is rounded off in the same way as were its sections (776–7n.).

immediately from where he sat: i.e. 'without rising' (cf. Hom. *Il.* 19.77, *Od* 21. 420), not (Jebb) '<rising> from his seat'.

782 **we have been frustrated:** lit. 'deprived <of our intention>'. There is no exact parallel for this use of the verb (see, however, Kannicht on Eur. *Hel.* 577; at *OT* 771 the object is more easily supplied).

783 **if Calchas is a wise man:** the second 'if' clause qualifies the whole preceding complex of 'if' clause + apodosis. 'Wise' here implies 'knows what he is talking about', 'speaks with expert knowledge'. The adjective is often applied to seers (see Coray 112–18).

784 **Wretched:** the same word meant 'the foe' at 365. For the different meanings see Garvie on Aesch. *Cho.* 429–30. Stanford here takes it to mean 'war-bride'.
offspring of an unhappy family: δύσμορον γένος, 'unhappy offspring', is unlikely to be right. γένος in this sense of an individual offspring is not uncommon (LSJ II; cf. 357 of a plurality), but, as A.E. Housman pointed out (*JPh* 20 (1892) 33), it is usually accompanied by a reference to the family of which the person is an offspring, as at Hom. *Il.* 6.180 'divine offspring', i.e. 'offspring of the gods'.

785 **see:** more logically we should expect 'hear'.

786 **This will be a close shave...rejoicing:** lit. 'this shaves on the skin that...', with the infinitive consecutive. The expression is odd. It is not the same as, but related to, the proverbial expression, 'to stand on a razor's edge', i.e. to be in a delicately balanced position between two opposite fates (see Garvie on Aesch. *Cho.* 883–4). For shaving close to the skin cf. Hdt. 4.175.1, Xen. *Hell.* 1.7.8. The meaning may be, 'there is great danger that someone [i.e. you and I] will find cause to grieve at this'. But more naturally, a 'close shave' implies the avoidance of a danger, and we should perhaps interpret, 'this will be a close shave if someone [i.e. Ajax' enemies] is not going to rejoice'. For the sinister use of the vague τις, 'someone', often in a threat, cf. 1138 and see Garvie on Aesch. *Cho.* 58–60.

787 Heath 191 n. 54 is probably right that Tecmessa is not accompanied by the child. 809, like 944, is merely 'a distraught apostrophe'. There is nothing for him to do in this scene, and his separate departure (with an attendant?) into the hut at 814 would be distracting.

788 **from where I was sitting:** the echo of 780 seems to be fortuitous. **unwearying trouble:** cf. Pind. *Py.* 4.178.

790 **an affair concerning Ajax:** cf. Aesch. *Pers.* 248, φέρει...τι πρᾶγος, 'he brings news of some event'.

791 **man:** Fraenkel 27–8 remarks that the vocative ἄνθρωπε (elsewhere in Sophocles only at 1154) is a coarse expression used only to an inferior: Tecmessa is in a state of agitation.
surely we are not undone: μῶν introduces a question that expects the answer 'no'. Tecmessa cannot yet bring herself to believe that her new-found happiness is illusory.

792-3 **how *you* are faring:** picking up Tecmessa's 'surely we are not undone' (so Σ 792a). Ajax' name, which emphatically begins its clause, is separated from its governing preposition which comes at the very end.
if...out of doors: after the slight hope of 778–9 the anxiety returns.

794 **Yes:** for καὶ μήν, 'usually with an echoed word, in substantiating a required condition' see Denniston 353.
full of anguish: cf. Aesch. *Cho.* 211, Eur. *Hcld.* 644. The expression properly describes the pangs of childbirth.

796 **in the shelter of:** the compound adjective comes from the same root as that at 611 (n.). For the polarisation of expression see 753–4n.

797 Tecmessa's question, as at 342, alerts the audience to expect the arrival of Teucer. τῷ = τίνι, 'what?'

798-9 **this going out...his death:** we may recall Ajax' earlier disastrous *exodos* referred to at 287. In 799 among a host of emendations of the (despite Kamerbeek and Stanford) untranslatable MSS reading the obvious sense is best provided by Jebb's (after Blaydes' ὄλεθρον εἰς Αἴαντος); cf. Eur. *Supp.* 295.

800 τοῦ = τίνος.

801-2 **son of Thestor:** Calchas is the son of Thestor at Hom *Il.* 1.69. **a pronouncement which:** the antecedent is the understood object of 'learned' at 800, 'a thing which'. The expression is not easy, but better than what the MSS provide. A subject for 'brings' cannot easily be understood.

803 **protect me from:** lit. 'stand in front of'.
this misfortune...forced upon me: cf. 485–6n.

804-5 No longer the timid, submissive woman, Tecmessa takes the initiative and gives orders to the chorus, and becomes as it were the protectress of Ajax; see Synodinou 105–6, Scott 283 n. 172. The chorus is apparently to divide into three groups, one of which (presumably with the Messenger) is to fetch Teucer, while the other two look for Ajax (for the rare division of a chorus for the purposes of the action cf. Eur. *Or.* 1246–1320 and see Taplin (1977) 190). There being only two *eisodoi*, two groups must leave in the same direction. Jebb takes the first group to consist of the πρόσπολοι (attendants) of Ajax and the Messenger (see also Seale 162, for whom the exit of Tecmessa and the Messenger by the two *eisodoi* is followed by that of the two groups of the chorus), but there is no evidence that such attendants are on stage.
the east: lit. 'facing the (rising) sun'. For the compass-directions cf. Eur. *Or.* 1258–60.

807 **I have been deceived:** Tecmessa refers to Ajax' speech at 646–92. Despite Segal (1981) 433 n. 13, her acceptance that it was deceitful is sufficient to refute the view that Ajax was honest then, and only later changed his mind.
in the man: for the genitive cf. 1382. Some render 'by the man', but the genitive of the agent without a preposition is dubious Greek (at 1353 it is a genitive of comparison). For a full discussion see Moorhouse 75.

808 Cf. 522n. Tecmessa finally understands that her plea in that speech has been unsuccessful.

809 **what am I to do:** deliberative subjunctive. This characteristic cry of the tragic hero is sometimes, as here, put into the mouth of one of the other characters (cf. *Phil.* 908, 969). **I must not sit still:** the verbal adjective (cf. 690) here is intransitive, but transitive at Ar. *Peace* 923.

811 **Let us go, let us hurry:** the asyndeton adds to the sense of urgency; cf. 988, *Tr.* 1255.

812 **if we wish** (θέλοντες) can, despite Lloyd-Jones and Wilson 27–8, be taken with the subject of 'let us go, let us hurry', with 'it is no time for sitting down' in parenthesis. It is ironical that Tecmessa is so anxious to *save* Ajax from the death which he himself sees as his only salvation (691–2, 778–9nn.).

813-14 The emphatic polarisation of expression in 813, and the stress on the necessity for speed, mark the unusual (see 719–865n.) departure of the chorus in the middle of the play. The antithesis between word and action is very common in sophistic thought.

After the departure of Tecmessa and the chorus there must be a pause, so that Ajax does not meet them as he enters.

815-65 The suicide of Ajax presents a major problem of staging. In no other surviving tragedy does violent death take place before the eyes of the audience, and it is not certain that it does so here. Three questions have to be answered: (1) How is the change of scene managed to the lonely place where Ajax falls on his sword? (2) Is the suicide visible to the audience or somehow concealed (Seale's compromise, 165, 179 n. 47, which has the sword concealed only at the end of the suicide-speech is hardly feasible)? (3) If the suicide was carried out on stage, and since the actor who plays the part of Ajax will be required later to take the role of Teucer, while the corpse will remain on stage, how was the substitution of the necessary dummy managed? That a fourth actor was not permitted has occasionally been questioned; so here R. Sri Pathmanathan, *G&R* 12 (1965) 14, implausibly proposes that the actor who plays Ajax remains lying on stage until the end of the play.

The simplest solution is for scene-shifters to bring on a simple screen, which they place parallel to the stage-building so that it conceals the door, and behind which the grove is supposed to be located. If this is done at 814, it would coincide with the change of scene. Ajax can disappear behind it to fall on his sword. Scholars are divided as to whether the full description of the sword indicates that it must be visible to the audience (as the deictic 'this' at 828 may suggest, though it is possible that Ajax is pointing offstage), or whether it is a substitute for what the audience cannot see (so e.g. Camerer 321 n. 62, K. Joerden, in Jens 404 n. 35, Heath 192–3). If it was invisible this would provide the simplest explanation of the chorus's inability to see the corpse at 912–14. But this leads to problems later. At 891 Tecmessa finds the body and screams, but the chorus cannot see her. If this is because she is hidden by the screen, she must emerge from it at 894, leaving the corpse improbably unattended. At 915 she says that she is going to cover the corpse, and this is surely done before the eyes of the audience. Probably it is this talk of shrouding the body that provides the cue for the screen to be brought on. Till now the corpse has been fully visible, the suicide having taken place in full view of the audience (perhaps by means of a sword with a retractable blade, such as is attested for the later theatre, the συσπαστόν or ἀνδρομητόν; Hesych., Achilles Tatius 3.20.7, 21.4). Many have suspected that the covering of the corpse somehow provides the means of substituting the dummy, but Tecmessa's holding up of the shroud would hardly by itself be sufficient to conceal so elaborate a manoeuvre. Rather, while she covers the body, the scene-shifters bring on the screen. The actor walks off unseen through the door and the dummy is substituted. For the rest of her exchange with the chorus Tecmessa must speak from behind the screen. When Teucer arrives at 975 the corpse is revealed to him in two stages. At first he cannot see it (978), or Tecmessa who must still be with the body. At 992 the shrouded corpse becomes visible to him, and his cry is his reaction to the removal of the screen, but only at 1004 is the shroud removed and he sees properly his brother's face.

Scullion, who provides a useful summary of scholarly opinion on the staging, denies that there is any change of scene: when Ajax departs at 692 he merely hides behind bushes which have been on stage from the beginning of the play, and does not leave the stage at all. He now emerges to make his final speech. The corpse is subsequently found by Tecmessa as she returns through the grove. But at 654–9 Ajax tells us that he is going to the seashore, and the audience has no reason to disbelieve him. How are we supposed to know that when he disappears into the bushes he has gone no further? Scullion's theory requires the grove to have access to the backstage area, so that the actor can walk off, and the dummy be brought on, out of sight of the audience. But it is hard to see how this could be done, given that there is only one door, as Scullion rightly maintains. Pickard-Cambridge 49 (see also Kamerbeek, Ley 88, 92), proposed an elaborate use of symbols or painted panels at the end of the back-wall. He did not make up his mind as to whether they were there from the beginning of the play, or were brought on by attendants at 814. The latter is the view of Stanford and Seale 163, for whom the hut is now concealed by scenery, painted on canvas, carried on by scene-shifters. E. Pöhlmann, *A&A* 32 (1986) 20–32, envisages the use of two side-doors, one representing the entrance to the hut, the other the entrance to the grove, so that there are two separate acting areas, but see 594–5n. Most probably the audience simply imagines the change of scene (so A.L. Brown, *PCPhS* 30 (1984) 10–11). If we are told that we are now in a lonely place, that is all that is necessary.

As for the actual suicide and the substitution of the dummy, the numerous theories which involve the use of the *eccyclema* and/or the central door are all to be rejected. T.B.L. Webster, for example, *Greek theatre production* (London 1956) 17–18, thought that the *eccyclema* is pushed forward with a screen in front, representing a bush, behind which the dummy is already concealed. The actor commits suicide behind the bush, then crawls off unobserved through the door. For Stanford (on 865–6) and Seale Ajax kills himself beside the door, which is perhaps partly masked by bushes or screens. Later, when the audience's attention is distracted by the entry of the chorus, a dummy is substituted inside the *skene*, and pushed forward on the *eccyclema* or simply revealed at the door. Similarly for P.D. Arnott, *Greek scenic conventions in the fifth century B.C.* (Oxford 1962) 131–3 (see also Mills), Ajax kills himself by the door, which shuts on him as he ends his speech. The most serious objection to all this is that the central door has been identified from the beginning as the entrance to Ajax' hut. It would be impossibly confusing if it should continue to be used now that the scene has shifted to a lonely place. The *eccyclema* in tragedy always presents an indoor-scene, and the door through which it emerges must represent the entrance to some specific building. But there is no such building in the lonely place.

815 the killer: i.e. the sword personified, perhaps (Stanford) with a sacrificial association; cf. Eur. *HF* 451, *IT* 623, and see Segal (1981) 139, 439 n. 106. The key-word comes at the beginning of the speech, and provides immediate confirmation of Tecmessa's words at 812: Ajax is intent upon the death from which his friends are vainly trying to save him. We first heard of Ajax' sword in a very different context at 10 (n.). Now it is to perform its final task. According to Σ 864a the actor Timotheus of Zacynthus was called *Sphageus* because of his celebrated acting in this scene.
where: rather than 'in the way in which'. The fact that it is buried in enemy soil (819) is likely to make it more effective.
816 if one...for calculation: the Greek says 'also for calculation' (i.e. as well as for action). Perhaps this is a signal to prepare the audience for a long speech before the suicide. Certainly Ajax' tone is calmer and more reflective than before, and it allows him to proceed to a logical analysis of the situation. But the expression is rather flat, and

COMMENTARY 205

Herwerden may have been right to delete the whole line (also Taplin (1978) 188 n.8). For earlier suspicion of it see Christodoulou p. 37*).

817-18 See 661–2, 664–5, 1026–35nn. The exchange of gifts established a kind of guest-friendship between Hector and Ajax. Cf. Glaucus and Diomedes, and their grandfathers, at Hom. *Il.* 6.216–20, 230–6. For Ajax Hector's gift has now turned into the instrument of his destruction, and the enemy who became a guest-friend is now once more his enemy; cf. 679–82n. For gifts which destroy in tragedy see Seaford 388–95. In this case (392) 'the sword reacquires the original hostility of its donor'.

819 Again, as at 420n. and 459, Ajax sees his environment as hostile to him.

820 In this three-word trimeter the heightened language marks the importance of the sword for Ajax. Both epithets, with 'iron-consuming' purely ornamental, occur only here.

821 **I fixed it:** picking up 819. After the deception-speech, with all its talk of alternation and change, the sword remains the immovable fixed point in Ajax' world; see Knox (1979) 144.

822 **be very kind...death:** lit. 'be very kind for me to die'. The two ideas frame the line in an effective oxymoron. Death for Ajax is a favour, and his enemy's gift has turned once more into a friend.

me: the Greek says 'this man', a common way of referring to oneself, but here perhaps marking Ajax' final assertion of his status as a hero (see 77, 1236nn.).

824-34 Ajax' prayer to the gods for help should not be taken (as by March 20 n. 102) to show that he has learnt *sophrosyne*; see 685–6n. Whether he kneels, as in the Basel lekythos (Intro. 3), it is impossible to say. He makes no prayer to Athena. His first request is perhaps granted (998–9n.), but it will be Odysseus, not Teucer, who prevents his body from being left for the dogs and birds. It is beyond his own power to control his burial (see L.R. Cresci, *Maia* 26 (1974) 222).

824 **for that is reasonable:** perhaps because it is natural to begin with Zeus (so Podlecki 46), but more probably because Zeus, as father of Aeacus, is the ancestor of Ajax' family (cf. 387). For the phrase thus used in a prayer cf. *El.* 659, Ar. *Thesm.* 1144.

must help me: the verb is the same as that of 590. Ajax, who there refused to serve the gods, now pathetically asks them to help him.

825 **no large gift:** but, ironically, it will become the central issue of the second part of the play.

826 **the bad news:** the same noun at 173 described the rumour of Ajax' disgrace. The news about him will again be bad.

827-30 Sophocles prepares us for Teucer's role later in the play; see 688–9n.

to lift me up: the verb is used of carrying a corpse also at 920, Eur. *Alc.* 724. **fallen around:** the body wraps itself round the sword; cf. 899, 907, Hom. *Od.* 11.424, Pind. *Nem.* 8.23 (of Ajax).

freshly-sprinkled sword: a grim reminder of 30 (n.).

cast out...birds: the dogs and the birds are conventional elements in the description of a corpse left unburied: e.g. 1064–5, *Ant.* 29–30, 205–6, Hom. *Il.* 1.3–5, 22.354. Cf. ἕλωρ at *Il.* 1.4, *Od.* 3.271, 5.473, Aesch. *Supp.* 800–1 (the only other occurrence in tragedy).

831 **That is all my prayer to you:** lit. 'I turn towards you in supplication as to so many things'. For the concluding phrase, rounding off the prayer, cf. 780n.

832 For Hermes as a chthonic god, whose function in particular is to conduct souls to Hades, see Garvie on Aesch. *Cho.* 1, and cf. Hom. *Od.* 24.1–10. He is also the god who sends sleep and dreams (see Garvie on Aesch. *Cho.* 22–83, and on Hom. *Od.* 7.136–8), so that Ajax' prayer is particularly appropriate. Hermes will combine both his functions by bestowing on Ajax the sleep that is death; see 674–6n. and cf. Hom. *Il.* 11.241.

833 At 30 Ajax leapt over the plain with his freshly-sprinkled sword. Here he plans to leap upon that sword (for his leap cf. Eur. *Hel.* 96). ἀσφάδᾳστος, 'struggle-free', occurs elsewhere only at Aesch. *Ag.* 1293, in a similar prayer by Cassandra for an easy death.

835-8 Ajax calls on the Erinyes (Furies) as a preliminary to his curse. The Furies were probably not originally identical with curses but are regularly associated with them; see Garvie on Aesch. *Cho.* 406–9 and cf. *El.* 111–12.

as helpers: the word is used of help provided by an underworld power also at *El.* 454, 1392, Aesch. *Cho.* 376, 477. Ajax rejected the help offered by his human friends (329), and can turn only to the Furies.

the everlasting virgins: rather than 'virgins who live for ever'. For their virginity cf. *OC* 127, Aesch. *Eum.* 68–9.

who forever...suffering: they are similarly described at *El.* 113–14, *OC* 42.

the holy Furies: Sophocles no doubt identifies the Erinyes with the originally distinct 'holy goddesses' who were worshipped in a cave near the Areopagus at Athens. The identification was perhaps first made in Aesch. *Eum.* (cf. 1041, and see the editions of Sommerstein 10–11, Podlecki 5–6; also A.L. Brown, *CQ* 34 (1984) 260–81); cf. *El.* 112, *OC* 89–90, 458.

·with their long strides: the epithet, which is used elsewhere (in a slightly different form) only of sheep (e.g. Hom. *Od.* 9.464), suggests the swift and relentless pursuit of the victim. At *El.* 491 the Fury has bronze feet; cf. also Aesch. *Sept.* 791. In a similar context Ruin (*Ate*) is 'sound of foot' at Hom. *Il.* 9.505, and a curse is 'terrible-footed' at *OT* 418.

839-42 Σ tells us that some ancient critics suspected interpolation, probably of 841–2, these lines being added to clarify the sense. The suspicion is justified for several reasons: (1) Nowhere in the tradition is Agamemnon killed by one of his descendants, and it is most unlikely that Sophocles should have made Ajax utter a curse which the audience knew would not be fulfilled. (2) αὐτοσφαγής can, depending on the context, describe either suicide or murder by a blood-relation, but hardly both in the same line. (3) The superlative form φιλίστων, 'closest', is nowhere else attested. If, with Bothe, Jebb, and Fraenkel 29, we delete only 841–2 ('falling...closest descendants'), 'even as they look upon me' provides an unpleasantly abrupt ending to the sentence, and it is unclear whether the subject is the sons of Atreus or the Furies. Pearson and Kamerbeek retain τὼς ὀλοίατο, 'so may they perish' (841–2), and delete what comes between. There is force in West's argument, *Gnomon* 50 (1978) 240, that ὀλοίατο does not look like the language of an interpolator. But then 'so' ought to imply that the Atreidae will, like Ajax, commit suicide. The most satisfactory solution is to delete the whole of 839–42 (so Lloyd-Jones and Wilson, following the eighteenth-century scholar P. Wesseling). 'The wretches in utter wretchedness' may have been inspired by 1177, 1391 (cf. *Phil.* 1369). After the appeal to the Furies to note his treatment at the hands of the Atreidae, Ajax proceeds immediately to his all-embracing curse. That Odysseus is not singled out may be part of the preparation for the end of the play. So for Machin 388 the passage marks the beginning of the separation of Odysseus from the Atreidae, and of the evolution of his moral authority.

843-4 This is not the language of a man who has learnt *sophrosyne*. Ajax' desire for vengeance is as strong as ever, and it embraces the whole army; cf. 722n., and see Heath 194–5.

avenging Furies: the epithet derives from ποινή, 'requital', which is sometimes personified as a synonym for 'Fury': e.g. Aesch. *Ag.* 58–9, *Eum.* 321–3 (see Garvie on Aesch. *Cho.* 946–7). The same adjective is applied to Δίκη, 'Justice' (coupled with the Fury), in a curse at *Tr.* 808.

devour them: lit. 'taste them', i.e. probably drink their blood. For this vampirical tendency of the Furies see Garvie on Aesch. *Cho.* 577–8, and cf. fr. 743. Some take 'the whole body of the army' as the object of both verbs.

845-9 Ajax appeals to the Sun, who as he travels about the sky sees everything (cf. [Aesch.] *PV* 91–2), and can report what he has seen to Ajax' parents. The idea is common; cf. *Tr.* 94–102, Hom. *Od.* 8.270–1, 302, Aesch. *Ag.* 632–3.

steep: a Homeric epithet applied to Olympus (*Il.* 5.367 etc.); cf. Bacchyl. 3.36 of *aither*.

846 you Sun: a tragic trimeter rarely begins with a dactyl formed by a single word. Ἥλιε (or -ος) is thus used at fr. 582, and by Aeschylus at *Cho.* 986; cf. also *OC* 1634.

847 gold-decked rein: lit. 'with gold on its back'. The epithet occurs only here, but the two-word phrase is an adaptation of the Homeric single-word epithet χρυσήνιος, 'with golden rein' (cf. *OC* 693 of Aphrodite). Ajax' use of the purely ornamental epithet may suggest that the fury of his curse has moderated, and he has returned to the comparative calm of the beginning of his speech (816n.).

848-51 Ajax has not after all been deaf to Tecmessa's appeal (506–9) that he should remember his old father and mother. The picture of their grief recalls that painted by the chorus at 621–45.

my ruin: rather than 'my madness' (Winnington-Ingram 45) or 'infatuation' (Segal (1981) 123).

my death: in tragedy μόρος normally connotes not 'fate' but 'death' or 'fated end'.

nurse: τροφός, unlike τρέφω, is rarely (but cf. Aesch. *Eum.* 659) used of a mother. After all the talk of Ajax' responsibility for the nurture of Eurysaces (499, 511), and of the nurture of his mother in her old age (621–5n.), there is pathos in this sudden reminder of the nurture of Ajax by his mother when he was a little boy.

850 news: the same word as at 826 (n.).

851 The line recalls Hom. *Il.* 22.408–9, 24.703; cf. also Eur. *Med.* 1176.

852-3 Ajax quickly suppresses his compassion, and reminds himself that there is a job to be done. His sudden sense of urgency matches that of the chorus-leader at 814 (cf. also 823, 833, 843). But then his mood changes again, and he ends with a final, more leisurely, appeal.

854-8 J.F.C. Campe, who deleted all five lines, is followed by Lloyd-Jones and Wilson. Dawe (3rd edn. Teubner) removes also 853 (Bergk's elimination of the whole of 855–65 is certainly too drastic). Good reasons for deletion are given by Fraenkel 30 and West 113–15. In particular, (1) 855, which lacks a caesura (but cf. 969, 994), is a frigid sophism (there is no need for Ajax to address Death now, as he will soon do so 'there' - i.e., as often, in the underworld) which anticipates the more effective 865. (2) The article τό at 856 is hardly possible after ὦ introducing an address. (3) 857 involves a pointless repetition of the appeal to the Sun as charioteer (845–6), and διφρευτής, 'charioteer', occurs only here. (4) 'For the last time' (858) weakens the reappearance of the same idea at 864. The line is probably modelled on such passages as Eur. *Alc.* 206–7, *Hec.* 411–12, Ar. *Ach.* 1184 (cf. also *Ant.* 808–10, *OT* 1072). But 854 deserves to be retained. The appeal to Death (for which cf. *Phil.* 797) is effectively juxtaposed with that to the light of day (859). I do not understand why C. Macleod (*apud* Fraenkel) found it strange in the mouth of a suicide. 'Visit' probably suggests the visit of a doctor, summoned by Ajax to attend him (so Kamerbeek and Stanford; *contra* Holt (1980) 31 n.14); see D.S. Robertson, *CR* 58 (1944) 34–5, and cf. Xen. *Cyr.* 5.4.10, 8.2.25, Dem. 54.12. For Death as a healer cf. Aesch. fr. 255, Eur. *Hipp.* 1373, Diphilus fr. 88 K–A. Death may be represented in the winged figure with Athena and Ajax on a stamnos in Palermo (L. Séchan, *Études sur la tragédie grecque dans ses rapports avec la céramique²* (Paris 1967) 130–1); so Podlecki 81 n. 70. This arrangement leaves us with six lines (854, 859–63) containing six resolved feet, half of all the resolutions in the speech. Passion underlies the apparent calm (see 457–9n.).

859-63 Oh light: i.e. the light of day, which symbolises life. But we already know that the only light which Ajax can envisage for himself is the death to which he has just appealed; see 394–5n. The final appeal is to the two environments that have shaped him, Salamis and 'famous Athens' (for which see 596–8n.), and the Trojan plains. The former symbolises his former happiness, as at 134–5 (where βάθρον is echoed here), the latter the world which has turned hostile to him (cf. 420, 819nn., and see Taplin (1978) 87–8), but is to be the only witness of his lonely death. The same contrast was applied by the chorus to its own situation at 596–9. The springs and rivers of Troy recall 418–20, the Trojan plains 459. In this final appeal the idea of nurture appears yet again (848–51n.), at 861, where it signifies the unity of Athenians and Salaminians (see 202n.), and more strikingly at 863, where, set apart by the parenthetic 'farewell', it brings the long appeal to an end. The hostile soil of Troy (819) is paradoxically also his nurse. For the appeal to his environment see 348–595n., and for the emotional effect of such apostrophes 412–13n. For the succession of vocatives and (beginning probably with 'famous Athens') nominatives, followed by an accusative governed by 'I call on', and ending with a return to the vocative, see Moorhouse 25 and cf. [Aesch.] *PV* 88–92.

foundation of my father's hearth: in Greek the adjective 'my father's' agrees with 'foundation', 'foundation of hearth' being taken as a single expression.

864-5 After the long appeal the final short two-line sentence has a ring of dignified simplicity, as does Ajax' third-person reference to himself (cf. 98). Σ remarks that he speaks of his life on earth in the third person, but uses the direct first person for his life below. These are the last words that we hear him speak, as he leaves the sunlight for the darkness of Hades.

866-973: Epiparodos

Epiparodos, according to Pollux 4.108 is the technical term for the second entrance of a chorus. Jebb and Kamerbeek mark 866–78 as the *epiparodos*, 879–93 as a separate *kommos* (see 201–347n.), while for K Aichele, in Jens 51, 55 n. 34, 891 is the beginning of the fourth episode. But, as Heath 197 remarks, there is no formal break at either 879 or 891, and the whole composition is a structural whole (contrast the clear distinction between parodos and dialogue at 201). The hurried and disorderly arrival of the chorus in two sections corresponds to its departure at 813–14, so that the sense of frustration and anxious urgency frames the calm suicide-speech of Ajax. This *epiparodos* is not unlike that which begins at Aesch. *Eum.* 244, in which the chorus arrives in search of, and hunting, Orestes, and is at first unable to see him (cf. esp. *Eum.* 249 and see Scott 286 n. 199). The search for Ajax takes us back to the beginning of the play.

From 866–90 the chorus describes in highly-wrought poetic language its inability to find Ajax. Tecmessa enters at 891, and, unseen by the chorus, discovers his body. The remainder of the composition is devoted to the shared lamentation of Tecmessa and the chorus. For the audience it marks a period of waiting. While Ajax' friends, not surprisingly, express their grief and their fears for their own future, we are kept in suspense as to the reaction of his enemies. Ajax has remained true to himself, and has obtained the death that he desired. But, unless his *arete* is recognised by others, he will not be restored to his status as a hero. The all-important question of his burial is introduced here at 920–2, picking up 827–30, and pointing forward to the long-delayed arrival of Teucer. But it is the thought of the laughter and *hybris* of his enemies that ominously brings the composition to a close.

For the highly complex structure, with the unusual arrival of Tecmessa between the choral and dialogue sections of the first strophe see Taplin (1977) 385 (also 379–80, (1978) 148–9, K. Popp, in Jens 252, 254). The introduction (866–78) is astrophic (though some have tried to restore strophic responsion between 866–9 and 870–2: e.g. R.M. Rattenbury, *PCPhS* 160–2 (1935) 6–7), with the isolated iambic trimeters spoken probably by the leaders of the two semi-choruses. 879–90 and 925–36 correspond as strophe and antistrophe, while 891–914, a mixture of spoken iambic trimeters and emotional lyrics, correspond to 937–60, with the same division of lines between Tecmessa and the chorus (that the chorus in each section has six utterances is not a sound indication that it had twelve rather than fifteen members – so Camerer 318 n. 15 – against this Jebb liii). Each section is rounded off by an iambic speech of Tecmessa, but 915–24 comprises ten lines, while the final speech at 961–73 contains thirteen. The deletion of 866–8 to produce total symmetry is arbitrary; see 961–73n., Jebb's Appx., Dawe 158–61. There is much repetition of words and sounds in the corresponding positions or lines, a feature which may have been characteristic of a formal dirge (see Garvie, Aesch. *Cho.* p. 55): 879/925 (the repeated 'which' and 'you were to'), 885/930 ('fierce-hearted'/ 'savage in your heart', 891 = 937 (see Coxon cited on 414), 893/939, 900/946, 912/958 (the repeated 'where' and 'alas'). The metre of the lyrics is largely dochmiac, the characteristic metre of tragic lamentation.

866-8 The weariness, frustration, and excitement of the chorus are marked at the outset by the triple repetition of 'trouble' (πον-) in different cases, with the panting alliteration of *p* continued in the triple 'where' (π). cf. 1197 and see Fraenkel on Aesch. *Ag.* 268. 'Trouble' will be a keynote of the whole composition (876, 879, 888, 928; cf. also 934, 938, 954, 957, also Aesch. *Eum.* 127, probably 133, 248). γάρ ('for') is delayed to fourth position in the sentence because the triple 'where' is treated as a single unit; see Denniston 96.

869 The text is uncertain. All the MSS have ἐπίσταται, 'no place *knows* that I share its knowledge <of where he is>' (or perhaps, 'no place knows where he is that I might share its knowledge'), which is a scarcely intelligible way of saying 'I do not know where he is'. And nowhere else does Sophocles use ἐπίσταμαι in lyrics or without a person (or representative of a person, *OC* 1006) as its subject (see Coray 77–8). Wecklein's ἐπισπᾶται, 'draws me', i.e. 'attracts me' (cf. 769), is only slightly easier.

870 **Listen listen:** lit. 'see see'; of sound also at *El.* 1410, *OC* 1477; see also P. Holt, *Hermes* 116 (1988) 486–8 on *Tr.* 693–4.

872 Lit. 'our common-sailing company of the ship', a highly poetic way of saying 'your shipmates' (cf. 357). For this kind of Sophoclean periphrasis, in which a compound adjective is combined with an abstract noun 'to produce a personal reference which completes the latter part of the line', see Long 59, 111–12.

873 The combination of οὖν and δή is common in Herodotus and Plato, but appears elsewhere in tragedy only at *Tr.* 153; see Denniston 468–9.

874 The language recalls the prologue (esp. 5–6, 18–20, 31–3). Again Ajax is being tracked down, but this time by his friends.

875 **Do you have anything, then:** 'anything' means 'any news', but the other semi-chorus at 876 understands it differently; cf. Eur. *Supp.* 818, *Cyc.* 683, and see Denniston 137–8.

876 **of trouble:** see 866–8n. Again there is alliteration with *p*.

877 **on the road...rising sun:** lit. 'from the direction of the sun's beams', i.e. the east; see 804–5n., Eur. *Or.* 1259. For the accusative of extent after a verb that does not describe motion see Moorhouse 44.

879–80 **Which, then:** the interrogative with ἄν + optative is equivalent to a wish (cf. *OC* 1100 and see 388–91n.).

the toiling sons of the sea: a poetic expression for 'fishermen'. 'Toiling' is lit. 'trouble-loving' (see 866–8n.), while 'sons of the sea' is a patronymic adjective that occurs only here. For this kind of descriptive periphrasis see Broadhead on Aesch. *Pers.* 576–8, where fish are the 'voiceless children of the undefiled' (i.e. the sea).

engaged in sleepless hunting: cf. 564. Fishing is a profession pursued by night as well as by day (cf. Pl. *Soph.* 220d). The chorus, in its fruitless hunt for Ajax, calls on professional hunters for information.

881–4 **the goddesses of Olympus:** probably not the major Olympian goddesses, but the minor local nymphs of Mount Olympus in Mysia, east of Troy.

the Bosphorus: the reference must be to the Hellespont, the modern Dardanelles, which is sometimes confused in Greek poetry with the Bosphorus (e.g. Aesch. *Pers.*, 723, 745–6), the entrance to the Black Sea. For the local rivers as part of Ajax' environment cf. 420, 859–63nn. After this phrase almost all the MSS add ἴδρις, which would give 'or who *with knowledge of* the flowing rivers of the B.' The deletion provides more exact responsion with the antistrophe than does Pearson's deletion of λεύσσων, 'if he sees', at 886, and the genitive is better taken as introducing a second category of goddesses, parallel with the Olympic goddesses in the preceding phrase.

885–6 Lit. 'seeing if <he sees> anywhere'; see Kühner-Gerth II 573–4 and cf. *Phil.* 1204. The masculine participle evidently agrees with the τίς of 879, despite the intervention of the goddesses at 881.

the fierce-hearted man: cf. 205, 548–9nn., 930.

887 **it is hard:** Sophocles often uses the neuter plural of a predicative adjective; cf. 1126.

888 **despite...wanderings:** lit. 'the wanderer as to long troubles'. For the expression cf. perhaps [Aesch.] *PV* 900 (but see Griffith's n.), Eur. *Andr.* 305–6.

889 **come near to success in my course:** less probably (Jebb and Stanford), 'come near <him> with prospered course'. The metaphor is derived from a voyage with a favouring wind.

890 **the feeble man** is certainly Ajax, not (Σ 890c) the chorus. The epithet, which, if right, provides a pathetic contrast with 'fierce-hearted' above, reflects the depth to which, in the chorus's eyes, their hero has fallen. In Homer it is most often applied to the dead in, or going to, Hades, so that its choice here makes a fitting prelude to the discovery that Ajax is dead. However, even in such a context, the description of the mighty hero as 'weak' is not entirely happy, and μεμηνότ', 'mad' (N; gloss in P), while probably an emendation, is at least an intelligent one..

  the whereabouts of: see 33n.

892 **nearby:** lit. 'dwelling beside'; cf. *OC* 785, fr. 503. *Aj.* contains a remarkably large number of compounds from this root; cf. 611n. I do not understand why Pickard-Cambridge 49 thought that the word indicates that 'the grove was at the *side* of the main scene'. Kamerbeek (and hesitantly Stanford) derives it from αὐλός, 'pipe', and takes it to mean 'ill-sounding'. Σ records both interpretations (cf. *Suda* Π 480). Tecmessa is evidently meant to be not yet visible to the chorus, which must be looking in the wrong direction.

894 **the captive of his spear:** the same compound epithet described the booty at 146.

895 **steeped in:** lit. 'mixed with', a metaphor probably derived from a mixing-bowl, and often found in such contexts of trouble: e.g. *Ant.* 1311, *El.* 1485; see Garvie on Aesch. *Cho.* 744–6.

896 The three synonymous verbs in asyndeton, each longer than the preceding (2–, 3–, 6–syllables) mark the intensification of Tecmessa's grief; cf. *El.* 13, fr. 774.1. οἴχωκ(α) is an Ionic form of the perfect, as at Aesch. *Pers.* 13.

898 **newly slaughtered:** cf. 546, *Tr.* 1130. For the possible sacrificial implication see 815n.

899 **folded round his hidden sword:** see 827–30n. The sword is hidden partly in the ground, partly in Ajax' body (see 658–9n.)

900-2 Even more than at 142–3, 245–56, 600–607nn. the chorus's first thought is for itself. Without its leader it sees no prospect of ever returning home. Ajax has found release from his troubles, but the cost to his friends is great. For the idea that somebody 'kills' one by his death cf. *El.* 808, *Ant.* 871.

  return: plural in the Greek, as at *El.* 193 (see Moorhouse 4).

  your shipmate: a much easier way of saying the same thing as 872 (cf. also 349).

903 The chorus's second thoughts are for Tecmessa, whose share in suffering will be developed at 966–73.

904 **This being his situation:** cf. 281n.

  lament: cf. 430–3n., also 982, *El.* 788. The choice of verb prepares us for the reference to Ajax' ill-omened name at 914.

905 The chorus-leader assumes that Ajax must have arranged for someone else, perhaps a servant, to stab him (cf. 361).

  ill-fated: the choice of the same epithet as at 894 unites Tecmessa in her suffering with Ajax; cf. also 923.

906 For αὐτοῦ rather than αὑτοῦ in this kind of expression see Garvie on Aesch. *Cho.* 221.

907 **of having fallen on it:** Musgrave's emendation brings the idea into line with 899 (see 827–30n.). For the construction after κατηγορεῖ, 'accuses', cf. Aesch. *Ag.* 271.

909 **Alas for my delusion:** the genitive of exclamation picks up 900.

910 **unprotected by your friends:** the chorus has failed in the duty of which Tecmessa reminded it at 329–30, and more particularly at 803–12 (cf. also 741–2, 752–5, 795–6). For the genitive see 321–2n.

912-14 Ajax' corpse is invisible to the chorus. For the staging see 815–65n.

inflexible; lit. 'difficult to turn', the opposite of εὐτράπελος. The chorus now realises that it was vain to suppose that Ajax was really converted in his deception-speech at 646–92.

915-19 The covering of the corpse, which is not Sophocles' own invention (see Intro. 3), is at least partly a conventional gesture (see Heath 199 and cf. Eur. *El*. 1231, and the unveiling of Clytaemestra's corpse at Soph. *El*. 1466). Tecmessa uses probably her own cloak or veil. φᾶρος, 'cloak', can also mean 'shroud' (see Garvie on Aesch. *Cho*. 1010–11). Her motive is perhaps not only to spare her friends, but to forestall the gloating of his enemies.

enfolding: the same adjective as at 899. 'The deadly "embrace" by the "hidden sword" contrasts with the lovingly spread "embracing cloak" with which Tecmessa would "cover" the grim sight' (Segal (1981) 117; also *CW* 74 (1980-1) 128–9).

who is really his friend: καί following the relative pronoun 'gives an effect of limitation, by imposing an additional qualification' (Denniston 295).

he gasps his blackened blood: the language resembles that at Aesch. *Eum*. 248–9, where, if Podlecki is right, Orestes, the prey of the Furies, gasps out his guts. Cf. also *Ant*. 1238, Hom. *Od*. 22.18–19, Aesch. *Ag*. 1389, and see 1411–13n.

slaughter: see 898n.

920-1 **Alas, what am I to do:** the same cry as at 809 (n.), where Tecmessa wondered how to save Ajax. His death has not resolved her problems.

Which...Teucer: for the long-awaited arrival of Teucer see 797n., where Tecmessa asked the same question. The juxtaposition of this question with the preceding, together with the following 'for' clause, makes it clear to the audience that the question of the burial is going to be of crucial importance in the remainder of the play, and confirms (cf. 827) that Teucer will have a major role to play.

if he came...timely: this, the emendation of Pantazides, is the easiest way to restore ἄν, which the MSS omit before the potential optative.

922 **to join in composing for burial:** this double compound occurs only here, but cf. Eur. *El*. 1228 for a single compound used in a similar context.

this his fallen brother: the deictic 'this' may indicate that, if there was a screen, it has already been removed. But Tecmessa could merely point to the screen behind which Ajax lies; see Garvie on Aesch. *Cho*. 893.

923-4 **what a man...such a fate:** see 500–4n. Tecmessa's confidence that even his enemies will mourn so great a hero (for the idea cf. *OT* 1296, for the expression 557 above), will soon be shown, as far as Menelaus and Agamemnon are concerned, to be misplaced. It is also pathetically inconsistent with the unspoken implication of her words at 915–19 (n.). Already at 961 she more realistically accepts the chorus's prediction that his enemies will laugh (cf. also 616–20). Surprisingly Odysseus will not laugh, and, as far as he is concerned, her hope here will be justified.

925-7 **stubborn:** the same idea as at 913.

so you were...: ἄρα marks the chorus's realisation that its earlier hopes were in vain. For what Ajax has accomplished see 712n.

to accomplish your evil destiny: the chorus may mean that his fierce character was bound to bring him to this end (see Winnington-Ingram 163 n. 31). More probably it assumes, fatalistically, that, since it has happened, it must always have been fated to happen.

troubles: see 866–8n.

928-32 The groans are no doubt those described by Tecmessa at 321–2.

I heard you: μοι is the ethic dative.

fierce in your heart: again Ajax' character is emphasised. The first part of the compound picks up 885, the second part 926.

by day: a bold use of the neuter plural participle, lit. 'shining', used adverbially like the neuter plural adjective 'all night long'.

full of hatred for: rather than 'hateful to'.

deadly passion: οὔλιος is an epic form that occurs only here in tragedy. πάθος meaning 'passion' is only doubtfully attested for the fifth century, but Kamerbeek compares Democr. 68 B 31.

934-6 Yes: the same ἄρα as at 926. For time personified as responsible for the events that happen in time, or that began, as here, at a moment in time see 646–7n., 714. For the competition for the arms of Achilles see 442–6n. The chorus here gives no indication as to whether the judgement was corrupt.

for the arms: the corresponding 890 shows that a word with choriambic shape, probably an adjective agreeing with 'arms', has dropped out from the MSS. Triclinius' Ἀχιλλέως (∪–∪–) does not provide the correct responsion.

for the best fighter: a compound adjective which occurs only here, agreeing with, and defining the nature of (cf. 64n.) the 'competition', lit. 'of the best hand'; cf. *El.* 699, *OC* 1062.

938 noble: or perhaps rather 'genuine', 'true to its type'; see Fraenkel on Aesch. *Ag.* 1198.

to your heart: lit. 'liver', which was often thought to be the seat of the emotions.

940 you wail twice: as did Ajax himself at 432; cf. *OT* 1319–20.

941 such a loved one: or, less well, 'a man who loved you'. In any case, the relationship is reciprocal. For the genitive of separation after 'bereft', lit. 'hindered from', cf. Aesch. *Ag.* 120.

942 Tecmessa objects to the chorus-leader's attempt to articulate the reason for the double lamentation. The chorus can only form an opinion, whereas for her it is a matter of understanding that is based on her own experience. Ajax has already told us (554) that the pleasantest life is that in which there is no awareness.

944-5 Tecmessa apostrophises the offstage child (see 787n.). He will be fetched from the hut at 985–6. The fears which she expressed at 496–505, 510–13 are now to be realised. She forgets that Ajax has already entrusted Eurysaces to the protection of Teucer (560–4).

a yoke of slavery: a common metaphor: e.g. Aesch. *Pers.* 50, *Ag.* 1071, Hdt. 7.8.γ.3; see also 735–6n.

overseers: lit. 'watchers'. Cf. Hom. *Od.* 22.396.

946-9 with this woe: the dative is thus best explained by Jebb, 'by the mention of'.

unspeakable deeds: Hermann's emendation, which is necessitated by his deletion of ἰώ at 902, produces a straightforward lekythion at 948. ἄναυδος usually means 'speechless', and only here is it equivalent to ἀναύδητος (715). It describes that 'for which (for describing which) there is no speech' (Fraenkel on Aesch. *Ag.* 238). **heartless:** see 1333n.

950-4 Tecmessa argues that the chorus's wish (949) is futile, as it is the gods who are responsible for all the troubles of Ajax and his friends (cf. 489), or at least that they are in accordance with their will.

Yes: for μέντοι with assentient force after τοιόσδε etc. cf. 1246, and see Denniston 400. **produces:** the same verb is used of trouble at Hom. *Il.* 15.134 etc. That Athena's intention was to give pleasure to Odysseus is confirmed by her attitude in the prologue (cf. esp. 79). The lines contradict the view of Stanford that Athena did not will the death of Ajax.

955-60 The chorus does not share the confidence expressed by Tecmessa at 924. It takes it for granted that Ajax' enemies will laugh, and it describes this laughter as a form of *hybris*; cf. 79 (where too it is Athena who invites Odysseus to laugh), 153, 198–9, 364–7, 379–82, 454. The final part of the play will reveal the actual attitude of Ajax' enemies in the context of his burial. For their laughter see 988–9, 1040–3nn. As at 153 and 379–82 Odysseus is uppermost in the chorus's thoughts, and the sons of Atreus come in almost as an afterthought (contrast 839–42n.). But it is 959–60 that will turn out to be true, whereas Odysseus' attitude will come as a complete surprise to the characters of the play.

955 no doubt: for ἦ ῥα see 172n.

in his black heart: the accusative of respect has papyrus support. 'Black' is lit. 'black-faced'. The second part of the compound perhaps adds nothing to the sense (cf. Pind. *Py.* 1.7), but Jebb may be right to envisage Odysseus' heart as watching from a place of concealment (cf. *Suda* K 1288). 'Black' suggests villainy in general, and more particularly the darkness of deceit.

956 much-enduring: the use of the Homeric formulaic epithet for Odysseus strikes a sardonic note, as does 'man' with the implication 'hero' (see 77n., Seale 168).

961-73 Tecmessa's speech has suffered from various deletions by editors. Some have removed three lines to make it correspond with 915–24. Thus Taplin (1977) 385 n. 1 (see also (1978) 190 n. 3), follows Schöll in deleting 971–3, so that we are left with two speeches, each divided into two five-line sections. Against this approach A.C. Pearson, *CQ* 16 (1922) 125, argues that 971–3 are transitional and serve as the introduction to the next scene. Others are more concerned with difficulties in the Greek at 966, with the lack of caesura at 969, and with the supposed incoherence of Tecmessa's arguments; see esp. Reeve 160–1. But the development in her thought is natural enough: 'let them laugh – they will not do so for long – I suffer and they are temporarily pleased, but Ajax has got what he wanted – why then should they laugh? – they can take no credit for his death – so let Odysseus laugh if he wants to, but it is empty laughter – I am the one who suffers'. It does not help with several MSS to give 969–73 to the chorus-leader.

961-3 Then let them...: for this use of δ' οὖν see 114n. After the defiant assertion that the laughter of his enemies does not matter, a view that Ajax himself is unlikely to have shared, Tecmessa comforts herself with the thought that in any case the laughter will not last for long. So at Hom. *Il.* 1.240–4 Achilles predicts that he will soon be missed by the Achaeans, and that Agamemnon will come to regret having dishonoured him.

did not miss him: ποθέω is normally to yearn for something absent or lost, but if it could mean 'be anxious to keep what one already has' (cf. perhaps *El.* 822), that sense would fit better with 965.

while he was alive: lit. 'seeing the light', a very common expression; cf. 1067. Tecmessa refers apparently to the period of Ajax' inactivity (193–4) after the award of the arms.

when...his spear: so Kamerbeek. Jebb and Stanford (after Σ) prefer 'in the straits of war'.

965 **until they are thrown away:** for the omission of ἄν in the indefinite clause cf. 552–5n.

966-8 Paradoxically Ajax' death pleases both his enemies and himself (cf. 473–80, 686). But for Ajax it will be in vain if his enemies do not come to recognise his *arete*. For ᾗ, 'as', 'in the manner in which', the MSS have ἤ, 'than', which Jebb and Kamerbeek defend, 'to my pain hath he died more than for their joy'. But the omission of μᾶλλον, 'more', is hardly supported by such passages as Hom. *Il.* 1.117, Hdt. 3.40.2, where the preliminary 'I wish' makes all the difference (Thgn. 577 is perhaps closer to the present instance).

970 **It is for the gods:** i.e. his death concerns only the gods (see Moorhouse 84); or perhaps, with a dative of the agent (Pearson, *CQ* 16 (1922) 126–7, Kamerbeek), 'he is the gods' victim'.

no not: for the repetition of the negative cf. *OC* 587, fr. 846, Ar. *Ach.* 421, *Frogs* 1308 (cited by Reeve 161 n. 36).

971 Tecmessa returns to the thought of 961, but with the significant addition that such behaviour is 'in empty things', i.e. futile (cf. 287). For ἐν + neuter dative (not masculine, 'bereaved', as Lloyd-Jones and Wilson take it) cf. *OT* 287 and see Moorhouse 106.

972-3 **For them:** the dative, of advantage or of the person interested (cf. 970, *El.* 1152, *Phil.* 1030), is ambiguous. It might mean either that they consider his *death* an advantage or that Ajax no longer lives for them to use.

in his passing...lamentation: Tecmessa ends with the same thought as at 966, the effect of Ajax' death upon herself (for this kind of implied reproach that the deceased has 'abandoned' his survivors see M. Alexiou, *The ritual lament in Greek tradition* (Cambridge 1974) 182–4). Once more (cf. 266) Ajax has what he wants, but at the expense of his friends. These are the last words that we hear Tecmessa speak.

974-1184: Fourth Episode

The episode, the first, and shorter, section of which begins with the arrival of Teucer, the second with that of Menelaus, presents contrasting attitudes to Ajax. Teucer's appearance has been long awaited (688–9, 797, 827–30, 920–1nn.), and thus provides something of a dramatic climax. At Hom. *Il.* 8.266–72 he was protected by Ajax, but now the situations are reversed, as (Dalmeyda 8) he plays the part of a Homeric hero protecting the corpse of a dead companion. He has failed to prevent Ajax' suicide, but we still hope that he will be strong enough to ensure his burial, in accordance with Ajax' own request (826–30), and to defend his son (560–71). He begins with a series of poignant questions, which will culminate at 1024–7 (for this as a characteristic of the lament see Alexiou 161–2); cf. the chorus's questions at 879–86, 1185–91, 1215, and those of Tecmessa at 920–1. Teucer's expressions of grief unite him with Tecmessa and the chorus (974, 981–2nn.), while his reluctance to face his father Telamon reminds us of Ajax' fears at 434–40, 462–6, and thus establishes the bond between the two brothers. From now until the end of the play Teucer will, in a sense, represent Ajax. It has been suggested (by Z. Pavlovskis, *CW* 71 (1977–8) 113–23, esp. 116–17, M. Kaimio, *Arctos* 27 (1993) 26–33, esp. 31) that, if both parts were played by the same actor (see Intro. 17), this would serve to convey the point more clearly to the audience, with Teucer's voice echoing that of Ajax. We cannot, however, be certain that the distribution of parts in Greek tragedy was ever arranged for this kind of dramatic purpose. By the end of the first section Teucer has taken the expected steps to protect Eurysaces, and his summoning (985–9) prepares us for the end of the episode. But he says nothing about the burial, and it is left to the chorus-leader to remind him of this duty, thus providing the transition to the second section of the episode.

Menelaus arrives with the express purpose of preventing the burial, and the second section is largely occupied with the angry quarrel. The fears of Tecmessa and the chorus that Ajax' enemies will gloat are fully confirmed. In other contexts, expressed in a different way and by a different person, some of Menelaus' arguments might be acceptable (see 1073–6, 1091–2nn.). Like Creon in *Ant.*, whose opening speech (162–210) seems sound enough in its sentiments, but who soon emerges as a tyrant, he has a taste for sententious utterances (for their sophistic character see Long 72–3). And he too (cf. *Ant.* 639–80) preaches sermons on the value of discipline. In some respects he is a typical Spartan as seen through Athenian eyes (see esp. Rose 72–4, who stresses that 'it is by tapping [the] enormous reservoir of anti-Spartan hostility in his audience that Sophocles consolidates his defense of Ajax'). In refusing to recognise Ajax' stature he shows himself to be one of the 'small' men whom the chorus distinguished from Ajax at 158–71. Particularly repulsive is his version of *sophrosyne* and of alternation, which Ajax made (646–92) to seem so attractive, even though he rejected these principles for himself. Menelaus preaches *sophrosyne* for others while acting hybristically himself, and all that alternation means for him is that it is now his turn so to behave (1088; see 131–2, 132–3nn.). It is not to Athena's credit that Menelaus' attitude resembles hers, as she expounded it in the prologue. It may be significant (see above) that the same actor probably plays both Athena and Menelaus. Yet we are left with the uncomfortable feeling that if the situation had been reversed Ajax would have been just as happy to gloat at Menelaus; see 304n., and cf. 586 where Ajax too recommended *sophrosyne* for others but not for himself. It is Odysseus who will behave differently, as the prologue has led us to expect. There is little doubt that Teucer, who 'makes no appeal to general principles' (Long 156), wins the argument. In any case the audience is already prejudiced against Menelaus (for the importance of the audience's emotional engagement in forming its moral judgement see Heath 80–1, 84). Still, there is something unpleasant about the petty wrangling with which the argument ends. Teucer is after all only 'a pale approximation' of his brother (Gellie 22–3). We should like to think that Ajax himself would never have descended to this level. This may be why Sophocles has not shown us Ajax in confrontation with his enemies. The mediocre Teucer, who despite his disgrace does not commit suicide, though he will be prepared to die in defence of the corpse, is what Ajax might have become if he had not committed suicide. With the hero gone 'what follows is the pettiness of the unheroic' (Rosenmeyer 189–90). There will be only one further choral ode to raise the level beyond that of prosaic debate. For the limited role of the chorus in the final scenes see Scott 91.

The corpse was covered by Tecmessa at 915–19, then uncovered by Teucer at 1003–5. After Menelaus' departure Tecmessa returns with Eurysaces, and Teucer places the child beside the corpse in the position of a suppliant, thus ensuring that from now till the end of the play Ajax will remain at the centre of our attention, and at the same time suggesting that his son, rather than Teucer, is the real heir of his heroic father (see 574–6, 985, 986nn.). Tecmessa too will have her place beside the corpse and at the funeral (see Rose 84 n. 32). In the last lines of the episode Teucer defiantly repeats his intention to bury Ajax, but the audience realises that such a burial by itself will not be enough to restore Ajax to his status as a hero. First his greatness must be recognised by others than his friends. We thus look forward to the final scene, to the confrontation with Agamemnon, whose entrance is prepared at 1116, and to the intervention of Odysseus.

974 Alas, alas: Teucer's opening cry repeats exactly that of Tecmessa at 891 and 937. The two are united in their grief. Cf. also the cry of Ajax himself at 333, 336.

976 that bears on: lit. 'reaching the target of'; cf. Aesch. *Eum.* 903, of prayers appropriate to a victory, and, literally, Hdt. 3.35.4.

977 beloved face of my brother: lit. 'my brother's eye'. Teucer does not yet see Ajax (for the staging see 815–65n.), 'but the imagery of sight prepares the ground for a literal use of the word' at 1004 (Long 125). The eye is commonly used to denote a beloved or precious person, or as a source of light or comfort; see Long 101–2, Garvie on Aesch. *Cho.* 238, H. Lloyd-Jones, in G.W. Most et al., *Philanthropia kai Eusebeia*, Festschr. A. Dihle (Göttingen 1993) 300–4 on *El.* 903. So we might translate 'brotherly source of light to me'. Probably the literal and metaphorical senses are combined. The eye of Ajax, which so terrified his enemies (167–8, 190–1nn.), and which he was ashamed to show to his father, is an object of love for Teucer.

978 have you fared: a metaphor from bartering or trafficking; cf. Aesch. *Eum.* 631, Eur. *Cyc.* 254. For a similar metaphor see 445–6n.

as the prevailing rumour suggests: once again, as in the parodos (173, 191), Ajax is the subject of an unpleasant rumour. For the expression cf. Aesch. *Pers.* 738, *Supp.* 293.

979 you must know this: for the present imperative of ἐπίσταμαι, confirming the supposition of the previous speaker, see Coray 65–9; cf. also 281, and the rather different 1370, 1399.

980 my heavy fortune: like the chorus (900–2n., 909) Teucer thinks first of himself. The line in its shape is similar to *El.* 1179.

981-2 Since this...may well lament: at 904 Tecmessa used similar language to the chorus-leader, but here the sentence is interrupted by Teucer's cries. For the excited *antilabe* see 591n.

over-hasty misfortune: the misfortune is that of Ajax, not Teucer (Kamerbeek, who translates 'vehement'; Σ and *Suda* Π 1292 explain it as βαρύ, 'heavy').

983 unhappy one: cf. 902, 925. But the Greek could mean also 'unhappy me', as at 981.

983-4 Teucer's thoughts turn from Ajax (or himself) to Eurysaces, whom we last saw entering the hut at 595. For the ethic dative, 'where is he for me?', cf. 102, 733.

985 alone: the temporary isolation of the child perhaps reminds us of the more fundamental isolation of his father (359, 467nn.), who earlier expressed the wish that Eurysaces might inherit his heroic qualities, as he is to inherit also his shield (574–6).

985-9 The sense of urgency with which Teucer summons the child is reminiscent of 803–14 (cf. esp. 988 with 811). The command is addressed to Tecmessa. For the staging see 815–65n. If the screen is removed before these lines, she may go into the hut through the central door, which will now have resumed its normal role. But 'beside the huts' is not the same as 'into the hut', and more probably she departs by an *eisodos*. The screen will not be removed until 992. From then on the distinction between the two settings will be blurred. Tecmessa's departure not only draws our attention to the importance of Eurysaces, but also makes possible the substitution of a non-speaking 'extra' when she returns at 1168. All three actors will be required in the final scene to play the parts of Teucer, Agamemnon, and Odysseus.

986-7 like the whelp of a bereaved lioness: the simile is probably modelled on Hom. *Il.* 18.318–23, where Achilles mourns the loss of Patroclus (cf. also 17.132–7, where Ajax with his broad shield (132) defends the corpse of Patroclus, while here it is left to Teucer to defend the son who takes his name from the shield; see Garner 60–1). In these passages the lion is male, but Gilgamesh mourning over Enkidu is compared to both a lion and a lioness who have lost their cubs (J.B. Pritchard, *Ancient Near Eastern texts*[3] (Princeton 1969) 88, M.L. West, *JHS* 108 (1988) 171). Here it is a lioness because Teucer is addressing the child's mother, who is already 'bereaved' by the death of her husband (not, Jebb, 'robbed of her young'). The simile suggests that Eurysaces has inherited the qualities of his father, the implied lion. Cf. the simile of the vultures who have lost their young at Aesch. *Ag.* 49–59, and the orphan nestlings of the eagle father at *Cho.* 246–51.

988-9 Go...the labour: for the asyndeton see 811n. If 'share' is the correct force of συν- here, the command must be addressed to a female attendant. But the prefix may merely reinforce the sense of urgency (see 310n.), so that only Tecmessa is addressed.

to laugh at: Teucer shares the fear of the chorus and Tecmessa that his enemies will laugh at Ajax. In the second section of the episode that fear will be realised. For the perhaps proverbial idea that it is natural to kick a man when he is down cf. Aesch. *Ag.* 884–5 (with Fraenkel's note), Ar. *Clouds* 550, and for the case of Ajax in particular cf. 1348.

990-1 The reference is to Ajax' words at 562–71; cf. also 689. The fact that Teucer has already anticipated Ajax' wishes testifies to his harmony with his brother.
Indeed: see 539n.

992-7 Seale 169 remarks that 'the high concentration of visual terms...conveys in a climax of pathos his terrible absorption with the sight before him'.

993 seen with my eyes: cf. *Ant.* 764. The tautology is common in Homer: e.g. *Od.* 6.160.

994-5 Teucer, like the Messenger at 738–9 (cf. *Ant.* 1212–13), complains about the journey which he has just made. 994, like 969, lacks a regular caesura, but this line, like 855 and 1091, has a medial caesura, i.e. it divides equally in the middle (see West, *CQ* 32 (1982) 295, *Greek metre* (Oxford 1982) 82–3). A normal caesura can be restored by rearrangement of the words, but there are probably enough instances of the irregularity to make this unnecessary. For the σπλάγχνα (internal organs) as the seat of anxiety, fear, or grief, see Padel 13–18.

997 hunting and tracking you down: Teucer has been engaged in the same enterprise as Tecmessa and the chorus (879–80n.), and here even more clearly we are reminded of the opening of the play where it was an enemy who tracked Ajax (5–6, 32) as the result of a report.

998-9 a keen rumour: Teucer uses the noun that Tecmessa used at 494 of the talk of Ajax' enemies. We should not enquire too closely how the rumour of Ajax' death (cf. 978) has already reached the Greek army. At 826–7 Ajax prayed to Zeus to send a messenger to Teucer, and we simply take it for granted that this prayer has somehow been answered. But we may, if we wish, suppose that the army has drawn the correct conclusion from the report of the men who were sent to fetch Teucer at 804.

1000-1 Teucer means that the report was bad enough, but the actual sight is worse.

I mourned low: the same compound verb was used of Ajax at 322. The two brothers share the same reaction to their grief.

1003 uncover him: the order must be addressed to an attendant who has accompanied Teucer. For Tecmessa's covering of the corpse see 915–19n.

1004-5 The beloved face of Ajax (977n.) has become one on which Teucer cannot bear to look. 'The light of comfort has become the light of bitter truth, the light which cannot be faced' (Seale 169). The language picks up that which Teucer used at 992–4, and the description of the effect of the sight now leads on to the consequences of Ajax' death for him. The sudden disclosure of Ajax at 346–7 (n.) was equally horrific. We may surmise that the corpse lies face upwards, as in the cup by the Brygos Painter (see Intro. 3, Golder 27 n. 20).

which reveals: the qualitative genitive, 'of cruel rashness', describes the characteristic which Ajax' face reveals; cf. 616–17, *OT* 533, and see Fraenkel on Aesch. *Ag.* 1535f, Moorhouse 54. Eust. 409.46 took it as a genitive of exclamation.

have sown for me by dying: for both the thought and the structure of the sentence cf. 972–3n.

1006-21 Teucer's despairing question corresponds to that of Ajax at 403–4, his reluctance to face Telamon to that of Ajax at 434–440, 462–6. The unfavourable, and perhaps traditional, impression that we are given of Telamon in these passages is counterbalanced by the picture of his grief at 641–5, and by Ajax' concern for his parents' welfare at 567–71. Telamon's predicted anger is a measure both of Ajax' disgrace and of Teucer's failure to support his brother, which for Teucer means a serious loss of honour, comparable to that which Achilles feels in *Iliad* at his failure to protect Patroclus (cf. esp.18.80–2, 98–102). On a lower level the chorus feels similarly affected (see 910n.). All that Teucer can now do to restore his honour is to ensure a proper burial for Ajax.

1007 supported: the same word as at 329. For the accusative participle, agreeing with the implied subject of the infinitive, see Moorhouse 241, Garvie on Aesch. *Cho.* 140–1, 704–6, 1031–2nn.

1008-11 There is much confusion in the MSS; see the *apparatus criticus*.

1010 Of course he will: lit. 'for how <will he> not <receive me>?' The question, whose form is perhaps colloquial (see Garvie on Aesch. *Cho.* 753–4), expects the answer 'yes', but here it is sarcastic. With similar sarcasm Medea imagines the reception which she will receive if she returns to the daughters of Pelias (Eur. *Med.* 504–5).

1010-11 Telamon is no more cheerful in good fortune than in bad. Arist. *Rhet.* 1390a 22–4 describes reluctance to laugh as characteristic of old men. Page (on Eur. *Med.* 659) takes πάρα (= πάρεστι) here to denote 'the possession of a habit or characteristic' ('he who is not wont to smile'). But Telamon's *inability* to smile is just as appropriate.

1013 the bastard...spear: see 434–6n. and cf. 894.

1017 a bad-tempered man...age: for the idea that old men are particularly bad-tempered cf. Hom. *Il.* 24.237–64, Eur. *Ba.* 1251–2.

stern: lit. 'heavy'; cf. 41n. Others take it as 'tiresome' (cf. Tr. adesp. F 1c).

1018 for the sake of a quarrel: i.e. for the pleasure that it gives him; see Gow on Theocr. 15.10.

1019 According to the tradition Teucer's prediction was to come true. Having been banished by Telamon he founded Salamis in Cyprus; see Eur. *Hel.* 90–104, Σ Pind. *Nem.* 4.26, *Hor. Odes* 1.7.21–32. The story probably formed the subject of Sophocles' *Teucer.*

1020 having been reduced...free man: cf. Aesch. *Ag.* 593, Σ Pind. *Nem.* 4.76. Teucer's fear is similar to that of Tecmessa at 499.

1023 For ἄφαντα, 'to disappear', all the MSS have πάντα or ἅπαντα, 'all', which is not certainly wrong. The sense would be, 'and all this I have gained now that you are dead'; so T. Pearce, *RhM* 139 (1996) 351–2, who punctuates with a stop at the end of 1022, and takes 1023 as summing up everything from 1005 (for the ring-composition 1023/1005 see also Blundell 81). But it is more natural to take the neuter 'and these' with the neuter 'advantages' which immediately precedes. Jackson's simple emendation (219) gives excellent sense. Teucer already knew that he had enemies and few advantages before the death of Ajax, but with that death even the advantages have vanished.

1024 Alas, what am I to do: Teucer's cry again unites him with his brother (457–9n.), as with Tecmessa (920–1n.).

1025-6 glittering: the adjective is used of armour elsewhere only by Homer, of Ajax' shield at *Il.* 7.222, 16.107. Garner 63 remarks that the echo thus brings the sword of Hector and the shield of Ajax together in the one epithet; see also 147n.

sword: at Xen. *Cyn.* 10.3 the κνώδοντες are teeth into which the shaft of a hunting-spear fits. Here it may be the point of the sword (Σ; cf. *Ant.* 1233), but more probably it is used by synecdoche for the sword itself (so *Suda* K 1882; cf. Lycophr. 466).

the killer which: Greek 'by which as killer', or 'the killer by which'. The idea of the sword as killer, which echoes the personification at 815, then leads on to the further thought that the real killer is the donor. At this stage Teucer pulls the sword from the corpse.

1026-39 See 817–18n. Lloyd-Jones and Wilson (see *Sophoclea* 32–3) follow Morstadt in bracketing 1028–39 as containing too much 'empty bombast'. They believe that the lines were composed for a fourth-century revival of the play (see also Pearce (1023n.) 352 n. 2, who remarks that the passage is more reflective in spirit than what precedes). Certainly 1027 makes a more effective ending to the speech than do the rather flat 1038–9. But the expansion of the underlying notion, that an enemy is always an enemy even in death, is by no means irrelevant to this play, and helps to prepare us for the final scene in which Agamemnon will adopt this attitude, while Odysseus will take a different view. Cf. also the sentiments expressed by Ajax at 679–82n. From another point of view, Hector who became the guest-friend of Ajax has now again become his enemy.

1027 was going to: cf. 925. The future of -φθίνω with short ι occurs only here, but is rightly defended by West 116 against Hermann's emendation to the aorist ἀποφθίσαι. For the paradox of the dead killing the living see 664–5n.

1028 Consider: the imperative is addressed to the world at large, especially no doubt to the chorus, and certainly not directly to the audience; see Taplin (1977) 131 and cf. Eur. *Hipp.* 943.

1030-1 In *Iliad* (22.395–404, 464–5, 24.15–16) Achilles ties the already dead Hector to his chariot with thongs of ox-hide, and drags him to the Greek ships, and later round Patroclus' tomb. The version which Sophocles adopts here, in which Hector is still alive when Achilles ties him to the chariot (cf. *A.P.* 7.151, 152, probably V. *Aen.* 2.273, perhaps Eur. *Andr.* 399), could be his own invention (March 17), but more probably goes back to the Epic Cycle (Jebb; see 664–5n.). It may even have been known to Homer himself, who seems often to have deliberately eliminated the more horrible elements of his tradition.

fastened: lit. 'gripped'; for this sense cf. 310, D.S. 17.92.3 (of a dog's teeth).

mangled: a metaphor from carding wool; cf. Aesch. *Pers.* 576, Pl. *Rep.* 616a, and 728 above.

until...life: only here, until late Greek (*A.P.* 12.72) does the verb govern an accusative.

1032 Ajax...of Hector: the Greek uses pronouns, 'this man...of that man', with the two juxtaposed to mark the reciprocity of the gifts. For δωρειάν rather than δωρεάν as the fifth-century form see K. Meisterhans, *Grammatik der attischen Inschriften*[3] (Berlin 1900) 40, 44, L. Threatte, *The grammar of Attic inscriptions* I (Berlin and New York 1980) 311.

1033 in fatal fall: cf. 828, 833. He who 'fell on' the animals (184, 300) has now fallen himself; cf. 323–5n. Long 45 remarks that 'lines which conclude with a -ma noun generally have a slow and weighty effect'; cf. *OT* 560, *Phil.* 267, which too are 'expressions of violent and disastrous action'.

1034-5 a Fury: the idea is that the Fury forged the sword with Hector's vengeance already in mind. Cf. Aesch. *Cho.* 646–7 where 'Fate who makes the sword does the forging in advance', also *Ag.* 1535–6. Again the pronouns 'this' and 'that' mark the reciprocity, but this time they are not juxtaposed.

craftsman: 'one who works for the people'; cf. Hom. *Od.* 17.383, 19.135. The application of the term to Hades is bitter and sardonic. There is a kind of zeugma: strictly speaking the belt was not 'forged'.

1036-7 Teucer agrees with the judgement of Tecmessa and the chorus-leader (950–4n.). The notion that the gods are responsible for all human success and failure is Homeric (383n.).

1039 his opinion...mine: again the Greek uses simple pronouns, 'those things...these things'. According to Σ the expression became proverbial. For the thought in general cf. Euenus fr. 1.4 W, Eur. *Supp.* 466, and for this kind of conclusion to a speech *Ant.* 469–70, *Tr.* 373–4.

1040-3 Do not prolong your speech: for this common type of expression see Fraenkel on Aesch. *Ag.* 916, A.N. Michelini, *Hermes* 102 (1974) 524–39, esp. 532–3. No noun is to be supplied with the feminine adjective. As Fraenkel says, it denotes an indefinite abstract. The phrase marks the transition to the second section of the episode. By the usual tragic convention the chorus-leader introduces the new arrival. The prediction that he will laugh like a scoundrel (cf. 955–60, 988–9nn.) will soon be fulfilled. The chorus-leader also reminds Teucer of the necessity for action (Ajax himself would have required no such reminder; see Ebeling 302), and thus introduces the theme of burial which will dominate the remainder of the play.

1044 For the attraction of the antecedent into the relative clause cf. *El.* 1040, *Tr.* 1060–1.

1045 Teucer will deny this at 1111–14.

1047-8 Menelaus is probably accompanied by one or two attendants (see 1115).

You there: for his peremptory beginning see 71n.

put...burial arrangements: the simple κομίζω means to carry out a corpse for burial at 1397; cf. Eur. *Andr.* 1264, Isaeus 8.21. for the accusative and infinitive of indirect command after φωνῶ cf. (after λέγω) *Phil.* 101, and contrast the dative at 1089. Here the compound συν- ('with') probably implies that Teucer will be assisted in the deed (cf. 922, 1378–9). Kamerbeek takes the compound to mean simply 'compose' (see 310, 361nn.). But, as Blundell 103–4 remarks, the co-operative nature of the funeral is characterised in the play by the repeated use of συν- words.

with your hands: see 27n.

to leave it: cf. in a similar context *Ant.* 29, 205.

1050 **Because that is my decision:** the neuter participle in the accusative absolute gives the reason.

the one who: sc. ἐκείνῳ as the antecedent of the relative pronoun ὅς.

1051 **Won't you then:** for οὔκουν thus used with optative + ἄν in impatient questions, at the beginning of a speech, see Denniston 431. Some verb meaning 'he has decided' has to be understood in the indirect question.

1052-4 Menelaus begins with his version of the theme of alternation as it relates to friends and enemies (see 1026–39n.). Ajax considered the Trojans to be his enemies, but now Menelaus considers *him* to be a worse enemy than the Trojans to the Greeks.

in our dealings with him: all the MSS have 'seeking', 'in our search'. But, despite Pearson (1922) 27, and Kamerbeek, it is difficult to see how the Greeks' discovery was the result of a search. Triclinius explains it by ἐξετάζοντες, 'putting to the test', but that is not the same as 'seeking'. The corruption was caused by the regular association of 'search' and 'find' (see Dawe 163–4).

Phrygians: synonymous with Trojans in tragedy (e.g. Eur. *Hec.* 4, *Or.* 1480).

1055 **against the whole army:** an exaggeration perhaps, but it is true that Ajax' anger was not confined to his immediate enemies; cf. 722n.

1057 **one of the gods:** Menelaus, like the chorus in the parodos, merely guesses. He is in no position to know that the god was Athena.

quenched: probably like a forest-fire; see 196–7n. Menelaus is thinking in terms of Ajax' *hybris* (see Fisher 314).

this attempt: Tecmessa used the same word of Ajax' enterprise at 290.

1058-9 **died and suffered this fortune:** lit. 'dying as to this fortune', but the accusative of respect does not go easily with 'dying', and the participle has been variously emended.

be lying exposed: the verb is often thus used of a corpse; see 426–7n.

in a most shameful death: in accordance with the Homeric conception the disgrace is to the victim, not the perpetrator; cf. Aesch. *Cho.* 494.

1060-1 **a god:** see 1057n.

has turned: the same verb as at 208. Kamerbeek prefers 'has changed the state of things so that his *hybris* has fallen etc.'

outrageous behaviour: for the first time in the play *hybris* is used unequivocably (but see 304n.) of the behaviour of Ajax. That the intended victim should use the term is natural, and we should not assume too readily that Sophocles intends *us* to share his outrage.

1062-3 his body: the Greek says 'him...his body', with 'him' coming early in the sentence for emphasis, and 'body', picking up the pronoun, placed more naturally inside the consecutive clause; cf. 1147–9.

1064-5 cast out...for the birds: see 827–30n. For ἐκβάλλω, 'cast out', as a key-word in the context of a Sophoclean hero's relationship with his community see M. Mantziou, ΔΩΔΩΝΗ 24 (1995) 70 n. 2.

1066 make...of might: lit. 'stir up no terrible might'. The language recalls 129, and serves again to portray Teucer as the natural successor of Ajax. For the 'raising' of anger etc. cf. *OT* 914, Eur. *IA* 919.

1067-9 The lines show how crucial is the issue of burial for Ajax. If Menelaus has his way, Ajax will after all have been forced to yield to his enemies (cf. 667–8).

when he was alive: see 961–3n., where there was the same antithesis between 'living' and 'dead'. Here it is made even more emphatic by the placing of the two participles in the same position in successive lines. Tecmessa there predicted that his enemies would eventually lament his death, but Menelaus is far from doing so.

disciplining him with our hands: cf. 542. Ajax will be reduced to the docility of a child or an animal (cf. 1254). The prefix παρ-, as Kamerbeek suggests, may indicate that he will forced aside from his intended course.

1071-2 characteristic of: see 319–20n.

a bad man: for the ambiguity in the meaning of κακός see 132–3, 319–20nn., where the vital question of Ajax' status was already raised. The implied conclusion is, 'therefore Ajax was a *kakos*' (see Denniston 563). If Menelaus, and Athena there, are right, Ajax has lost his status as a hero. But the grotesquely insulting description of Ajax as a 'commoner', whose only duty is to obey his superiors' orders, leaves us in no doubt that Menelaus is wrong.

though he is: the participle ὄντα is Reiske's correction of ἄνδρα, 'a man <who is> a commoner'. The juxtaposition of the repeated 'man' is awkward and pointless, and probably arose from dittography, or from a reminiscence of *Ant.* 690; cf. however 1093. For the accusative see 1007n.

to those set over him: cf. 945.

1073-6 Menelaus' argument about the necessity for discipline and *sophrosyne,* and obedience to the laws, in both a city and an army, is not unlike that of Creon at *Ant.* 663–76 (cf. also fr. 683). For its sophistic characteristics see Long 72–3. For its use by Thucydides, e.g. at 3.37.3 (in Cleon's speech), and especially in connection with Sparta and with the oligarchs at Athens, see Coray 394–9. In this context *sophrosyne* refers primarily to the right relationship between superiors and inferiors (Coray 184).

have a successful course: probably a metaphor from a ship at sea; cf. Thuc. 2.60.3, 5.16.1.

where there is no fear established: see 552–5n. The optative provides more normal sequence, but the less remote subjunctive is more appropriate than 'where fear was not established'. Menelaus doubtless speaks as a Spartan. Plut., *Agis and Cleom.* 9, tells us that at Sparta there were temples of Fear, and that it was considered that the whole constitution was held together by fear. The sentiment in itself is unobjectionable. When Athena at Aesch. *Eum.* 696–9 (picking up 517–30) praises the mean between anarchy and despotism and stresses the necessity for fear in a city (cf. also 691–2), the audience is meant to approve. What revolts us is Menelaus' application of the principle to the particular case of Ajax, and the context in which he expounds it. For him *sophrosyne* (for which cf. *Eum.* 521) means no more than the obedience of others to himself.

fear or respect as a defence: lit. 'a defence consisting in (defining genitive) fear and respect'. 'Respect' (αἰδώς) is 'that which renders one sensitive to the general values of society and which inhibits departure from them' (Cairns 154). It is not indeed the kind of virtue favoured by a hero like Ajax; cf. 506–7 and see 485–524n. Paus. 3.20.10 mentions an image of *Aidos* near Sparta. αἰδώς and αἰσχύνη (1079) are often coupled with 'fear': e.g. Hom. *Od.* 7.305, *Cypria* F 24 Davies, Thuc. 2.37.3, Pl. *Ep.* 7.337a. For the association of αἰδώς with *sophrosyne* cf. Thuc. 1.84.3.

1077-8 even if...a great body: for Ajax' size cf. Hom. *Il.* 3.229. The implication is that this is his only accomplishment. Cf. 1250–4, and contrast the chorus' view of his 'greatness' in the parodos (134–200, 160–1nn.). Even Athena was not so dismissive of his qualities (118–20n.). But the notion that such a man might easily fall (cf. 758–61n., *Ant.* 1045–7) is in harmony with her words at 131–2. For the, perhaps sophistic, idea that a trivial cause can have serious consequences cf. 1148–9, 1253, *Ant.* 477–8, *El.* 415–16.

even of: in this kind of expression (1058) κἄν (= καὶ ἄν) is scarcely distinguishable from καί ('even'), and has become a mere formula in which ἄν cannot be precisely explained; see Kamerbeek, Kühner-Gerth I 244–5, comparing ὡσπερανεί = ὡσπερεί.

1079-80 who enjoys security: for salvation as the result of discipline and *aidos* cf. Creon's words at *Ant.* 675–6, and those of Athena at Aesch. *Eum.* 700–2 (also Hom. *Il.* 5.530–1 = 15.562–3, spoken by Ajax himself, and Pl. *Prot.* 322b–c). Ajax had a very different idea of salvation for himself (see 691–2n.).

fear...a sense of shame: for the combination see 1073–6n. αἰσχύνη and αἰδώς mean much the same.

1081 act outrageously: 'commit *hybris*'. For the second time Menelaus uses this term, here in a generalisation but with obvious reference to Ajax. For the subjunctive see 552–5n.. For a similar picture of what happens to a city if everyone is allowed to do what he pleases see [Dem.] 25.20–1.

1083 before fair winds: the metaphor of the ship of state is very common (e.g. *OT* 22–4, *Ant.* 162–3, 189–90), and picks up 1074. Here a prosperous voyage turns unexpectedly into disaster (as at Men. *Sam.* 206–8), the implication being perhaps that it is prosperity itself which leads to disaster. For the expression cf. Arist. *Mech.* 851b 6, Polyb. 1.47.2.

falls: the infinitive of the gnomic aorist, used frequently in proverbs and generalisations.

1084 let timely...established: the language picks up 1074. For the fourth time in eleven lines Menelaus uses a word meaning 'fear'.

1085-6 what pleases us...that will cause us pain: the ponderous balance of ἄν ἡδώμεθα with ἄν λυπώμεθα, at the ends off the two successive lines, is perhaps meant to convey the banality of Menelaus' utterance.

1087-8 in alternation: a prosaic adverb that occurs only here in tragedy. But the idea is of fundamental importance for the play (see de Romilly (1968) 94). For what it means to Menelaus see 974–1184n.

hot-tempered insolence: lit. 'was a hot-tempered committer of *hybris*'; for the epithet see 221n.

to be proud: 'to think big'. Menelaus cannot bring himself to admit that he himself is now committing *hybris* – the word is more naturally used by the victim than by the aggressor – but that (despite Dickie 105–6, Fisher 315–16) is what he really means, as the chorus-leader recognises at 1092. He thus goes further than even Clytaemestra at *El.* 523, who denies that in reciprocating insults she is committing *hybris* (for reciprocal *hybris* see Intro. 13, 304n.). At *OC* 883 Creon momentarily admits the charge, but very rarely does anyone boast of it (see Fisher 107, 251, 313). Unlike the Messenger (758–61n.) Menelaus does seem to equate 'thinking big' with *hybris*, and the passage is used, not unreasonably, by D.L. Cairns (*CR* 44 (1994) 78–9, *JHS* 116 (1996) 10–13) in support of his argument that *hybris* may describe a disposition as well as behaviour (see Intro. 13 n. 48). In the eyes of the victim there is only a fine line between the aggressive self-assertion of another and the outrageous behaviour that results from that self-assertion. To Menelaus Ajax' pride seems itself to be an offence against him. This is very different from saying that Ajax is objectively guilty of *hybris* for which he is rightly punished by the gods.

1089-90 Menelaus returns to his starting-point (1047–8).

before everyone: or 'in advance'.

fall...into your grave: so Kamerbeek; not (Jebb) 'come to need funeral rites'.

1091-2 Two speeches in a quarrel are regularly thus divided by two or three lines from the chorus-leader, giving the audience a moment to relax. Here the chorus-leader acknowledges the soundness of Menelaus' principles, but condemns his behaviour as inconsistent with them. His 'wisdom' is in fact directed primarily to his own ends (see Coray 95–6).

having laid down: perhaps a metaphor from laying the foundations of a house. At Pind. *Ol.* 6.1, 8.26 the verb is used metaphorically of pillars. For the absence of caesura in 1091 see 994–5n.

1093-6 In the modern phrase *noblesse oblige.* The well-born should show a good example to their social inferiors.

nobody: cf. 767–9n.

who seem to be born noble: Teucer implies that, despite his birth, Menelaus is not really entitled to be called 'noble' at all. Nobility of birth does not necessarily go with nobility of character; see Denniston on Eur. *El.* 253, 367–72, and, for this kind of distinction in sophistic rhetoric, Goldhill 162–3, 228.

speak words...so wrong: lit. 'are wrong as to such words in their speeches'. For this kind of internal accusative in which a cognate is replaced by another noun cf. 1107 and see Moorhouse 40.

1097-9 Teucer answers the argument of Menelaus at 1052–4. He cannot deny that Ajax came to Troy as the ally of the Greeks. All the emphasis is on 'took and brought'. The answer, as at 1234, is that Ajax came on his own initiative.

1100-8 Teucer takes issue with Menelaus' assumption that Ajax owed any duty of obedience to Menelaus, who is ruler only of his own Spartan contingent. For a similar complaint against Menelaus cf. Eur. *Andr.* 581–2, and esp. Eur. *Telephus* fr. 723, the first line of which, 'you have got Sparta, govern it', apparently became a proverb. The play was produced in 438 B.C., but there is no good reason to suppose that it must have been the model for 1102 here (see Intro. 6–7, Reinhardt 234 n. 3). Teucer's argument largely corresponds with the conditions of the *Iliad*, in which each contingent had its own independent commander, and there is no hierarchy of rank among them, except that all are subject, in a way that is never really explained, to Agamemnon as commander-in-chief.

1101 he led: most MSS have ἡγεῖτ', which breaks Porson's Law, according to which a fifth-foot spondee should not be divided between two words. It is doubtful if the elision mitigates the abnormality (so W.J.W. Koster, *Traité de métrique grecque* (Leiden 1966) 105). The best corrections are ἦγετ' (anon.), which is palaeographically easy, and ἦγεν (Porson), which gives the same verb in the same active voice as in Menelaus' accusation at 1053, and may be a reminiscence of Hom. *Il.* 2.557, where Ajax *brought* twelve ships from Salamis.

1102 our commander: the word picks up 1067.

1103 discipline: the noun κοσμήτωρ, which derives from this verb, describes Menelaus and Agamemnon at Hom. *Il.* 1.16 = 375. For the regular association of κόσμος and obedience in a military context see H. Diller, in *Festschrift B. Snell* (Munich 1956), esp. 52–5.

1104 of command: picking up 1068, 1075.

for his part: for this nuance of καί see Denniston 299.

1105-6 Schneidewin was probably right to delete these lines (see Reeve 162). 1107 follows better after 1104. And, while the argument that Menelaus himself is a subordinate (i.e. to Agamemnon) is not irrelevant, it carries with it the unfortunate implication that Ajax too is subordinate to Agamemnon, if not to Menelaus. At 1109 and elsewhere in the play we have the impression that Menelaus and Agamemnon are joint commanders. On the other hand, at 1116 Agamemnon alone is 'the general'.

of the whole army: this is what the genitive plural, whether masculine or neuter, must mean, but there seems to be no real parallel in classical Greek for the word in the plural meaning 'everybody' or 'everything'.

1107 For this offensive way of saying 'mind your own business' cf. *OC* 839, Hom. *Il.* 1.180, Aesch. *Eum.* 574.

with those proud words of yours: see 1093–6n. The article is used with demonstrative force.

1109-10 or the other general: the words help to prepare us for the appearance of Agamemnon in the final scene.

I shall…in his grave: Teucer picks up Menelaus' words at 1089–90.

1111-14 Here too interpolation is a possibility. Wecklein deleted the lines, Reichard the whole of 1111–17 (see also Fraenkel 33–4, for whom Teucer should end his speech at 1110 by replying to the last lines of Menelaus' speech at 1089–90). 1115–17, however, make a not ineffective ending to the speech. The reference is to the oath sworn to Tyndareus by Helen's suitors that they would support the successful suitor if he should be robbed of his wife (the oath is first attested at Hes. fr. 204; see Stockert on Eur. *IA* 57ff.). But it is hard to find any real distinction between 'for the sake of your wife' and 'for the sake of the oath'. And the notion that Ajax was constrained by his oath merely weakens the argument at 1099 that he came voluntarily to Troy. On the other hand, the triple structure, 'not for the sake of…, but for the sake of…, not for the sake of…', with the third element more or less repeating the first, is typical of Sophocles; see Jebb on *El.* 363f., *Ant.* 465–8.

those who have their fill of labour: i.e. apparently the ordinary soldiers, those who were conscripted. But the expression is odd. Jebb compares Eur. *Andr.* 695, where there is a distinction between the generals who get the credit and the ordinary soldiers who do the work. But Teucer can hardly mean that Ajax did not take his share of the work. At 637 *all* the Achaeans, including Ajax himself, were described as πολύπονοι, 'much-suffering', 'toiling'. For the triple alliteration of π see 866–8n.

for he placed no value on nobodies: cf. 1094 and the words of Ajax himself at 767–9n.

1115-16 Therefore: if these lines, but not 1111–14, are genuine, they follow on from the mention of Agamemnon at 1109. But a logical connection with the insulting 1114 is clearer: 'you are a nonentity; so come back with reinforcements and the more important Agamemnon'. Again we are prepared for the appearance of the latter.

1116-17 pay attention to: lit. 'turn'; cf. μεταστρέφω + genitive at Eur. *Hipp.* 1226, and other compounds of στρέφω (e.g. *OT* 728, *Phil.* 599), also ἐντρέπω 90 (see Moorhouse 65).

for any noise you make: a genitive of cause. So Teucer dismisses the empty words of Menelaus; see Long 156.

as long as...you are: for a similar phrase cf. Pl. *Phaedr.* 243e.

1118-19 Again: referring back to 1091–2. The role of the fair-minded conciliator is conventional for the chorus-leader in such quarrel scenes; cf. 1264–5n., Eur. *El.* 1051, and see Burton 4, 35. The emphasis on talk and words sets the tone of the whole quarrel (cf. 1124, 1142, 1162, 1226, 1272, and see Torrance 279). Contrast Ajax as the man of action.

1120 For Teucer's prowess as an archer cf. *Phil.* 1057, Hom. *Il.* 8.266–334, 13.313–14, 23. 859–69. But few major heroes in *Il.* fight with the bow, and Menelaus' insult is in line with the general epic conception that archery is less honourable than close-quarter fighting with sword or spear; cf. *Il.* 11.385–90 and see Garvie on *Od.* 8.215–28. In fifth-century Athens too archers were considered inferior to hoplites. The Scythian archers who formed the police-force were slaves. After 1088 it ill becomes Menelaus to taunt Teucer with pride.

1121 vulgar: a prosaic word that occurs only here in tragedy. At Hom. *Il.* 15.440–1 we learn that Teucer's bow and arrows were a gift from Apollo.

1122 Once more the language associates Teucer with, but reminds us that he is not the same man as, Ajax himself, the boastful owner of the mighty shield (cf. 18–19n., 96).

if you were to get a shield: i.e. 'if you were to fight like a proper man'. In fact Teucer did take up a shield at Hom. *Il.* 15.479, and fought with a spear, leaving his damaged bow in his hut.

1123 lightly armed...fully armed: in the fifth century the first word regularly describes archers or slingers, the second someone armed as a hoplite with breastplate and shield. Σ criticises the sophism as inappropriate to tragedy. For this kind of ancient criticism see Heath 35.

1124 terrible: cf. 1066. Menelaus means that Teucer is brave *only* in his tongue.

1125 The line answers 1120 as much as 1124. Teucer, like Menelaus (1087–8n.), but with more justification, believes that he is entitled to 'think big'. His opponent will consider this to be *hybris* directed against himself.

1126 What: γάρ in an incredulous question 'implies that the speaker throws doubt on the grounds of the previous speaker's words' (Denniston 77). Menelaus uses the idea of justice in a different way. For Teucer it meant the claims to which he and Ajax were entitled through their status, whereas for Menelaus it is a matter of what Ajax deserves for his crimes.

1127 Menelaus' exaggerated 'after killing me' (so at Eur. *Ion* 1291, 1300, 1500 'kill' means 'intend' or 'try to kill') gives Teucer the opportunity for this highly sarcastic reply.

1128 god is my saviour: see 1057n.

as far as he is concerned I am dead: the language resembles 970 and 972, but the sense is not quite the same. Menelaus means that he *would* be dead if Ajax had had his way.

1129 dishonour the gods: by forbidding that the corpse be buried. For such behaviour as a form of *hybris*, 'an illegitimate extension of revenge', and as an offence against the gods, see Fisher 147–8, and cf. 1343–4, *Ant.* 450–60, 519, 998–1032, 1070–6; see further Mastronarde on Eur. *Ph* 1663, R. Parker, *Miasma: pollution and purification in early Greek religion* (Oxford 1983) 43–8. ἀτιμᾶν occurs only here in tragedy, but it is common in Homer.

by the gods...saved: the phrase is in antithesis with 'as far as he is concerned I am dead'. There is some bitterness in the thought that the gods allowed Ajax to die, but saved the villainous Menelaus. Cf. *Phil.* 416–18, 436–7, 446–52.

1131 If you stand here: i.e. 'by your personal intervention' (Moorhouse 253).

do not allow: one expects μή (cf. 1108) rather than οὐκ in the conditional clause, but the negative goes closely with the verb, in the sense 'forbid'; cf. *OC* 935 and see Goodwin § 384.

1132–4 At 1132 Menelaus uses the word πολέμιος, which is usually an enemy in war, whereas ἐχθρός is usually a private enemy; but sometimes they are interchangeable (at *Phil.* 1302–3 Philoctetes applies both terms to Odysseus). This gives Teucer an opportunity to quibble: how could Ajax, who was on the same side in the war as Menelaus, be his πολέμιος? Instead of replying that by his attack on the booty of the army Ajax has indeed turned into a public enemy, Menelaus weakly replies, 'well, if he was not a πολέμιος, we still hated each other'; i.e. in effect 'he was my ἐχθρός' (see Winnington-Ingram 64 n. 20, Blundell 39, 92). Like Creon in *Ant.* (cf. 284–9) Menelaus assumes, not only that it is acceptable to treat an enemy in this way, but also (not unreasonably in the light of 1057, 1060) that the gods agree with him. But Creon learned eventually that the gods require that *all* the dead be buried; see 1343–4n.

1133 really: for ἦ γάρ introducing a surprised question see Denniston 284. The question is a little disingenuous. Ajax himself was in no doubt that as a result of the judgement of the arms Menelaus and he were enemies.

1134 He hated me as I hated him: Greek says it in only two words, both of them denoting 'hate', clearly marking the reciprocity of the relationship.

1135 to have cheated...votes: lit. 'to be a vote-making thief of him'. So Pind. *Nem.* 8.26 describes the votes as 'secret'. It is not clear whether Teucer means that Menelaus bribed the judges to vote in favour of Odysseus, or that he somehow tampered with the votes after they had been cast, perhaps by adding false ones. Sophocles seems to think of the placing of votes in urns, according to fifth-century Athenian practice. He leaves us in doubt as to whether there is any substance to the accusation; see Intro. 5, 442–6, 1336–41nn. For Machin (see 719–65n.) the uncertainty is deliberately contrived by Sophocles, to give us the impression at the beginning of the play that the sons of Atreus are innocent, an impression which will be reversed by the end as the culpability of Ajax is correspondingly reduced and his moral authority increased.

1136 lay with: i.e. 'depended on'; cf. the use of ἐν at 519.

1137 good at: καλῶς, the reading of L alone, gives an effectively sarcastic paradox ('you would do evil well'); cf. *Ant.* 1047. Most MSS, more tamely, have κακῶς, 'badly', i.e. 'you would do evil in an evil way'.

performing much furtive mischief: lit. 'stealing many evil things'; cf. 187–9n.

1138 for someone: the vague τις, 'somebody' (cf. 404), is common in threats: e.g. Aesch. *Sept.* 402, Eur. *Andr.* 577, Ar. *Frogs* 552, 554; see Jebb on *Ant.* 751.

1140-1 As at 1089–90 Menelaus tries to bring the argument to an end by simply repeating his command. But Teucer replies in kind, reiterating his determination to disobey.

he *shall* be buried: see 577n.

1142-6 Menelaus' fable perhaps owes something to Eteocles' parable (Aesch. *Sept.* 602–4) of the good man who goes on board a ship with wicked sailors and perishes with them, but here it is the individual who turns out to be the fool. The fable, 'a rhetorical device of low character' (Heath 200), was probably a common element of early iambic and elegiac poetry (cf. Cleobulina fr. 1 and 2 W, where we find 'I saw a man'). For its popular character and form see Fraenkel 35–6, *Kleine Beiträge* (Rome 1964) I 235–9; cf. e.g. Ar. *Wasps* 1427–32.

1142 I once saw: for this kind of beginning with ἤδη cf. Hdt. 4.77.1, Pl. *Gorg.* 493a, and, with ἤδη and ποτε combined, Aesch. *Eum.* 50.

bold of tongue: cf. 1124.

1143 in a storm: or 'in winter'. At *Acts* 27.9–12 it is St Paul who advises against putting to sea after winter has begun, but he is overruled by the captain and ship-owner.

1144 you would have found: Hartung's compound verb ἐνηῦρες removes the pointless repetition of ἄν, but it is by no means certain, as the compound is not otherwise attested before Josephus, unless a conjecture at Ar. *Ach.* 1037 is correct.

1146 by any...who wished: for the expression cf. Eur. *IA* 340. Pl. *Tht.* 191a similarly uses the picture of a seasick sailor who allows himself to be trampled on, while Synesius of Cyrene 4.163d (p. 15 Garzya) quotes the line in his story of a ship in a storm.

1147 So also with you: for this formula in the fable cf. Ar. *Wasps* 1432.

you and your violent mouth: each man finds fault with the 'mouth' or words of the other (cf. 1110). For the expression cf. *Ant.* 95, 573, *OT* 905 etc., and see Long 108 n. 155. The adjective is similarly used at Pind. *Ol.* 2.86, *Py.* 2.87, Simon. 177 B. It is especially appropriate to the imagery of a storm; cf. Eur. *Or.* 341–4, *HF* 861.

1148-9 See 1077–8n. **extinguish:** the same verb as at 1057.

your loud shouting: the object is best explained (with Jebb) as resuming 'you and your violent mouth'; cf. 1062–3n.

1150-8 Teucer responds to Menelaus' fable with what is hardly a parable at all. Avoiding the metaphorical language of Menelaus, he more directly, and less imaginatively, says merely, 'I have seen a man, who...It is in fact you whom I have in mind'.

1150 And: for δέ γε in 'retorts and lively rejoinders' see Denniston 153.

full of folly: cf. 745.

1151 triumphed insolently in the misfortunes: after 1087–8 (n.) the charge of *hybris* is obviously justified. As usual in this play, the term describes the behaviour of Ajax' enemies (see 955–60n.). For the expression and the thought cf. Aesch. *Ag.* 1612.

1152 For 'and then', marking the intervention of the wise adviser in the fable, cf. Ar. *Wasps* 1430.

1154-5 Man: see 791n.

treat...suffer: the underlying idea that 'he who does must suffer' is a very common and ancient one; see Garvie on Aesch. *Cho.* 306–14, and cf. in Sophocles *Ant.* 927–8, *OC* 951–3, fr. 223b, 962; also 1085–6 above.

1156 stood : a curious echo of 1131, which contributes little to the sense of this line; cf. also 1384.

1159-62 That Menelaus has lost the argument is clear from the fact that he is the first to break it off and can resort only to threats of force. That Teucer has the last word shows that he remains in control. Menelaus has probably already begun to leave after 1160. For such lines 'cast after a departing back' cf. *Phil.* 1259–60 and see Taplin (1977) 221–2 ('the device tends to lack dignity, and is often used to lower the tragic or heroic tone'). But the recognition by his enemies of Ajax' status as a hero remains unresolved. Like Ajax himself both Menelaus and Teucer show concern for their own honour. The idea of Menelaus that failure to harm one's enemies is disgraceful, repulsive though it may be in this context, is yet in harmony with normal Greek values (see Blundell 55, and cf. Hom. *Od.* 24.433–6, [Dem.] 59.12), and indeed with those of Ajax himself. But Menelaus fails to recognise that there are limits to the maltreatment of an enemy when he is dead; cf. Hom. *Od.* 22.411–12, Ar. *Clouds* 549–50, Lys. 2.8. For Teucer's attitude to Menelaus' words see 1147n.

1160 that I am...to use force: παρῇ (subjunctive) would turn the line into a general statement, 'that one chastises...when he has the power...'. But πάρα is almost certainly correct.

1162 φλαῦρος, 'petty', 'is used especially of ill-treatment, abuse, and slander' (Dover on Ar. *Clouds* 834).

1163-7 As at 1040–3 the chorus-leader, so here probably the whole chorus, in this brief anapaestic passage which separates the departure of Menelaus from the arrival of Tecmessa and Eurysaces, gives practical advice to Teucer. But his departure to arrange for the funeral is prevented by the arrival of Tecmessa and the child.

1163 There will be: the quarrel in fact began some time ago, but the chorus's words warn us that there is more to come.

a very contentious quarrel: the genitive 'of strife' defines the nature of the contest; cf. *Tr.* 20, Eur. *Andr.* 725.

1165 see to: i.e. 'look for', 'provide'. For this sense of ὁράω cf. *Phil.* 843, Theocr. 15.2.

hollow trench: Homer has the same combination of words at *Il.* 24.797, of the cavity in which Hector's bones were placed (the only passage in which he uses the noun of a grave). Once more Hector and Ajax are linked in their deaths; see P.E. Easterling, *Metis* 3 (1988) 96–7.

1166-7 where he will possess: for the semi-final use of the relative with future indicative see 658–9n. The same verb describes the occupants of graves at Aesch. *Supp.* 25, *Ag.* 454, 1540. Normally it is the earth which 'possesses' the corpse (*Ant.* 409, Hom. *Il.* 16.629, Archil. 196a 12), but in this case the heroic Ajax will be the possessor (see Henrichs 171, 173–5).

dank: the word is regularly used of the underworld or the grave: e.g. Hom. *Il.* 20.65, *Od.* 10.512, Archil. 196a 12 (and the noun εὐρώς at Simon. 26.4).

that mortals will always remember: for the supposed tomb of Ajax near Cape Rhoeteum in the Troad see Strabo 13.595, Dio Cass. 17.17.3. 'The "enemy" soil does not reject his corpse, but, like the hateful sword, plays its part in his reinstatement' (Taplin (1978) 88; see 859–63n.). This contrast, between the dank corruption of the grave and the eternal memory of the hero buried in it, is the most specific reference in the play to the hero-cult of Ajax, and forms an appropriate prelude to the setting up of the tableau that follows; see Segal (1995) 23, 1172n. For the association of grave and memory cf. Simon. fr. 26, *IG* 9.2.252, and see Henrichs 172–3. But Agamemnon, who no longer 'remembers' Ajax (1268–9), has still to be persuaded to allow the funeral. For the word-order, article, epithet, noun, second epithet, see Jebb on *OT* 1199, Kühner-Gerth I 622.

1168-9 Look...here come: the usual tragic formula for the introduction of a new arrival (cf. 1223, *Ant.* 1257, etc.). For the dramatic convention of someone's *opportune* arrival on stage cf. *Ant.* 386, Eur. *Hipp.* 899, *HF* 701. Tecmessa and Eurysaces probably emerge through the central door; see 985–9n. It is unusual for a major character to enter without saying anything (see Taplin (1977) 284), but the role of Tecmessa, now played by an 'extra', is no longer to speak but merely to form part of the tableau beside the corpse.

1170 to arrange the burial: the verb is more often used of laying out the corpse which is to be buried: e.g. *Ant.* 903. Ajax used the same word with a more general sense at 821.

1172 in supplication...father: for the symbolism of the child's position see 974–1184n. Although Jebb was certainly wrong to find the main theme of the play in the establishment of Ajax as a cult-hero (see Intro. 6), Burian and Henrichs have shown that the cult is at least implied in the tableau which is now arranged by Teucer, with its three ritual elements of supplication, offering, and curse. The corpse will (despite Henrichs 166) be protected by the child who clings to it in supplication (anyone who tries to remove the child by force will be committing an offence against Zeus the protector of suppliants), but, more important, the dead hero, who a few moments ago was so helpless, is now, even before he is buried, in a position to protect his dependants and to do harm to his enemies. Henrichs 176 (cf. 165) remarks that we see the tragic hero in the process of becoming a cultic hero, a process which Sophocles will present much more explicitly and fully in *OC* at the very end of his life. In the final scene 'those who love Ajax enact, at least symbolically, [Ajax'] consecration as a hero' (Burian 151). But Ajax himself is unaware of all this. For the belief in the power of the dead hero to grant such aid cf. Aesch. *Cho.* 306–478, where Orestes and Electra appeal as suppliants (336) at their father's tomb. There, as at Eur. *Hel.* 64–5, 800–1, the tomb is probably conceived as a kind of altar, which normally provides sanctuary for suppliants.

1173-80 For the widespread practice of offering hair on a tomb cf. Hom. *Il.* 23.141–53, and see Garvie on Aesch. *Cho.* 6. The idea may be (Jebb) that Eurysaces is to perform a symbolic self-immolation on behalf of the three mourners. Or it may involve a removal of what is defiled by the *tabu* of death. Most probably it is part of the process which links the child to his father and confirms his heritage (see 574–6n., L. Gernet, *The anthropology of ancient Greece* (tr. Baltimore and London 1981) 177–9. 'The mourners' hair, unlike the mourners themselves, will stay with the dead' (Seaford 168). At 1175–9 Teucer gives his own twist to the custom, turning it into a kind of sympathetic magic with which to curse his enemies: 'may they be cut off as now I cut off this hair'.

For 'even as now', emphasising the 'law of homoeopathy', see Fraenkel on Aesch. *Ag.* 1602, and cf. Hom. *Il.* 3.300, Theocr. 2.28.

1173 Sit: not 'kneel' (Jebb). Both positions are adopted by mourners in Attic Geometric vases; see T.B.L. Webster, *ABSA* 50 (1955) 46–7, who thought that the present scene is modelled on an epic original. But he wrongly imagined that Tecmessa has Eurysaces on her knee. All the emphasis in Teucer's speech is on the child (cf. 1409–11), and this should be reflected in Tecmessa's position further from the corpse; see Seale 171, Blundell 93 n. 168. The great hero is protected by a small child.

as a suppliant: lit. 'turned towards', a term regularly used of a suppliant; cf. 831 and see Fraenkel on Aesch. *Ag.* 1587, Garvie on *Cho.* 287.

1175 a suppliant's treasure: it is the offering that gives the suppliant his power.

1177 the wretch...wretchedly: the polyptoton emphasises that his fate is commensurate with his deeds; cf. 839, 1154–5n., 1391, *OT* 248, *Phil.* 1369.

1178 with the root mown down: the same idea is expressed in similar language at *Ant.* 599–602; cf. also *El.* 765, Ar. *Frogs* 587.

1180 keep close: i.e. to the body, not 'guard the hair' or even 'guard the body'. Henrichs 167 is probably right (but see 1172n.) to argue that this line does not refer to protective power invested in the suppliant. Rather it suggests the child's dependence on the corpse; cf. Aesch. *Eum.* 242–3, 439–40, Eur. *HF* 51.

1182-3 stand near him: the chorus may move nearer to the stage, on which the body lies, but it must still be in the orchestra to sing the third stasimon.

when you should be men: lit. 'instead of men' (cf. 1020). For this kind of reproach cf. Hom. *Il.* 7.96, 8.163. Conversely at *OC* 1368 Oedipus says that his daughters are men, not women, but at *El.* 997 Electra is reminded that she is a woman, not a man.

support him: Tecmessa used the same word when she appealed for the chorus's help at 329.

until I return: see 552–5n.

1184 The episode ends with Teucer's defiant statement of his intention; cf. the end of Aesch. *Sept.* (1066–9). He exits by one of the side-passages.

1185-1222: Third Stasimon

The ode makes no comment on the events of the preceding episode. Instead, the chorus dwells upon its own sufferings at Troy, and curses the man who invented war. Now that Ajax is dead its plight is worse than ever, and it ends with the wish that it were at home. This theme of the chorus's suffering, and the contrast between Troy and home, has formed a permanent undercurrent throughout the play (cf. esp. the first stasimon, 596–645; these two stasima together frame the joyous second stasimon, 693–718, in an A-B-A pattern; see Burton 24, 38–9). Its fullest and final development here provides a melancholy moment of equilibrium between the two passionate quarrel-scenes. Agamemnon's entrance has already been prepared (1109–10, 1115–16nn.), but we are kept waiting for it. The reminder of Ajax' greatness from the sympathetic chorus (1211–13) forms a fitting prelude for the exodos.

1185-6 Which...the last, when will it stop: the sentence is best thus punctuated as two separate questions, with 'number' as the subject of both. Others (e.g. LSJ) take 'last' proleptically with 'stop' ('so as to be the last').

the wandering years: the primary idea is probably that the years go pointlessly on and on. But the phrase may suggest also the long period of time in which the chorus has wandered far from home. For this kind of ambiguity cf. *Ant.* 615 and see Garvie on Aesch. *Cho.* 523–5. It is odd that three stasima begin with this kind of compound (see 694–8n.).

1187-90 imposes on...bane: the same phrase is found at Aesch. *Cho.* 403–4 (ἄτην...ἐπάγουσαν); cf. also Hes. *Op.* 242.

in wide Troy: an adaptation of the Homeric εὐρυάγυια, 'with wide streets'. The adjective, which occurs only here, may, however, be corrupt. The line as it stands in the MSS does not correspond with the glyconic at 1197. At the very least ἀνὰ τὰν has to be changed to either ἀν τὰν (Ahrens; ἀν by apocope for ἀνά is found in Aeschylus and Euripides but not elsewhere in Sophocles) or τάνδ' ἀν (Lobeck).

battle-toil: lit. 'toils in which spears are brandished'.

1191 a sad reproach for the Greeks: the accusative 'reproach' is in apposition with the sentence. The reproach is that they cannot bring the war to an end.

1192-5 For the common wish that someone (usually the speaker himself) might disappear, or have disappeared, into the sky or beneath the ground cf. *OC* 1081–4, Eur. *Hipp.* 732–4 (with Barrett's note), 1290–3, *Ion* 796–7, *Or.* 1376–7. It is a commonplace to curse the first inventor of some unpleasant feature of human life; see Barrett on Eur. *Hipp.* 407–9, F. Leo, *Plautinische Forschungen*[2] (Berlin 1912) 151–4. For the inventor of war in particular cf. Tibullus 1.10.1.

hospitable: lit. 'common to many', a euphemism for 'everyone'; cf. *El.* 138, Aesch. *Sept.* 860. For the thought cf. Men. fr. 538.8 K.

1196 warfare...for all to share: lit. 'common Ares'. At Hom. *Il.* 18.309 ξυνὸς Ἐνυάλιος the adjective means 'impartial' (cf. Archil. fr. 110 W); cf. also the Homeric formula ὁμοιίου πτολέμοιο ('war which makes everyone equal'). War too is the shared experience of all mankind; not (Jebb) '"public" warfare, in which all the Greeks make common cause (as against the Trojans)'.

1197 For the idea, that trouble engenders trouble, and the alliteration cf. 866–8n.

1199-204 He did not dispense: i.e., by inventing war he has deprived the chorus of these pleasures. The easiest way to restore correspondence with 1211 is to accept Hermann's οὐ, 'not', for the MSS οὔτε, 'neither'.

of garlands: they would be worn at the banquets at which the deep cups are drunk and the pipes played.

deep cups: for modern art historians a *kylix* is a *shallow* cup, but there is no reason to suppose that the sense was thus restricted in antiquity.

to consort with: predicative or epexegetic infinitive, in prosaic terms 'to get used to'; cf. Pind. *Nem.* 10.72 and see Moorhouse 239.

the sweet sound of pipes: for the power of music in the symposium to impose peace and calm see Dickie 92–3, and cf. Pind. *Py.* 1.5–12.

ill-starred as I am: the MSS have the adjective in the nominative, agreeing with the inventor of war. Blaydes' conjecture provides an attractive contrast between the pleasures which the chorus so beautifully describes and their unhappiness now that it is cut off from them. The long final syllable is shortened in hiatus as regularly in Homer.

the pleasures of sleep at night: lit. 'to sleep as to pleasure in the night', or 'the pleasure of night for sleeping' (cf. ὁμιλεῖν above). The chorus may mean literally that it cannot sleep (cf. the effect of the end of the war at Aesch. *Ag.* 337), but the following clause suggests rather that it is thinking of sexual pleasure (cf. 520–1n.), of the 'night ritual' of Aesch. *Sept.* 367. For ἰαύω, 'sleep', in this sense cf. Hom.*Il.* 14.213, *Od.* 11.261.

1205 the passion of love: Burton 36 is probably wrong to suppose that ἐρώτων includes all the delights mentioned in the previous lines.

1206-10 The description of the discomforts of life in the camp recalls 601–5 (n.), and may, like that passage, owe something to the Herald's similar description at Aesch. *Ag.* 555–62 (cf. 335–7), ἐξ οὐρανοῦ δὲ κἀπὸ γῆς λειμώνιαι | δρόσοι κατεψάκαζον (560–1), 'from the sky and from the ground dews drizzled on us in the meadows'.

I lie like this uncared for: cf. the state of Ajax himself at 426–7, also Hom. *Od.* 20.130. Σ 1207 took α- as intensive, 'with many anxieties'.

to make me remember: accusative in apposition with the sentence.

1211-15 Things were bad before, but with the death of Ajax they will be still worse.

in the night picks up 1204: formerly the chorus was denied the pleasure of sleep at night, but at least Ajax was there to keep it from being afraid. Similarly **pleasure** (1215) echoes 1201, and, in the same position in the line, 1204: there is no longer any hope that pleasure will return.. Correspondence with 1199 is best restored by emendation there (see 1199–1204n.).

impetuous Ajax: see 212n.

defence: the word is related to that used by Menelaus at 1076. For the idea of Ajax as a defence cf. 158–9.

given up to: perhaps (Jebb) like a consecrated animal which is allowed to roam at liberty (cf. Eur. *Ph.* 947), hence 'consecrated to his fate'.

a hateful fate: see 534n.

will...be my portion: lit. 'will be set over me' or 'will attend upon me'.

then: for οὖν delayed to fifth position in the sentence see Denniston 427. It is less common in Aeschylus and Euripides.

1216-22 A tragic chorus frequently expresses the wish to escape to some distant place, usually a kind of fantasy-world, which is described in terms of great beauty that contrasts with the horror of what is happening on stage: e.g. Eur. *Hipp.* 732–51, *Hel.* 1479–86, *Ba.* 402–16. Here the chorus wishes to escape to Attica, a very real place for the audience, but one which to the chorus seems as distant and unattainable as the Garden of the Hesperides seems to the chorus of *Hipp.* Here, as at 202 (n.), the chorus seems to think of itself as Athenian. But perhaps it pictures itself merely as rounding Cape Sunium, the south-east tip of Attica, on the voyage home to Salamis.

sea-washed promontory: the compound adjective recalls 412, 597, while the noun is the same as at 1076, lit. 'that which is thrown in front'. Home is perhaps thought of as a defence to replace Ajax (see 1211–15n.).

stands over the sea: the MSS have a genitive, 'promontory of the sea', but Morstadt's dative goes better with the verb.

flat top: others prefer 'projecting cape' (cf. Hom. *Od.* 3.278 where Sunium is the ἄκρον Ἀθηνέων), but the fact that Sunium is a promontory is sufficiently indicated by πρόβλημ'.

holy Athens: cf. Pind. fr. 75.4, Ar. *Knights* 1319. The name comes emphatically at the end of the ode, and contrasts with 'Troy' at the end of the preceding stanza (1210).

Again we are reminded of the two landscapes that have formed the background for Ajax' life.

1223-1420: Exodos

The scene that follows the final choral ode is divided into two sections which present the second and third confrontations of Teucer with Ajax' enemies. Since, however, the third enemy, Odysseus, turns out after all to be a friend, the scene balances the fourth episode (974–1184n.), which likewise presented contrasting attitudes to Ajax, but with the friend appearing before the enemy. Agamemnon's arrival was prepared in the previous episode (1109–10, 1115–16nn.). In many ways the quarrel with him is a doublet of that with Menelaus, and the differences (for which see Dalmeyda 8–9, Rosenmeyer 192, Leinieks 200–1) are mainly minor. The length and duplication of the quarrel reflect the importance of the issue of Ajax' burial. We need to see the opposition of both sons of Atreus, who have been consistently paired throughout the play, if the very different attitude of Odysseus is to have its full effect. The parallelism leads us to expect that the second scene will lead to the same deadlock as the first. But this one will dramatically change direction with the sudden appearance of Odysseus. See Holt (1981) 282–6, Davidson (1985) 21–5. The same actor probably played the parts of both Menelaus and Agamemnon, as well as that of Athena. His voice throughout is the 'voice of heartless brutality' (Pavloskis 116; see 974–1184n., Intro. 17).

Agamemnon is almost as repulsive as Menelaus, particularly when, at the beginning and end of his speech, he taunts Teucer with his slave-mother and his unintelligible barbarian speech. Teucer still represents his brother, and for most of the time it is Ajax whom Agamemnon has in mind; both men are described as nonentities at 1231. The idea that they are slaves (1235) is even more offensive than Menelaus' description of Ajax as a commoner (1071–2n.). His condemnation of Teucer's *hybris* (1258) sounds unconvincing after 1087–8 (n.). His complaint that Teucer will not learn *sophrosyne* (1259) reminds us of Ajax himself, but appears equally hollow after Menelaus' use of that term (1073–6n.). Nevertheless, Agamemnon's arguments do represent an advance on those of Menelaus, in that he attempts to evaluate, though negatively, the services and worth of Ajax (1236–8). He argues too that Ajax was properly defeated by a majority decision in the contest for Achilles' arms, and, since Sophocles never makes this issue clear (see 442–6, 1135nn.), the argument is strong enough to make us uneasy. The view (1250–4) that intelligence is more valuable than brawn is not unreasonable in itself, though we may question whether it applies to Ajax.

Teucer's reply is as effective as it can be. He easily defends the past services of Ajax, and shows that he was a greater warrior than Agamemnon. But, while we may agree with his condemnation of Agamemnon's ingratitude (1266–71), and our sympathy is certainly with him, we are uncomfortably reminded that Ajax too rejected Tecmessa's appeal to gratitude (see 1266–9n.). Lines 1290–8 create an unfavourable impression. Not content with defending his own worth and that of his family, Teucer descends to Agamemnon's level by making a vulgar attack on Agamemnon's family-history. He may have won a rhetorical victory (see Heath 202, 204–8, who provides a more favourable assessment of Teucer than do most modern scholars), but he has not persuaded Agamemnon to allow the burial. This second confrontation therefore ends in impasse. All the hopes of Tecmessa and the chorus, as of Ajax himself, were placed in Teucer, whose arrival had been so eagerly awaited. But he has failed them; he has not succeeded in reaching the heart of the matter. While it is true that Ajax' *arete* must depend on what he has done, in the last resort it depends also on what he is, and on its recognition by other people. Even if Teucer should succeed in burying him against the orders of the generals, his status will remain unrecognised.

Our disappointment over Teucer's failure makes the third confrontation all the more remarkable. Instead of the angry stichomythia that followed the quarrel-speeches of Menelaus and Teucer, here the stichomythia of 1316–31 serves to introduce the third and final stage and to prepare the solution which it will present. The intervention of Odysseus comes as a complete surprise to Teucer and the chorus, who all along, like Tecmessa and Ajax himself, have taken it for granted that he is on the same level as the sons of Atreus. But Odysseus does not laugh, and he commits no *hybris* (971), as Teucer recognises with amazement (1382–8). The audience is less surprised, having been prepared for this reversal in the prologue, but, since for most of the play we have seen Odysseus through the eyes only of his enemies, even for us the effect is striking enough. It is Odysseus, the worst enemy of Ajax, not Teucer his friend, who secures his burial and his recognition as a hero. He does so because he has learnt well the lesson of alternation, the idea which was so repulsive in the mouth of Menelaus, but which returns now in its most attractive form (1336–45, 1355–60, 1377). Their former enmity no longer matters. Odysseus is not even greatly interested in what Ajax did, but only in what he was, the best of the Achaeans (always excepting Achilles 1340–1), and he will therefore treat him henceforth as a friend. For the bearing of all this on the tragedy see Intro. 15–17.

1223-4 Look: simultaneous but separate entries are comparatively rare in tragedy (see Taplin (1977) 148–9, 176–7, 351–2, Bond on Eur. *HF* 701). It is unusual that this formula of introduction (1168–9n.) should be used not by a person who is already on stage or in the orchestra, but by someone who is himself arriving. Dawe follows Morstadt in giving 'look' to the chorus-leader and positing a lacuna after it in which he introduces Teucer. But the transmitted arrangement allows Sophocles to bring on both men simultaneously, probably by the same *eisodos*, while reserving the formula for Agamemnon, who alone needs to be introduced to the audience.

I have hurried...rushing: the two verbs convey a sense of urgency as the climax of the play approaches; cf. 811.

1225 it is clear to me: cf. 326n.

his foolish tongue: lit. 'mouth'. The adjective σκαιός is explicitly contrasted with σοφός, 'wise', at fr. 771.3, 921, Eur. *Med* 190, *El.* 972, etc. It, or its noun, seems to describe someone who is stubborn, narrow-minded, and inflexible, and unwilling to learn from good advice (*Ant.* 1028, cf. *OC* 1213); see Coray 112–13, 136, 143.

1226-7 You there: Agamemnon's peremptory beginning is similar in effect to that of Menelaus at 1047. He virtually repeats it at 1228.

to open your big mouth...to say: lit. 'to open your mouth wide as to these terrible words'. The verb 'implies contempt for what was spoken' (MacDowell on Ar. *Wasps* 342); cf. Aesch. *Ag.* 920.

these terrible words: see 312n. Agamemnon doubtless speaks sarcastically, but we may recall the terrible words of Ajax himself at 312.

against us: probably both Agamemnon and Menelaus, but the plural could signify simply 'me'.

1228 Yes you I say: for τοι with the accusative of the second person singular pronoun, 'conveying a summons to attention, often peremptory in tone', see Denniston 542, Moorhouse 35, and cf. *El.* 1445.

the son of the captive-woman: Agamemnon begins as he means to go on, insultingly. Teucer's mother Hesione was in fact the daughter of Laomedon, and sister of king Priam. But she was given to Telamon by Heracles as a slave; see 434–6n.

1229 no doubt if...: i.e. 'how much more so, given that you behave like this when you are *not* nobly born'. For ἦ που in an *a fortiori* argument see Denniston 281–2.

bred: the word reminds us of Ajax' preoccupation with his own breeding or nurture (848–51, 859–63nn.), and with that of his son which he entrusted to Teucer (562, cf. 557). In the mouth of Agamemnon it has become an insult.

1230 you would be speaking: for this, rather than ἐκόμπεις, 'you would boast', as the transmitted reading see Dawe 169.

proudly: lit. 'high things'; cf. Eur. *Hipp.* 730.

on tiptoe: cf. Eur. *El.* 840, *IT* 266, *Ion* 1166 (with Owen's note), fr. 570. Here the Greek says merely 'on the tips', with the toes understood from the context. Agamemnon means that Teucer would draw himself up to his full height. For this as a sign of pride cf. *Suda* Υ 747.

1231 nonentity...on a nonentity's behalf: not (Σ and Kamerbeek) 'on behalf of the dead'. At the very beginning of the movement which will end with the recognition of Ajax' status Agamemnon asserts both his and Teucer's worthlessness. For this kind of expression see 767–9n., where Ajax used the same expression of the man with whom he contrasted himself, and 1093–6n., where Teucer compared Menelaus to such a man (cf. 1114). Here, if there is any subtle difference between οὐδέν (= Teucer) and μηδέν (= Ajax), the latter is perhaps even more contemptuous.

1232-4 we did not come...as you claim: the reference is to Teucer's argument at 1097–1106, esp. 1099. 1226 shows that what he said there to Menelaus has been reported offstage to Agamemnon. For the omission of 'either' in the Greek before 'of the Achaeans' see Denniston 511.

as his own commander: for the expression cf. Ar. *Wasps* 470.

1235 of slaves: so at *Ant.* 479 Creon describes Antigone as a slave. Agamemnon goes further than Menelaus, who was content to describe Ajax as a 'commoner'. The plural may be 'poetic', referring to Teucer alone (cf. 1226–7n.), but it is better to take it of both brothers (cf. 1242); Ajax though dead still speaks through Teucer's mouth. At 1020 Teucer himself feared that his own father would reduce him to this status.

1236 what kind of man: Agamemnon's question raises the vital issue, but it will not receive the answer that he expects. Ever since 77 (n.) we have been encouraged to consider what it means to call Ajax an ἀνήρ, 'man'. For the simple genitive meaning 'about' after a verb of saying see Denniston on Eur. *El.* 228, Moorhouse 72–4. More often it depends on an accusative noun, as at 221, 998, or a subordinate clause (e.g. *El.* 317).

1238 The answer is that the Greeks do not in fact have any other 'men' like Ajax.

1239 to our sorrow: lit. 'bitter', i.e. with painful results. For the adjective thus used predicatively cf. Hom. *Od.* 17.448, *El.* 470, Eur. *Ba.* 357.

1241 if we are to be denounced...as knaves: the verb is that used by Teucer at 1020 of Telamon's expected denunciation of himself; cf. *El.* 367, *Tr.* 1129, 1251 (for its use with ἐκ, 'on the part of', cf. *OC* 51). Like Teucer and Ajax Agamemnon is concerned for his own status and reputation. As at 132–3 (n.) κακοί has both moral connotations (Teucer has accused him of behaving badly) and those of status. Agamemnon realises that if he loses the argument his reputation will suffer. On both counts he will emerge as inferior to Ajax.

1242 be content: the word, in different senses, is unusually common in this play; cf. 439n. The negative in the εἰ clause is οὐ rather than μή because its force is more causal than conditional; see Moorhouse 322 and cf. 1268.

1243 to submit: such submission was impossible for Ajax (666–7n.), with whom Agamemnon here couples Teucer.

1245 who lost the decision: lit. 'who were left behind' (as in a race), i.e. 'defeated' (cf. Hom. *Il.* 23.407, 409, 523, *Od.* 8.125, Polyb. 1.62.6).

1246-9 Whatever our doubts may be about the fairness of the judgement of the arms, Agamemnon's argument, that the stability of law in society depends on the acceptance of a majority verdict, is unexceptionable in itself. We may think of the problems that could arise from a situation like that in the Funeral Games at Hom. *Il.* 23.536–8, where the second prize for the chariot-race is to be given to Eumelus, who came in last, simply because he is 'the best'. The argument is, however, weakened by the use made by Menelaus of similar arguments at 1073–83.

Yes...such: see 950–4n.

no law...soundly established: lit. 'there could not be a firm settlement of any law'. For the political connotation of the abstract noun κατάστασις, and for the use of such abstract subjects in sophistic style, see Long 72–3.

those who are behind: probably the racing metaphor continues from 1245.

1250-4 The idea that brains are better than brawn is again acceptable in itself, but not its application to Ajax, nor the comparison with the ox, as if Ajax' greatness consisted only in his physical size (the imputation made also by Menelaus at 1077–8n.), that he is 'great' only as to his flanks. In *Il.* Ajax is indeed characterised as a strong rather than a clever warrior, and his size and broad shoulders are mentioned at 3.226–7. At 11.558–63 he is compared to a donkey beaten by children for straying into a harvest-field, but there the tone is not derogatory, and even in *Il.* there is more to him than this (see Intro. 1). Athena has already admitted that he is capable of thinking (118–20n.). Agamemnon therefore is wrong. And yet the idea that Ajax was only an ox to be controlled by whipping (cf. 1069; at *Ant.* 477–8 Creon's opponents are compared to horses which require to be controlled) reminds us uncomfortably that this is how he in his madness had tortured his supposed enemies.

1250 this: i.e. 'these tendencies' (Stanford) rather than 'the funeral rites' (Kamerbeek).

1251 broad-backed: the compound occurs only here.

safest: perhaps in two senses: they are unlikely to fall themselves (cf. 1136), and they will not fail their friends. Cf. *OT* 617 (negatively) of those who are too hasty in thought.

1252 of sound mind: the antithesis shows that this is the primary meaning (cf. 746, 1330, and see Coray 155–6), but the Greek in itself could also mean 'well-disposed', 'loyal' (cf. 491). For Agamemnon loyalty to himself *is* the mark of the sensible man.

1253-4 See 758–61, 1077–8nn.

1255-6 is soon on its way for you: the same word (lit. 'is creeping on') as at 228n. The whipping appropriate to Ajax will befall his representative Teucer.

if...some sense: this too links Teucer with his brother. The Sophoclean hero is as regularly, and vainly, urged to acquire sense as to yield (1243n.): e.g. *El.* 1013, *Ant.* 68.

1257 the man...a shade: probably genitive absolute, rather than (Stanford) a genitive of reference. This is a clear echo of 126. But, whereas Odysseus identified himself compassionately with Ajax and with all humanity, Agamemnon is content to crow over what 'the man' (1236n.) has now become, a mere shade (cf. *El.* 1159). According to the normal Greek conception the only kind of immortality for which a man may hope is posthumous glory, and this is what, despite Agamemnon, will be guaranteed for him by Odysseus.

1258 behave...outrageously: again Agamemnon equates Teucer with his brother, who was accused of *hybris* by Menelaus at 1061, 1081, 1088. The audience realises that the term describes his own behaviour.

speak so freely: the same verb, but without the prefix, is coupled with the idea of 'confidence' at [Aesch.] *PV* 178–80; cf. also Eur. *Andr.* 153. An Athenian democratic audience would be more inclined to think of freedom of speech as a virtue than a vice; cf. Aesch. *Supp.* 948 (with the note of Friis Johansen and Whittle). For Agamemnon, however, Teucer is only a slave. For this kind of compound verb with ἐξ-, filling the second half of the three-word trimeter, see E. Tsitsoni, *Untersuchungen der EK-Verbal-Komposita bei Sophokles* (Kallmünz 1963), 30, 35.

1259 learn to be reasonable: once more Teucer is urged to do what Ajax all along refused to do, to acquire *sophrosyne* (132–3, 646–92nn.), which, in this context, means to recognise his own social position, and to exercise restraint in his dealings with his superiors (see Coray 182–3, and cf. 1073–6n.).

recognise what kind of man you are: for this idea cf. Pind. *Py.* 2.72.

1260-1 someone else, a free man: not 'some other free man'. In Athenian law no slave was allowed to plead in court. The same idea may underlie *OT* 408–11 (cf. fr. adesp. 304). Teucer himself ended his speech to Menelaus (1115–17) with the demand that he should send someone more qualified to speak. Robert 213–15 supposes that there is here an allusion to Pericles' citizen-law of 451–50, by which no one could be an Athenian citizen unless both parents were Athenian (Plut. *Per.* 37).

who will plead: see 470–1n. Agamemnon has no idea that the man will turn out to be Odysseus.

1262-3 For μανθάνω, 'learn', thus used of someone's readiness to accept another's arguments see Coray 315–16. The pretence that Teucer does not speak intelligible Greek brings the speech to its offensive end, and for the audience removes any lingering doubts that Agamemnon's arguments may have been sound.

1264-5 The chorus-leader picks up the words used by Agamemnon at 1256, 1259. It is slightly odd that he should implicitly criticise Teucer as well as Agamemnon, especially when the former has not yet spoken to the latter. But this kind of neutral intervention between the two speeches of a quarrel is conventional in tragedy; see 1091–2, 1118–19nn.

1266-9 Teucer's argument and language are reminiscent of Tecmessa's at 520–4. He who there refused to show gratitude to his concubine is now being treated with ingratitude for his warlike services (see Winnington-Ingram 30 n. 56). We may feel uneasy that Ajax and Agamemnon are alike in rejecting the obligation to show gratitude, but we feel also that, while Ajax was right to subordinate it to his own honour, Agamemnon, the lesser man, is being merely petty and vindictive.

gratitude: χάρις seems to combine here the reciprocal ideas of the favour performed by the dead and the gratitude owed him by the recipient.

it proves treacherous: for the phrase cf. *Ant.* 46, Eur. *Andr.* 191. The verb is a technical legal term for conviction and condemnation.

no longer...remembers you: despite the chorus's hopes at 1166 the remembrance of Ajax is still in doubt. For οὐ, not μή, see 1242n.

for a brief mention: Reiske's emendation of the intolerable MSS reading is the most satisfactory that has been proposed; see Lloyd-Jones and Wilson 37–8, and cf. *El.* 414, *OC* 620.

1269-70 The emphasis on Ajax' services is perhaps modelled on Hom. *Il.* 9.322, αἰεὶ ἐμὴν ψυχὴν παραβαλλόμενος πολεμίζειν, 'always risking my life in war'.

1271 is thrown away: the verb is similarly used at Aesch. *Eum.* 215, Dem. 25.75.

1272 senseless: or 'foolish'. Agamemnon fits the chorus's description at 162–3.

1273-80 This does not correspond in detail to any single incident in *Il.* It comes closest to the battle at the ships in *Il.* 15, but Sophocles probably combines this with episodes from Book 13 and e.g. 9.241–3, 16.123–4. There is no good reason to suppose that he is following a different tradition. In fr. adesp. 569 Teucer himself stops the Trojans as they leap over the trench.

1274 inside your defences: ἐντός, 'inside', is superior to the reading of most MSS, οὗτος, 'this man', which provides an unnecessary subject for 'came and protected', and leaves 'your defences' to be taken as a partitive or locative genitive of place, which is dubious except after a verb of motion (but cf. Eur. *Ph.* 451 and see Moorhouse 59).

1275 were now reduced to nothing: Teucer rebuts the argument of Agamemnon at 1231 (n.): on that occasion it was Agamemnon and Menelaus who, compared with Ajax, were nonentities.

when the battle turned: lit. 'at the turning of the spear'. The same expression appears at [Eur.] *Rhes.* 82, and a similar one at Aesch. *Ag.* 1237; cf. also *Ant.* 674, and for the prepositional phrase 963 above. The noun is common in this kind of military context.

1276 alone: as usual; see 29n.

1277 the tops of the ships: cf. Alc. 34a.9, εὐσῦγων θρῴσκοντες [..] ἄκρα νάων, 'leaping to the tops of their well-benched ships'. At Hom. *Od.* 8.111 a seafaring Phaeacian is called *Akroneos*, 'Ship's top'. This sense is made possible by Bothe's insertion of θ', 'and'. With the MSS reading ἄκροισιν has to be taken with ἐδωλίοις ('round the edge of the quarter-decks'), and ναυτικοῖς is awkwardly repetitive after νεῶν.

ships' quarter-decks: the lexicographers (e.g. Hesych. E 547, *Suda* Σ 255, *Et.Magn.* 317.5, *Et.Gud* 401.26) explain the word as 'the rowers' benches', but no passage in classical Greek clearly points to that sense.

1279 over the trenches: in Hom. *Il.* 7 on the advice of Nestor the Greeks build a wall and dig a trench to protect their ships. Hector and the Trojans cross the wall at 15.384.

1281 you claim: at 1237.

1282 was this: for ἄρα = 'surely it was' see 277n.

1283-7 Teucer gives an example of a second service performed by Ajax. The two together serve to counterbalance, and to remove any doubts we may have felt about, the two negative examples of Ajax' behaviour which the Messenger reported at 762–75. This second instance is derived from *Il.* 7, where Hector challenges any Greek to single combat, and Nestor recommends that the choice of champion be made by the drawing of lots (171–4). Homer tells us merely (182–3) that the lot which jumped out of the helmet first was that which the Greeks hoped for, namely that of Ajax, and that he himself rejoiced in his heart (189, 191–2). As a result of the ensuing duel Ajax and Hector made their fatal exchange of gifts (661–2, 664–5, 817–18nn.).

1283 in single combat: lit. '[he himself] alone [faced Hector] alone'. For the emphatic repetition and juxtaposition of 'alone' cf. 467n.

1285-7 a clod of wet earth: which would be likely either to crumble in pieces or to sink, and perhaps stick to the bottom of the helmet when it was shaken. No doubt he means to contrast Ajax' honesty with the crooked voting which gave Achilles' arms to Odysseus, and thus tacitly denies the validity of Agamemnon's argument at 1246–50. Homer seems to envisage a potsherd inscribed with some kind of mark to identify its owner. The clod of earth is probably Sophocles' own invention. Σ says that he is thinking of the story of Cresphontes, who, when lots were drawn among the Heraclids for the possession of Argos, Lacedaemon, and Messenia, to ensure that he received Messenia, which was to go to the owner of the last lot to emerge, put a lump of earth instead of a stone into the urn (Apollod. 2.8.4; cf. Paus. 4.3.4–5).

a runaway's lot: lit. 'a runaway lot'. The epithet is transferred from the person to the object that marks his cowardice. Since it is particularly appropriate to a runaway slave, Teucer effectively prepares his reply to Agamemnon's insult at 1235, 1260. Neither Ajax nor he himself was a slave.

to jump lightly: cf. Aesch. *Pers.* 305, and, for the vivid expression, Eur. *El.* 861, *Supp.* 1047. So the lot *jumps* out of the helmet at *Il.* 7.182.

well-plumed: cf. fr. 341. Although the word is not itself Homeric, the ornamental epithet gives a suitably epic tone to the narrative.

1288 It was he who did this: both examples (cf. 1280) are summed up in similar language.

along with me...beside him: Teucer passes neatly from Ajax to his own defence, Agamemnon having attacked them both.

1289 the slave...barbarian mother: Teucer sarcastically picks up Agamemnon's taunts at 1228–9, 1235, 1259–63.

1290 you *say* it: for καί emphasising the verb, and calling in question 'the ground or motive of an action' see Denniston 315. 'It' is Agamemnon's charge that Teucer is the son of a barbarian mother.

where can you look: i.e. Agamemnon ought to hide his face in shame for saying such things. For this as the proper response to shame cf. Hom. *Od.* 8.85–6, *Hy. Aphro.* 156, and see 462-5n., Cairns 98 n. 151, 158 ('*Aidos* is manifest in the eyes because the feeling of shame or inhibition naturally causes one to avert one's gaze'), 292–3, Richardson on *Hy.Dem.* 194.

1291-2 Pelops, son of Tantalus, came to Greece from Sipylus in Maeonia, which was part of Phrygia 'in the older and larger sense' (Jebb); cf. *Ant.* 824, Hdt. 7.11.4. In claiming that it is really Agamemnon's family that is barbarian, and thus answering 1263, Teucer insinuates also that Agamemnon is related to the Trojan enemies of the Greeks (cf. 1054), and that he is as much a barbarian as Teucer the son of Hesione. Lydians and Phrygians are cowardly stereotypes at Ar. *Birds* 1244; cf. Eur. *Or.* 1351–2, 1447.

1293-4 When Thyestes, brother of Atreus, committed adultery with the latter's wife, Atreus took revenge by inviting him to a dinner at which he served up Thyestes' children.

most impious is better taken with 'banquet' than with either 'Atreus' or 'you'.

1295-7 Aerope was the daughter of Catreus, king of Crete. On catching her with a slave, her lover, Catreus sent her to Nauplius, king of Euboea, with instructions that he should drown her. He, however, spared her and she married Atreus (in another version Pleisthenes). Euripides evidently handled the story in his *Cretan Women* in 438 B.C. (see Σ 1297a), but there is no good reason to suppose that *Aj.* must have been composed with that play in mind; see Reinhardt 234 n. 3.

she had brought in: the adjective describes someone who is imported from outside and does not belong, hence here an 'adulterer'; cf. Pind. *Ol.* 10.89, Eur. *Ion* 592.

to be a prey: lit. 'as a destruction', a remarkably bold example of the Sophoclean use of an abstract noun in apposition with a person, here to describe what was to happen to the object of the verb; see Long 120–3, and cf. Eur. *HF* 458–9. At *Ant.* 533, where Creon uses the abstract noun 'ruin' to describe Antigone and Ismene, he means that they will cause, not suffer, ruin; cf. also *OT* 1248. For the idea of feeding someone to the fish cf. [Aesch.] *PV* 583.

dumb: fish are 'voiceless' at Aesch. *Pers.* 577 and Soph. fr. 762 (cf. fr. 1072). But this is only one of the possible meanings assigned to ἐλλός and ἔλλοψ by Hesych. E 2167, 2168, and the derivation is obscure. LSJ prefer 'scaly' (cf. *Et. Magn.* 593.1, but also 331.49). It is used of fish already in the *Titanomachy* (fr. 8 Davies), and in the pseudo-Hesiodic *Shield* 212.

1300-3 See 434–6n.

as a choice gift: she is like Cassandra at Aesch. *Ag.* 954–5; cf. also *Eum.* 402.

1304-5 Teucer's desire not to disgrace his birth (cf. Hom. *Il.* 6.208–10) matches Ajax' shame at apparently having done so (434–40). For Teucer the disgrace would be in allowing his brother to lie unburied, combined no doubt with his failure to support him while alive (1007); not (Jebb, Kamerbeek), 'how would it dishonour Ajax to have me plead on his behalf?' However, if he can ensure the burial he will restore Ajax' honour and at the same time maintain his own.

blood-relations: lit. 'those from my blood'. For this use of πρός see Kühner-Gerth I 516, and cf. *El.* 1125. The phrase, unless it is a 'poetic' plural, may include the whole of Teucer's family, but the following relative clause shows that he is thinking primarily of Ajax.

1307 are not ashamed of saying: the idea that it is Agamemnon, not Teucer, who ought to feel ashamed picks up 1290 at the beginning of the comparison between their two families. For the participle with ἐπαισχύνομαι see 652–3n.

1308-9 three people: Teucer himself, Tecmessa, and Eurysaces who is still clinging to the corpse. All will be prepared to die and join Ajax where he lies in death (1306). **lying together:** cf. 1058–9n.

1310-12 to die conspicuously: cf. 229n., with perhaps the same implication that his death will be glorious as well as public. So too for Antigone it is better (καλόν) to die for burying her brother (*Ant.* 72).

labouring on his behalf: an echo of the troubles undertaken by Ajax' friends on his behalf even before he died (866–8n.).

than on your wife's behalf: i.e. fighting on behalf of the Greeks against the Trojans, for the sake of a mere woman. Teucer means that they are fighting in an unworthy cause (cf. 1111–14), and he increases the insult by pretending to confuse Menelaus' wife with Agamemnon's woman, implying that she was unfaithful to Menelaus.

or am I...brother's wife: Teucer pretends to correct himself, by alleging that both brothers shared the bed of Helen.

1313 my case...your own: for this use of the article with neuter possessive pronoun cf. *El.* 251–2.

1314-15 you will wish...bold: at 1241 (n.) Agamemnon revealed his concern for his own reputation. Teucer ends with bluster, rudely warning him that he will one day regret having tried to be a 'hero' in his quarrel with Teucer.

at my expense: cf. 1092, also 366, 971.

1316-17 The final stage begins with the abrupt appearance of Odysseus. He is not announced in the usual way (see 1223–4n.), but addressed directly by the chorus-leader (see Taplin (1977) 288, 346). The latter's hope that he may have come to reconcile the quarrel is scarcely consistent with the hostile view of Odysseus shared by all Ajax' friends throughout the play. It is probably fruitless to try to explain this change of attitude in terms of the chorus's psychology (Stanford). Sophocles merely uses the chorus-leader to introduce the sudden change of mood and to prepare the audience for what in fact is going to happen.

timely: cf. 34n.

to join in the quarrel: the Greek says merely 'to join', with 'the quarrel' understood. So the verb can be used with (Hdt. 6.108.5) or without (Hdt. 4.80.2, Ar. *Ach.* 686) a noun, meaning 'to join battle'.

1318-19 Odysseus' polite request for information, and his complimentary reference to Ajax, contrasts with the rude opening words of Menelaus (1047–8) and Agamemnon (1226–8). Already he begins to reveal his sympathies, by mentioning the shouting, not of Teucer, but of the sons of Atreus. Taplin (1978) 41 (cf. Seale 171) contrasts this entry of Odysseus with his first in the prologue: 'when he returns there is nothing cautious or devious about him'. J. Irigoin, in *Entretiens Fondation Hardt* 29 (Vandoeuvres-Geneva 1982) 45, points out the symmetry of the composition: the 14 lines of stichomythia which begin at 1318 are followed by a speech of 14 lines (= 28 altogether). This is followed by a 24-line stichomythia, which concludes with four lines from Agamemnon, again making a total of 28 lines. Despite Webster 121 n. 2, 1319 does not indicate the presence of Menelaus as a mute in this final scene, in which he would be quite superfluous.

1320-1 Blundell 37 remarks that 'the question of who started a quarrel is crucial'. If one's opponent started it one has a right to retaliate.

1322-3 It is clearly Teucer, not Agamemnon, for whom Odysseus is prepared to make allowances, and the attitude of Agamemnon that he is trying to change. At this stage he is content to argue from the traditional moral code that it is natural and right to reciprocate injuries or insults. What Odysseus means is that if Teucer insulted Agamemnon it must be in response to insults from the latter.

when he is the recipient of insults: lit. 'when he hears petty words'. Cf. the complaint of Teucer at 1162 (n.), *Phil.* 607.

matches them: like 'to join' at 1317, an expression proper to engaging in military conflict; cf. Eur. *IA* 830.

1324-6 Agamemnon admits that he did insult Teucer, and uses Odysseus' argument (1322–3) to justify his conduct. The 'kind of thing' that Teucer did was to insult him. Kamerbeek and Stanford think that there is an antithesis between speaking and doing: Teucer deserves to be insulted because of his disgraceful *behaviour*. But Teucer has not in fact *done* anything against Agamemnon (cf. 1326), and Kamerbeek's 'wanted to do' is not in the Greek. In 1325 it is Odysseus who insists on taking 'was doing' in the narrow sense of action as opposed to words, and in 1326 it is only Teucer's words that Agamemnon can adduce. For the periphrastic imperfect in 1324 see Kühner-Gerth I 38.

1328-31 Odysseus cleverly begins by establishing that Agamemnon is prepared to treat him as a friend and to observe the traditional code of friendship. By agreeing to do so Agamemnon dooms himself to lose the ensuing argument. And by reminding us that Odysseus is the natural friend of Agamemnon (and Menelaus) Sophocles ensures that his support of Ajax will be all the more surprising.

remain your partner: lit. 'row with you', but the nautical sense is probably no more strongly felt than in ὑπηρετεῖν, 'to serve'.

for otherwise: for this elliptical use of γάρ see Denniston 62–3 and cf. Eur. *Hipp.* 90.

show sense: see 1252n. The sensible man is one who understands how to behave correctly, in this case how to treat his friends.

1333 to cast out...unburied: picking up 1307–8.

so insensitively: lit. 'without feeling pain'. The word was used by the chorus at 946 to describe the 'heartless' Agamemnon and Menelaus.

1334-5 At 1327 Agamemnon attributed 'violence' to Teucer in the idiomatic expression 'in despite of me'. Now Odysseus warns Agamemnon that it is he who is in danger of behaving violently. The idea of violence or strength or might is sometimes paired with that of justice (see Garvie on Aesch. *Cho.* 244–5, and cf. *El.* 476), but here they are in natural antithesis. It is a mark of a tyrant to prefer violence to justice; cf. the words of Menelaus at 1159–60. For the idea of 'trampling' on justice cf. Aesch. *Cho.* 641–2, *Eum.* 540–1; also *Ant.* 745 where Haemon accuses Creon of trampling on the honours of the gods.

1336-41 Odysseus argues, not that it was wrong for Agamemnon to hate Ajax – he shared that hatred himself – but that justice now requires that hatred be laid aside.

I would not so dishonour him: the sense is clear, although the MSS provide a variety of readings. For the corruption cf. *Ant.* 747. The dishonour of which Ajax was so keenly aware (98, 426–7, 440) is expunged by Odysseus, who thus fulfils Tecmessa's prediction at 923–4 (n.); with his recognition that he was the best of the Greeks Odysseus restores his status as a hero, and accepts Ajax' own judgement of himself at 423–6 (n.), adding only the qualification 'except for Achilles'. Odysseus tacitly admits that the judgement of the arms, though not necessarily fraudulent (see 1135n.), was wrong; see Winnington-Ingram 58, Machin 38–9, Seidensticker 128 n. 67. It remains, however, to persuade Agamemnon to allow the burial which will symbolise the restoration.

the single most excellent man: for 'one' thus used to intensify the superlative see Kühner-Gerth I 28, and cf. *OT* 1380, *Phil.* 1344–5.

1342 to be dishonoured by you: picking up 1339 (Agamemnon should feel the same way as Odysseus), as 'it would not be right' (lit. 'not justly') picks up 1335.

1343-4 the laws of the gods: which require that all the dead be buried (1129, 1132–4nn., 1154), the 'unwritten laws' to which Antigone appeals at *Ant.* 453–60 (cf. also 1070 and 'Justice' at 451). 'With the prohibition of burial...the *hubris* of Aj.'s enemies...takes on a more objective character (it is no longer just a term which Aj.'s party apply to their opponents' conduct') (Cairns 237 n. 73).

1344-5 After the more general argument that all the dead should be buried Odysseus returns at the end of his speech to 'justice' as it concerns the particular case of the 'good man' (ἐσθλός), a word which, like 'most excellent' (ἄριστος) at 1340, refers more to Ajax' status as a hero than to his moral virtue. He means, not that the gods would be offended by denial of burial only to an ἐσθλός, but that Ajax' status makes the general denial even worse; see Fisher 320. 'The good man' is certainly the object, not the subject, of the infinitive. It is the status of Ajax, not that of Odysseus, that is in question. Odysseus does not go as far as to say that it is no longer right for Agamemnon to hate Ajax; he means only that he should no longer treat him as an enemy.

if he should die: for the optative see 520–1n.

1347 I hated him: as did Menelaus (1134) and Agamemnon. But by adding that it is no longer right (or 'good', 'acceptable'; cf. 1132, 1310) to hate him Odysseus goes further than he did at 1345.

1348 Agamemnon does not even mention Odysseus' argument that Ajax was the 'best' of the Greeks. He completely fails to understand how a hated enemy can become a friend just because he is dead. Rather, now that he is dead Odysseus should not only hate but also trample on him (cf. 988–9n.). The position of καί rules out the meaning 'trample on him in death as well as in life'. Agamemnon, like Athena at 79 (n.), is in effect inviting Odysseus to commit *hybris* against Ajax. For the idea of trampling cf. 1146, *El* 456, Soph. *Eurypylus* (Page, *Greek literary papyri* 4.12), Aesch. *Pers.* 911, Eur. *Hipp.* 668.

1349 an advantage that is not right: cf. Moschion fr. 7.1, 'what advantage is there in committing *hybris* against those who are no longer alive?' κέρδος, 'gain', 'advantage' (cf. 107) is often used of profit of an unworthy kind or dishonestly acquired; cf. *Ant.* 1056 and see Garvie on Hom. *Od.* 8.164. Odysseus uses the same kind of language to describe it as he has used at 1347.

1350 Agamemnon cannot deny the truth of Odysseus' argument. With perhaps particular reference to 1343–4 he takes refuge in the difficulties imposed upon him by his position and its responsibilities (cf. Oedipus at *OT* 628). No doubt he uses τύραννος in a neutral sense ('ruler'), but a fifth-century Athenian audience would certainly hear the word as 'tyrant'; cf. 1334–5n.

1351 when they give good advice: cf. *Ant.* 723 and contrast 1137. Odysseus presses home the admission already made by Agamemnon at 1330–1. He is as much under an obligation to respect his friend Odysseus as to harm his enemy Ajax.

1352 The good man: Agamemnon belatedly attempts to answer the argument of Odysseus at 1340, 1344–5: Ajax cannot have been a 'good' man; for otherwise he would have recognised Agamemnon's authority. But his definition of 'goodness' and 'badness' is like that of Menelaus at 1071–2 (n.) (cf. also Creon at *Ant.* 666, Neoptolemus at *Phil* 925–6). For Odysseus, as for Ajax, it means something very different. It is less likely that by 'the good man' Agamemnon means Odysseus, with the implication that it is now *his* duty to accept the decision of his superior.

1353 by yielding to your friends: his decision to be overcome by his friends rather than by his violence (1334) will show that he is a responsible ruler. At Aesch. *Ag.* 943 Clytaemestra used a similar argument to her husband (cf. also fr. adesp. 40). It is ironical that Ajax will secure his burial only because Agamemnon will accept the obligation which Ajax had rejected for himself (330, 481–4nn.). For τοι in a statement, 'hortatory, deprecatory, persuasive, soothing, or remonstrating' see Denniston 540–1.

1354-6 the kind of man: Agamemnon recognises that this is what the argument is really about, and Odysseus merely has to repeat what he has established at 1340, 1345, 1355.

you give the favour: Odysseus is prepared to do for Ajax what Ajax declined to do (522) even for Tecmessa, and what Agamemnon's failure to do was lamented by Teucer (1266–7).

was my enemy: not 'is my enemy'. For Odysseus Ajax is now his friend; cf. 1377 (n.). But the omission of the verb in the Greek leads Agamemnon to a further misunderstanding: if Ajax *is* Odysseus' enemy, how can he show him this respect?

Do you have such respect: we may remember that Tecmessa appealed in vain to Ajax' sense of shame or respect (506–7n.). Again Agamemnon's values are closer to those of Ajax than to those of Odysseus.

1357 This is perhaps the most important line in this final scene. Although 'his' is omitted in the Greek, there can be no doubt that the *arete*, 'excellence', is that of Ajax. With 'prevails over' Odysseus echoes both 1353 and also 1334: he takes his own advice.

1358 unstable: i.e. 'fickle', 'capricious', as at Eur. *Tro.* 1205 (of fortune); cf. Hom. *Od.* 20.132, Thuc. 3.82.4. That Agamemnon is referring to Ajax, who changed from friend to enemy, is shown by Kitto (1956) 194, Winnington-Ingram, *BICS* 24 (1979) 3–4, Blundell 85–6, 98 n. 190. 1354, 1358, and 1360 should all describe the same person, and the question is whether it is proper to treat Ajax as a friend. As Blundell remarks, it is ironical that Ajax has to be excused by his enemy Odysseus for the fickleness which he himself despised.

1359 For this alternation cf. Ajax' words at 679–82 (n.); for its formulation here cf. esp. *OC* 614–15, Aesch. *Cho.* 234 (with Garvie's note). We might expect Odysseus to say rather that enemies often turn into friends. His main concern, however, is to defend the charge that Ajax changed from friend to enemy. But at the same time he implies that the opposite change is equally natural. For ἦ κάρτα, strongly emphasising πολλοί, 'many', see Denniston 280 , Garvie on Aesch. *Cho.* 929.

1360 such men: i.e. unstable men like Ajax.

1361 an unyielding soul: the opposite of an unstable one. Heracles describes his own soul in the same way at *Tr.* 1260; cf. also *Ant.* 473 (for the term see Knox (1964) 23). Thus Odysseus condemns Agamemnon's inflexibility, but at the same time leaves us with the uncomfortable feeling that the description fits Ajax better than does Agamemnon's charge of fickleness. Agamemnon and Ajax are alike in their stubbornness; cf. 594–5, 649, 913, 926.

1362 You will show us up: Teucer used the same verb at 1020 in the context of his father's reaction to his disgrace, as did Agamemnon (1241n.) when he displayed the same fear that, if he should give in and permit the burial, his reputation would suffer. Here δειλούς, 'weaklings', corresponds to κακοί, 'evil', at 1241. But Teucer has already warned Agamemnon (1314–15n.) that it is not in his interest to play the hero. 'This day', the day which seemed to his friends to be so vital for the salvation of Ajax (753, 756, 778), will in fact re-establish Ajax as a hero and prove Agamemnon's weakness as a leader.

1363 Odysseus cannot really reassure Agamemnon that if he surrenders he will be acting like a hero. All that he can say is that in others' eyes he will be doing the right thing. He thus in effect repeats the argument of 1335, 1342.

1364 Agamemnon has no more counter-arguments. His simple question implies that he is now ready to give in.

1365-7 shall also come to that: i.e. to death and the necessity for burial. Odysseus' enlightened ability to see himself in others (cf. *OC* 567–8 and see 124n.) was already revealed at 121–6 (n.). Agamemnon's cynical and terse reply, with its alliterative πᾶς...πονεῖ, has a proverbial ring (see W. Bühler, *Zenobii Athoi proverbia* IV (Göttingen 1982), 100). He, like Ferguson 26, Nielsen 26–7 (see also Machin 391–2), dismisses Odysseus' attitude as purely selfish, and the latter does not bother to put him right. Rather, he is content to use an argument which Agamemnon evidently understands (see Stanford, Evans 82 n. 39). But Sophocles does not intend us to share Agamemnon's cynicism. That there is always an element of selfishness in compassion was well understood by Greek writers (cf. *OC* 309, Hom. *Il.* 19.301–2, Eur. *Med.* 86, Men. *Mon.* 407): we pity someone because we see ourselves in him (see J. Jones, *On Aristotle and Greek tragedy* (London 1962) 186–91). What matters is that Odysseus does show compassion, and this is something that Agamemnon cannot understand. It is now Odysseus' turn to 'labour' on behalf of both Ajax and himself (see 1310–12n.).

1368-9 Agamemnon disclaims all responsibility (much as he does at the end of Eur. *Hec.*; cf. esp. 850–63), and, although Odysseus replies that he will be 'worthy', 'good', he uses a weaker word (χρηστός) than ἀγαθός or ἐσθλός, one which implies merely 'useful' or serviceable' (cf. however *Phil.* 476, where it is opposed to that which is disgraceful (αἰσχρόν), and results in glory; also *Phil.* 437). Agamemnon will be doing the right thing, but it will not really enhance his reputation (cf. 1241n.).

at all events: i.e. 'whether or not you accept the responsibility'. H.D. Broadhead, *Tragica* (Christchurch 1968) 72, prefers 'altogether good' (cf. [Aesch.] *PV* 198).

1370-3 Agamemnon returns to the point at which the argument began (1328–31n.): he will do his friend the favour which he asks (cf. also 1351), but his attitude to Ajax will remain unchanged to the end, and he never learns the lesson of alternation; see Blundell 99.

both in...and in this: the Greek says simply 'both there and here', with 'there' referring to Hades (see 854–8n.).

what you wish: all the MSS have χρή, 'what you should', which, even if it means merely 'what is necessary for the burial' (cf. *Ant.* 247), would make Agamemnon concede more than he is clearly prepared to concede. At 1348 he has explained what he thinks 'should' be done to the dead. Dindorf's χρῆς is certainly correct. The rare use of the word in this sense made corruption inevitable, as it did at *El.* 606, *Ant.* 887. Odysseus will not in fact be allowed to do all that he wishes (1394–5, 1400n.).

1374-5 The chorus-leader acknowledges that his hopes at 1316–17 have been fulfilled. Odysseus is no longer one of 'the people of poor judgement' of 964. This praise prepares us for the more important reaction of Teucer. Odysseus' traditional cleverness is often in tragedy presented as a vice (cf. *Phil.* 431–2), and throughout the play he has been consistently abused for it by Ajax and his friends (cf. 103n.). In Sophocles in general σοφός more often has negative than positive connotations (see Coray 122–3, 131–2, 385–6). It is therefore ironical that it is this quality of Odysseus, together with his persuasiveness (151n.), that has restored Ajax to his status as a hero. See further Blundell 103, Coray 145.

1377 Odysseus makes it clear that his change of attitude applies to Teucer as well as to Ajax.

1379-80 to share...all the labours: the polarisation of expression stresses the remarkable fact that Odysseus has joined the friends of Ajax; see 1047–8, 1365–7nn. Contrast the 'task' (πόνος) of tracking down his enemy to which he yoked himself at 24.

to fail in none: cf. Xen. *Cyr.* 1.2.14.

who are the best: cf. 1340–1, 1345, 1355, 1357.

1381 Most excellent Odysseus: it is striking that Teucer uses the same word (ἄριστος) to describe Odysseus as the latter has in the preceding line applied to Ajax. This (cf. 1399) does provide some support for the view (see Intro. 15) that in Odysseus Sophocles is setting up a new model of *arete* to set against that of Ajax; cf. *OT* 1432 where Oedipus is equally surprised to discover that he can describe Creon as ἄριστος. See, however, 1344–5, 1357nn. For Teucer Odysseus' recognition of the *arete* of Ajax entitles Odysseus himself to be called *aristos*, but all the emphasis is on the status of Ajax, not on that of Odysseus.

when I speak: this does not imply 'only in my words'. Jebb and others understand 'for your words' (dative of cause). But Teucer is praising Odysseus also for his deeds (1384; cf. Σ).

1382 you have deceived: again (cf. 1374–5n.) it is ironical that Odysseus, the man of 'many wiles', should here be shown to have deserved his reputation for deceiving, but to have turned out to be better than was expected.

1384 you alone stood by him: Odysseus' isolation reminds us of that of Ajax himself (1276n.).

with helping hand: lit. 'with your hands', i.e. 'you gave him practical help'; cf. 115n., Hom. *Il.* 1.77.

to stand...beside: see 1131, 1156nn.

1385 though he was dead: i.e. 'when it was in your power to treat Ajax as you would not have dared when he was alive' (cf. 1348).

to treat him with great outrage: as throughout the play Ajax and his friends, as well as Athena, expected Odysseus to do (see 950–4, 955–60nn., 971). His enemies' *hybris* includes the pleasure which they take in inflicting the dishonour (see Fisher 321). Despite the view of Menelaus and Agamemnon (1258n.) it is *their* behaviour that is clearly established as *hybris* at the end of the play. For *hybris* applied to the wrong treatment of the dead cf. Eur. *Ph.* 1663, *El.* 902; also 1092, 1151 above.

1386 crazy: lit. 'thunderstruck', so that he has lost his wits. ἐπιβρόντητος occurs only here, while ἐμβρόντητος occurs in comedy and prose but not in tragedy.

1388 disgraced: see 560–1n., and cf. also 181, 217.

1389 the father: i.e. Zeus.

the sky above us: lit. 'this Olympus', Olympus and the sky being thought of indiscriminately as the home of the gods; cf. *Ant.* 758, *OC* 1655.

rules over: lit. 'takes precedence over'; cf. fr. 270.

1390 The appeal to the Fury reminds us of Ajax' curse in his final speech at 835–44.

who remembers: the same adjective is used of the Furies at Aesch. *Eum.* 383, *PV* 516; cf. *Ag.* 155 (of Anger).

who brings accomplishment: at *PV* 511 it is Μοῖρα, 'Fate', who receives this adjective; cf. *Hom. Hy.* 23.2, Aesch. *Sept.* 655 (of curses), and see Fraenkel on *Ag.* 997. For the association of the Fury and Justice cf. *Tr.* 808–9, Aesch. *Ag.* 1432–3 (where Justice is τέλειος, 'accomplished', or 'that accomplishes').

1391-2 even as they wished to cast him out...in disgrace: the language picks up 1387–8, so that, by a typically Sophoclean arrangement the curse itself is both preceded and followed by its grounds. For 'cast out' see 1064–5n.

1393 aged: the word, as in Homer, combines the notions of age and dignity.

Laertes: for the form of his name see 1–3n. Odysseus is no longer described as son of Sisyphus (see 187–9n.), but as the true son of a noble father. Contrast the petty insults levelled by Agamemnon and Teucer at each other's family (1228–30, 1259–63, 1291–8).

1394 to touch: the verb means essentially 'to touch lightly on the surface'. Odysseus is not even to lay a finger on the corpse'.

1396 do join: Teucer picks up Odysseus' ξυμπονεῖν, 'to share the labour', at 1379. For καί thus used to stress the contrast between what Odysseus is and what he is not to do see Denniston 321–2.

the rest: the expression is vague, but presumably it includes (Stanford) everything that does not involve the actual touching of the corpse. The line can hardly mean (Jebb) that Teucer is inviting him only to be a spectator at the funeral, or even that his task will be to see merely that it is not interrupted.

1396-7 anyone from the army: no doubt to join Odysseus. Although this role is limited, it does indicate at least some degree of reintegration for Ajax into his community.

1398 everything else: i.e. everything that Odysseus is not allowed to do.

1399 Teucer ends with a tactful, and no doubt sincere, compliment, for which see 1381n.

1400 I wanted it: the imperfect tense, and the μέν...δέ antithesis, imply a sorrowful acceptance that his wish has not been granted. The addition of ἄν at 88 (n.) produces a slightly different effect.

1401 accept your word: lit. 'approve' of it, the same verb as at 1360, 1361, 1381; cf. also 536, Aesch. *Eum.* 469. As at 99 'word' is omitted in the Greek.

and go: the language is similar to that of Menelaus at 1159, but the nature of Odysseus' departure is very different.

1402-20 The play, like *El.*, *Ant.*, *Tr.*, and *OC*, ends with anapaests. They contain a number of linguistic and metrical difficulties that have led to the deletion of various lines, and to that of the whole passage by Dawe. It is unlikely that the original ending came at 1401, with the tableau still present on the stage. The passage may conceivably have replaced a different ending (the final lines of a play seem to have been peculiarly liable to alteration), but for the most part corruption is a better explanation than interpolation (see Lloyd-Jones and Wilson 41, Heath 204 n. 81). Either way, it is a pity that for the modern reader it spoils the effect of what was almost certainly an impressive ending to the play. A further problem for the modern reader, though not for the original audience, concerns the staging. At 1403–8 Teucer issues instructions to three separate groups, and it is unclear whether he is addressing the chorus, which is to split into three groups, or (Seale 173) attendants, or a mixture of both. More important is the question of whether this triple division takes place before the eyes of the audience, with two groups departing by the two *eisodoi*, while the third enters the hut by the central door to fetch the armour. After or before the departure of the chorus the corpse would then be carried off by

Teucer, Eurysaces, and Tecmessa (or with Tecmessa following), perhaps helped by one or two attendants (so Webster 120, Gardiner (1979) 13–14, who has them go through the central door, perhaps by means of the *eccyclema*). This arrangement would duplicate the triple division at 804–6: everyone is now as anxious to arrange for the burial as they were there to save Ajax' life (for the triple division of a chorus into three bodies see Lloyd-Jones, *SIFC* 87 (1995) 140–2 on fr. 314.174 (*Ichn.*)). However, the total effect of all this is one of fragmentation, instead of the unity that the conclusion seems to demand (cf. esp. 1413–14). It is therefore preferable to envisage a single funeral procession in which all take part, a ritual action which 'can be seen as a demonstration of the civilised community's shared (ideal) values' (P.E. Easterling, *Metis* 3 (1988) 95, cf. 91). The unity *contrasts* with the disarray of the chorus's earlier departure (see Taplin (1978) 42). Either (Seale) we wait while attendants bring the armour from the hut, and then the whole procession moves off together by an *eisodos*, or, more simply, we are left to imagine that all three groups will separate to their allotted tasks after the end of the play. The sense of finality, however, is not quite complete. We remain conscious that Agamemnon and Menelaus will not attend the funeral, and that the role of Odysseus will be limited. Segal (1995) 25 remarks that the blood is still flowing from Ajax' mortal body.

1403-4   quickly prepare a hollow trench: at 1164–5 (for Dawe the source of the interpolation here) 'hurry *to see to* a hollow trench' is much easier than the present expression, 'hurry a trench', which is as dubious in Greek as it is in English. At Eur. *Alc.* 256 the accusative τάδε is not comparable.

1404-5   others: τοί, an epic and Doric form of οἱ, is found in Aeschylus, but is attested nowhere else in Sophocles (unless at fr. 555b.20); cf. τώς in the interpolated 841.
   high: lit. 'set on high', a compound found elsewhere only at Pind. *Nem.* 10.47 (of cities). Here it is purely ornamental.
   in the middle of the fire: lit. 'with fire all round'. So at Hom. *Od.* 8.437 the fire surrounds a tripod. But it may be that it is the tripod-legs which bestride the fire, as probably at *Il.* 18.344, *Od.* 8.426, 434.
   for the holy bath: for the ritual washing of the corpse cf. *El.* 1139, *Ant.* 901, 1201. Ajax' defilement (654) is to be removed at last.

1408   the armour...shield: but not the shield itself, which Ajax has bequeathed to his son (574–6), with the further instructions that the rest of his armour is to be buried with him (577), as Teucer now arranges. The language here is unexceptionable, and, if the present passage is to be attributed to an interpolator, he was at least intelligent enough to remember the earlier passage accurately.

1409-11 γ'(ε), apparently somehow stressing 'your father', is hard to explain. It is omitted in some MSS, but is metrically indispensable. Denniston 155 doubtfully classifies δὲ...γε here as 'weakly adversative or purely continuative'.
   to raise: it is curious that Euripides uses the same verb ἐπικουφίζω at *El.* 72, but in the commoner metaphorical sense 'alleviate', immediately after 'as far as I have strength'. At *Ant.* 43 the simple κουφίζω is used of raising a corpse for burial.

1411-13 The description resembles that at 918–19, and, if part of an interpolation, may have been borrowed from that passage. Whoever wrote it, Sophocles or an interpolator, ignores the improbability that Ajax is still pumping up blood so long after his death. For 'black strength' in the sense of life-blood see Padel 25 and cf. Hom. *Il.* 4.149. The word translated 'channels' (σύριγγες), originally a pipe, comes to be used of any pipe-like object. Commentators here are divided as to whether it refers to nostrils (Σ; cf. 918, Hom. *Od.* 22.18), or to veins or arteries (cf. A.R. 4.1647), which were probably not distinguished from each other in the fifth century, or to the bronchial passages of the lungs (see A. Platt, *CQ* 5 (1911) 30–1). The last is perhaps the likeliest; cf. *Tr.* 1054, Arist. *Resp.* 478a 13, 480b 7. Stanford finds a connection with Empedocles' account of breathing, in which there is a reference to channels filled with blood (31 B 100; see N.B. Booth, *JHS* 80 (1960) 10–15). A further problem concerns the logical connection. It is hard to see why the fact that Ajax is still bleeding provides a reason (γάρ) for the raising of the body. See Dawe, *PCPhS* 14 (1968) 13–14.

1413-14 everyone present who claims to be a friend: Teucer addresses the chorus and attendants, but there is a sense that the wider army is also involved. Ajax is no longer unprotected by his friends (910).

let him hurry, let him go: for the asyndeton see 811n.

1415 labouring: see 1365–7, 1379–80nn.

1416-17 Even this sense (with Blaydes' τόδε), which seems to imply absurdly that Ajax is no longer so good now that he is dead, is hard to extract from the Greek, which says 'and (sc. 'having laboured') for nobody yet better of mortals than Ajax, when he was alive, then (or 'once') I say it'. With a comma after 1416, we might take 1417 to mean (with Kamerbeek, Segal (1981) 144) 'I speak of Ajax at a time when he was alive' (cf. Eur. fr. 311), but the sense is still feeble. There are also metrical objections. Two successive paroemiacs (catalectic anapaests) are not permitted in recitative anapaests, and word-end after initial – ∪∪ – (κοὐδενί πω) is avoided; see L. Parker, *CQ* 8 (1958) 86. It is certainly tempting to attribute these lines, or at least 1417, to an interpolator, but even an interpolator must have meant something by them. For discussion see Lloyd-Jones and Wilson 40–1.

1418-20 The final conventional choral anapaests, which, along with other such Sophoclean codas, were first deleted by Ritter as a post-Euripidean interpolation, are not very different from those which end *El.* and *Ant.* It is idle to look for profundity in the closing lines of a Sophoclean or Euripidean tragedy. For the closural function of such codas see D.H. Roberts, *CQ* 37 (1987) 51–64: 'the final lines of tragedy may be seen as part of a closural strategy, with significance both for our experience of the end as an end and for our recognition of its limitations'. The chorus's comment that 'it is all very surprising, who could have predicted it?', may be compared with fr. 590, probably the conclusion of the *Tereus*, and with the formula with which Euripides ends several of his plays; cf. also *Ant.* 1160, Thgn. 1075–8, and the words of Ajax himself at 648, also 715–18). What has surprised the chorus is the restitution of Ajax after his humiliation, together with the behaviour of Odysseus.

before he sees them: for πρίν + infinitive (instead of the normal ἄν + subjunctive) depending on a negative main clause see Goodwin, *MT* § 628, Kühner-Gerth II 458. For the postponement of δέ see 116–17, 169–71nn.

Metrical Appendix

My analysis of the lyric metres is according to the text printed in this edition. For other analyses see A.M. Dale, *Metrical analyses of tragic choruses* (*BICS* Suppl. 21.1 (1971); 21.2 (1981); 21.3 (1983)); Dawe's Teubner edition; W.C. Scott, *Musical design in Sophoclean theater* (Hanover NH 1996). Disagreements about text or colometry will often account for different explanations of the metre. Helpful also are Dale, *The lyric metres of Greek drama* (2nd edn. Cambridge 1968); M.L. West, *Greek metre* (Oxford 1982), and *Introduction to Greek metre* (Oxford 1987).

Parodos (172–200)

172–81 = 182–91

172/182	– ∪ ∪ – ∪ ∪ – ∪ ∪ – ∪ ∪	4 dactyls
173/183	– ∪ ∪ – ∪ ∪ –	D (hemiepes)
174/184	– ∪ – – – ∪ –	E
175/185	– – ∪ – – – ∪ ∪ – ∪ ∪ – –	x e x D x
176/186	– – ∪ – – – ∪ – – – ∪ –	x E x e
177/187	– ∪ ∪ – ∪ ∪ –	D (hemiepes)
178/188	– – ∪ – – – ∪ ∪ – ∪ ∪ –	x e x D
179/189	– – ∪ – – – ∪ ∪ – ∪ ∪ –	x e x D
180/190	– – ∪ – ∪̄ – ∪ ∪ – ∪ ∪ –	x e x D
181/191	– ∪ – ∪ – ∪ ∪ – –	aeolic enneasyllable

For the interplay of dactylo-epitrites with separate dactylic cola see Dale (1968) 44.

192–200		
192	– ∪ ∪ – ∪ ∪ –	hemiepes
193	∪ – ∪ – – –	iamb spondee
194	– – – ∪ ∪ – ∪ – ∪ – ∪ –	glyconic iamb
195	– – – ∪ ∪ – ∪ –	glyconic
196	– – – ∪ – ∪ – –	spondee cretic bacchiac
197	– – ∪ ∪ – – ∪ – – –	anceps choriamb cretic spondee
198	– – – – – –	2 molossi (or 3 spondees)
199	– – ∪ ∪ – –	reizianum
200	∪ – ∪ ∪ – – –	telesillean dragged

Amoibaion (201–262)

201–220 anapaests (Tecmessa, Chorus, Tecmessa)

221–232 = 245–256

221/245	− − ∪ − − −	iamb spondee
222/246	− ∪ ∪ − ∪ ∪ − ∪ ∪ −	dactylic tetrameter catalectic
224/247	∪ − ∪ − ∪ − −	iamb bacchiac (iambic dim. catalectic)
225/249	− ∪ ∪ − ∪ ∪ − ∪ ∪ − ∪ ∪ −	dactylic pentameter catalectic
226/250	− ∪ ∪ − − ∪ ∪ − −	choriambic enneasyllable
227/251	− − ∪ − − ∪ ∪ − − ∪ ∪ − ∪ − −	choriambic dimeter B + aristophanean
230/253	∪ − − ∪ ∪ − − ∪ ∪ − ∪ − −	dodrans B + aristophanean
231/255	∪ − − ∪ ∪ − ∪ ∪ −	glyconic (see Dale (1971) 16)
232/256	∪ − ∪ − ∪ − −	iamb bacchiac (iambic dim. catalectic)

233–244 and 257–262 anapaests (Tecmessa, Chorus)

Amoibaion (348–429)

348–55 = 356–363

348/356	∪ −	extra metrum
349/357	∪ − − ∪ − ∪ ∪∪ − ∪ −	2 dochmiacs (correption in hiatus)
350/358	∪ ∪ ∪ ∪∪ ∪ − ∪ − − ∪ −	2 dochmiacs (correption in hiatus)
351/359	∪ − ∪ − ∪ − ∪ −	iambic dimeter
352/360	∪ − ∪ − ∪ − ∪ −	iambic dimeter
353/361	− ∪ ∪ − ∪ − −	aristophanean

354–355/362–363 trimeters (Chorus-leader)

364–378 = 379–393

364/379	∪ – – ∪ – ∪ – – ∪ –	2 dochmiacs
365/380	∪ – – ∪ – ∪ – ∪ – – ∪ –	2 dochmiacs
366/381	∪ ∪ ∪ – ∪ – ∪ – – ∪ –	2 dochmiacs
367/382	– – ∪ – ∪ – ∪ – ∪̄ – ∪ –	3 iambs
368–371/383–386 trimeters (370/385 – – – – 2 spondees)		
372/387	– – ∪ ∪ – ∪ –	telesillean
373/388	∪ – ∪ – ∪ – ∪ –	iambic dimeter
374/389	– ∪ ∪ – ∪ – ∪ –	choriambic dimeter A
375/390	∪ – ∪ – – ∪ ∪ –	choriambic dimeter B
376/391	∪ – ∪ – ∪ – –	iamb bacchiac (iambic dim. catalectic)

377–378/392–3 trimeters

For the structure of these first two strophic pairs see D. Korzeniewski, *RhM* 104 (1961) 193–7.

394–411 = 412–429

	∪ –	extra metrum
394/412	∪ ∪ ∪ – ∪ –	dochmiac (correption in hiatus)
395/413	∪ ∪ ∪ – ∪ – ∪ ∪ ∪ – ∪ –	2 dochmiacs
396/414	∪ – ∪ – ∪ – – ∪ –	iamb dochmiac
397/415	∪ – ∪ – ∪ – – ∪ –	iamb dochmiac
399/416	– – ∪ ∪ – ∪ – ∪ –	choriambic enneasyllable
400/417	∪ – ∪ – ∪ – ∪ – – –	two iambs spondee
401/418	– ∪ – ∪ –	hypodochmiac
402/419	– ∪ – ∪ –	hypodochmiac
403/420	∪ ∪ ∪ ∪ – – –	dodrans A? (see 403n.)
404/421	– ∪ – ∪ –	hypodochmiac
405/423	– ∪ – ∪ –	hypodochmiac +
(423)	– ∪ – ∪ –	hypodochmiac?
406/424	† †	iambic dimeter?
407/425	– – ∪ – ∪̄ – ∪ –	iambic dimeter
408/426	– – ∪ – ∪ – ∪ –	iambic dimeter
409/427	∪ – ∪ ∪ – –	reizianum

410–411/428–429 trimeters

For the accumulation of hypodochmiacs see West (1982) 111

First Stasimon (596–645)

596–608 = 609–620

596/609	– – – ∪ ∪ – ∪ – –	hipponactean
597/610	Ū – ∪ ∪ – ∪ – – –	telesillean spondee
598/611	– – ∪ ∪ – ∪ – –	choriambic enoplian A
600/612	∪ – ∪ – – ∪̲ – ∪ ∪ – ∪ –	iamb glyconic
601/613	† ∪ – ∪ – – – – ∪ ∪ – ∪ –	iamb glyconic
604/615	– ∪ – ∪ ∪ – ∪ – – –	glyconic spondee
605/616	∪ – – ∪ ∪ –	dodrans B
606/617	∪ – – ∪ ∪ –	dodrans B
608/620	∪ ∪ ∪ ∪ ∪ ∪ ∪ – ∪ ∪ ∪ ∪ ∪ ∪ ∪ ∪ trochaic tetrameter
	– ∪ – –	catalectic

622–634 = 635–645

622/635	– – ∪ – – – – ∪ ∪ – ∪ –	iamb glyconic
625/636	Ū – ∪ – – – – ∪ ∪ – ∪ –	iamb glyconic
626/637	∪ ∪ ∪ ∪ – ∪ – –	iamb bacchiac (iambic dim. catalectic)
627/638	– ∪ ∪ – ∪ –	dodrans A
628/640	– – – ∪ ∪ – – ∪ ∪ – –	asclepiad catalectic
630/641	– – – ∪ ∪ – – ∪ ∪ – ∪ – –	dodrans B + aristophanean)
631/642	– – – ∪ ∪ – –	pherecratean
632/643	– – – ∪ ∪ – –	pherecratean
634/645	– – – ∪ ∪ – ∪ – ∪ – –	phalaecean

An alternative colometry of 629–34 gives ionics; see U. von Wilamowitz-Moellendorf, *Griechische Verskunst* (Berlin 1921) 510.

Second Stasimon (693–718)

693–705 = 706–718

693/706	∪ – ∪ – ∪ ∪ ∪ ∪ – ∪ – ∪ –	3 iambs
694/707	∪ – ∪ – – –	iamb spondee
695/708	– – – ∪ ∪ – ∪ –	glyconic
696/709	– ∪ – ∪ ∪ – ∪ –	glyconic
697/710	∪ – – ∪ ∪ – ∪ – ∪ – –	phalaecean
698/711	– ∪ ∪ – ∪ – ∪ – –	dodrans A bacchiac
699/712	– ∪ ∪ – ∪ –	dodrans A
700/713	– ∪ – ∪ ∪ – ∪ – ∪ – –	phalaecean

701/714	– ∪ ∪ – ∪ – ∪ – – ∪ – ∪ –	dodrans A bacchiac iamb
702/715	† – ∪ ∪ – ∪̲ – ∪ ∪ – †	choriambic dimeter B?
703/716	∪ – ∪ – ∪ – –	iamb bacchiac (iambic dim. catalectic)
704/717	∪̲ – ∪ ∪ – – –	telesillean dragged
705/718	∪̲ – ∪ – – ∪ ∪ – ∪ – –	iamb aristophanean

Amoibaion (866–960)

866–878
866	∪ – ∪ – ∪ – ∪ –	iambic dimeter
867	– –	spondee
868	– ∪ – ∪ – ∪ –	lekythion
869	iambic trimeter	
870	∪ – ∪ –	iamb
871	– ∪ – ∪ – ∪ –	lekythion
872	iambic trimeter	
873	∪ – –	bacchiac
874	iambic trimeter	
875	∪ – –	bacchiac
876–8	iambic trimeters	

879–914 = 925–960
879/925	∪ – – ∪ – ∪ – ∪̲∪̲ ∪ –	2 dochmiacs
880/926	∪ ∪ ∪ – ∪ – ∪ – – ∪ –	2 dochmiacs
882/928	– ∪ ∪ – ∪ ∪ – ∪ – – ∪ –	hemiepes dochmiac
884/929	– ∪ ∪ – ∪ ∪ –	hemiepes
885/930	∪ – ∪ – ∪ – ∪ –	iambic dimeter
886/931	– ∪ ∪ – – –	dochmiac
887/932	– ∪ – ∪̲∪̲ ∪ –	2 cretics
888/934	∪ ∪ ∪ – ∪ – ∪ – – ∪ –	2 dochmiacs
889/935	– ∪ – – ∪ ∪ – ∪ –	cretic dochmiac
890/936	– ∪ ∪ – ∪ – ∪ – ∪̄ – ∪ –	choriambic dimeter A + iamb
891/937	– – – –	2 spondees
892/938	iambic trimeter	
893/939	– – – –	2 spondees
894–6/940–2	iambic trimeters	
897/943	∪ – –	bacchiac
898–9/944–5	iambic trimeters	

900/946	– ∪ ∪ – – –	dochmiac (correption in hiatus)
901/947	– – ∪ ∪ – ∪ ∪ –	enoplian
902/948	– ∪ – – – ∪ –	lekythion
903/949	– ∪ – – ∪ –	2 cretics
904–907/950–953	iambic trimeters	
909/955	– ∪ ∪ – – – – ∪ ∪ – – –	2 dochmiacs (correption in hiatus)
910/956	∪ – – ∪ –	dochmiac
911/957	∪ – ∪ – ∪ – ∪ ∪ – ∪ ∪ –	iambelegus
912/958	∪ – ∪ – ∪ – –	iamb bacchiac (iambic dim. catalectic)
913/959	– ∪ ∪ – ∪ ∪ –	hemiepes (correption in hiatus)
914/960	∪ – ∪ ∪ – –	reizianum

Third Stasimon (1185–1222)

1185–1191 = 1192–1198

1185/1192	∪ ∪ ∪ ∪ ∪ ∪ – ∪ ∪ –	choriambic dimeter B
1186/1193	– ∪ ∪ – – ∪ ∪ – ∪ – –	2 choriambs bacchiac
1187/1195	– ∪ – ∪̲ – ∪ ∪ – ∪ – ∪ –	choriambic dimeter B + iamb
1189/1196	– – – – – ∪ ∪ –	choriambic dimeter B
1190/1197	– – – – – ∪ ∪ –	choriambic dimeter B
	= – ∪ – ∪ ∪ – ∪ –	= glyconic
1191/1198	– – ∪ ∪ – ∪ – – –	aeolic enneasyllable

1199–1210 = 1211–1222

1199/1211	∪̲ – ∪ – ∪ ∪ – –	iamb ionic
1200/1212	∪ ∪ – – ∪ ∪ – –	2 ionics
1201/1213	∪ ∪ – – ∪ ∪ – –	2 ionics
1202/1214	– – ∪ ∪ – – ∪ ∪ – –	spondee 2 ionics
1203/1215	∪ ∪ – – ∪ ∪ – – ∪ ∪ – –	3 ionics
1205/1217	∪ – – ∪ – – ∪ ∪ – ∪ – –	bacchiac hipponactean
1206/1219	∪̄ – ∪ ∪ – ∪ – –	enoplian
1208/1220	∪ – ∪ ∪ – ∪ –	telesillean
1209/1221	– ∪ ∪ – ∪ –	dodrans A
1210/1222	∪ – – ∪ ∪ – –	pherecratean

Index

Numbers in italics refer to pages of the Introduction, all others to line-numbers in the Commentary.

Gifts 825, 1300-3
  See also *Hector*
Gilgamesh 986
Gods, power of 118-20
  relationship of Ajax with 589-90,
    646-92, 654-6, 666-7, 719-865,
    764-5
  responsible for Ajax' troubles 136-8,
    185, 278-9, 611, 950-4
  for human failure and success 383,
    455-6, 648-9, 1036-7
  for Tecmessa's troubles 485-6, 504-
    5
  resentment of 758-61
  reverence of Ajax to 685-6, 713,
    824-34, 824
  See also *Burial*; *Hybris*
Gorgon 450-2
Grove 815-65, 892

Hair 1173-80
Hand 27, 35, 40, 230, 310, 364-7,
    729-30, 1384
Hearth 490-3
Hector, and Achilles 1030-1
  and Andromache and Astyanax
    485-524 and *passim*, 545-82,
    545-7, 550-1, 558-9, 579-80
  exchange of gifts with 661-2,
    664-5, 817-18, 822, 1025-6,
    1026-9, 1032, 1283-7
  linked with Ajax in death 1165
Helen 1310-12
Heracles *10*, 651, 1361
Hermes 832
Hero-cult *5-6*, 646-92, 670-3, 719-
    865, 1166-7, 1172
Hesione 434-6, 569, 1228
Homer, Ajax in *1-2, 17*, 1273-80,
    1283-7
  borrowings from *8*, 134-200, 147,
    179-81, 239-42, 485-524, 500-4,
    545-82, 652-3, 1025-6, 1165,
    1269-70
  epithets 175, 190-1, 237-9, 239-42,
    249-50, 286-7, 372-6, 706, 708-

10, 847, 956, 1187-90
  hybris in *12*
  See also *Achilles*; *Hector*
Honour, importance of *13 n. 48, 14-15,*
    98, 134-200, 405-6, 430-80
  of Menelaus and Teucer 1159-62,
    1304-5
  See also *Ajax*; *Arete*; *Burial*;
    Disgrace
Hope 430-80, 477-8, 606, 693-
    718, 778-9, 792-3, 925-7,
    1223-1420, 1374-5, 1382
Hunting See *Imagery*
Hybris 12-16, 127-33, 719-865, 758-61,
    760-1
  of Ajax *13-16*, 1057, 1060-1, 1081
  of Ajax' enemies *13*, 134-200, 153,
    196-7, 560-1, 866-973, 974-1184,
    1129, 1151, 1258, 1343-4, 1348,
    1385
  laughter as form of 79, 304, 364-7,
    866-973, 955-60
  not committed by Odysseus 79, 127-
    33, 134-200, 1223-1420, 1349,
    1385
  reciprocal *13*, 304, 364-7, 1087-8
  of Teucer *13*, 1125, 1223-1420, 1258

Imagery *7-8*
  agricultural, pastoral, fishing 239,
    302, 369, 412-13, 508, 611, 614-15,
    767-9
  barter 978
  birds 134-200, 140, 142-3, 169-
    71, 190-1, 196-7, 282
  building 159, 160-1, 1091-2
  fire 196-7, 1057, 1148-9
  horses and yoking 24, 123, 275,
    548-9, 735-6, 944-5
  hunting 1-3, 5-8, 18-19, 20, 32, 60,
    64, 92-3, 172, 308-9, 562-4, 874,
    879-80, 997
  lion 986-7
  medical 362-3, 545-82, 854-8, 912-
    14

nautical 251-3, 683, 889, 1073-6,
1083, 1328-31
sport and games 475-6, 610, 1245,
1246-9
storm 206-7, 257-8, 351-3, 558-9,
114*l*
technological and domestic 131-2,
651, 728, 895, 1030-1
See also *Darkness, Eye*
Irony *16*, 103, 116-17, 342-3, 364-7,
379-82, 481-4, 506-7, 693-718,
778-9, 812, 1216-22, 1353, 1358,
1374-5, 1382

Joy, of Eurysaces 558-9
of Tecmessa and the Chorus 646-92,
693-718, 693, 719-865
See also *Chorus, longing for home*;
Disease; *Madness*
Judgement of arms, Athena's part
in 719-865
cheating in 445-6, 447-9, 934-6,
1135, 1285-7
fairness/unfairness of 74-90, 442-
6, 444, 1223-1420, 1246-9, 1336-
41
in tradition *1-5*
Justice 1126, 1334-5, 1336-41, 1344-
5, 1390

Laertes 187-9, 1393
Lamentation, language and conventions
of 310, 627-31, 631-4, 866-973,
974-1184
unheroic 319-20, 321-2, 579-80
Laughter, of Ajax 303
of his enemies 1-133, 66-7, 134-200,
198-9, 303, 348-595, 379-82, 485-
524, 923-4, 961-73, 988-9, 1040-3
See also *Hybris*
Law 1073-6, 1246-9
See also *Burial*
Light See *Darkness; Eye*
Little Iliad See *Epic Cycle*
Lot 1283-7, 1284, 1285-7

Madness, Ajax' joy in 1-133, 51-2,
348-595
association of Artemis with 172
cessation from 201-347, 206-7, 256,
257-8, 259, 263, 265-7
hard to distinguish from sanity 331-2,
354-5, 371, 611, 635
inflicted by Athena 1-133, 611
symptoms of 447-9
in tradition *2-3, 5*
Man 68-9, 77, 78, 118-20, 520-1, 822,
956, 1236, 1257
Meadows 601-5, 654-5
Menelaus, arguments of 974-1184
character of *13, 15-16*, 127-33, 974-
1184
status of 1100-8, 1105-6
Metre, anapaest or dactyl in first foot
of trimeter 571, 846
caesura 430-3, 485-524, 854-8,
961-73, 994-5, 1091-2
diaeresis 146
hiatus 190-1, 192, 196-7, 1199-1204
lyric 134-200, 348-595, 364-7, 403,
702-5, 1187-90
paroemiac 1416-17
Porson's Law 1101
prosody 210-11, 514-15
resolution *7*, 30, 403, 457-9, 485-
524, 569, 854-8, 866-973
Miltiades *6*
Mourning See *Lamentation*
Mysia 342-3, 698-700, 720-1, 881-4

Necessity 485-6
Neoptolemus 646-92
Nightingale 627-31
Nonentities 767-9, 1093-6, 1115-16,
1223-1420, 1231, 1275
Nurture, of Ajax 638-40, 641-5, 848-
51, 859-63
of Ajax' countrymen 859-63
of Eriboea 621-5
of Eurysaces 499, 510-13, 556-7,
558-9, 562-4

of Tecmessa 499, 500-4
of Teucer 1229

Oaths 648-9, 1111-14
Odysseus *passim*
cunning and unscrupulousness of
103, 379-82, 388-91, 445-6, 646-
92, 955, 1374-5, 1382
enlightened compassion of 121-6,
124, 1318-19, 1365-7
intelligence of *1*, 1-133, 1-3, 16-17
persuasiveness of 151, 1374-5
sophrosyne of *15*
surprising behaviour of *5*, *15-16*, 1-
133, 79, 134-200, 364-7, 923-4,
955-60, 974-1184, 1223-1420,
1328-31, 1418-20
Optative 185, 313, 520-1, 1216-22,
1344 -5
Ornamental language *8*, 16-17, 143-
4, 357, 866-973, 872
See also *Epithets*; *Homer*
Oxymoron 394-5, 517, 822

Pan 693-718, 694-8, 698-700
Papyri *18*
Paradox *12*, 47, 214, 348-595, 548-9,
646-92, 719-865, 859-63, 966-8,
1137
Parodos *7*, 134-200
Parts, distribution of *17*, 815-65, 974-
1184, 985-9, 1168-9, 1223-1420
Pathos 313, 360, 392-3, 485-524, 514-19,
545-7, 683, 687-8, 824, 848-51, 890,
923-4, 992-7
Pericles *6*, 1260-1
Personal construction 76, 326, 635,
1225
Persuasion *14*, 330, 481-4, 485-524,
592
See also *Odysseus, persuasiveness of*
Pindar *4-5*, *7*
Polarisation 20, 23, 96, 113, 192, 523-
4, 627-31, 676-7, 753-4, 796, 813-
14, 1379-80

Political relevance *6-7*, *15-16*, 132-3,
1073-6, 1246-9
Pollution and purification 654-6, 658-
9, 712, 713, 1404-5
Polyptoton 619-20, 1177
Preparation and foreshadowing, of
Ajax' suicide 229, 326, 361, 388-
91, 421-2, 426-7, 440, 577, 735-6
of appearance of a character 201-
347, 329, 339-41, 525-44, 562-4,
688-9, 719-865, 742, 797, 920-1,
974-1184, 1109-10, 1115-16
of a later speech or scene 330, 345,
403-4, 481-4, 499, 586, 827-30,
839-42, 974-1184, 1026-39, 1374-
5
Pronouns 485-524, 514-15, 518, 530,
1032, 1034-5, 1039
Proverbs and generalisations 292-3,
362-3, 635, 648-9, 664-5, 679-82,
746, 786, 988-9, 1039, 1100-8

Relative clause with final-consecutive
force 470-1, 658-9, 1166-7
Repetition, for emotional emphasis
349-50, 359, 396-7, 593, 619-20,
866-8
of information 201-347, 296-7, 299-300
of language 111, 403, 669-70, 970
in strophic response 414, 707-8,
866-973
Rhea 698-700
Rhetorical effect 430-80, 485-524,
1223-1420
Rumour, of Ajax' suicide 826, 850,
998-9
of attack on animals 134-200, 142-3,
148, 173-4, 185-6, 187-9, 201-347,
226, 264

Sack of Troy See *Epic Cycle*
Sacrifice 239, 712, 815
Salamis *5*, 134-5, 202, 204, 595-645,
596-8, 694-8, 859-63
battle of *5*, 596-8
in Cyprus *4*, 1019